Developing Global Health Programming

A Guidebook for Medical and Professional Schools, Second Edition

JESSICA EVERT, PAUL DRAIN, THOMAS HALL

ISBN: 978-0-578-12721-7 (sc)
ISBN: 978-1-4834-0377-9 (e)

Library of Congress Control Number: 2013916909

Editors
Jessica Evert, MD
University of California, San Francisco
Child Family Health International

Paul Drain, MD, MPH
Massachusetts General Hospital
Harvard Medical School

Thomas Hall, MD, DrPH
University of California, San Francisco
Consortium of Universities for Global Health

Photo Editor
William Bynum, MD
National Capital Consortium Family Medicine Residency
Medical Students for Burn Care International

Foreword by
Andres-Jacques Neusy
CEO and Co-Founder
Training for Health Equity Network

Suggested Citation:
Evert J, Drain P, Hall T (eds). Developing Global Health Programming: A Guidebook for Medical and Professional Schools, 2nd Ed. San Francisco: Global Health Education Collaborations Press, 2014.

Lulu Publishing Services rev. date: 01/13/2014

Contents

Supporting Organizations

Child Family Health International (CFHI)

www.cfhi.org

Child Family Health International (CFHI) is a leading non-profit provider of Global Health Education Programs. CFHI Programs utilize a community-engaged approach, affording students from resource-rich countries transformative educational opportunities in developing countries that spotlight local experts and re-invest in host communities. CFHI provides pre-health, social science and health science professional students exposure to Global Health through the eyes of native health care providers, populations and local champions. In doing so, CFHI lays the foundation for participants to see global health solutions through a collaborative, asset-based perspective. CFHI programs not only provide first hand exposure to clinical, NGO and public health settings, they emphasize cultural immersion, health systems and a broad view of social determinants of health. CFHI Academic Partnerships allow schools and universities to partner with CFHI to expand global health offerings and utilize best-practice standards.

CFHI has over 25 programs in 6 countries that focus on a variety of topics including Palliative Care, Primary Care, Infectious Disease, Maternal/Child Health, Indigenous Health, Rural/Urban Comparatives and Universal Access. CFHI is an NGO in Special Consultative Status with the ECOSOC of the United Nations, and is recognized for its financial integrity by the Better Business Bureau and Independent Charities of America. CFHI's emphasis on sustainability is evidenced by its 20-year anniversary celebrated in 2012.

Consortium for Universities for Global Health (CUGH)

www.cugh.org

The Consortium of Universities for Global Health (CUGH), founded by leading North American university global health programs, aims to:

- Define the field and discipline of global health
- Standardize required curricula and competencies for global health;
- Define criteria and conditions for student and faculty field placements in host institutions;
- Provide coordination of projects and initiatives among and between resource-rich universities and less-developed nations and their institutions.

CUGH is dedicated to creating balance in health resources and in the exchange of students and faculty between institutions in high and low-income countries, recognizing the importance of equal partnership between the academic institutions in low-resource nations and their resource-rich counterparts in the planning, implementation, management and impact evaluation of joint projects.

Global Health Learning Opportunities (GHLO)

www.aamc.org/ghlo

GHLO's vision is to be a community of health professionals transformed by global experiences. Institutions that join the Association of American Medical Colleges' GHLO Collaborative are members in an innovative global network of leading caliber institutions around the world that value cultural contexts in medical education. The Collaborative facilitates educational mobility of health professionals and promotes standardization of quality with special consideration to institutional autonomy. This engagement allows the cadre of institutions to enhance dialogue, exchange ideas and best practices, and conduct joint research towards innovation and building global understanding.

The GHLO application service facilitates global mobility for final year students pursuing clinical, research, or public health electives outside their home country. This service utilizes a Web-based platform that streamlines the application process for students, enables home schools to endorse student applications and track progress, and host institutions to publish and manage elective offerings, student selection and evaluation.

International Federation of Medical Student Associations (IFMSA)

www.ifmsa.org

Founded in 1951, the International Federation of Medical Students' Associations (IFMSA) is the world's oldest and largest independent organization representing medical students from around the world. With an estimated membership of 1.2 million medical students, IFMSA currently maintains 108 National Member Organizations from more than 100 countries. IFMSA is recognized as an international nongovernmental organization by the United Nations and the

World Health Organization and is a proud partner of various international bodies such as the World Medical Association.

Created to make a positive impact on the world, IFMSA has inspired generations of medical students to develop knowledge, skills, and attitude needed take on current and emerging challenges in medicine and global health. Annually, IFMSA provides opportunities to medical students through its two general assemblies, five regional meetings, around 15,000 exchange program slots, hundreds of national and international projects and trainings, and dozens of international campaigns on issues ranging from climate change to global health equity. We have standing committees that focus on medical education, public health, sexual reproductive health, including HIV/AIDS, human rights, and clinical/research exchanges.

Ride for World Health (R4WH)

www.r4wh.org

Ride For World Health is a 501 3 (c) non-profit with three important goals: Education, Fundraising and Advocacy. R4WH was created with a few, very simple ideas in mind. 1) There are a great many people across the globe, in the U.S. and abroad, who are not receiving proper healthcare. 2) There is a significant link between poverty, disease and lack of access to healthcare. 3) Something can be done about it...and it starts with education. During the ride, we deliver a coast-to-coast lecture series to all age groups, from elementary school students to medical school faculty. The lectures are on topics as diverse as always washing your hands when you use the bathroom and trying to eat fruits and vegetables every day (elementary school) to the pathophysiology of infectious diseases or the politics of foreign aid (medical school faculty). We also fundraise and make sizeable donations to local and global health nonprofits. Ride For World Health's third focus is advocacy. We advocate for the freedom and health of all people. At home that means we support the efficient and safe delivery of health care to anyone in need.

Contributors

Jonathan Abelson, MD
New York Presbyterian Hospital/Weill Cornell Medical College

Natasha Altin, MscOT
Dalhousie University

Baharak Amanzadeh, DDS, MPH
University of California, San Francisco School of Dentistry

Kelly Anderson, MD, CCFP
University of Toronto

Timothy Anderson, MD, MA
University of Pittsburgh Medical Center

Leann Andrews, MLA, Certificate of Global Health
University of Washington

Hrishikesh K. Belani, MPH
University of Minnesota

Laura Bertani, BS
Northeast Ohio Medical University

Susan Bolton, MS, MSCE, PhD
University of Washington

Meaghan Bond, BS
Rice University

Timothy Brewer, MD, MPH
University of California, Los Angeles
Consortium of Universities in Global Health (CUGH)

Carrie Bronsther, BA
Weill Cornell Medical College

William Bynum, MD
National Capital Consortium Family Medicine Residency
Medical Students for Burn Care International

Kaitlin Carlson, DPT
University of Alabama at Birmingham

Benjamin W. Chaffee, DDS, MPH
University of California, Berkeley

Jack Chase, MD
University of California, San Francisco

Karen E. Gieseker, PhD, MS
Child Family Health International

Kerry Adele Gillette, PA-S
University of Utah

Mera Goodman, MD
Mount Sinai School of Medicine Department of Pediatrics

Johanna Gusman, MS, JD
University of Washington School of Law

Nilofer Khan Habibullah
The Lancet-University of Oslo Youth Commission on Global Health Governance
International Federation of Medical Students' Associations (IFMSA)

Thomas Hall MD, DrPH
University of California, San Francisco
Consortium of Universities for Global Health (CUGH)

Rachel Hanle, BSW-candidate
University of Alabama at Birmingham

Robert Huish, PhD
Dalhousie University

Paula Johns, OD
Zuni Indian Hospital

Andrea Johnson, DPT
University of Alabama at Birmingham

Evaleen Jones, MD
Stanford University School of Medicine
Child Family Health International (CFHI)

Sarah Kleinfeld, BA
Louisiana State University School of Medicine

Michael Kron, MD, MSc.
Medical College of Wisconsin

Amita Kulkarni, BA
Dartmouth Center for Health Care Delivery Science

Heidi Lauckner, PhD, OT Reg (NS)
Dalhousie University

Amy Lockwood, MBA, MS
Stanford University

Kate W. Read, PhD
University of San Francisco

Lynda Redwood-Campbell, MD, FCFP, DTM&H, MPH
Association of Faculties of Medicine of Canada Resource Group
McMaster University

Tania Rezai, MPH
Stanford University School of Medicine

Rebecca Richards-Kortum, PhD
Rice University

Alfonso J. Rodriguez-Morales
Universidad Tecnológica de Pereira

Brittany Rohrman, BA
Rice University

Pamela Runestad, ABD
University of Hawaii at Manoa

Sarpoma Sefa-Boakye, MD
Birthing Project USA

Sharon E. Shaw, PT, DrPH
University of Alabama at Birmingham

Ben Spencer, MLA
University of Washington

Predrag Stojicic, MD, MPH
ReThink Health
The Fannie E. Rippel Foundation
Serbia on the Move

Geren Stone, MD, DTM&H
Indiana University School of Medicine
Moi University

Nicole Sussman
Wake Forest School of Medicine

Daniel Tobón-García
Universidad Tecnológica de Pereira

Herica M. Torres, RN, MSN, PhD-candidate
University of South Alabama

Diane C. Tucker, PhD
University of Alabama at Birmingham

Rachel A Umoren, MB.BCh, MS
Indiana University School of Medicine

William Cherniak, BSc, MD
University of Toronto

Eileen Cheung, MD
University of Toronto

Mark Clarfield, MD
Medical School for International Health
Ben-Gurion University

Michael S. Cordray, BS
Rice University

Erin Corriveau, MD
University of New Mexico

Zachary Crannell
Rice University

Madhavi Dandu, MD MPH
University of California, San Francisco

Allan Davison, BSc, MS, PhD
Simon Fraser University

Kyle Dempsey, AB
Harvard University

Elizabeth Dohrmann
University of Tennessee Health Science Center

Paul K. Drain, MD, MPH
Massachusetts General Hospital/Brigham and Women's Hospital
Harvard Medicine School

Mei Elensary, MD, MPhil
Boston Combined Residency Program in Pediatrics

Jessica Evert, MD
University of California, San Francisco
Child Family Health International (CFHI)

Mariam O. Fofana
Johns Hopkins University School of Medicine/Bloomberg School of Public Health

Amy Forrestel
Yale School of Medicine

Marcela Frazier OD, MPH, FAAO
University of Alabama at Birmingham

Tate Lowrey, MPH
University of Cape Town, South Africa

Mary MacLennan, MSc, BA&Sc
International Centre for Diarrhoeal Disease Research, Bangladesh

David Matthews, MPhil
University of Toronto

Kate McCalmont, MD
University of New Mexico

Cathy Gilbert McElderry
University of Alabama at Birmingham

Ranit Mishori, MD, MHS
Georgetown University School of Medicine

Brian T Montague, DO, MS, MPH
Warren Alpert School of Medicine at Brown University

Mazheruddin Mulla, B.S., M.P.H.
University of Alabama at Birmingham

Ndidiamaka L Musa
Medical College of Wisconsin

Shawna O'Hearn, MA, MSc (OT)
Dalhousie University

Donald M. Pedersen, PhD, PA-C
University of Utah School of Medicine

Kathy J. Pedersen MPAS, PA-C
University of Utah School of Medicine

Michael J. Peluso
Yale School of Medicine

Jorge Alarcon Piscoya, BArch
UNMSN, Instituto de Medicine Tropical, Daniel A. Carrion

Kevin Pottie, MD, CCFP, MClSc, FCFP
University of Ottawa

Mirriam Rafiq Braden, MPH
Child Family Health International (CFHI)

Mena Ramos, MD
Contra Costa Family Medicine Department

Anvar Velji, MD,FRCP (c),FACP,FIDSA
California Northstate School of Medicine
Kaiser Permanente, South Sacramento
Global Health Education Consortium (now CUGH)
University of California, Davis

Lauren Wempe, BA
University of Colorado School of Medicine

Lynda Wilson, RN, PhD, FAAN
University of Alabama at Birmingham School of Nursing

Michael Windle, MPH-candidate, JD-candidate
University of Washington

HaruYamamoto, BS

Bingnan Zhang
Yale School of Medicine/ Yale School of Management

Foreward

"The measure of a country's greatness should be based on how well it cares for its most vulnerable populations"
Mahatma Gandhi

THE EFFECTS OF GLOBALIZATION—the rapid global interdependency of economic, political, cultural, social and religious factors—on population and individual health is profound and complex. Health threats can be exported and imported like commodities. Poverty generates insidious public health risks for populations everywhere. As health professionals and educators, one of the greatest challenges of our times is to understand and manage this ever-changing complexity while maintaining clarity of purpose on keeping people healthy. This encompasses providing access to food; water; sanitation and shelter; human rights; gender equity; financial and personal security; education; as well as host of environmental, economic and political factors. Yet, what should be a major concern to us all is how these determinants of health, if not adequately addressed, produce gaping health inequities between and within nations.

Health inequity refers to the differences in population health that are systemic, socially produced, and preventable, therefore inherently unjust and unfair. Such health inequities are not only unacceptable—causing unnecessary and preventable suffering and deaths—but also costly—limiting individual opportunity and slowing economic growth. In the U.S. alone companies lose more than $1 trillion a year in productivity due to chronic illness. This put health equity squarely at the center of the global health agenda. There is now growing global support to address health inequities by achieving universal health coverage i.e. providing everyone with access to quality health services without individuals having to risk financial destitution. For this to happen, nations must build strong equitable health systems with a well-trained health workforce that is equitably distributed and capable of working collaboratively across sectors and disciplines.

What can we as health professions educators do to reduce health equity gaps?

This book *Developing Global Health Programming: A Guidebook for Medical and Other Professional Schools* represents a significant step to engage health professions schools in addressing global health challenges. At the root of global health is human security and concern for society's most vulnerable groups. There is no simple solution to breaking the cycle of poverty and disease but health professional schools can and should play a central role. However, business as usual is no longer acceptable. The Independent Global Commission on Education of Health Professionals for the 21st Century, in a 2010 report points out that predominant models of health professional education are not producing the people, research and services needed to meet the needs of the 21st century. It calls for the re-design of institutional and educational strategies within the framework of health system reform shifting the focus from a curative to preventive approaches; fragmented to integrated comprehensive care and hospital-oriented to secondary and primary care levels.[1] With health expenditures rising everywhere, offering universal health coverage while containing costs requires health systems to focus more on keeping people healthy. Moreover, governments and taxpayers investing in educating the health workforce will increasingly demand that schools be held accountable for producing what the communities and societies they serve need. This was reinforced in 2011 by the Global Consensus for Social Accountability of Medical Schools urging schools to reorient their activities and align them to evolving needs of society.[2]

Today, more than ever, a global perspective is critical when preparing health professionals to responds to health threats that endanger communities at home and abroad. Consequently this book *Developing Global Health Programming: A Guidebook for Medical and Other Professional Schools* is of great importance. It argues that medical education needs to expand its borders. Health inequalities are complex, expensive and hard to solve. Hence, global health challenges require effective and coordinated international efforts and partnerships between parties sharing mutual interests in improving public health outcomes. In addition to the health sciences, it involves an ever-increasing number of disciplines such as engineering, sociology, anthropology, economics, and management and law. The space created by the cross fertilization of these disciplines provide new opportunities to come together with a focus to solving health problems and making health equity a reality.

Keeping individuals and communities healthy requires people to take responsibility for their own health; hence communities are essential partners of academic institutions. This calls for a major change in the academic mindset still entrenched in the traditional "ivory tower," and for developing solid partnerships between academic centers and the communities they serve. In this book, experiences across the globe offer valuable lessons. As mentioned in chapter 5, notably a number of schools in poor countries, precisely due to limited funds, have recognized the importance of tapping the resources their communities offer; including knowledge, social networks and other local resources often overlooked by academia. These schools work with communities and local stakeholders as equal partners to identify community health related priorities. This results in planning, designing, implementing and evaluating agreed upon interventions, and deciding the best use of available technologies. Several of these health profession institutions in underserved and rural regions of Africa, Asia, Europe, the Americas and Australia have created a peer-to-peer partnership, pioneering innovative approaches. Community engagement is hardwired in all their educational, research and service activities. These schools, striving towards social accountability, measure their success not by how many graduates they produce or how many of their articles are published but by whether their graduates have the right competencies to meet the needs of their reference populations and whether a large proportion of them stay and work in medically underserved communities post-graduation.

They also measure whether their research and services positively affect health policies and practices all to one end—to improve over-all access and quality of health care delivery in their communities. Compared with traditional health professional schools in their regions these schools are achieving consistently higher retention rate of graduates with the right skills to work where they are needed and are making a difference in health outcomes. [3, 4]

The growth of academic programs in global health in North American universities provides valuable opportunities to foster such partnerships and cross-border learning. This book discusses some of the challenges in building partnership and developing collaboration. A paradigm shift is emerging where global partnerships are based on commitment of institutions to solve common challenges affecting their communities, irrespective of geographic location and differences in resources. What make such collaboration stronger than traditional aid-oriented partnerships are opportunities to learn globally and re-invent locally to solve specific problems. For example, vast areas of the North American continent are suffering from severe health workforce shortage, unable to attract and retain well-trained health workers in areas of great needs. Similar workforce crisis is particularly acute in low and middle-income countries some of which have developed innovative solutions to respond to their needs that can be applied in high-income settings.

The second edition of *Developing Global Health Programming: A Guidebook for Medical and Other Professional Schools* builds on such efforts, providing valuable resources for policy makers, academic leaders, faculty, and students engaged in global health programs. Importantly, this edition has expanded to include the voices of a variety of disciplines and toward a conversation necessary for trans-disciplinary program development. It provides an overview of the global health education landscape in North America. It covers a wide range of topics from ethical issues and advocacy to collaboration building and gives examples of partnership-based, interdisciplinary programs that integrate education, training issues and research that are beyond the traditional ways at solving global health problems. As this book emphasizes, the future of global health will depend to a great extent on how academic institutions join forces with all relevant stakeholders to help build local and global capacity to make societies healthier.

AJ Neusy
Co-Founder, THEnet

References

1. Frenk, J., Chen, L. et al. Health professionals for a new century: transforming education to strengthen health systems in an interdependent world. Lancet 2010:376(9756):1923-58
2. Global Consensus for Social Accountability of Medical Schools. 2011. Global consensus for social accountability of medical schools. Available from http://www.healthsocialaccountability.org.
3. Larkins SL, Preston R, Matte MC, Lindemann IC, Samson R, Tandinco FD, Buso D, Ross SJ, Palsdottir B, Neusy A-J. Measuring Social Accountability in Health Professional Education: development and International Pilot Testing of an Evaluation Framework. *Medical Teacher.* 2013; 35: 32-45.
4. Palsdottir B, Neusy A-J. Global Health: Networking Innovative Academic Institutions. *Infectious Disease Clinic of North America.* 2011; 25(2):337-346. Available from http://www.ncbi.nlm.nih.gov/pubmed/21628049

CHAPTER 1

An Introduction to Global Health in Education and Practice

Mary MacLennan, MSc, BA&Sc
Health Economist
International Centre for Diarrhoeal Disease Research, Bangladesh

Elizabeth Dohrmann
MD-candidate
University of Tennessee Health Science Center

Editor

Timothy Brewer, MD, MPH
Vice-provost for Interdisciplinary and Cross-campus Affairs
University of California, Los Angeles

THE NOTION OF MEDICINE AND health spilling beyond geographic boundaries is not novel. Discussions have been carried out for centuries on the spread of diseases, the far-reaching impacts of political decisions and the influences of increasingly inter-linked people and economies. Nevertheless, the concept of "global health" as an academic discipline is relatively recent. This chapter will first provide a brief background of how the current global health landscape came to be, and subsequently describe the evolution of global health education.

The Rise of the World Health Organization and International Organizations

Global health, which considers the health needs of the entire planet above the concerns of individual countries, has progressed greatly over the past 150 years.[1] Its origin may be traced back to the mid-1800s, when several cholera outbreaks led to the first International Sanitary Conference in 1851. Years later, in response to yellow fever, countries of the Western hemisphere created the Pan American Sanitary Bureau in 1902 (now called the Pan American Health Organization—PAHO).

After World War I, the League of Nations Health Committee helped expand the concept of "international health" from one focused on epidemics and outbreaks to a broader vision that included maternal and infant health and nutrition among other issues.

The World Health Organization (WHO) was formed in 1948 as a specialized agency of the United Nations. Its goal was to create a single governing body in charge of creating cooperation and collaboration between nations to address health problems. Its stated mission was a novel idea: health is not merely the absence of disease, but the promotion, attainment and maintenance of physical, mental and social well being.

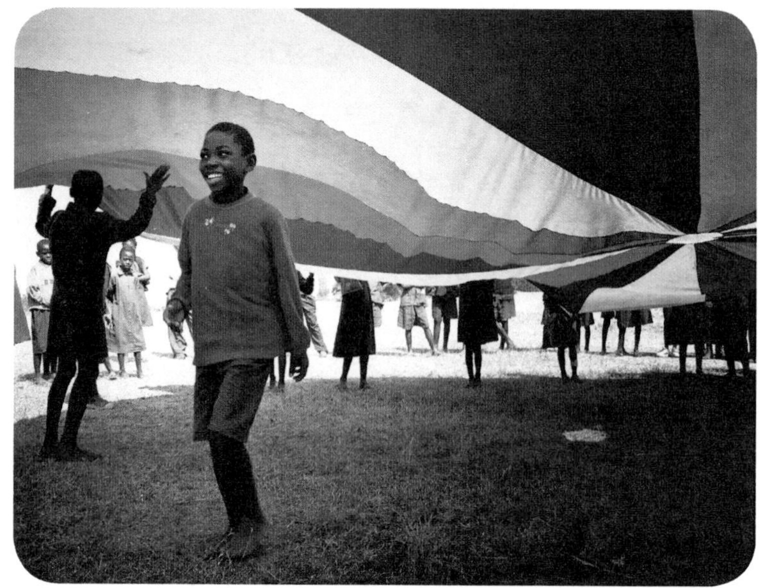

A Zambian boy participates in a village-wide game of parachute outside a temporary medical clinic
Photographer: *Will Bynum*

During the 1960s and 1970s, the WHO began to focus on long-term socioeconomic growth as opposed to short-term technical interventions. The importance of the interplay among health, infrastructure, culture and economy was highlighted in many of their projects, such as the eradication of small pox and control of malaria.[2] In 1978, the International Conference on Primary Health Care (PHC) was held in Alma Ata with an idea of "health for all," which was based on equity, social justice, community participation, prevention/health promotion, inter-sectorial collaboration, appropriate use of resources and sustainability.[2]

Less than a year after the Alma Ata conference, the World Bank and others leveled heavy criticism of the conference's conclusions by stating that the costs of the comprehensive health care discussed were too high (between 5.4 to 9.3 billion USD by the year 2000).[2] The PHC subsequently focused on a subset of diseases with cost-efficient interventions that could be made easily available, such as vaccinations or oral rehydration.

Amidst the economic recession of the 1980s, a strategy proposed by the World Bank and the International Monetary Fund called for "structural adjustment", which set requirements for receiving loans. The requirements included large cuts in consumption and public spending, including spending on healthcare, with the intention of decreasing inflation and public debt. These financial adjustments greatly reduced public spending for health at the same time the HIV/AIDS virus was becoming a global pandemic.

The Playing Field Opens: The Rise of Public-Private Partnerships

In 1990, the WHO had an annual budget of almost $1.2 billion and was the primary player in global health. The US Government, which had the next largest budget, was spending $850 million annually on global health assistance.[3] At that time, however, funding dedicated to the WHO's ordinary budget began to decrease while programs financed through "extra-budgetary" means, i.e., commitments made by member states to specific programs, were increasing (54% by the early 1990s). This shift meant that wealthy donor countries and multilateral organizations gained a significant influence in the WHO health agenda.[1]

At the turn of the millennium, the concept of global health as an academic discipline began to emerge. There was an explosion of global health activity financed by extra-budgetary funding that eventually was greater than the regular budget of the WHO.[2] Public-private partnerships became a common and new method of financing global health, and governmental and multinational organizations were no longer the only major players. For example, in 2002, the Bill and Melinda Gates Foundation invested $2.8 billion in global health initiatives; one such initiative, Roll Back Malaria, had more than 80 international partners (including WHO).[2] The growth in public-private partnerships resulted in a great diminution of the role of WHO and changed the global health landscape.

Although the WHO made significant contributions to the global health landscape in the 2000s—including the Framework Convention on Tobacco Control, the Millennium Development Goals and the Commission on Macroeconomics and Health–by 2010 their budget had fallen back to its 1990 level. This placed WHO fourth in funding, behind the massive $7.5 billion US President's Emergency Plan for AIDS Relief (PEPFAR) program, the $3 billion Global Fund to Fight AIDS, Tuberculosis and Malaria (GFATM) and the $2.2 billion collection of smaller nongovernmental organizations.[3]

Among the many key players in global health that have achieved a great deal of tangible success are the Global Alliance for Vaccine Initiative (GAVI) and the GFATM. Launched in 2000 using private and government funding, GAVI negotiates low prices and bulk purchases of vaccines for 70 of the world's poorest countries. After only a decade, its programs have provided 326 million vaccinations and have prevented more than 5.5 million deaths. In 2010, $4.3 billion USD was pledged by private and governmental sources to maintain GAVI programs until 2016.

A child rescued from the streets in Ethiopia is excited to welcome the non-profit Invest in Children to come and teach music and the arts to her and 50 others like her.
Photographer: *Kimberly Krauk*

The idea for the GFATM was initially discussed at the special UN assembly on HIV/AIDS in 2001. Its purpose is to finance projects related to fighting HIV, tuberculosis, and malaria, which are three of the world's most devastating infectious diseases. The GFATM receives funding from governments and philanthropic organizations, including the Bill and Melinda Gates Foundation.[2] The GFATM has supported programs that have treated 3.3 million people with antiretroviral drugs, detected and treated 8.6 million new cases of tuberculosis, and distributed 230 million insecticide-treated nets.

Additionally, numerous product-development partnerships focusing on pharmaceutical product development are playing a large role in developing and delivering new drugs and technologies needed in resource-limited settings. Examples include the Drugs for Neglected Diseases Initiative and the Meningitis Vaccines Project.

Many people have suggested that the WHO should play a role in evidence-based ideas, surveillance, technical assistance and cooperation.[3,4,5] Current resources dedicated to global health could have a greater impact if there is a more cohesive global health strategy, particularly to foster collaboration among health disciplines, stakeholders, and countries.[5] At the 2012 World Health Assembly, the committee proposed the following as the WHO's core responsibilities: i) initiating collaboration for better health; ii) generating evidence on health trends and determinants; iii) providing advice for health and development; iv) coordinating health security; and v) strengthening health systems and institutions.[6]

If history is a guide, it has become clear that global health is a complex discipline with many inter-related issues and players. The concept's origins began with a focus on protecting the health of individual nations followed by a shift toward recognition of co-dependency among nations. This change was followed by a move from a disease-focused approach to a more broad view of health. Subsequently, and most recently, there has been a rise in collaboration among and within countries recognizing mutually shared problems. An emphasis on health systems and an integrated approach (both nationally and among nations), which involves cooperation, collaboration and partnership between countries, health care professionals, medical researchers, public health specialists, corporations and individuals, has been recognized as necessary. Trained individuals from many fields are needed to address the multifaceted challenges to the world's health. Essentially important are the continued contributions and training of healthcare professionals.

The Integration of Global Health into Medical Education

Today nearly one million healthcare professionals (including physicians, nurses, and public health providers) graduate annually from 2,420 medical schools, 467 schools or departments of public health, and numerous nursing institutions across the globe.[7] The distribution of these health care graduates, however, is relatively uneven, which affects the quality and efficiency of care provision both at home and abroad. In sub-Saharan Africa for example, 3% of the world's health workers struggle to address 24% of the global disease burden.[8] In North America, more rural areas also have struggled to retain medical practitioners. In response, medical schools have been established in resource-limited settings and encourage graduates to serve in their immediate communities. For example, Northern Ontario School of Medicine was founded in 2004 with the explicit mission to recruit students from and to serve in its rural communities. Although such efforts are one way to address healthcare worker shortages, initiatives on a global scale are needed. This is especially true given the increasing interdependency of previously isolated regions of the world through immigration, commerce, technology, and information. In this current landscape imbalances in healthcare availability must be addressed by redefining priorities, recruitment and training of future medical professionals. This is a challenge for all professional schools and requires a redefined approach towards training providers who are willing and able to practice in the areas of most need. These new approaches may be most easily analyzed in the context of medical education, where the changing trajectory of global health training reveals patterns that may apply not only to future generations of physicians, but professionals in allied disciplines as well.

There has been a clear movement towards increasing global exposure and awareness in medical education. In the early twentieth century many American medical students completed clinical rotations in Germany or Great Britain for exposure to new technologies and practice.[9] During

World War II, the recognition of tropical diseases in war regions fostered a new discipline of study of parasites and related diseases. In 1944, for example, the American Association of Medical Colleges (AAMC) reported 96% of medical schools as teaching aspects of tropical medicine and international health.[9] Later during the Cold War in the 1960s, programs such as the Peace Corps were created to provide American aid to foreign partners. In response to such social trends, some American medical schools modified their teaching and curricula. International experiences for medical students, however, did not become commonplace until easier travel, increasing interest, and institutional collaborations burgeoned over the next few decades.

One of the first opportunities for an international health elective was in 1960. With the aim to support promising fourth year medical students in a placement in a developing country, Smith, Kline and French Laboratories provided an $180,000 grant for 3 years to the AAMC.[10] Over time, other opportunities followed from both private and public funding sources. For example, in 1980 the Department of Preventive Medicine and Community Health at the State University of New York, Downstate Medical Center implemented a 6-8 week international health rotation that has since trained over 217 students.[9] Additionally at Yale University in 1981, two physicians founded the Yale University International Health Program (IHP) to provide global placements to Yale internal medicine residents. This program was subsequently sponsored by Johnson & Johnson in 2001 and expanded its focus to providing overseas opportunities to outside and practicing physicians.

During the 1990s, many people and organizations worked to increase international opportunities for medical students. The International Health Medical Education Consortium (later known as the Global Health Education Consortium, and presently as the Consortium of Universities for Global Health) was founded, as was the Global Health Action Committee of the American Medical Student Association (AMSA). Both of these organizations are dedicated to enhancing opportunities for global health education in the training of medical professionals through advocacy, curricula development and facilitation of international exchanges. A key component of AMSA's global health programming, for instance, relies on its status as a National Member Organization (NMO) with the International Federation of Medical Students' Associations (IFMSA). The IFMSA was established in 1941 as the body representing medical students around the globe, and it currently includes NMOs from over 100 countries worldwide. The IFMSA's exchange program supports over 10,000 medical students a year in international placements.

Many international electives emphasize skills and awareness in the areas of public health, primary care and preventive medicine. Interest in these electives has increased consistently over time, reflecting a trend in medical students' valuation of these disciplines. According to the AAMC exiting student survey from 2010, 30.8% of graduating students in 2010 participated in global health experiences, up from 27.2% in 2006.[11] Likewise, students indicated a consistent increase in "appropriateness" of instruction in the areas of public health (64.9% in 2006 to 73.4% in 2010) and global health issues (42.1% in 2006 and 49.2% in 2010). A survey of 96 allopathic US medical schools in 2008 showed that 87% had international clinical elective opportunities; this figure alone demonstrates the recognized importance and demand for such global exposure.[12]

The high demand for content modifications and the endless scientific advances make it difficult to smoothly orchestrate curriculum revisions in health science education. Global health curriculum is only one of many competing additions to healthcare instruction. To date there have been few clear analyses of the preparation, educational objectives, and downstream benefits from international health electives or other key aspects of global health programming.[13] Should this programming be important enough for schools to invest in? What skills do they really impart to students, and how, if at all, do they change professional outcomes?

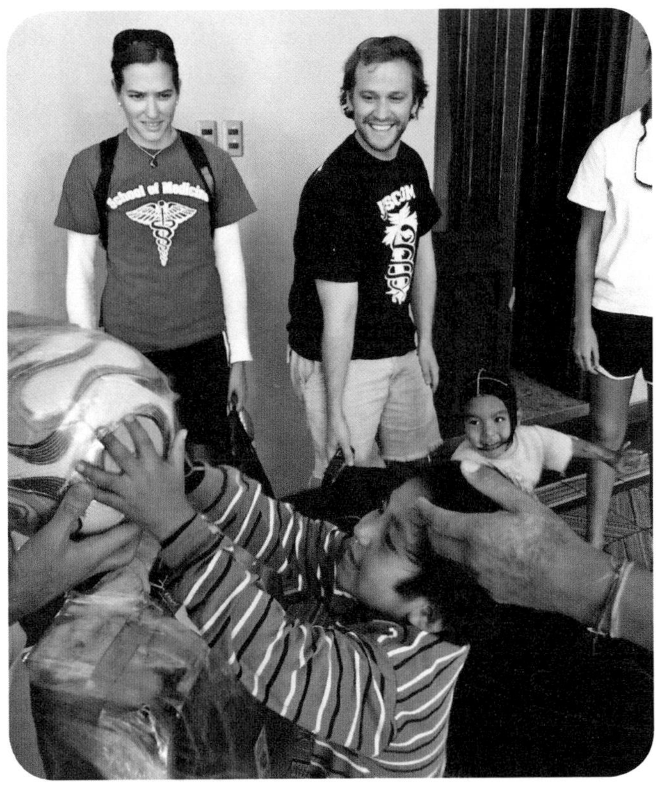

Medical students from the University of South Carolina donate sports equipment to children at a Bolivian orphanage
Photographer: *Alvin Strasburger*

Preliminary answers to these questions can be found in a recent literature review of outcomes of international exposure spanning almost two decades of medical students.[14] Although not reflective of global health curricula as a whole, data from international electives are widely available and offer a starting point for analyzing an aspect of this curriculum's effect on students. In this review, a total of 893 participants in international electives were identified, 43% of whom were in their fourth year of medical school. Program duration ranged from 4–32 weeks, and most evaluations were based on self-reports. Significant outcome trends among participants in these reports included 1) enhanced history-taking and physical exam skills (due to less reliance on technology), 2) higher scores in the public health and preventive medicine portion of Step II USMLE exam, 3) attitudinal changes reflecting increased cultural awareness and sensitivity, and 4) a high percentage opting for careers in primary care, underserved populations, and joint MPH degrees.[13,15,16]

While the qualitative results regarding the benefits of international health electives are encouraging, students and faculty still find difficulty securing funding for these experiences.[17] This lack of funding may play a large role in the inability of medical universities to keep up with student demand for international electives and other global health curricula opportunities. Recognizing this paradox, a number of students and faculty have proposed strategies for implementing a more standardized global health curriculum that would allow competencies to be defined and measured. Central to this proposal is that basic global health content varies considerably among medical schools and as such, the actual preparation and outcome of students completing abroad rotations may be highly variable in terms of quality and skills obtained.[18]

Following a literature and peer review to identify recommended approaches for teaching global health curricula, a joint Association of Faculties of Medicine of Canada Resource Group on Global Health and GHEC committee proposed six areas of core competencies for all medical students: 1) global burden of disease, 2) health implications of travel, migration and displacement, 3A) social and economic determinants of health, 3B) population, resources and the environment, 4) globalization of health and healthcare, 4) healthcare in low resource settings, 6) human rights in global health.[19] These expanded on the initial three domains proposed by Houpt et al.: 1) global burden of disease, 2) traveler's medicine, and 3) immigrant health.[20]

In addition to asking what global health training should impart to healthcare students, it is also useful to ask what those students wish to gain from their global health training. Again, as an initial barometer, student responses following global health electives appear to provide insight into their attitudes towards global health training as a whole. Holmes et al., at the University of Buffalo, retrieved five general objectives from a cohort of medical students pre- and post-international elective experiences. These students shared the aims of 1) observing the practice and organization of healthcare in another country, 2) improving medical/surgical skills, 3) improving language skills, 4) learning about another culture, and 5) deepening knowledge of infectious diseases.[21] Additionally, students identified native language, politics, housing, and travel expenses as the most challenging aspects of their international clinical rotations.

All these findings must be considered when constructing and implementing global health curricula and electives. As we move towards developing mainstream global health curricula for all healthcare professionals, several key components should be emphasized. Brewer et al. point out that pre-departure training (PDT) prior to all international health electives is essential to securing successful and safe outcomes but is often overlooked or lacking institutional support.[22,23] As global health teaching and training become more comprehensive and systematic, it will be increasingly valuable to ascertain population health outcomes related to international placements and training.[23] These data, among other standardized measures of improvement in core competencies and professional development, will be central to carving out a permanent niche for global health education in medical training.

Among the many initiatives currently underway, six Family Medicine residency programs in Ontario recently convened to establish a framework for global health curricula in their training programs.[25] The product of their efforts included delineations of competencies, values, training, and learning approaches that will be the basis of global health training at all six institutions. Other institutions are focusing their efforts on strengthening global partnerships, a key factor in the continued success and evolution of international rotations. The University of North Carolina-Malawi Surgical Initiative, for instance, has developed a partnership where one surgery resident is placed full time in Malawi to teach a basic surgical care curriculum to local medical providers.[26] This model for sustained institutional presence is particularly noteworthy for its cultural sensitivity and integration with local provider networks, an aspect sometimes inadvertently overlooked by outside programs eager to assist.

Still other medical training sites, such as the University of California system, have received private support to develop a School of Global Health, which will likely help set the standards for comprehensive education and training.[27] There is hopeful movement on many fronts to address the imbalance of health resources, health professionals, and global health training. In 2010, the Commission on Education of Health Professionals for the 21st Century was launched and released a detailed report of general strategies to achieve international healthcare integration via education across the health professions.[28] Every effort will be needed to create a unified system capable of evolving with the challenges of the future.

Redefining Professional Paths

As opportunities and training for global health continue to develop, one of the most exciting changes will be the trajectory of professional healthcare careers. For either correlated or causative reasons, students with global health experiences veer towards serving the underserved in primary care, often with an additional MPH degree as described above. Many of these providers complete their MPH degrees through part-time study while maintaining a practice, which has led to an increase in the average length of time for completing over the past 30 years.[28] This change in timeframe and a significant increase in popularity have transformed schools of public health, the first of which initially formed following the 1914 Welch-Rose report.[8]

One of the long-standing concerns remaining for medical practitioners who choose to practice primary care internationally is the limited number of job placements available. As the global health market develops to respond to the changing need and supply of trained practitioners, an instrumental force continues to be non-profit organizations. In 2013, for example, the Global Health Service Corps will join the Peace Corps in providing a short-term (one year per assignment) professional force of clinical services. This program aims to target resource-poor settings by supporting international placements for licensed medical practitioners, many of whom will receive loan repayment or other stipends to support their service in global health and medicine. Although not a permanent placement, this program emphasizes international partnerships and the development of a national network of placements for physicians and other medical providers. Other efforts, such as Partners in Health and Doctors Without Borders have defined missions addressing global health disparities due to socioeconomic and political inequalities. With initiatives such as these, modified and standardized professional school curricula, and more international electives for students, it is likely that the impact of global health practice will multiply many fold in the ensuing years.

References

1. Brown T., Cueto M. and Fee E. "The World Health Organization and Transition from 'International' to 'Global' Public Health" *American Journal of Public Health.* 96.1 (2006): 62-72.
2. Maciocco, G. "From Alma Ata to the Global Fund: The History of International Health Policy" *Social Medicine.* 3.1(2008): 36-48.
3. Pang T., and Garrett L. "The WHO must reform for its own health" *Nature Medicine.* 18.5(2012): 646.
4. Bollyky, T. "Reinventing the World Health Organization" Expert Brief. *Council on Foreign Relations.* May 2012.
5. Dybul M., Piot P., and Frenk J. "Reshaping Global Health" *Hoover Institution, Stanford University, Policy Review (2012):173.*
6. World Health Organization. "The future of financing for WHO: World Health Organization reforms for a healthy future". 64th World Health Assembly Agenda, May 2012. <http://apps.who.int/gb/ebwha/pdf_files/WHA64/A64_ID5-en.pdf>
7. Frenk, J., Chen, L., Bhutta, Z.A., et al. "Heath professionals for a new century: transforming education to strengthen health systems in an interdependent world." *The Lancet* 376 (2010): 1923—1958.
8. World Health Organization. *The world health report: working together for health.* Geneva: World Health Organization Press, 2006.
9. Imperato, P. "A third world international health elective for U.S. medical students: the 25-year experience of the State University of New York, downtown medical center." *Journal of Community Health* 29 (5) (2004): 337—373.
10. Luter J. "Fighters of disease, poverty and malnutrition." *Today's Health* 40(9) (1962): 48-53; 60-61.
11. American Association of Medical Colleges. "GQ Medical School Graduation Questionnaire: All Schools Summary Report FINAL." 2010.
12. McKinley DW, Williams SR, Norcini JJ, et al. International exchange programs and U.S. Medical Schools. *Acad Med* 2008;83(10 suppl):S53-S57.
13. Miranda, J.J., Yudkin, J.S., and Willott, C. "International Health Electives: Four years of experience." *Travel Medicine and Infectious Disease* 3 (2005): 133-141.
14. Jeffrey, J., Dumont, R., Kim, G. "Effects of international health electives on medical student learning and career choice: results of a systematic literature review." *Family Medicine* 43 (1) (2011): 21—28.
15. Ramsey, A., Haq, C., Gjerde, C., et al. "Career influence of an international health experience during medical school." *Medical Student Education* 36 (6) (2004): 412- 416.
16. Global Health Resource Group of the Association of Faculties of Medicine of Canada. "Towards a medical education relevant to all: the case for global health in medical education." 2006.
17. Grudzen, Corita and Eric Legome. "Loss of international medical experiences: knowledge, attitudes and skills at risk." *BMC Medical Education* 47 (7) (2007): http://www.biomedcentral.com/1472-6920/7/47
18. Izadnegahdar, R., Correira, S., Ohata, B., et al. "Global health in Canadian medical education: current practices and opportunities." *Academic Medicine* 83(2) (2008): 192—198.
19. Arthur, M, Battat, R, Brewer, T. "Teaching the basics: core competencies in global health." Global Health, Global Health Education, and Infectious Disease: The New Millennium, Part 1. Ed. Anvar Velji. *Infect Dis Clin N Am* 25 (2011) 347–358: doi:10.1016/j.idc.2011.02.013 id.theclinics.com

20. Houpt, E.R., Pearson, R.D, Hall. T.L. . "Three Domains of Competency in Global Health Education for All Medical Students." *Academic Medicine* 82:3 (2007): 222-225.

21. Holmes, D., Zayays, L.E., Koyfman, A. "Student Objectives and Learning Experiences in a Global Health Elective." *J Community Health* (2012): DOI 10.1007/s10900-012-9547-y

22. Brewer, T. "Preparing medical students for low-resource setting electives: a template for national pre-departure training guidelines." *Report to Association of Faculties of Medicine of Canada*. 2008.

23. Anderson K.C., Slatnik, M.A., Pereira, I. "Are We There Yet? Preparing Canadian Medical Students for Global Health Electives." *Academic Medicine* 87:2 (2012): 206-209.

24. Celletti, F., Reynolds T., Wright, A. et al. "Educating a New Generation of Doctors to Improve the Health of Populations in Low- and Middle-Income Countries." *PLoS Med* 8(10): e1001108. doi:10.1371/journal.pmed.1001108.

25. Redwood-Campbell, L., Pakes, B., Rouleau, K., et al. "Developing a Curriculum Framework for Global Health in Family Medicine: Emerging Principles, Competencies, and Educational Approaches." *BMC Medical Education*, 11:46 (2011): http://www.biomedcentral.com/1472-6920/11/46

26. Qureshi, J.S., Samuel, J., Lee, C.., et al. "Surgery and Global Public Health: The UNC-Malawi Surgical Initiative as a Model for Sustainable Collaboration." *World Journal of Surgery* 35 (2011): 17-21.

27. Rosenberg A. UC receives Gates Foundation grant to plan a School of Global Health. 2008. http://www.universityofcalifornia.edu/news/article/19077.

28. Frenk J, Chen L. *Health professionals for a new century: transforming education to strengthen health systems in an interdependent world. The Lancet* 376;: 2010: 1923–58.

29. Imperato, J, LaRosa, J, Schechter, L. "The development of a master of public health program with an initial focus on urban and immigrant health at the state university." *Journal of Community Health* 30(6): 2005: 417—449.

CHAPTER 2

Ethics and Global Health Education

Nicole Sussman
MD candidate
Wake Forest School of Medicine

Mei Elensary, MD, MPhil
Boston Combined Residency Program in Pediatrics
Urban Health and Advocacy Track

HaruYamamoto, BS

Jessica Evert, MD
Executive Director, Child Family Health International
Clinical Faculty, Department of Family and Community Medicine
University of California, San Francisco

Editors

Evaleen Jones, MD
Associate Professor, Stanford University School of Medicine
Founder, Child Family Health International

Anvar Velji, MD,FRCP (c),FACP, FIDSA
Associate Dean of Global Health Sciences, California Northstate School of Medicine, Elk Grove, California
Chief Infectious Disease, Kaiser Permanente, South Sacramento,
Co-Founder Global Health Education Consortium (now CUGH)
Clinical Professor of Medicine, University of California, Davis

ETHICS PERMEATES GLOBAL HEALTH EDUCATION and training in multiple ways- as a curricular topic, as the underpinnings of tensions that arise when programs are operationalized, and as the foundation of the wider 'global health' movement. More specifically, domains of Applied Ethics can be seen as a framework for global health ethical considerations and education. Perhaps the simplest definition of Applied Ethics is "The philosophical search (within western philosophy) for right and wrong within controversial scenarios."[1]

Ethics in the field of global health and global health education embodies multiple domains of

Applied Ethics. Importantly, Applied Ethics is not about absolute moral correctness or endpoints, rather it focuses on the intent and process of working through ethical tensions and dilemmas. These ethical issues can be constants during the establishment of training partnerships of equals, but drawn from programs and institutions at different levels of development and/or disparate access to resources both human and financial.

Ethics, as Russell Porter (the creator of the typology used in this chapter) puts it, is "an aggregate of morals within a specific group used to solve conflicts, with reasons on why a solution was chosen."[2] Ideally, explicit ethical content and discussions of hypothetical or actual ethical tensions should be introduced to students within any global health curriculum. While there is an overlap between these ethical content and tensions, they are both distinct and important considerations for operationalizing any new or existing global health program.

Over the last two decades as globalization and the global health movements have gained significant momentum, ethical concepts and diplomacy have taken precedence over the historically lopsided relationship that exists between the well developed countries and the low middle income countries (LMICs). A comprehensive perspective of core principles must be the foundation for sustainable gains toward health for all.

In our experience, ethical tensions encountered in developing and executing global health programs are often evident during the preliminary planning, realization, and subsequent reflection on experiences. Such ethical issues arise from and inform program implementation and engagement. These tensions are important and relevant in guiding academic and non-academic institutions, and for informing administrators, faculty and students.. Optimal program composition will mitigate these tensions, while poor design runs the risk of exacerbating dilemmas.. This chapter discusses a multitude of ethical considerations for global health educational programs from a variety of perspectives. Chapter 8 in this volume also provides a framework for the practical application of these theoretical concepts during international medical electives.

Ethical foundations and tensions inherent within global health programs and education can be viewed through the 6 Domains of Ethics Training articulated by Porter's framework for structured ethics education for those involved in all areas of healthcare:[2]

1. Social ethics (ethics between/within nations/among the global community)
2. Professional ethics (ethics underlying professionalism)
3. Clinical ethics (ethics underlying health care provision)
4. Business ethics (moral and ethical considerations of business conduct)
5. Organizational ethics (ethics of organizations that informs internal and external responses)
6. Decision ethics (ethical decision making processes to address an ethical dilemma)

Below we articulate and outline concepts that are relevant for global health education and educational programs using Porter's typology. These training paradigms, along with the resources listed at the end of the chapter, are useful when developing or improving global health education programs and training.

Two siblings stand outside their home in a large neighborhood in Lusaka, Zambia
Photographer: *Will Bynum*

Social Ethics

Health as A Human Right

Human rights can be understood as the set of freedoms inherent to every person: they are not earned, but, rather, are intrinsic to the dignity of personhood. Health as a human right was established for all in the 1948 UN Declaration.[3] Yet some believe the right to even basic healthcare is fundamentally different because, unlike other human rights that address protection against an act such as slavery or torture, healthcare is a professionally provided service. Critics also argue that it is difficult to determine the minimum standard of healthcare that could be considered a human right.[4] For example, international consensus on an appropriate guaranteed basic minimum has been elusive. Such criticisms, however, pale in comparison to the widespread reality of health inequality among populations on an international scale. Ideally, the consensus would be to provide the highest standard of affordable care for all humans. Despite the difficulties inherent in their ambitions, proponents of the ideal that healthcare is innate to humanity argue that universal access to and basic care for preventable and treatable diseases should be the realistic expectations of health systems across the globe.

To accept a global basic minimum of healthcare requires accepting the possibility that the responsibility of reaching this ideal falls to the international community as a whole. The premise of "shared responsibility" is often critiqued. Underlying this debate is the question of exactly who bears responsibility for the health of the earth's population. Unfortunately, as sovereign states focus inward, they might fail to understand that international boundaries are human-made distinctions that protozoa, bacteria, and mosquitoes do not appreciate. Understood in this way, shared responsibility may be in a sovereign state's best interest.[5] For example, processes such as globalization can contribute to pandemics, but a broader conception of the responsibilities of the international healthcare community might help mitigate the risk or magnitude of pandemics. The toll of human disease is not merely a local problem: it is a global problem, and the available benefits of aid should be viewed as support for the global community.

The impact of globalization has expanded the roles and responsibilities of healthcare professionals worldwide.[6]In a world of permeable borders and increasing migration and travel, physicians are now responsible for the care of patients from a wide array of cultures. As the world becomes more interconnected, physicians from developed countries have the unique opportunity to work with and learn from global communities to address the morbidity and mortality caused by poverty and preventable illnesses.

Social Justice

Social justice is the recognition of a "historically deep and geographically broad" understanding of gross inequities, and power imbalances that underlie causes of ill health.[7] International experiences foster and reinforce a commitment to care for underserved groups. Medical students should prepare for and reflect on their global health activities through the lens of social justice. Pre-departure preparation should include an understanding of geopolitical, historical, and other determinants of health and health care. The content of this preparation should be as locally specific as possible, as each region and even community within a region is unique. Importantly, national boundaries may be less definitive for local populations than connectors such as faith, language, tribe, or clan. This is particularly true in previously colonized regions. Social justice can be intertwined into competencies and learning objectives to help articulate the multiple learning dimensions that result from immersion experiences.

With regard to outcomes of global health rotations, social justice captures both opportunities and limitations of short-term engagement. For short global health experiences, it may be difficult to have an impact that diminishes inequality in health care globally. However, these opportunities can help students develop a sense of social responsibility and gain a better understanding of the concept of a 'world village.' This, in turn, garners an appreciation of how behaviors/actions in one part of the world affect the entire world as a whole. Short global health experiences for medical students help 'connect the dots' and define their roles as future physicians who have the potential to be productive and beneficial in articulating and advocating for the marginalized both at home and abroad.

Distributive Justice

Distributive justice principles are defined as "providing moral guidance for the political processes and structures that affect the distribution of economic benefits and burdens in societies."[8]Previously, distributive justice in the area of health was looked at from a national perspective. In the past 30 years, the field of international justice has blossomed to include consideration of distributive justice, and justice more generally, on a global scale.

Principles of distributive justice often call for the equitable distribution of scarce or finite resources among all socioeconomic groups. When looked at globally, this challenges the gross health inequities that exist between and within countries for access to limited health care workforce, medications, and technologies. Some health care systems have prioritized distributive justice over other principles, such as individualism, to try to create an equitable health system. Global organizations such as Medecins Sans Frontiere's (MSF's) Campaign for Access to Essential Medications is an excellent example of efforts to address distributive justice issues globally. Over the last two decades, for mostly economic reasons, drug company research and development was disproportionately focused on profitable drug development, rather than drug development that reflects needs of the populations of LMICs. Known popularly as the 10/90 Gap, this reality led to only 10% of the worlds expenditures on health research and drug development being spent on problems that affect the poorest 90% of the world's population that live in the LMICs. MSF and others have advocated for more focus on low-cost drugs and issues disproportionately affecting LMICs. In addition, the changing disease burdens in the LMICs (including a rapid increase in the chronic conditions of chronic obstructive lung disease, emphysema, diabetes, cardiovascular disease, and obesity) and disabilities due to multifactorial causes have now put much more emphasis on provision of drugs that prevent and treat diseases previously thought to be more prevalent in affluent countries. Non-profit drug companies and advocacy groups, such as MSF, are also campaigning for the suspension of drug patents to allow medications to get to the poorest, most suffering patients, at a reasonable price and following an expedited timeline.

Professional Ethics

Professionalism

"Professionalism" relates to responsibilities and obligations one has by virtue of one's role in their "profession." Prior to embarking on a global health experience, it is important to clearly define one's role as an observer, a practitioner, or a researcher. Medical and other health science students often have limited training about clinical practice in a developing country and lack familiarity with endemic disease conditions. These differences in how medicine is practiced globally make it important to reflect on one's limited ability and restricted role on 'the healthcare team.' Professionalism embraces the same set of parameters in the global health setting as one would in their home institution, even if these parameters do not formally exist in the foreign setting. Students and residents should not take on responsibilities that they have not been trained for, or take advantage of lack of oversight to practice beyond their level. It is essential to establish appropriate connections within the host community to ensure accurate interpretation and transparency of roles of all health care providers.

Respecting the privacy and dignity of patients is an important aspect of professionalism that transcends most cultures. Often in developing countries, students may forget the basic right to privacy that is practiced very deliberately in the Western world. Students may be overwhelmed with new and interesting disease presentations and may be tempted to document such conditions with photographs to share with others. While local people may not openly object to it, considerations for patient's privacy and dignity must be assessed and deliberated. Both patients and native health care workers may be so grateful to have a Western medical provider that they may forfeit usual customs in an effort not to offend. Therefore, as an outsider, one must take extra consideration not to exploit individuals in the host community. Such exploitation can come in many forms—taking staff away from job duties to translate or assist with logistics, providing unskilled care in 'the cloak of expertise' a white coat can impart, or speculative treatment on patients who do not have ability to choose a more seasoned provider.

Students must be mindful of the inherent lack of clarity around their level of expertise by both host institutions and patients. Patients may take a western-trained health care provider's advice without question, so students need to be aware of this when discussing care, explaining a procedure or obtaining informed consent. Before embarking on their journey, students should work with their home institution to complete appropriate pre-departure training. The home institution or organization providing support for the clinical rotation should make sure the student's level of training and role is clearly defined with the host institution and the relevant community. Pre-departure training is essential (see chapter 8 for more details). This might include correspondence with someone at the home institution or program who has previously traveled to that location. This should most certainly include contact with the host community, either directly or through a facilitator. Prior knowledge of cultural differences can enrich interactions with local community members and help build trust and rapport with patients, key components of cultural competence and humility. Subtle violations of certain cultural norms may be perceived as disrespectful and this information is rarely found in books but gained only through experience and critical reflection.

Leading ethical standards suggest that students rotating in global setting **should be placed as learners, not health care providers**.[9] While this may seem obvious, it is actually an explicit discussion that needs to occur to optimize the students understanding of one's role based on one's experience and level of training. Inherent to all clinical training is practice caring for patients and doing procedures. However, this should not include capitalizing on the well-known cliché "See one, Do one, Teach one". The boundaries, expectations, and supervision of students need to be clear for both the host and guest institution. Importantly, the level of clinical practice, types of procedures, and other independence the student has at home may be appropriately very different when they are abroad. The overlays of a new culture, novel language, and less resources may be important reasons for the student to require more supervision and be in a more observational capacity, at least initially. Utilizing sites with established relationships, either with an academic institution or a third-party organization, helps to ensure these complex considerations are revisited every year or even more frequently, as well as facilitates program quality improvement and ongoing feedback from host communities.

Altruism

Medical students and institutions often portray global health engagement with underserved people, both locally and abroad as an altruistic activity. This is most commonly in reference to the historical definitions of altruism as conceptualized by Auguste Comte in the 1800's who defined altruism as self-less "Living for the sake of others."[10] In actuality, the nature of benefits in global health engagement may be more aligned with contemporary definitions of altruism. One such contemporary definition of altruism is that of Mendoca, who states that acts of altruism are actually "mutually beneficial" and represent "an enlightened form of self-interest." As such, actions often conceived of as being self-less (such as volunteering at a clinic in a developing country) are actually self-benefiting. This understanding of altruism captures the benefit to both the underserved patients and communities, as well the benefits for the physicians and others 'helping' patients/communities in the context of global engagement and outreach.

This shift in the understanding of benefit challenges many of the presumptions underlying global health programming. One way for students and faculty to evolve their understanding of the impacts and rationale for global health experiences is to examine their motivations. Before beginning a global health experience, students should engage in honest self-reflection. Jane Philpott developed a useful exercise to facilitate reflection on their reasons/justifications for participating in a global health elective.[11] Philpott's exercise asks trainees to qualify motivations as those to which they aspire, those they tolerate, and those they try to suppress. Through this exercise most trainees realize that there is much they gain in the service of others and thus come to understand that they often "get more than they give"

Many students are motivated by traditional notions of altruism – i.e., to provide help and "do good" for a medically and socio-economical underserved population. However, one can rightly question whether students (and perhaps outsiders more generally) have the ability to do "enough" good, or whether this comes at such a cost to qualify as "altruism." Most students lack the training and skills needed to effectively make contributions at such an early stage in their medical career. It may be more useful to look at global health opportunities as an educational experience rather than a service experience.

Developing clear learning objectives that can be attained in a short amount of time helps formalize global health experiences as learning experiences. For example, a realistic learning objective could be a) to understand generally how resource limitations influence medical care in a LMIC context or b) to identify presentations of tropical diseases rarely seen in the West.

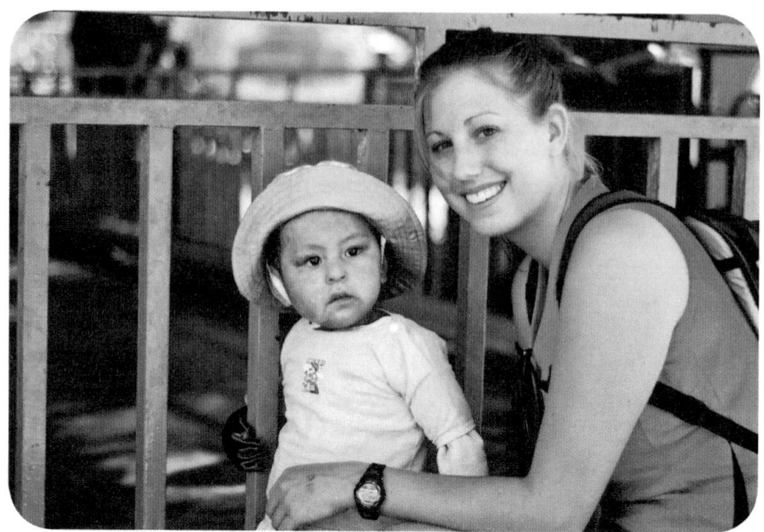

An American medical student bonds with a young child who was burned in a kitchen fire at her rural South American home
Photographer: *Julius Cronin*

Humility

Humility involves an ability to recognize one's limitations in training, experience, and one's potential to do harm.[12] Training of medical students primarily occurs in a resource-rich setting that may not easily translate to global health settings. In addition, students often have limited exposure to many diseases endemic in developing countries. It is paramount to respect the expertise of host medical personnel as they have greater experience in managing most medical conditions in this setting. Hosting practitioners may overestimate students' skills and may fail to provide adequate supervision. Humility can help deflect neocolonial behavior and avoid potential harm to patients.

Performing beyond one's medical training can potentially lead to bad outcomes, resulting in harm to the patient and/or family members and emotional turmoil to the student. Visiting students frequently underestimate local practitioners' skills. This underestimation is not intentional, rather, it is usually a reflection of the characterization of LMIC and native populations made by Western institutions, media, and other influential sources. Appropriate humility can serve as a counterweight for this tendency. Furthermore, humility can moderate the student's desire to help and avoid inadvertently finding themselves in a position to care for patients beyond their level of training. Dr. Evaleen Jones reminds students ***'don't just do something, stand there!"*** An effect of humility and inaction is that students can be anthropological in their approach to learning about global health and the realities that underlie this nebulous term. As such, students can learn to observe reality before they try to change it. This nurtures global health leaders that embody characteristics necessary for a successful, just partnership. As articulated by Shah and Wu, "This desire to help, combined with relative inexperience, can pose ethical conflicts and leave both patients and students vulnerable to negative outcomes"[13] This is a concern particularly with students early in their training, when they have limited clinical exposure. As Crump and colleagues wrote, "In resource-constrained health care settings, trainees from resource replete environments may have inflated ideas about the value of their skills and yet may be unfamiliar with syndromic approaches to patient treatment that are common in settings with limited laboratory capacity."[14]

Students have an ethical obligation not to practice outside of their scope of training. This is particularly important with regard to patients in resource-poor settings who are particularly vulnerable to "dis-symmetries of power" in medicine.[15] This situation illustrates the common misconception that "people who live in poverty will benefit from any medical services, irrespective of the experience or lack thereof, of the provider."[13] This perspective assumes incorrectly that low resource settings do not share the same ethical and professional standards for the care of patients. As a part of medical education, it is important to model that all patients in all settings deserve the highest quality of care.

Academic institutions and other sending organizations have an important role in emphasizing the place and value of humility. This is challenging because inevitably there arise conflicts between an institution's desire to emphasize their own central role in 'global health' and the need to engender humility on both institutional and individual levels. This tension may be remedied by partnering with third-party organizations or other NGOs that represent and advocate for the host community. This will help to balance the agendas of Western institutions and host communities and create a framework for establishing local capacity and ethical engagement. Importantly, medical educators are now candidly teaching that humility is not a sign of weakness in medicine, but rather "on the contrary, humility requires toughness and emotional resilience."[16] If humility can be strongly embraced by academic institutions and Western organizations, it will be an ethical tenant that students will be more likely to understand and practice.

Codes of Conduct

Many medical trainees are well aware of the Hippocratic Oath. Historically it has been a moral and ethical guide for the field of medicine. As such, many medical students make this pledge during graduation. The Oath reads as follows:[17]

> *I will respect the hard-won scientific gains of those physicians in whose steps I walk, and gladly share such knowledge as is mine with those who are to follow.*
>
> *I will apply, for the benefit of the sick, all measures which are required, avoiding those twin traps of overtreatment and therapeutic nihilism.*
>
> *I will remember that there is art to medicine as well as science, and that warmth, sympathy, and understanding may outweigh the surgeon's knife or the chemist's drug.*

I will not be ashamed to say "I know not," nor will I fail to call in my colleagues when the skills of another are needed for a patient's recovery.

I will respect the privacy of my patients, for their problems are not disclosed to me that the world may know. Most especially must I tread with care in matters of life and death.

If it is given me to save a life, all thanks. But it may also be within my power to take a life; this awesome responsibility must be faced with great humbleness and awareness of my own frailty.

Above all, I must not play at God. I will remember that I do not treat a fever chart, a cancerous growth, but a sick human being, whose illness may affect the person's family and economic stability. My responsibility includes these related problems, if I am to care adequately for the sick.

I will prevent disease whenever I can, for prevention is preferable to cure.

I will remember that I remain a member of society, with special obligations to all my fellow human beings, those sound of mind and body as well as the infirm.

If I do not violate this oath, may I enjoy life and art, respected while I live and remembered with affection thereafter. May I always act so as to preserve the finest traditions of my calling and may I long experience the joy of healing those who seek my help.

This oath strives to reflect the essence of medicine. A complimentary professional code is that of Carl Taylor's Free Version of the Hippocratic Oath that reflects many of the tenants of global health. It offers an alternative and practical perspective on the priorities and considerations of professionals working in the area of global health. Along with the Hippocratic Oath, it is useful as a tool for students, faculty, and institutions to benchmark their embodiment of professional ideals. It further clarifies common goals of global partnerships as follows:[18]

I will share the science and art by precept, by demonstration, and by every mode of teaching with other physicians regardless of their national origin.

I will try to help secure for the physicians in each country the esteem of their own people, and through collaborative work see that they get full credit.

I will strive to eliminate sources of disease everywhere in the world and not merely set up barriers to the spread of disease to my own people.

I will work for understanding of the diverse causes of diseases, including social, economic, and environmental.

I will promote the well-being of mankind in all its aspects, not merely the bodily, with sympathy and consideration for a people's culture and beliefs.

I will strive to prevent painful and untimely death, and also help parents to achieve a family size conforming to their desires and to their ability to care for their children.

In my concern with whole communities I will never forget the needs of its individual members.

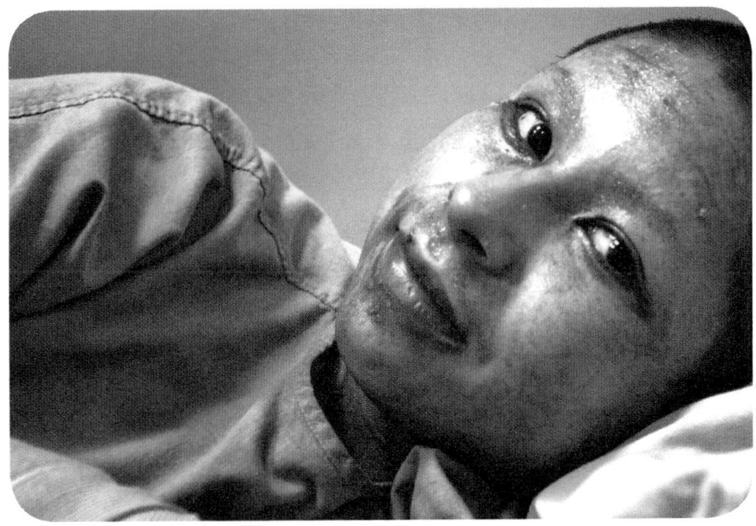

A Bolivian child burned in a kitchen fire rests comfortably in the burn center where Bolivian physicians provide her medical care despite her family's inability to pay.
Photographer: *Will Bynum*

Clinical Ethics

Health Equity

Former WHO Director-General Margaret Chan astutely proclaimed, "Greater equity in the health status of populations within and between countries should be regarded as the key measure of how we, as a civilized society, are making progress."[19]Measuring success by this metric is far from current reality in spite of the fact that many global health programs are based on a 'health equity' mantra. In fact, the lack of health equity in countries, particularly the United States, offers a rich opportunity to more closely appraise both local and global health enterprises. With the passage of the Affordable Health Care for America Act of 2012 it appears there is greater intention to mitigate the enormous gap in health care accessibility.

Non-Maleficence

The proverbial "First, Do No Harm" is the colloquial version of the ethical term non-maleficence. Sending institutions, in principle, must ensure that host institutions, at a minimum, are not left worse off as a result of global health collaborations. In addition, supervisors, institutions, and students themselves have an obligation to assure individual patients will not be worse off due to the students' activities and presence. Such a situation may arise when the burdens and expectations placed on host institutions are not adequately considered by sending institutions or not clarified between host and sending institution. For instance, local physicians may be required to spend considerable time and effort in supporting and educating visiting students, which may result in a physician being diverted from his/her clinical responsibilities. Physicians in low-resource settings are always in high-demand, and any diversion of their clinical time may be detrimental to patient care.[20] Moreover, it is often expected that local staff will orient medical trainees, arrange for housing and transportation, locate translation services, and provide general logistical support. Besides expending significant amounts of time and energy there may be additional financial burdens, "such as unaccounted-for-costs associated with hosting trainees that may include paying for visas, food, and incidental costs".[21]

Further complicating such challenges, host institutions with fewer resources may be hesitant to address such concerns with wealthier, "sending institutions" to avoid jeopardizing relationships. Electives have been described as a "one-way opportunity" favoring students who visit from wealthier institutions.[22] The potential for disproportionate benefit for visiting students rather than for the host institution may paradoxically reinforce the same disparities in wealth and opportunity that global health programs seek to address.[23] Sending institutions should be required to incorporate a natural and continuous feedback system for host institutions. This will facilitate open communication and help ensure that partnerships are mutually beneficial and do not cause harm for individual patients or the larger institution.

Business Ethics

Sustainability

Sustainability is a major goal of global health aid and service. For medical students, this may mean working within an existing collaborative initiative between their home institution and the host institution. Ideally, a sustainable academic partnership would be a long-term interaction between institutions with funding and resources provided as needed. In addition, knowledge transfer between institutions would facilitate changes on both sides to create improvements in delivery of healthcare. Ideally this would include medical students, residents, and faculty from both institutions in some form of bilateral exchange. During their global health experience, medical students can act as diplomats and representatives from their home institution and help build a stronger relationship between the two institutions. These continuous, long-term interactions help maintain solidarity between programs and ensure that personal and community goals are in alignment and prioritized to the mutual benefit of both institutions.

Global health electives are usually short-term, however some students strive to complete a research project or make some quantifiable contribution in a short amount of time. Students may attempt to institute change or implement new protocols in the existing healthcare setting of local communities during their visit. In such instances, it is necessary to evaluate the local capacity to embrace, implement, and identify local personnel to take on leadership roles. This may require ongoing communication on leaving the country and perhaps in future visits. Finally, it is important that medical students maintain these ethical obligations during their global health experiences and create a strong and ongoing rapport that allows for future students to also participate in such opportunities.

Recognizing the limitations of medical students to affect host communities during short-term rotations in the areas of health metrics does not mean that medical students' activities in global health do not lead to sustainable outcomes. Sustainable outcomes include motivating students to serve the underserved, culturally diverse populations at home, providing health diplomacy through student's positive interactions with host communities, and elevating local preceptors as 'experts' in optimally structured rotations.

Transparency

Global health education programs benefit a multitude of stakeholders. However, these benefits are not often made explicit in agreements, reflections, and program materials. As mentioned previously, more often than not, global health activities, including education and research, are undertaken in the hopes of "helping" the less fortunate. However, these endeavors have great benefits for the US-based universities such as increased funding (both public and private) for research and programs, heightened prestige, and increased ability to attract competitive candidates. These benefits ethically should translate into greater advantage to the host partners. Similarly students need to be transparent in their motivations and the benefits of their global health education. One common situation is students who want to get a clinical experience, but instead go abroad under the guise of doing research because of more expansive funding opportunities.

Students enlist in global health education programs out of a variety of motivations, and have various expectations of benefit. For instance some students will try to work around the constraints of their research to get clinical exposure, even though it may not be an explicit expectation of the host institution or a well-supported program framework. Students may also be motivated to enhance their resume.

Medical tourism has been defined as "exotic travel to a developing region with a brief opportunity to practice medicine on local residents."[24] Many consider global health education to be synonymous with Medical Tourism. Under optimal structure and transparency, Medical Tourism is not the goal of short-term global education programs. In addition, ethically sound institutions and organizations will ensure that this paternalist approach is forbidden. Once the motivations are unroofed and the intentions are made clear, both for individual students and institutions, transparency can permeate partnerships, student and institutional activities. A useful resource list designed by Jane Philpot for trainees and institutions on motivation activity is listed in the resource section of this chapter.

Economic Justice

A very nuanced definition of Economic Justice is "giving to each what he or she is due."[25] When it comes to global health programs the economic units can be measured in dollars, recognition, publications, employee promotions, travel support, access to professional development and many other valuable tangible and non-tangible benefits. For a university or organization to practice economic justice they must make certain to 1) Recognize the efforts that lead to the compensation 'due' 2) Adequately give, in either financial or other economic units, to those that are 'due.' This concept is directly related to the ideas of transparency, altruism, and professionalism. If the benefit of global health education program is mainly for the student, then one must look at who is providing those benefits. In many respects, these benefits are provided by the local community, hosting health care facilities, local medical staff/supervisors, and those administering the program either from the US or locally. Then one must examine how to appropriately recognize that these benefits are being provided and address how to appropriately compensate for them. More often short-term global health educational placements are becoming tuition-based. This is due to an enlightened sense that students are the net beneficiaries and there is a great amount of work that goes into supporting, hosting, organizing, overseeing, and educating them.

Organizational Ethics

Organizational Ethics are those principles, commitments and morals on which organizations are founded and operate. Four elements of creating an ethical organization have been suggested:[26]

1. Written code of ethics
2. Ethics trainings for leaders and staff
3. Mechanisms to field and address ethical concerns
4. Systems of confidential reporting

Importantly, these elements are not stagnant entities, but rather dynamic processes that have ongoing revisions, reference, and consideration. Critics have pointed out that large organizations considered very unethical, such as Enron, had glowing codes of conduct and ethical behavior that they did not follow.[27]

There are various situations where organizational ethics can pertain to global health programs. Obviously for those programs housed within a University, the wider University context can be a driving force. In many circumstances a smaller University division, be it a school, department, division, or other administrative construct is much more the determinant for the nature of global health programs and education. In this case, it may be appropriate to look at the unique ethical codes and constructs necessary for building global health activities. Chapter 8 helps institutions consider and examine their ethical framework, which lays the groundwork for a code of ethics. For non-profit organizations that are running global health education programs, the above elements may be appropriate for the entire organization, ideally involving both domestic and international team members and viewpoints.

Developing mechanisms to recognize, address and confidentially report ethical concerns is critical for global health engagement of any kind. There are often wider University-based systems for such reporting, however these may not be readily apparent or accessible to global health program participants. It also may be appropriate to have a mechanism to facilitate such dialogues within the Department or entity that oversees the global health educational programming. Making such reporting easily available to international partners may be logistically difficult, but certainly would be a gold standard to allow them to voice their concerns about ethical breaches precipitated by the students, faculty, or administrators.

Decision Ethics

Decision Ethics involves using sound decision-making processes to approach problems, questions, or other relevant judgment-based issues. There are multiple ethical frameworks through which to base decisions, these include distributive justice theory, obligationism, positivism, utilitarian theory, and many more. For those not expertly versed in ethics, this terminology may be overwhelming. A more practical way to approach Decision Ethics is to have a general algorithm or framework that is followed when decisions are made. There are multiple ethical decision making models that exist. One of the more easily understood is the PLUS Decision Making Process espoused by the Ethics Resource Center.

There are 6 Steps to any Decision-Making Process:[28]

Step 1: Define the Problem

- » Clearly state the problem.
- » Why is a decision called for?
- » Identify the most desired outcome(s) of the decision-making process.

Step 2: Identify a minimum of 3 alternative solutions to the problem

- » Go beyond obvious solutions

Step 3: Evaluate the identified alternatives

- » Recognize the role of assumptions and beliefs (rather than facts)
- » Consider the positives and negatives of each alternative
- » Try to evaluate which alternative one is most confident about—which one is based on the most fact/s and most likely to have the anticipated outcome.

Step 4: Make the Decision

Step 5: Implement the decision

- » Recognize that there is a difference between deciding or intending to do something and actually doing it.

Step 6: Evaluate the Decision

- » Consider what new problems arose?
- » What problems were solved?
- » Were short-term problems solved at the expense of long-term considerations?

While this process is very deliberate in nature, the manifestation of Decision Ethics in real situations might require more expediency. This process can occur in the minds of individuals, in the context of group work, or at an organizational level. Particularly when students are required to make decisions about how to act in a novel, global setting, having a process to evaluate when there is a choice (as it is not always obvious that a choice exists), how to process alternative decisions, and how to evaluate their decisions is very useful.

There are multiple exercises that may help students consider their decision-making processes and allow for past decisions to influence future courses of action. Louise Aronson's structure for Critical Reflection is a means to this end.[29] In addition, using case-based preparation materials can help students to anticipate situations and decisions they might face and consider alternative ways to approach them before they find themselves in a high-stakes situation. See the resources section of this chapter for more information.

Summary

The underpinnings of global health education, how our institutions operationalize the concept, and the 'on the ground' realities of education and training activities are all rich with ethical ideals, tensions, and opportunities. The onus is on the institutions and organizations that facilitate these educational opportunities and tout global health activities to ensure that we are doing our "ethical homework". We must strive to walk our talk. Ethics is not an end. As presented in this chapter, ethics is the application of concepts, processes, and fundamentals to help guide our organizations, faculty, students, and partnerships in a way that navigates ambiguities and seeks moral soundness. At the heart of global health is a foundational belief in health as a human right. Importantly, our actions and efforts to promote wellness and alleviate suffering worldwide must be accompanied by scrutiny and mindfulness of ethical principles and processes.

Acknowledgement

A special thanks to Matthew DeCamp MD PhD for his contribution to this chapter through thought-leadership and editorial advice.

Resources (a select, not exhaustive, list of useful resources)

Web-based Resources

The EIESL Project Web-Based Guidebook (www.ethicsofisl.ubc.ca): A comprehensive guidebook on teaching and considering ethics of international engagement and service learning. Includes basic concepts, case-based learning, and in-depth theoretical frameworks.

Ethical Challenges of Short-Term Global Health Training Case Studies (www.ethicsandglobalhealth.org): A collaboration between Stanford University and Johns Hopkins providing 10 cases with 5 survey questions per case- a Certificate of Completion is provided. Supported by Doris Duke Charitable Trust.

AMSA Global Health Ethics Student Curriculum (www.amsa.org/AMSA/Homepage/About/Committees/Global/Ethics.aspx): A case-based curriculum that explores some of the ethical challenges posed by global research and clinical experiences.

PLUS: The Decision Making Process (www.ethics.org/resource/plus-decision-making-process): A more detailed version of the 6 step decision making process outlined above.

Articles

Aronson L. Twelve tips on teaching reflection at all levels of medical education. Med Teach. 2012 Aug;46(8):807-814.

Brenda A and Walker P. The obligation of debriefing in global health education. Med Teach (2012);online published 26 Oct 2012.

Crump J, Sugarman J, Working Group on Ethics Guidelines for Global Health Training (WEIGHT). Ethics and best practice guidelines for training experiences in global health. Am J Trop Med Hyg (2010);83(6):1178-82.

Elansary M, Graber L, Provenzano A, et al. Ethical Dilemmas in Global Clinical Electives. The Journal of Global Health. Spring 2011.

Gostin LO. A framework convention on global health: health for all, justice for all. JAMA (2012);307(19);2087-92.

Lowry, C. Two Models of Global Health Ethics. Public Health Ethics (2009). 2(3):276-284.

Pinto A and Upshur R. Global Health Ethics for Students. Developing World Bioethics (2007). 9(1);1-10.

White M and Evert J. Developing Ethical Awareness in Global Health: Four Cases for Medical Educators. Developing World Bioethics (2012);e-published online 1 Oct 2012.

Film

First Do No Harm: A Qualitative Research Documentary (www.vimeo.com/22008886): A documentary produced by Alyson and Timothy Holland that can be used with an accompanying discussion guide to facilitate student, faculty, and institutional considerations of the ethical challenges of global health education programs.

References

1. Gowdy L. Applied Ethics. http://www.ethicsmorals.com/ethicsapplied.html, June 2012. Accessed December 11, 2012.
2. Porter R. *A Typology of Ethics Education in Healthcare.* University of North Texas, 2004.
3. UN Declaration of Human Rights, 1948. http://www.un.org/en/documents/udhr/. Accessed December 28, 2012.
4. Wolff J. The Human Right to Health. Amnesty International Global Ethics Series, 2012.
5. Helble M. The movement of patients across borders: challenges and opportunities for public health. WHO, 2011. http://www.who.int/bulletin/volumes/89/1/10-076612/en/index.html. Accessed December 27, 2012.
6. Frenk J, Chen L, Bhutta ZA, et.al. Health professionals for a new century: transforming education to strengthen health systems in an interdependent world. *Lancet* 2010; 376: 1923-58.
7. Pinto AD, Upshur RE. Global health ethics for students. Dev World Bioeth. 2009 Apr;9(1):1-10.
8. Lamont, Julian and Favor, Christi, "Distributive Justice", *The Stanford Encyclopedia of Philosophy* (Spring 2013 Edition), Edward N. Zalta (ed.), http://plato.stanford.edu/archives/spr2013/entries/justice-distributive/. Accessed Dec 12, 2012
9. Crump JA, Sugarman J, WEIGHT. Ethics and best practice guidelines for training experiences in global health. Am J Trop Med Hyg. 2010 Dec;83(6):1178-82
10. Steinberg, D. Altruism in Medicine: its definition, nature, and dilemmas. Cambridge Quarterly of Health Care Ethics. 19(2);2010:249-257.
11. Philpott J. Training for a Global State of Mind. *Virtual Mentor,* 12;3: 231-236.
12. Coulehan J. *PerspectBiol Med.* A gentle and humane temper: humility in medicine. 2011 Spring;54(2):206-16.
13. Shah S, Wu T. The medical student global health experience: professionalism and ethical implications. J Med Ethics 2008;34:375-8.
14. Crump JA, Sugarman J. Ethical considerations for short-term experiences by trainees in global health. JAMA : the journal of the American Medical Association 2008;300:1456-8.
15. Farmer P, Campos NG. Rethinking medical ethics: a view from below. Developing world bioethics 2004;4:17-41.
16. Coulehan J On Humility. *Ann Int Med.* August 3, 2010 vol. 153 no. 3 200-201.
17. Lasagna L. Hippocratic Oath (modern version). http://guides.library.jhu.edu/content.php?pid=23699&sid=190964. Accessed December 12, 2012.
18. Taylor, C. Ethics for an International Health Profession. Science. 12 August 1966:
19. Vol. 153 no. 3737 pp. 716-720 World Health Org 2009 Greater equity in health should be a progress indicator.
20. Elansary M GL, Provenzano AM, Barry M, Khoshnood K, Rastegar A. Ethical dilemmas in global clinical electives. The Journal of Global Health 2011;1:24-7.
21. Crump JA, Sugarman J. Ethical considerations for short-term experiences by trainees in global health. JAMA : the journal of the American Medical Association 2008;300:1456-8.
22. Mutchnick IS, Moyer CA, Stern DT. Expanding the boundaries of medical education: evidence for cross-cultural exchanges. Academic medicine : journal of the Association of American Medical Colleges 2003;78:S1-5.

23. Graber LK EM, Khoshnood K, and Rastegar A. With So Much Need, Where Do I Serve? . Virtual Mentor: American Medical Association's Journal of Ethics 2010;12:149-58.

24. Bishop R, Litch JA. Medical tourism can do harm. BMJ. 2000;320:1017.

25. Center for Economic and Social Justice. http://www.cesj.org/thirdway/economicjustice-defined.htm. Accessed December 12, 2012.

26. Clark, Margaret. "Corporate Ethics Programs Make a Difference, but not the only difference," HR Magazine, July 1, 2003, 36.

27. Johnson, Craig. Meeting the Ethical Challenges of Leadership. Sage Publications, 2012.

28. Ethics Resource Center. 2010. www.ethics.org/plus-decision-making-process. Accessed December 12, 2012.

29. Aronson L. Twelve tips on teaching reflection at all levels of medical education. Med Teach. 2012 Aug;46(8):807-814.

CHAPTER 3

The Global Health Landscape at U.S. Medical Schools: Global Health Program Structures, Content, and Examples

Amy Forrestel
MD Candidate
Yale School of Medicine

Michael J. Peluso
MD Candidate
Yale School of Medicine

Bingnan Zhang
MD/MBA Candidate
Yale School of Medicine/ Yale School of Management

Carrie Bronsther, BA
Global Health Teaching Associate
Weill Cornell Medical College

Mariam O. Fofana
MD/PhD Candidate
Johns Hopkins University School of Medicine/Bloomberg School of Public Health

Mena Ramos, MD
Resident Physician
Contra Costa Family Medicine Department

Sarpoma Sefa-Boakye, M.D.
International Program Director
Birthing Project USA

Mark Clarfield, MD
Director, Medical School for International Health
Ben-Gurion University

Mera Goodman, MD
Resident Physician
Mount Sinai School of Medicine Department of Pediatrics

Amita Kulkarni, BA
Presidential Fellow in Global Health
Dartmouth Center for Health Care Delivery Science

Nicole Sussman
MD Candidate
Wake Forest School of Medicine

Nilofer Khan Habibullah
Member, The Lancet-University of Oslo Youth Commission on Global Health Governance

Editors

Michael Kron MD MSc.
Director, Global Health Pathway
Medical College of Wisconsin

Madhavi Dandu, MD MPH
Assistant Professor of Medicine
University of California, San Francisco

Introduction

OVER THE PAST 3 DECADES, largely in response to increased student interest, the prevalence, organization, and scope of global health education offered at many medical schools nationally and internationally have expanded significantly.[1] In a recent study, over one-third of recently graduated U.S. medical students participated in a global health experience.[2,3]

The nature and extent of this expansion has varied widely across institutions. The breadth of educational opportunities includes didactic courses,[4,5] international research, international clinical experiences,[3,5,6] "local global health" (experiences of working with underserved populations domestically),[7,8,9] cultural programs, and mentorship. These opportunities are often available in a fragmented, elective, "a la carte" manner for interested students to pursue on their own. However, some schools have made efforts to integrate global health topics into the required curriculum,[4,5] and other institutions are organizing global health education into structured elective curricula in the form of tracks, concentrations, or certificate programs that can be completed in addition to the MD degree.[10]

In this chapter, we provide a practical overview of the current global health education landscape. We first explore the principles behind and details of structured global health programs at some institutions that have already developed an organized curriculum. We then discuss the "a la carte" menu of global health offerings across U.S. medical schools, with a focus on the major types of opportunities available to medical students – didactic courses, research, clinical electives, cultural experiences, mentorship, and capstone projects. Each section of this chapter consists of a broad overview that attempts to consolidate some general principles from our review of many programs, followed by specific, in-depth profiles of individual programs that provide case examples illustrating common or unique approaches. We hope to provide the reader with a sense of what each element of a global health curriculum might look like, by using key examples from notable programs across a diverse spectrum of institutions.

The true prevalence of global health opportunities in U.S. medical schools is unknown, as accurate information regarding these programs is not readily available in the public domain. The overviews and specific institution profiles included in this chapter are based on the review of information available on the web and through discussions with key faculty and student stakeholders in global health.

Caption: *American medical students pose for a picture with the Bolivian residents, physicians, and nurses that hosted their clinical rotation*
Photographer: *Mandi Klein*

Section 1. Structured Global Health Programs

Section Overview

U.S. and other medical schools in the Global North often organize their global health opportunities into non-degree granting elective programs such as concentrations, tracks, or certificate programs. These structured opportunities have become increasingly common. Such programs are generally longitudinal and include some combination of (1) didactic coursework, (2) hands-on, experiential learning, (3) cultural competency training, and (4) requirements for scholarly work. At most schools, any student can participate in individual aspects of the structured program, but only those who fulfill all the requirements will be recognized as having completed a focus area in global health. In a minority of schools, the global health coursework is only available to a select group of students who undergo an application process.

In a recently published review of global health programs with information available on the web, 32/133 U.S. allopathic medical schools had some form of structured global health program.[10] Most of the programs had some combination of the above four criteria; however, there was clear variability among the programs. While all required at least one didactic course, one required as many as 12 courses. About 73% of programs required an international hands-on experience, though only 40% required that the experience be clinical. Cultural competency was a common core competency among programs; however, only one directly addressed this through an explicit requirement that was clearly delineated alongside clinical and research experiences. Not all programs required research, though students at most institutions had opportunities to do scholarly work. The variability between programs was attributed to program administration and financial resources, and also might be related to the availability of educators comfortable teaching global health subject matter.

The rest of this section will highlight examples of structured programs at medical schools throughout the U.S. These programs were selected based on the range of structures and content they offered. We have endeavored to include programs from schools that are diverse in size and location, and that vary in terms of program age and method of administration. We first describe the programs in the text and then provide reference tables for comparison.

Structured Program Examples: U.S. Medical Schools

University of Arizona College of Medicine, Tucson, AZ
Global Health Distinction Track

Basic Characteristics: southwest, public school, administered by medical school

Overview

This distinction track integrates the long-established College of Medicine (CoM) electives in global health with several newer elements. The track consists of the following educational components: externships, courses, participation in global health forum, and a scholarly capstone project. Students who complete the track receive a "Distinction in Global Health" at graduation.

History

Since 1979, University of Arizona College of Medicine has offered elective curricular activities focused on the underserved, and global health was included under the larger "Commitment to Underserved People" (CUP) Program. In 2003, the student-led Global Health Forum began to formalize the global health activities on campus and worked with faculty to create an autonomous program. In 2010, the medical school curriculum committee officially recognized the Global Health Distinction Track.

Notable Elements of the Program

Intensive clinical, interprofessional training for working in resource-poor settings. Started in 1982, the goal of the Global Health: Clinical & Community Care Course is to prepare fourth-year medical students, primary care residents, and other clinical and public health care professionals to "join the team" based at a rural district hospital or similar setting. Using a small-group, problem-based format, the intensive course (5-6 hours/day for 3 weeks) introduces participants to clinical, public health, cultural, and economic issues, which mold the lives and health of the people they will help serve. This course is open to all students, clinical residents and faculty in North America.

Leadership. The track explicitly requires participation and leadership in the Global Health Forum (GHF) Student Group. Leadership may be an important component of global health education, but it is rarely mentioned in program requirements.[10] Encouraging leadership among participants may contribute to the sustainability of the program and also ensures that students contribute to the program in a substantive way.

Global Health Distinction Track— University of Arizona College of Medicine	
Program Requirements	
Years 1-2	Global Health Externship Orientation Course Global Health Externship
Year 3 or 4	Global Health: Clinical and Community Care Course
Year 4	Global Health Clinical Preceptorship Capstone Global Health Project Paper
Any Year	Participation in student-led Global Health Forum
Program Administration	
Location	Housed at University of Arizona College of Medicine in Tucson
Leadership	Track Faculty Directors, with support of other faculty and GHF students
Participants	MD students
Mentorship	Mentored experience during Global Health Externship, informal mentorship through coursework
Admin Support	Global Health Distinction Track Administrator—50% time
Funding	20% Director, 50% Administrator, 20% MPH Co-Director; no current programmatic budget; no direct funding for international externships. Students are encouraged to apply for graduate student grants at University of Arizona; a database of funding sourced is maintained
Contact	Ron Pust, MD / Tracy Carroll MPH Global Health Distinction Track Directors rpust@email.arizona.edu / tcarroll@email.arizona.edu www.globalhealth.arizona.edu

Components
Didactic Coursework
Global Health Externship Orientation Course
Global Health: Clinical & Community Care This full-time, three week course integrates community public health aspects of global health with clinical practice challenges of developing nations or resource-poor health care settings in USA. Students may take the course to prepare for the Global Health Clinical Preceptorship.
Experiential Learning
Global Health Externship Emphasizes local health needs, culturally appropriate approaches, clinical observation, and linkages with community and government resources in faculty-approved sites in less-developed countries.
Global Health Clinical Preceptorship Preferred sites are district-level hospitals, especially those supervising community health programs. An updated database of evaluated program sites is maintained, but often sites suggested by students are approved if those facilities meet goals outlined by the medical school.
Research or Capstone Project
Capstone Global Health Project Each student completes an evidence-based meta-analysis focused on a specific clinical or community global health problem based upon his or her experience. The paper becomes the subject of an oral examination prior to graduation.
Other
Participation in Global Health Forum (GHF) Student Group GHF was created to increase awareness and involvement of students in global health and is a space for students to form connections for outreach, development, and advocacy while receiving training in public health and clinical skills for resource-limited settings. Students are expected to actively participate in GHF as an elected leader or by participation in seminars in Years 1 and 2.

Baylor College of Medicine, Houston, TX
International Health Track
Basic Characteristics: south, private, administered by medical school

Overview
The Global Health Track at Baylor College of Medicine (BCM) consists of courses, clinical

training, research opportunities, and electives abroad that are designed to give students a broader understanding of medicine in a global context and prepare them for a career in global health.

History

In 1998, a group of Baylor medical students approached a few Baylor faculty members with international experience, asking for help in developing a formal curriculum in global health. With a precedent of two other specialized tracks at BCM and support from key leaders at the institution, Baylor's International Track, now called the Global Health Track, became one of the first structured global health educational programs within a medical school in the nation.

Noteworthy Elements of the Program

Emphasis on tropical medicine. With required courses and experiential learning in infectious disease and tropical medicine, the track prepares students to sit for the American Society of Tropical Medicine and Hygiene Certification if they choose to do so.

International Health Track—Baylor College of Medicine	
Program Requirements	
Year 1	Overview of Global Health
Year 2	Readings in Global Health
Year 3 or 4	One month international clinical elective (2 for those taking the ASTMH exam Four half days in the Travel Medicine Clinic City-wide Infectious Disease Conference National School of Tropical Medicine (NSTM) course (optional)
Program Competencies	
Upon completion of the track, the student should be able to: 1. Discuss international problems of health and illness, with focus on the developing world. 2. Describe existing health care organizations and systems that are involved in international health, including the scope of their services and their interaction 3. Apply knowledge of epidemiology, diagnosis and treatment for common tropical and parasitic diseases and health problems of international travelers 4. Understand in a practical way the challenges of providing healthcare services in international settings 5. Utilize skills in cultural competency and understanding cross-cultural dynamics in caring for patients 6. Evaluate the impact of global health factors (e.g., economical, epidemiological, and cultural) on the provision of health care in the United States 7. Design and implement a research project in international health 8. Identify and critically utilize pertinent literature on global health issues	

Program Administration	
Location	Currently administrated through Family Medicine; housed in School of Medicine
Leadership	Two faculty directors oversee the track
Participants	MD students
Mentorship	In Year 2, students are assigned a mentor and begin one-on-one quarterly meetings
Admin Support	Academic Coordinator for International Affairs in Department of Family Medicine
Funding	Support from School of Medicine; track leadership supported by respective departments; private donations
Contact	G. Robert Parkerson III, M.D., MPH / Jose Serpa-Alvarez, M.D., MS Co-Directors of International Health Track grp@bcm.edu / jaserpaa@bcm.edu www.bcm.edu/medschool/internationaltrack

Components
Didactic Coursework
Overview of Global Health Class meets two times per week for six weeks at noon for one hour.
Readings in Global Health Class meets September through May. Students are required to make a presentation.
City-Wide Infectious Disease Conference Students must attend four meetings, which take place for one hour each Wednesday at noon.
Experiential Learning
One month clinical elective abroad in a developing country.
Four half-days in the Travel Medicine Clinic
Capstone/Scholarly Project/Thesis
None required.
Other
Students may register with the National School of Tropical Medicine (NSTM) to take the Diploma Tropical Medicine course.

The George Washington School of Medicine and Health Sciences, Washington, DC
Global Health Track
Basic Characteristics: east coast, private, administered by medical school

Overview
The Global Health Track (GHT) at George Washington University (GW) is an educational program designed to enrich students' experiences and leadership opportunities and provide a broader healthcare perspective. The track aims to increase students' awareness about international health systems, global diseases, and assessment techniques for the specific health needs of countries at various stages of development.

History
The GW Office of International Medicine Programs has been offering international experiential learning opportunities to medical students, residents, and faculty since its inception in 1995. These opportunities came about as the school began to respond to the increasing demand for U.S.-style medical education in other countries and requests for academic affiliations. In 2005, the School of Medicine created the Office of Student Opportunities and launched the track system using the global health track as a model for other tracks including research, medical education, emergency preparedness, and health policy. The first GHT cohort graduated in 2009.

Noteworthy Elements of the Program
Medical/Surgical Mission Trips. While GW offers full-fledged international clinical electives, students in the track may participate in short-term mission trips[12,13] to fulfill the international clinical experience requirement for this program.

Location. In the nation's capital and in close proximity to many embassies, non-governmental groups, and international organizations, including the World Bank, PAHO, Peace Corps, the State Department, and Health and Human Services, students have an array of resources and mentors at their fingertips. The track attempts to make use of these uniquely accessible resources.

Global Health Track—George Washington University School of Medicine and Health Sciences	
Program Requirements	
Year 1 and 2	Attend lecture series Participate in an 8-week international experiential learning opportunity in the summer following first year
Year 3 and 4	Practice of Medicine Scholarly Project related to Global Health International Clinical Elective (4-8 weeks) or global health medical mission (2 weeks)

Program Competencies	
At the completion of this track, students will be able to: 1. Gain a basic understanding of the relationship between demographics indicators to health and disease 2. Gain knowledge of various global diseases 3. Gain an introduction to the study of community and public health, primary care, health care for the underserved, epidemiology, as well as infectious and tropical diseases all over the world 4. Provide international experiences and training that expose students to diverse cultures and broaden their cultural perspectives 5. Learn how to communicate more effectively with the increasingly diverse patient populations students work with in the U.S.	
Program Administration	
Location	Developed, implemented, and administered by the Office of International Medicine Programs (IMP)
Leadership	Track Director, mentors, and faculty committee
Participants	MD students
Mentorship	Formal and informal mentorship provided by GW and non-GW faculty and medical doctors with expertise in global health
Admin Support	Dedicated office (Office of Student Opportunities) with 2 full-time employees that oversee track programs; support staff in the IMP office
Funding	Dean's Office, scholarships, and IMP funds
Contact	Huda Ayas, EdD, MBA, MHA Director and Mentor of the Global Health Track hayas@gwu.edu
Components	
Didactic Coursework	
Global Health Track Lecture Series Topics areas include: Basics of Global Health, Demography of Diseases, Infectious and Tropical Diseases, Women's Health, Child's Health, Gender Issues in Global Health, Global Healthcare Workforce, PEPFAR, Philanthropy in Global Health, Poverty and Hunger, Intercultural Sensitivity	

Experiential Learning
Summer Internship Students must submit a project proposal including scope of work, timeline, objectives/goals, and the organization/on-site mentor with which the student will be working. The project must be approved prior to student departure from the U.S. Projects are to be completed abroad over 8 weeks during the summer between first and second years. After project completion, students are required to submit a 4-6-page paper that includes the project's scope, the role the student played in the project, any unexpected outcomes, and reflections on the experience. Competitive scholarships are available and usually provided to most students traveling abroad for their international summer internships.
International Clinical Elective (4-8 weeks) or Global Health Medical Missions (2 weeks) Opportunities for electives through affiliated sites: 30 different sites, in 23 different countries. Students also have the option to plan their own internships through non-affiliate schools and organizations. Surgical/Medical missions are usually shorter in duration and are offered through GW partners: Operation Smile (globally) and Project Medishare (Haiti). Pre-trip orientation sessions are required of students going abroad.
Capstone/Scholarly Project/Thesis
Required Practice of Medicine Scholarly Project must be related to Global Health

The Medical College of Wisconsin (MCW), Milwaukee, Wisconsin
Global Health Pathway
Basic Characteristics: midwest, private, administered by medical school

Overview
The Global Health Pathway at MCW is a formal element of a newly revised "Discovery Curriculum." The "Pathway" concentration areas were originated in 2008, with students required to choose and participate in one or more of six pathways in addition to their general core curriculum. Currently the pathways are: Physician Scientist, Clinician Educator, Global Health, Academic Clinician, Urban and Community Medicine, and Quality Improvement and Patient Safety. Pathways are educational programs designed to enrich students' experiences with flexibility geared to a student's individual interests. The Global Health Pathway aims to increase awareness about an array of important global health topics and the opportunities and challenges of addressing public health priorities in low resource and low technology regions of the world.

History
The MCW Global Health Pathway originated four years ago through growth of a Department of Medicine program in international health that began in 2005 and was led by the former director of the International Health Institute at Michigan State University. Recently, the Global Health

Pathway has been enriched through the appointment of an Associate Dean for Global Health and corresponding interdisciplinary efforts to promote a variety of global health goals. MCW graduated the first cohort of students who completed the three-year curriculum in 2012.

Noteworthy Elements of the Program

Local Global Health. Wisconsin is home to five federally designated refugee relocation organizations through which academic-community linkages are promoted in order to provide students with the opportunity for local global experiences.

Medical/Surgical Missions and Electives. Both MCW sponsored and external international opportunities for clinical and research purposes are available for medical students, during vacation periods and primarily in the fourth year of medical school when the scheduling of away electives is more flexible.

Global Health Pathway—Medical College of Wisconsin	
Program Requirements	
Year 1	"Introduction to Pathways" orientation in first two months Choose a Global Health Pathway, advisor, and project mentor in first semester Participate in monthly pathway-specific core curricular sessions (3 hours/month) and track at least 6 hours per month of individualized "non-core curricular" study
Year 2	Continue a series of monthly core curriculum topics and track additional non- core curricular activities Define a scholarly project to be completed as a graduation requirement
Year 3	Optional participation in core curriculum and non-core curricular activities
Year 4	Submission and presentation of scholarly project as graduation requirement
Program Competencies	
1. Medical Knowledge: Acquire and apply medical knowledge specific to global health issues in order to expand understanding of unique problems. Expand awareness of a specific global health issue and country of particular personal interest. 2. Practice-based learning: Gain ability to investigate specific global health issues from local, foreign, and international data sets and apply this information to specific global health issues. 3. Interpersonal Communication: Strengthen communication skills with Limited English Proficiency (LEP) and deaf patients.	

4. Expand Awareness: Learn about a specific global health issue and/or country of particular interest.
5. Professionalism: Learn professional behavior and interpersonal interactions appropriate for specific global cultural contexts.
6. Systems-based practice: Understand the complexity of global health studies in terms of ethical human study regulations.

Program Administration	
Location	Developed, implemented, and administered by the Curriculum Evaluation Committee and Senior Associate Dean for Education
Leadership	Global Health Pathway Director, pathway advisory council, clinical advisors and project mentors
Participants	MD students
Mentorship	Formal and informal mentorship provided by MCW and community based faculty and staff
Admin Support	Curriculum Office with pathway-specific program administrators and support staff
Funding	Dean's Office, scholarships, and donations earmarked for international electives
Contact	Michael Kron / Hilary Chavez Pathway Director / Pathway Coordinator mkron@mcw.edu / hchavez@mcw.edu

Components
Didactic Coursework
Global Health Pathway Core Curriculum Series Topics include: Disaster preparedness and response, injury prevention, clinical tropical disease and medical parasitology, careers in global health, tropical ophthalmology and dermatology, pediatrics and malnutrition, Wilderness Medicine, global HIV topics, women's health, medical anthropology, working with Limited English Proficiency (LEP) patients, preparing for overseas work and cultural sensitivity.

New York Medical College, Westchester, NY
Certificate in Global Health
Basic Characteristics: northeast, private, administered by entity outside medical school

Overview

The School of Health Sciences and Practice offers a 12-credit Graduate Certificate in Global Health for MD and MPH students. The program aims to enhance healthcare providers' knowledge of the health, socio-economic, and political environments that affect the health status of individuals and population groups worldwide. The Certificate may be taken independently and upon completion may serve as an entry to Master's degree studies for those who may want to do so. Alternatively, the Certificate may be taken as part of an MPH degree in any of the degree program areas. Receipt of the Certificate does not require completion of a global health applied experience or project; however, opportunities for such experiences are available for MD and MPH students.

History
The online Graduate Certificate in Global Health was started in 2010. Prior to this, the courses were taught on campus. One of the reasons for the establishment of online courses was so that students beyond the Tri-State area who were enrolled in the online MPH program could complete the Certificate.

Noteworthy Elements of the Program
Exclusively coursework, available online. The fully online distance education format aims to be interactive. Each course is designed with video lectures and corresponding PowerPoint presentations. There is a discussion forum and students have the opportunity to interact with each other and the course instructor, and are kept up to date with the current events in global public health. While students are able to participate in an international field experience, this experience is optional. The entire program is completed within the first two years of medical school.

Location. Enrolled students who reside in the area have opportunities to attend and participate in international conferences and workshops at the United Nations and other NGOs, held in New York City.

Certificate in Global Health—New York Medical College	
Program Requirements	
Years 1 and 2	4 Courses, 12 Credits
Years 3 and 4	Optional Global Field or Clinical Experience
Program Competencies	

1. Identify, analyze, and challenge power structures that produce poverty, inequality, and disease. Describe the major underlying and proximate determinants of adverse health issues in developing countries. Apply community development skills, policy advocacy, and communication strategies to promote public health, while using human rights concepts and instruments to promote social justice.
2. Incorporate qualitative, quantitative, and operations research skills to design and apply reliable, valid, and ethically sound research to identify innovative solutions for international health problems. Demonstrate a mastery of epidemiologic and bio-statistical approaches to public health issues. Read and analyze health literature critically.

3. Design, manage, and evaluate programs in developing countries in close collaboration with local institutions to assure equitable access to quality health care. Use financial management techniques that promote program sustainability and cost-effectiveness of primary health-care systems.
4. Describe important health problems contributing to excess morbidity and mortality in developing countries, including their magnitude and distribution. Describe disparities in health by gender, race, ethnicity, rural/ urban status, and economic class
5. Use collaborative and culturally relevant leadership skills to advocate for evidence-based policies and plans to solve health problems in international settings
6. Develop tailored messages, intervention methods, and delivery channels for prevention and sustainable behavior- change programs. Design practical, culturally relevant, and communication programs for resource-constrained settings. Consider structural interventions where community-level interventions are more appropriate than at the individual level.
7. Be able to assess the appropriateness of intervention strategies to address major health problems in low-resource settings, including locally determined priorities their efficacy, cost-effectiveness and feasibility in reaching all segments of the population. Evaluate and establish priorities to improve the health status of populations in low-resource settings, with recognition of the importance of integrated strategies.
8. Analyze and explain the role of transnational networks and global institutions in the adoption and enforcement of international laws, conventions, agreements, and standards that affect health and safety. This should include the domains of trade, labor, food supply, and the environment, pharmaceuticals, international aid, human rights, and conflict.
9. Analyze and explain the economic, social, political, and academic conditions that can produce a strong health workforce. Address barriers to recruitment, training, and retention of workforce competent health resources in developing countries.

Program Administration	
Location	Housed in Health Policy and Management Division of New York Medical College and School of Health Sciences and Practice
Leadership	Program Director
Participants	Any interested student or faculty; MD or MPH Students; open to the public
Mentorship	Students who chose to do optional field experiences have faculty mentors
Admin Support	Departmental administrator and Program Director
Funding	Budget in School of Health Sciences and Practice

Contact	Padmini Murthy, MD, MPH, MS, MPhil Director, Global Health padmini_murthy@nymc.edu
Components	
Didactic Coursework	
Primary Care Around the World An introduction to primary health care in different areas of the world.	
Comparative Healthcare Delivery Systems This 11-session course offers a comparative analysis of healthcare systems in terms of the financing, organization, and delivery of acute, long-term, and mental health care, and public health services.	
Women and Health: A Global Perspective The social and health problems of women in developing countries are addressed in 15 weeks.	
Infectious Diseases in Public Health Epidemiologic principles are used to study the prevalence of infectious diseases.	
Experiential Learning	
None required; optional field experience for MD students.	
Capstone/Scholarly Project/Thesis	
None required.	

Weill Cornell Medical College (WCMC), New York, NY
Global Health Curriculum
Basic Characteristics: northeast, private, administered by medical school

Overview
The WCMC Global Health Curriculum is a longitudinal program featuring didactic coursework, experiential learning, and mentorship designed to enable students to make informed decisions about how they plan to address global health equity in their future careers.

History
Students who wished to contextualize and expand upon their global health experiences designed the Global Health Curriculum in 2009. With the support of faculty from the Office of Global Health Education, Center for Global Health, and Global Emergency Medicine program, it has developed into a highly popular elective program for medical students.

Noteworthy Elements of the Program
Domestic Global Health Preceptorship. One of unique aspects of the program is the required

domestic "global health" clinical preceptorship during the first year. Through the preceptorship, students must shadow a physician working with resource-poor populations in New York City. Students get a firsthand perspective on local health disparities through their interactions with immigrants, the uninsured, homeless, HIV-positive patients, those of low-socioeconomic status, and those on Medicaid.

Global Health Grand Rounds. The monthly lecture series gives students up close and personal access to global health leaders who speak on topics ranging from health policy to community engagement. Past speakers have included heads of state, UN and WHO officials, economists, journalists, and activists.

Global Health Curriculum—Weill Cornell Medical College	
Program Requirements	
Year 1	Introduction to Global Health Global Health Preceptorship Foundations in Global Service Applied Experience #1
Year 4	Clinical Skills in Resource-Poor Settings Applied Experience #2 (Clinical)
Years 1-4	Global Health Grand Rounds
Program Competencies	
1. Global Burden of Disease 2. Inequalities, Health, and Human Rights 3. Research and Evidence-Based Outcomes 4. Payers and Players 5. Health Systems and Health Care Delivery	
Program Administration	
Location	Housed in the Medical College
Leadership	Steering Committee of students and faculty from the Center for Global Health, Global Emergency Medicine Program, and Office of Global Health Education
Participants	MD Students; PA and Graduate Students can participate in aspects of program
Mentorship	Individual faculty provide mentorship on projects and career development
Admin Support	Two full-time, BA-level "Global Health Teaching Associates"

<table>
<tr><td>Funding</td><td>Dean's Office; Interdepartmental; International field experiences are funded by endowed donations and federal work-study support</td></tr>
<tr><td>Contact</td><td>Carrie Bronsther
Global Health Teaching Associate
cab2031@med.cornell.edu
med.cornell.edu/globalhealth</td></tr>
<tr><td colspan="2">Components</td></tr>
<tr><td colspan="2">Didactic Coursework</td></tr>
<tr><td colspan="2">Introduction to Global Health: A Case-Based Approach
Introduces first-year students to 13 key topics in global health through 14 weekly seminars.</td></tr>
<tr><td colspan="2">Foundations in Global Service
6-week introduction to hands-on global health work.</td></tr>
<tr><td colspan="2">Clinical Skills in Resource Poor Settings
This two week, full-time elective teaches high-yield skills in preparation for common clinical encounters in resource-poor settings.</td></tr>
<tr><td colspan="2">Experiential Learning</td></tr>
<tr><td colspan="2">Global Health Clinical Preceptorship
Students are paired with a clinician working with underserved populations in the US.</td></tr>
<tr><td colspan="2">Two Applied Experiences
Full-time, student-selected project that falls into one of the following categories: Field Experience (International or Domestic), Policy Project, Basic Science/Clinical Research, and Training Course.</td></tr>
<tr><td colspan="2">Capstone/Scholarly Project/Thesis</td></tr>
<tr><td colspan="2">Not currently required; however, a scholarly project requirement is being developed as the elective curriculum is moving towards official concentration status within the medical college.</td></tr>
<tr><td colspan="2">Other</td></tr>
<tr><td colspan="2">Global Health Grand Rounds
A monthly public lecture series that serves as a platform for dialogue on contemporary global health challenges relating to the Global Health Curriculum's Core Competencies.</td></tr>
<tr><td colspan="2">Careers in Global Health Seminars
Informal seminars highlight physicians who have pursued global health through research, fieldwork, or policy.</td></tr>
</table>

Yale University School of Medicine, New Haven, CT
Certificate in Global Medicine

Basic Characteristics: northeast, private, administered by medical school

Overview

Medical students are able to pursue a variety of didactic, research, and clinical experiences in global health at Yale. The Certificate program organizes coursework and international experiences into a longitudinal curriculum that a student can complete over four (or five) years of medical school, while maintaining flexibility in terms of both the timing and content of these opportunities. Each student compiles a Global Health Portfolio as he or she completes each portion of the curriculum.

History

The Certificate in Global Medicine at Yale was first mentioned as a long-term goal in the Global Health Curriculum Proposal, which was approved by the school's Curriculum Committee in 2007. Over the next five years, Yale made great strides in developing what would become the components of the program, including didactic opportunities and international clinical electives. In 2011, once sufficient global health infrastructure had been created, the students from the Global Health Working Group worked in conjunction with faculty from the Office of International Medical Student Education to organize the existing opportunities into a structured longitudinal curriculum. After receiving feedback from students and faculty stakeholders, their proposal was submitted to and approved by the Curriculum Committee, the deans of the School of Medicine, the University Provost, and the Yale Corporation.

Noteworthy Elements of the Program

Flexibility. Flexibility is a key component of the core medical curriculum at Yale, and this is reflected in the Certificate. While there is a recommended trajectory through the curriculum, each component can be completed at any time, and often in a number of different ways. Students compile a portfolio as they complete each requirement, and a faculty committee that grants the Certificate reviews this portfolio each year.

Broad definition of cultural competency. The program formally recognizes the value of language and cultural competency, but defines it broadly. This requirement is based upon the understanding that while it is beneficial to be able to speak fluently the native language of a specific population, in reality, language proficiency might not be the most practical skill of a global health practitioner. Instead, the program requirements reflect the belief that medical graduates must also be prepared to work with populations whose language they do not speak through the appropriate use of an interpreter.

Certificate in Global Medicine— Yale University School of Medicine	
Program Requirements	
Year 1	Global Health Seminar; start scholarly project
Year 2	2nd didactic elective; epidemiology and public health; medical microbiology; leadership
Year 4	International elective; additional experience; cultural competency; finish scholarly project
Program Competencies	

1. Describe the importance of social, political, economic, and cultural factors in the health of populations living outside the U.S.
2. Demonstrate an appreciation for the language and culture of a non-American and/or non-English speaking population.
3. Apply epidemiology to understand the incidence, prevalence, and risk factors for disease in international populations.
4. Compare and contrast the health care system and services of the United States with those in other countries.
5. Explain strategies for providing healthcare services, including health promotion, disease prevention, and medical treatment, to individuals and populations in resource-poor settings.
6. Recognize the extent of healthcare inequality in both the United States and other countries, and explain how inequality can impact the health outcomes of populations and their access to healthcare services.
7. Demonstrate how to conduct a focused, culturally appropriate medical history and physical exam with limited laboratory and supplemental tests in a resource-poor setting, and generate a focused differential diagnosis in this setting.
8. Develop and communicate a culturally sensitive plan of care that takes into account risks, benefits, alternatives, and financial consequences for a patient in a resource-poor setting.
9. Be aware of the challenges of serving as a provider for individuals from a cultural background other than your own.
10. Demonstrate leadership, organization, and collaboration that are crucial for engagement in global health activities.
11. Appreciate the physician's responsibility to society, both in our own country and throughout the world. These responsibilities should include not only service to the underserved or disenfranchised members of our own society, but also advocacy for the care of the disadvantaged persons in other nations, who bear a heavy burden of disease, death and disability.

Program Administration	
Location	Housed in the Office of International Medical Student Education
Leadership	A faculty committee reviews each applicant's portfolio
Participants	MD students
Mentorship	No formal mentorship program currently
Admin Support	Staff and Student Administrators responsible for program coordination
Funding	Program supported by global health education grants awarded to OIMSE
Contact	Robert Rohrbaugh, MD Director, Office of International Medical Student Education robert.rohrbaugh@yale.edu http://medicine.yale.edu/globalhealth/yale/certificate.aspx

Components
Didactic Coursework
1. Global Health Seminar
2. Elective Course (such as Tropical Medicine, Global Mental Health, or other graduate course)
3. Medical Microbiology
4. Epidemiology and Public Health
Experiential Learning
International Clinical Experience Students must complete one elective and can chose from 10 fully funded global health rotations.
Capstone/Scholarly Project/Thesis
Conduct basic science or clinical research that focuses on an important topic in global health
Other
Language/Culture Appreciation Demonstrate an appreciation for the language and culture of a global population by: a. Conducting research or providing healthcare services in a language other than English, OR b. Appropriately utilizing a translator in a healthcare interaction in an international setting.

Global Health Leadership Serve for 1 academic year as a member of the Global Health Working Group or another student organization that directly addresses global health issues internationally or locally.
Additional elective experience in global health Students must complete an additional didactic, clinical, or research experience in global health.

University of California, San Francisco School of Medicine, San Francisco, CA
Pathways to Discovery in Global Health
Basic Characteristics: west coast, public, jointly administered

Overview
The Pathway to Discovery in Global Health at UCSF aims to support and develop lifetime commitments to decreasing health inequities and disparities in populations throughout the world, prepare undergraduate and graduate trainees to be successful in global health careers, and support collaborative projects across disciplines and schools. The program achieves these goals by offering courses and educational opportunities to build a background understanding of the vocabulary, problems, and concepts in global health, and to develop tools for success in global health careers. The experiential focus of the program is a mentored project in an underserved population.

History
Since the mid 1990s, UCSF medical students had opportunities to concentrate in various areas of interest during their time in medical school, including in global health. In 2007, the Areas of Concentration were consolidated into a more centralized, cohesive, and longitudinal program called Pathways to Discovery. Global Health is one of five pathways. The change to "Pathways" allowed faculty and students to spend more time to develop interprofessional training programs, consider core competencies, and focus on long-term career development. Each pathway has at its core mentored projects, coursework, and focus on leadership and career development.

Noteworthy Elements of the Program
Interdisciplinary Nature. Throughout all aspects of the Global Health Pathways program, students from various UCSF schools are learning side by side. Additionally the pathway spans all levels of learners from undergraduate medical education to various levels of graduate education (masters students, residents, fellows, graduate level nurses, pharmacists, and dentists).

Pathways to Discovery in Global Health— UCSF School of Medicine	
Program Requirements	
Year 1-3	GHS 101: Introduction to Global Health Summer Project Identify a mentored scholarly project
Year 4	Officially apply to be in Pathways to Discovery in Global Health GHS 103: Advanced Global Health Work-in-Progress Seminars Completion of a legacy product and presentation at Research Symposium Students can go further in-depth with their legacy project and apply for MD with Distinction in Global Health during Year 4.
Program Administration	
Location	Jointly housed in School of Medicine and Global Health Sciences
Leadership	Pathways Faculty Director and Associate Director (10%-20% time)
Participants	Students in MD Program, Nursing, Pharmacy, Dentistry, and Graduate-Level (PhD/MS Biomedical Sciences, Anthropology, and Global Health Sciences)
Mentorship	Each student has a faculty mentor who oversees Pathway scholarly project
Admin Support	Administrator spends 30% of time coordinating Pathways Global Health program
Funding	Supported internally by Medical School & Global Health Sciences
Contact	Chris Stewart, MD, MA / Madhavi Dandu, MD, MPH Director / Associate Director, Pathways to Discovery in Global Health cstewart@sfghpeds.ucsf.edu / dandum@medicine.ucsf.edu
Components	
Didactic Coursework	
GHS 101: Introduction to Global Health elective [online course acceptable] This survey course reviews basic topics in GH through assigned reading and small group discussions.	
GHS 103: Advanced global health elective This course explores some key GH topics in-depth in the context of ongoing or completed student projects. Topics include project design, skill-building sessions such as leadership skills, literature searches, and human subjects protocol review in addition to core global health topics.	

Work-in-Progress Seminar A required seminar during Year 4 that allows students to discuss ongoing scholarly research for their legacy project. Seminar can be attended in person or remotely for those in the field conducting research.
Experiential Learning
Required Fieldwork for Legacy Project Experiential learning in an underserved area is required. This, which usually entails a project during the summer between Year 1 and 2 AND during Year 4 (or 5). No international *clinical* elective is required.
Capstone/Scholarly Project/Thesis
The Legacy Product To complete the Global Health Pathway, students must present their scholarly project and legacy work at the yearly Pathways Symposium and to the community/organizational partner. The scope does not require an additional year. For students who complete the MD with Distinction in Global Health (usually requires an additional year): 1. Dissemination—A first-authored manuscript is preferred, submitted to a peer-reviewed journal. Alternatives include an implemented curriculum, a policy paper or multi-media presentation with demonstrated impact. 2. Scope—The scope would ideally require additional time (i.e. an extra year), but may be longitudinal projects completed over 4 years, or a project that meets dissemination criteria above. 3. Impact—The student must demonstrate involvement of the affected/involved communities in the project, and dissemination of the project results to those communities. 4. Approval—Product must be approved by GH Pathway leadership and the MD with distinction committee.

Structured Program Examples: International Medical Schools

Escuela Latinoamericana de Medicina (ELAM), Havana, Cuba
A medical school dedicated to global health principles

The Escuela Latinoamericana de Medicina (ELAM) is an international medical school located in Havana, Cuba, whose primary mission is to produce doctors with training strongly rooted in public health and primary care to address the health crisis faced by medically underserved regions worldwide. ELAM was founded in 1998 as relief work that was done in the wake of devastating hurricanes revealed a need for a long-term solution to the shortage of healthcare providers in underserved areas.[13]

Before matriculating, one must be evaluated through placement exams and a one-year pre-medical course[14] that includes Spanish proficiency.[15] Graduates are conferred a Doctorate of Medicine (MD) following the completion of a six-year curriculum which includes two years of basic sciences, three years of clinical rotations, and a one year pre-professional internship which is followed by the Cuban State Medical Board Exams.[16] To date, ELAM has provided thousands of scholarships to students from Central and South America and the Caribbean, U.S., Africa, and Southeast Asia. As of 2010, over 8,500 doctors have graduated from ELAM.[13]

Primary care is emphasized within the curriculum through Comprehensive General Medicine (Family Medicine), which is comprised of an introductory course in the first semester and community-based rotations in each of the last three years. Students also participate in a public health rotation, which culminates in a health assessment of a local community. Participation in public health brigades, particularly in potential public health disasters including hurricanes and epidemics, is required of the student body.

International research projects are encouraged in the 4th and 5th years. While most ELAM graduates complete all rotations in Cuba, some complete the pre-professional 6th year internship in countries such as Venezuela, Honduras, Guatemala, and other countries with established Cuban health personnel to ensure academic requirements are met.[17]

University of Saskatchewan College of Medicine, Saskatoon, Canada
Making the links between local and global health

Started in 2005, the "Making the Links"[18] program began as a service learning experience which exposes students to health issues present in the urban (underserved community in urban Saskatoon), rural (northern remote communities in Saskatchewan), and international settings (Mozambique). A Certificate in Global Health was established in 2011 and modeled after the Making the Links model. The goals of the program are to give students the "knowledge, skills, and attitudes to help them work competently with marginalized, underserved communities locally and globally." It is available to first and second year medial students.

Requirements include didactic coursework and clinical work in both a local and international setting. The didactic curriculum includes two introductory courses that teach through lecture, case studies, and discussion. They cover concepts including development aid, social movements, indigenous health, emergency management, and the impact of gender, power, ecology, globalization, and education on health.

Students participate in three practicums: one urban, one rural, and one international. The Inner City Practicum is in an urban clinical experience affiliated with one of two student-run health clinics located in Saskatoon (Student Wellness Initiative Toward Community Health) or Regina (Student Energy in Action for Regina Community Health). The Northern Saskatchewan Practicum is a six-week experience in one of three remote northern Saskatchewan communities. A local field preceptor and the Global Health Certificate Program Director provide supervision. The International Practicum is 6-week mentored experience in a low resource country (options include Mozambique and Zimbabwe). To participate, students must have completed the urban and rural practicums, required GH coursework, and demonstrate language proficiency.

Registration for the program requires tuition fees from the student, with additional funding support from the College of Medicine, Saskatchewan Medial Association, and a bursary program for students. Recognition for completion includes an official certificate and mention in the student's Dean's letter.

Medical School for International Health, Ben Gurion University, Beer Sheva, Israel A mandatory global health curriculum

To address the need for medical training focused on diverse and under-served populations in resource-limited settings, Ben-Gurion University of the Negev (BGU) and the Columbia University College of Physicians and Surgeons (CU) collaborated on a new medical school in which students acquire the skills, attitudes, and knowledge to become global health practitioners. The Medical School for International Health (MSIH) provides training in cross-cultural issues, program development and management, individual- and population-based health promotion, and disease prevention and treatment. The goals are set by the faculty of both universities. Admissions are administered at CU and the degree is awarded from BGU, but both universities provide input in all facets of the school. The collaboration has been described in detail.[19]

In August 1998, MSIH admitted its first students and introduced them to a U.S.-style curriculum that included a four-year, required track in international health and medicine (IHM). The curriculum is centered on a working definition of IHM as visualized by an "IHM wheel" of interlocking domains,[20] the hub of which is a set of skills that help the clinician practice medicine outside the culture in which he or she grew up. These include communication skills, competence in foreign languages and the use of translators, knowledge of other cultures, and the influence of cultural factors in medical decision-making. Around this hub is a rim of disciplines that may help solve health problems when working in another culture.

The standard curriculum is focused on basic science, systems-oriented courses, and clerkships. IHM is taught as a required study track that includes four innovative components. Introduction to Concepts of Global Health and Medicine is a year-long course during year 1 that introduces students to patients in hospital, clinic, and community settings, medical anthropology, and skills in communication, clinical medicine, and cross-cultural issues. In year 2, students complete 4 modules, 6-20 hour courses in topics such as Medical Anthropology, Aging, Tropical Pediatrics, How to Write a Grant, and Water and Health. These modules have often been designed with the help of students. During year 3, the Workshop in Cross Cultural Communication sensitizes the student to cultural differences that influence communication, teaches how to use translators, and makes use of standardized patients. The International Clerkship in year 4 is a required experience in a developing country that is planned by BGU faculty and implemented by a coordinator at the local medical school, according to goals and objectives of MSIH. Students work both in the community and in the regional hospital. A few students each year do the International Clerkship in Israel or North America in a culturally relevant, resource poor setting.

Formal tracking data shows that 70% of responding graduates of the MSIH's first 5 classes are meaningfully involved in global health within 8 years after medical school. The model of using an international academic partnership to develop a medical school that graduates physicians with special skills in IHM has been transformed from a set of plans to reality.

Section 2. Components Of Global Health Programs

Section Overview

Few schools include comprehensive global health training in the core medical curriculum. Although some argue that all students should be exposed to global health, it is a challenge to find space in curricula already constrained by time and content[21,22] and to convince administrators that global health is any more essential than the other neglected components of medical education. The lack of global health in the core curriculum is likely responsible for the rise of a strong student role in advocating for the expansion of global health opportunities.

In this section, we review each of the key components of global health programs, including didactics, research, international clinical opportunities, cultural opportunities, mentorship, and capstone projects. Each section begins with a broad overview of that component, followed by specific notable examples of the component.

DIDACTIC / CLASSROOM EXPERIENCES

Overview

The expansion of student-led didactic courses is evidence of the crucial role that students have played in the development and implementation of global health programs.[23-25] While it might be a struggle for these courses to attain the physical (i.e., technological equipment) and human (i.e., compensated faculty time) resources available to core medical courses, in some cases, student-led didactic courses have received institutional support or been successfully integrated into a core or elective curriculum.[26] Unfortunately, student-led initiatives run the danger of losing momentum due to the lack of institutional memory and the rapid turnover of student leaders. Indeed, the course management programs at many institutions serve as catalogues of old syllabi for failed or transient global health courses.

Often, global health courses are offered outside the medical school proper—for example, at a school of public health, global health center or institute, or through an interdepartmental collaboration. Few are offered by a medical school department and targeted specifically at medical students. Schools where such courses are available often include them as requirements of structured certificate programs or specialized distinction tracks. Some schools with structured programs limit didactic opportunities to those students within the program.

The structure and content of global health didactic courses vary widely. While most courses target junior medical students in the preclinical portion of the curriculum, several schools offer courses specifically for advanced medical students (third and fourth year) with a more clinical perspective. The duration of courses runs the gamut from just a few days to several academic periods, as does the intensity of the courses: some feature hour-long sessions every few weeks whereas others are held as an intensive, full-time courses lasting several weeks. Some schools require didactic training as preparation prior to international clinical electives. Most courses use a lecture and discussion format. Similarly, the methods of evaluation vary: some courses are offered on a non-credit basis and require only attendance and participation, whereas others require formal academic work, including written assignments and student presentations. The variety of approaches to didactic global health education is illustrated in the detailed examples described below.

A rudimentary but functional schoolroom in a remote African village
Photographer: *Bynum*

Examples of Global Health Didactic Opportunities

Weil Cornell Medical College, New York, NY
Bringing global health into the core medical curriculum

Since 2000, Cornell has required a series of global health courses as part of the core medical school curriculum for all students at various stages of study.[27] First-year students take courses on "Health Interventions in Resource-Poor Countries," "Global Health Nutrition," and "**Epidemiologic and Biostatistics Research Methods"** as part of the required "Medicine, Patients, and Society" program. In their second year, students take a Parasitology course including three lectures and lab exercises as part of the Infectious Disease module. Finally, in their fourth year, students take a two-week clerkship in "**Public Health Systems." Although they are not exclusively focused on global health, these courses aim to give students perspective on the impact of globalization in healthcare, considerations for the delivery of care in resource-limited settings, the** social, economic, political, and clinical aspects of health care delivery, and clinical topics relevant to tropical a low-resources settings, in addition to equipping them with technical tools to address the evaluation of public health problems and health intervention design. This is an important example of a medical school achieving some level of integration of global health into the medical curriculum.

Yale University School of Medicine, New Haven, CT
An interdisciplinary, collaborative approach

The Global Health Seminar at Yale was originally conceived by the student-led Global Health Working Group during the 2007-2008 academic year. The course aimed to provide medical, physician associate, nursing, and public health students with the knowledge and skills to address the "Social, Economic, and Political Determinants of Global Health."

Initially structured as a series of bimonthly lectures, the course was modified in 2009-2010 in response to students' requests for more frequent meetings, greater detail, and more in-depth participation. With the advent of Yale's newly formed Global Health Leadership Institute (GHLI) and the Office of International Medical Student Education (OIMSE), the course also received greater institutional support, including joint funding from the medical, nursing, and public health schools. Today, the course is structured as a year-long, weekly elective course, which is jointly coordinated by the schools of Medicine, Public Health, and Nursing through the cooperation of students in GHWG, faculty from GHLI, OIMSE, and Department of Medicine, and guest speakers from outside institutions. Students continue to have significant input in curriculum design and execution, but now receive administrative support from the global health program manager at GHLI and the student coordinator for global health through OIMSE. The course draws students from across the health professions and content changes every year based upon student and faculty interests.

Each semester is divided into two longitudinal themes and one module. Each theme is covered in a series of 3-4 lectures that are tied together thematically, while the module comprises a series of 4-5 interactive sessions with a single faculty leader on a specific topic. Thematic topics covered have included global health history and architecture, global chronic diseases, global health innovation and technology, global burden of disease, global infectious diseases, vulnerable populations in global health, global health diplomacy, and emerging issues in global health. Modules have focused on advocacy and activism in global health, violent conflict and health, global mental health, maternal and child health, and global health program management and evaluation.

While each session has assigned readings, the modules require more active student participation through discussion and conclude with student projects presented to the whole class Although the course is open to all students, medical students wishing to receive a Certificate in Global Medicine[28] and public health students in the Global Health Concentration[29,30] must take the course for credit by attending 75% of sessions and completing both module projects during an academic year.

Johns Hopkins School of Medicine, Baltimore, MD
Fostering international exchange through technology

Initiated in the first year of the Johns Hopkins' new "Genes to Society" curriculum (2009-2010), the Global Health Intersession is one of several focused, intensive 4-day "breakout" courses offered every 6-8 weeks throughout the preclinical and clinical years. Like all other preclinical and intersession courses, the GH Intersession is required of all students and graded on a Pass/Fail basis. It is not associated with a specific department but rather directed by university's Center for Clinical Global Health Education.

With significant financial, administrative, and infrastructure support from the School of Medicine, the course has used innovative technological approaches to provide students both in the U.S. and abroad with a unique experience in group learning. Each day features a clinical case conference held simultaneously by faculty in Baltimore and at a selected international site via the use of videoconferencing. Faculty at both sites present two cases of the same condition, allowing students to discuss the differences in risk factors and management while taking into account locally relevant practices, resources, delivery systems, and socioeconomic factors.

The themes covered in the inaugural session of the course were maternal health, child health, emerging diseases, and chronic diseases. These themes were approached through the discussion of cases on high-risk pregnancy, pneumonia, MDR-TB, and coronary heart disease in collaboration with faculty and students in Addis Ababa, Ethiopia, Kampala, Uganda, Karachi, Pakistan, and Pune, India. In addition to the case conferences, the course features problem-based small-group exercises in which students discuss and solve cases focused on metrics for the burden of disease, multi-sector (clinical, public health and research) interventions for disease prevention, epidemiology and the role of the environment in emerging diseases, and international research ethics.[31]

University of Arizona College of Medicine, Tuscon, AZ
Intensive preparation for international experiences, with a clinical focus

The University of Arizona Department of Family and Community Medicine's course on "Global Health: Clinical and Community Care", or the "Arizona Course" as it is commonly known, is one of the oldest courses of its kind. An intensive, interactive course aiming to prepare senior medical students, residents, and other health care professionals for international experiences in rural hospitals, the course has a unique focus on the challenges of clinical practice encountered in resource-limited and underserved areas both in the United States and in the developing world.

Students are divided into 3 small groups of up to 8 people for the duration of the full-time, 3-week course. Using problem-based-learning, they are introduced to public health, cultural and economic issues, and clinical problems by faculty from a variety of primary care medical specialties (pediatrics, family medicine, internal medicine, obstetrics) as well as other healthcare-related fields (i.e., nursing, dentistry, public health) and non-healthcare fields (i.e., hydrology). The goal is for faculty to share not only their expertise, but also their personal and professional experiences in global health. Students are taught based on a process-oriented approach to solving global health–related problems.

Over three weeks, the course introduces students to four major problem areas: nutrition (assessment and management of malnutrition, micronutrients), population health (epidemiology, demography, health metrics, public health systems, family planning), infectious diseases (HIV, malaria, TB, "neglected tropical diseases", water-borne and diarrheal illnesses, pneumonia, meningitis), and chronic diseases (tobacco, the epidemiologic transition). Other areas of focus include obstetrical problems (complications of labor, maternal and child survival), child health (vaccines, integrated management of childhood illness), surgical and peri-operative care, mental health, and the role of women in health and development. Topics of discussion within these areas include approaches to health interventions (vertical vs. horizontal, clinical vs. community-based interventions, etc), cross-cultural issues, the impact of globalization, the roles of professionals (as clinicians, teachers, researchers, and advocates) and ethical controversies in international health work.

Students are equipped with practical skills in clinical diagnosis and management through parasitology labs and sessions on chest radiology, and a few sessions are devoted to region-specific travel preparation. Unlike most other global health courses, the "Arizona Course" is open to healthcare students and practitioners from other institutions, and an application is required. Tuition fees ($500) are waived for students at LCME-accredited medical schools.[32]

Research In Global Health

Overview

Global health lends itself to unique challenges and opportunities in terms of research, and the option to conduct scholarly work is an important aspect of many global health programs. Medical schools vary widely in their degree of support for and training in research related to global health.

The inclusion of research projects or training in global health curricula offers many benefits. On an individual level, it strengthens research skills, allows for the application of concepts learned at home institutions, and promotes networking that may result in valuable mentorship relationships. On an institutional level, global health research may result in additional grant funding, promote the expansion of ideas at research meetings, lead to valuable inter-institutional partnerships or collaborations, and make the institution appear more competitive among students and faculty interested in global health. Finally, on a systems level, global health research can contribute to overall learning and the development of interventions for a specific geographical area or medical problem, in some cases by building local research capacity.

Most commonly, medical students choose to participate in GH research during their summer between first and second year or during their 4th year elective time. Alternatively, students may take a gap year at some point during their medical training. Some medical schools offer a less traditional core medical school structure that creates a natural "flex" year or part of a year (i.e. modified three-year curriculum at **Duke University**[33] and **University of Pennsylvania**[34]) which some students elect to spend participating in global health research. In other cases, students may choose to add 1-2 years on to their training for committed research time abroad, during which they can be funded by specific grants/fellowships.

The degree of selectivity for research initiatives varies, and appears to relate most to the presence of a funded grant within the institution and the formality of the program. Some institutions offer a training program or class prior to participation in research, but it is rarely required. Such classes are typically in research methodology, ethics of research, surveillance techniques, and/or biostatistics.

In this section, we divide the models of GH research exposure into several basic categories rather than focusing on specific institutional case examples. While this allows for a broad conceptualization of how scholarly work is available and encouraged by institutions, these categories are not mutually exclusive and multiple approaches may be offered by any one institution.

Examples of Approaches to Scholarly Work in Global Health

Academic center associated with an institute for global research

Medical schools with significant research funding may have overseas facilities operating under broad research initiatives, and students may have the opportunity to pursue research projects or training within this infrastructure. The core training opportunities within this category often include a rigorous introduction to global health research. For example, **Johns Hopkins School of Medicine**[35] offers a number of courses through the Center for Global Health, including "Health Systems Research and Evaluation in Developing Countries" and "Ethics Issues In Human Subjects Research In Developing Countries." Medical schools that are part of an undergraduate campus also often offer research classes to all disciplines and degree programs. For example, courses are available at **Brown University**[36] through their Global Health Initiative and multiple disciplinary degree programs, including " Survey Research in Health Care," Introduction to Methods in Epidemiologic Research," and "Introductory Statistics for Social Research." These touch on topics of global health but are not specifically targeted to research in global health.

The Center for International Health (newly reorganized as the Center for Global Health and Diseases) at **Case Western Reserve University**[37] was established in 1987 to help link the numerous international health resources of the University, its affiliated institutions, and the Northern Ohio community in a multidisciplinary program of research, training, and clinical application related to global health. International health research has been a strength of CWRU for more than thirty years, involving the participation of scientists who helped define this field of global health academics as it emerged. Its mission is accomplished uniting the CWRU faculty in programs of collaborative research and education, student and faculty international exchanges, and community enrichment to promote health in the world and enrich the international community.

Structured global health research programs

Some institutions offer structured research programs in global health that are run from within the institution rather than from an associated entity at the university. For example, **Albert Einstein College of Medicine**[38] has a research program in Uganda to which medical students can apply. This program is selective, requiring application and interview, and requires a paper or poster presentation at the end. It includes research training at the site. **Yale School of Medicine**[39] offers the Downs Fellowship, which supports 10-week long research projects conducted by health professional students. In addition to funding, the Downs provides a structure for close mentorship with 2 academic advisors – one at Yale and one in the host country. Medical students most often participate in the summer after their 1st year, and spend up to 8 months ahead of their departure working closely with a project mentors to choose a research topic, location, and work through the methodological and practical details of their proposed research project.

Research training provided by international health or healthcare research organizations

Though not accredited, there are various opportunities for certificate achievement or basic training. Examples of resources of this nature include: the Institute for International Medicine, USAID Global Health Learning Opportunities, the Agency for Healthcare Research and Quality (AHRQ), Institute of Medicine, and Global Health Education Consortium teaching modules. The **University of Pittsburgh**[40] offers a super-course website where additional resources can be found.

International research fellowships affiliated with medical schools

The Doris Duke Charitable Foundation[41] offers 1-year research fellowships to medical students with an interest in conducting research abroad. These fellowships are competitive and provide full funding for a year of work. While the program sites are based out of 6 medical schools (Columbia, Harvard, Yale, University of Pennsylvania, University of California – San Francisco, and University of North Carolina – Chapel Hill), students from any institution may apply for a spot in the program. Similarly, the Fogarty International Research Scholars Program offers year-long mentored global health research opportunities at international NIH-funded research centers.

Informal research programs

The value of informal research opportunities in global health should not be understated. Even where no formal programs exist, medical students may be able to identify faculty mentors with projects abroad. While this type of training might be less formal, and while funding might be difficult to procure, such opportunities nonetheless can be valuable as long as the medical student has adequate guidance and supervision.

International Clinical Experiences

Overview

Many U.S. medical schools offer international clinical electives.[42] Such electives offer perspective on health and healthcare in a new context, and how it is affected by local and international cultural, political, and economic factors. They can also provide site-specific objectives based on location. For example, the focus of a rotation could be the understanding of the practice of medicine in a resource-limited setting, improvement of language skills, or exposure to a specific disease that is not prevalent in the U.S. While global health clinical experiences are traditionally held in international settings, some institutions have developed clinical electives working with underserved populations in the U.S., with the intention of exposing students to the same knowledge, skills, and sensitivity that is relevant in work with populations abroad.

In general, international clinical electives are achieved through partnerships between a U.S. medical school and a local university, non-profit organization, or hospital at the clinical rotation site. The amount of funding and administrative support available for these clinical electives varies from being fully supported and subsidized, to being entirely the student's responsibility. Considerations of logistics and funding include program fees at the hosting institution, housing, transportation, visas, immunizations, malpractice and health insurance. Students are often required to have completed some core clerkships before participating in international experiences, and are often selected based on some combination of applications and interviews which touch on a range of factors including career goals, previous experience abroad, relevant skills (including language skills), and academic qualifications.

Examples of International Clinical Electives

Yale-China Program, Yale School of Medicine—Xiangya Hospital, Changsha, China

Yale School of Medicine has several structured international electives in Asia, Africa, and South America. One of the well-established programs is jointly run between the Office of International Medical Student Education (OIMSE) and the Yale-China Association, which provide stipends to eligible students to cover travel and living expenses for a six-week clinical elective at Xiangya Hospital in Changsha, China.[43]

Medical students in their clinical years are eligible to apply. Selection is based on applications reviewed by a committee from OIMSE and the Yale-China Association. The objective of the elective is to develop an understanding of the practice of medicine in a large academic hospital in urban China. Approximately 6 students participate each year. A Yale faculty member and a mentor from Xiangya Hospital, as well as the staff of the Yale-China Association support students, during the trip.

Pre-departure logistical training is available through the Yale-China Association, and students are also able to required to participate in a pre-departure ethics course. Knowledge of Chinese language is not required. Levels of participation may differ depend on types of specialty. In general, students tend to participate as observers on the clinical team.

FACES-STEP Program, UCSF School of Medicine—Kenya

UCSF has over a dozen clinical electives spanning Africa, Asia, Europe, Latin America, Middle East and North America. Many of the programs include a combination of research and clinical responsibilities with language and cultural immersion opportunities.

One of the programs in Kenya is Family AIDS Care and Education Services (FACES) - Student Education and Training Program (STEP), a joint program of UCSF and Kenya Medical Research Institute (KEMRI).[44] It provides opportunities for medical student involvement in clinical and research activities with a focus on HIV/AIDS and sexually transmitted infections in Nyanza Province, Kenya. Sites include Kisumu, Suba, Rongo and Migori.

Medical students in their clerkship years and residents can apply for clinical and research electives. Clinical electives are a minimum of 6 weeks, and can include more than one site for electives of 8 weeks or longer. Applications are open to medical students and residents from any institution; however priority is given to those from University of Nairobi, UCSF and University of British Columbia. Students are responsible for all of their own expenses including travel, food and accommodations. Students are usually supervised by an assistant program coordinator at each site, and mentored by on-site medical staff and residents.

Pre-departure orientation materials can be accessed through the FACES website. Students are involved in taking care of HIV-positive adults and children in a family-centered outpatient clinic, home and hospital visits to follow-up patients in the community, multidisciplinary team meetings, weekly case-based clinical discussions, and are expected to complete one or two projects during their elective. At the end of electives, participants are required to complete a participant evaluation and are evaluated by their primary mentors.

UCSF Latina Health, UCSF School of Medicine—Cuernavaca, Mexico

After completion of their OB/GYN core clerkship, UCSF students may apply to a summer practicum experience in Mexico for 4-8 weeks where they can attain clinical and public health experience in Latina health.[45] Students participate in ongoing reproductive health research projects at the Instituto Nacional de Salud Publica (12 hours per week) while attending Spanish language school (20 hours per week). The students live with a family to facilitate language immersion and volunteer in a clinic for four hours per week. This elective is designed to train students to perform a women's health-focused interview in Spanish; converse with a patient in Spanish about basic issues such as lactation, pregnancy, contraception; understand the complexities of clinical research in an international setting; and identify the principal reproductive health problems and priorities in Mexico.

George Washington University—Alexandria University School of Medicine, Egypt

Established in 1942, Alexandria Medical School is one of the Middle East's pre-eminent institutions in medical education and research, and is the second largest university in Egypt with 10 affiliated facilities. The school is affiliated with four hospitals, specializing in obstetrics and gynecology, pediatrics, orthopedics, and neurology. Interested students also have the opportunity to gain a better understanding of schistosomiasis, which is a major health risk in Egypt. In addition to hospital specializations listed above, Alexandria offers clinical electives in the following areas: internal medicine and sub-specialties; community medicine; tropical medicine; surgical specialties; pediatrics and obstetrics-gynecology.[46] Medical students work with a designated faculty mentor who evaluates the student's progress.

Students must have completed the following rotations prior to participation: internal medicine, family practice, pediatrics, OB/GYN, surgery, and psychiatry. Selection of students is based on a range of factors, including but not limited to: career goals, previous experience, relevant skills (such as language skills) and academic qualifications. All tuition, fees, and living expenses are paid by the student.

University of Chicago Pritzker School of Medicine—West Africa

The University of Chicago Pritzker School of Medicine offers multiple options for elective rotation at sites in West Africa.[47] The first is a 3-week elective available to students through the University of Ibadan in Ibadan, Nigeria, with rotations at Lagos State University Teaching Hospital, Lagos and Igbo-Ora Community Health Center, Igbo Ora. Students rotate in Medicine, Surgery, Pediatrics and Obs/Gyn, and opportunities also include research experiences in the immunohistochemistry, genetics, radiology, and breast imaging. The second is a 1-week elective in an urban setting at the Lagos State University Teaching Hospital, focusing primarily on maternal child health and obstetrics. The third is a 2-week experience in a rural community center setting where students are exposed to rural and tropical medicine of all forms including diarrheal diseases, malaria, skin diseases, minor surgeries, and obstetrics.

Michigan State University College of Human Medicine—Local Global Health

Started in 2004, the Leadership in Medicine for the Underserved (LMU) program was designed as an option in the clinical curriculum to enable students to work with underserved and vulnerable populations.[48] The skills, knowledge, and sensitivity gained are meant to prepare students to address the medical needs of the urban, rural, and international underserved. The program involves core clerkship integration in rural and urban underserved clinics (including migrant clinics), monthly community service, weekly community involvement at various local organizations, as well as more standard electives at international sites.

For the international elective, students work in affiliation with the Foundation for International Medical Relief of Children (FIMRC). Prior sites have included Costa Rica, Nicaragua, Peru, El Salvador, India, and Uganda. If students do not wish to travel internationally, they are given the option of designing their own 8-week elective in a rural or urban setting in Michigan. An example of a possible schedule for this rural/urban elective is the following: migrant clinic family medicine every Monday/Wednesday, rural outpatient family medicine Tuesday, psychiatry at a jail Thursdays, rural emergency medicine Fridays.

Students apply for the LMU program in their preclinical years, and are required to have an intermediate Spanish proficiency. 18 students are accepted annually.

Cultural Opportunities In Global Health

Overview

The development of cultural humility[49] is one of the key goals of global health education programs.[50] Recently, accreditation standards have changed such that medical schools are encouraged to integrate multicultural training programs into their curricula.[51] The strive for cultural competency stems from the desire to create well-rounded doctors capable of treating patients from a wide variety of backgrounds and with a greater commitment to underserved populations both home and abroad.

On a local level, across the US, medical students have identified instances of culturally- based disparities in the health care system and attempted to remedy these disparities with education and outreach through student groups and student-run free clinics. Obviously, the issues of cultural diversity and inequality that are addressed on a local level are often relevant to health in a global context. However, it is important to recognize that cultural training specifically for the international setting may involve in-depth training that is unique to a certain population or location. In this vein, some schools require that medical students work through modules or online trainings as well as meet with faculty members before and after their participation in international electives or research.

A recent review of structured global health programs found that only one institution's program explicitly addressed cultural/language competency in its requirements.[10] This is often an unstated objective of global health education and we therefore highlight it here to focus attention on the need to explicitly acknowledge the development of cultural competency as a core goal in global health education programs.

Examples of Cultural Opportunities

Wake Forest School of Medicine, Winston-Salem, NC

Wake Forest School of Medicine recently created a Cultural Awareness Committee (CAC) that consists of administrators and elected representatives of each medical school class. In an attempt to increase cultural awareness among medical students, they host speakers and workshops and offer scholarships to students who pursue culturally enriching activities. One of the CAC's most popular events is its semi-annual lunch, during which a panel of speakers discusses a particular theme related to the intersection of culture and medicine. Past themes have included discussions on cross-cultural perspectives of end-of-life care, practicing international medicine, and socio-racial determinants of health. To enhance this cultural experience, the lunch is catered by both students and local ethnic restaurants. Students are encouraged to prepare dishes from their own culture and are reimbursed by the school for all expenses.

The CAC also sponsors educational programming for 1st and 2nd year medical students during their biweekly "Being a Physician" course. Each session begins with an upper level student sharing a culturally related experience from his or her clinical rotations that fosters discussions on cultural relativism, diversity, and ethics.

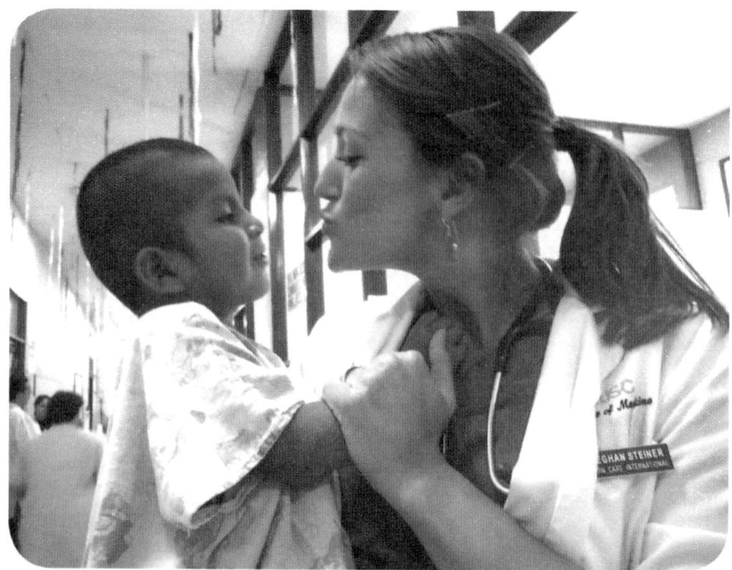

An American medical student poses with a child being treated for third degree burns in a South American hospital
Photographer: *Meg Steiner*

University of Wisconsin, Madison, WI

University of Wisconsin School of Medicine and Public Health[52,53] has established several programs that are designed to educate medical students in specific cultural paradigms. One program focuses on Training in Urban Medicine and Public Health (TRIUMPH) for students who wish to pursue careers in urban areas and are interested in combating health disparities. This program offers clinical rotations in inner city areas, as well as a Community and Public Health Enrichment Experience that addresses the cultural and historical context of Milwaukee. TRIUMPH lists cultural humility and sensitivity as a core competency of its students. Although this program focuses on the issues of urban areas of Wisconsin, skills and experiences gained are often relevant to the global community.

University of Washington, Seattle, WA

The University of Washington created the Center for Cultural Proficiency in Medical Education (CC-PrIME) in 2005 after it was awarded the Cultural Competence and Health Disparities Award by the NIH/NHLBI.[54] CC-PrIME sponsors courses addressing health disparities and houses an array of resources (DVDs, CDs, videotapes, books, journal articles, assessment tools, case vignettes) for additional information.

UW also contains the Native American Center of Excellence (NACoE), which promotes training of Native American and Alaskan students, teaches traditional Native American medicine, and supports research of Native Health Issues. The Indian Health Pathway (IHP) is a longitudinal curriculum that educates medical students in Alaskan and Native health issues through the use of a specialized lecture series, small group discussions, immersion in clinical experiences, and research opportunities. The Hispanic Health Pathway was created in 2008 to prepare students to care for the growing Hispanic population in the U.S. and culminates in an immersion experience in Central America to improve Spanish skills. General cultural awareness is included in in the "Introduction to Clinical Medicine" course required of all medical students.[55]

Mentoring In Global Health Programs

Overview

The formality and extent of mentorship in global health varies across institutions. Often, students are mentored by a research advisor supervising their capstone project. In specialized track programs, students may be formally matched with a mentor early in their medical school career and continue their relationship through graduation. While these more structured mentorship programs are often the best way to ensure appropriate guidance, many students are able to find significant informal mentors through research, coursework, or other mechanisms.

An obstacle often encountered in GH mentorship is that a single mentor may not be suited to advise students in the various realms of their career such as clinical work, community-based experiences, research or career planning. Ideally, students would be matched with several mentors, each providing guidance on a different aspect of GH training. Another problem can be a lack of defined relationships and roles for students and mentors. Many schools have addressed this problem by defining a set of mentor and student expectations, requiring signed mentor-student agreements, and establishing detailed mentorship guidelines.

Roles and Duties of Global Health Mentors

(Adapted from the University of California at San Francisco's "Mentorship Guidelines for Global Health")[56]

Mentors in global health are ideally faculty with significant expertise and field experience in international and underserved settings. They should serve as teachers, role models, advocates, guides, and even friends to their mentees. Because mentorship is a critical part of the learning experience, setting expectations early on and abiding by these expectations helps ensure a mutually beneficial mentoring relationship. Although a single person may combine any of these roles, students in global health education programs need several types of mentors (project mentors, career mentors, advisory mentors, consulting mentors) to guide them throughout their various stages of learning and experiences. In addition to the duties expected of all mentors, each mentor role involves specific responsibilities.

Project mentors work with students on defined supervised experiences. Their duties include:

- Helping students assess their learning needs and agree upon objectives for the project;
- Assisting students in the design, conduct, and analysis of the defined project;
- Communicating with students frequently to assist them with project-related work and decisions;
- Assessing and verifying students' progress through the project, including administrative requirements, and remediate or adapt the project plan as necessary;
- Guiding students in the elaboration of a final product based on the project (presentations, manuscript, etc...).

Career mentors provide students with guidance beyond the context and timeframe of individual projects. In the best of cases, these relationships will persist throughout students' careers. The responsibilities of career mentors include:

- Helping students set educational and professional goals;
- Helping students seek (and obtain) learning- and career-enhancing opportunities including networking such as in the search for training opportunities;

- Supporting student's scholarly activities, including offers of co-authorship, and encouraging them to seek avenues for recognition of their work (i.e., scholarly meetings);
- Communicating with students and meeting with them face-to-face, if possible, to review progress and exchange feedback.

Advisory mentors help guide students in defining their interests and goals. They should assist students in defining their areas of interest in global health and in finding appropriate project and career mentors. They may also provide additional support for students' work (without overtaking the role of the project mentor), for example by reviewing project drafts.

Consulting mentors should be available for focused advice on specific topics, offered either in one-on-one or group settings. Topics covered may include career planning, research workshops, negotiation workshops, guidance on applying to global health positions, etc. They should guide mentees in seeking further resources for career advancement.

In addition to the above duties, all global health mentors at are expected to:

- Meet regularly with mentees
- Help mentees navigate the university system and network
- Be available for emergencies that may arise
- Evaluate the mentoring interaction and provide feedback
- Get to know other aspects of mentees' lives including (family, outside interests)
- Discuss and maintain confidentiality

Examples of mentoring in a global health education

University of Michigan Medical School, Ann Arbor, MI

The Global Health and Disparities (GHD) Path of Excellence is among the few programs that systematically provide multiple "streams" of mentorship for students along the course of their studies. From the first year until graduation, students meet in small groups with two Small Group Facilitators. These faculty members lead didactic group sessions during the first two years, and serve as one-on-one Longitudinal Mentors for students in their group, providing them with guidance on their projects and career plans throughout medical school.[57]

Additionally, students choose faculty mentors for a summer project after their first year and a month-long disparities-focused project during their fourth year to fulfill capstone requirements. The summer project may be conducted at established sites or students may look for mentors through other avenues. An online "Faculty Clearinghouse" enables students to search for mentors specializing in global health-related research, including faculty involved with the University's international partnerships in Ghana and China.

Of note in this program, specific efforts are made to encourage and prepare faculty to mentor students. For instance, small group mentors in the GHD program receive specific training for their duties (including didactic teaching). Interested faculty throughout the university can also apply to become a Faculty Associate of the Center for Global Health (CGH), which requires 3-year commitment to activities that promote collaboration in global health work. Faculty who participate in the Center for Global Health have access to the Center's resources, including administrative, research, and practical support for their own scholarly pursuits related to global health. In return they are expected to present at and attend CGH events, providing another avenue for students to meet mentors.

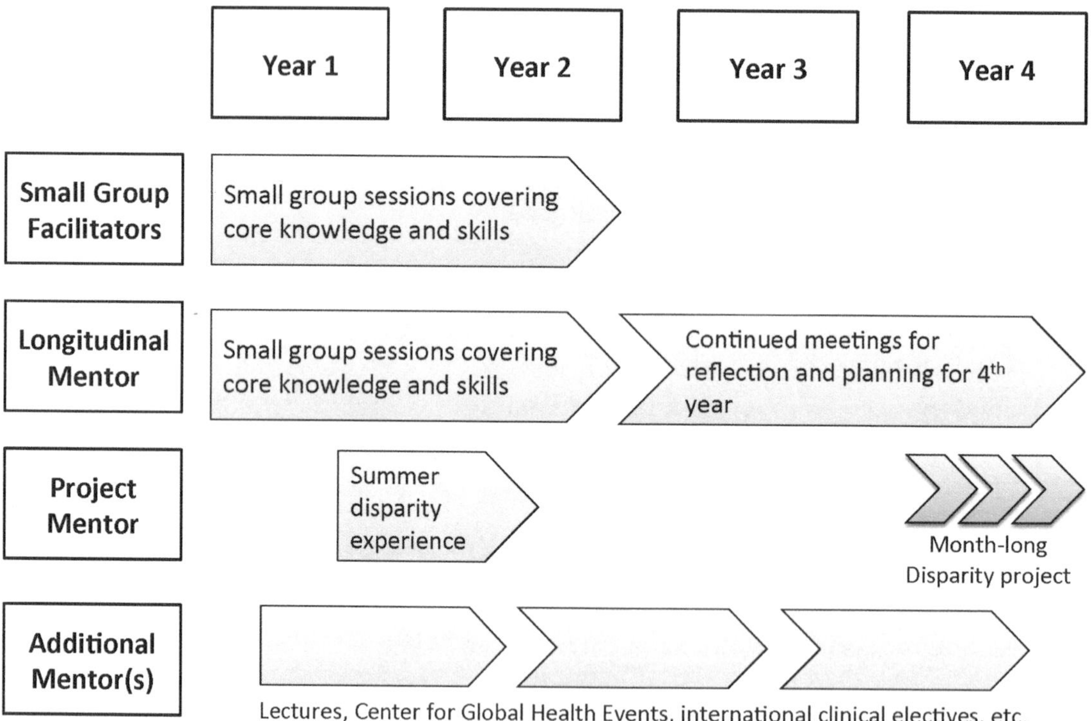

Figure. Global Health Pathway "streams" of mentorship[57] at the University of Michigan.

Capstone Experiences In Global Health

Overview

Capstone projects provide the opportunity for medical students participating in structured or unstructured global health programs to synthesize knowledge, skills, and attitudes acquired from a spectrum of global health experiences into a final product. As with all other aspects of global health curricula, the range of capstone experiences varies widely across programs, and all programs do not require such projects.

The two tables below provide examples of the content and timeline of capstone projects in global health. As a timeline, some programs require longitudinal involvement in a project throughout medical school, whereas others only require a few weeks. For content, some schools explicitly require research, while others allow more flexibility, with a choice of clinical, community, research, educational, and even creative projects. The final product of the capstone, if required, takes various forms including reflection papers, poster presentations, and research manuscripts that are a publishable quality.

Examples of Capstone Requirements

Program	Required final product(s)
Global Health Pathway *University of Rochester School of Medicine*[58]	» Presentation at Student Research Forum and submission of abstract to GHP, due Year 2 » 8- to 10-page summation paper due in Year 4, including (1) chronological description of student's experiences, (2) background on communities in which the student worked, (3) referenced discussion of potential interventions, and (4) optional reflection piece
Emphasis Program in Global Health *Vanderbilt Medical School*[59]	» Due in Year 2 » Research manuscript worthy of submission for publication » Presentations at extramural conferences may serve as additional or alternative products
Global Health Distinction Track *University of Arizona College of Medicine*[60]	» Due in Year 4 » Evidence-based synthesis paper focusing on a global health-relevant clinical or community health problem drawn from student's field experiences. Should be publishable, preferably meta-analysis style, fully referenced. » Oral examination based on capstone paper
Global Health Pathway *Medical College of Wisconsin*[61]	» Faculty mentored scholarly project completion as a graduation requirement. » Formal presentation of scholarly project at Student Research Forum by year 4 » Required participation in monthly core curriculum (3 hours) in years 1-3. » Independent learning (non core curriculum required 6 hours per month) based on an *Individual Learning Plan* » Structured local and international elective opportunities

Examples of Timeline for Capstone Experiences

	Required Scholarly Project *University of Southern California* *Keck School of Medicine*[5]	Scholarship and Discovery *University of Chicago* *Pritzker School of Medicine*[6]
Timeline for Capstone Project		
Year 1	» Students choose an area of focus and identify a mentor » Proposal for hypothesis-driven research project due in August	» Introductory coursework » Meetings with potential mentors
Summer 1	» Mentored research	» First international experience
Year 2	» Mid-year evaluation in January » Submit poster proposal to mentor by March » Present poster at Medical Student Research Day in April » Final evaluation in May	» Students apply to the GHST in the fall » Progress report with literature review, research proposal and pilot data due by end of year
Year 3		» Continued work on project under supervision of mentor
Year 4		» Second international experience (intended to constitute the basis of scholarly project) » Presentation at Senior Scientific Session (required) and dissemination of work at extramural conferences (optional)

Conclusion

The type, quantity, accessibility, and organization of global health opportunities vary widely in medical schools in the U.S. and abroad. It has been suggested that this variation is at least in part due to a lack of consensus on competencies that medical students should demonstrate in global health upon graduation from medical school.[5,64] Such competencies are addressed separately in chapter 4. In addition, unlike many medical school curricular topics, such as cardiology or microbiology, global health does not lend itself to a standardized, uniform, evidence-based knowledge set for the purpose of both educators and students. Consequently, there is not a readily apparent cohort of educators who feel comfortable teaching or are formally accredited to teach 'global health'- which is a topic that includes a wide variety of subjects and is wrought with opinions. Despite these challenges, it is imperative to discuss competencies and goals of global health education so that as the emphasis on global health education continues, the programs created and opportunities offered are designed to expand students' knowledge, skills, and attitudes in a meaningful and consistent way. It is also necessary to allow for customization of each institution's approach to global health to make the curriculum feasible for faculty to teach and locally relevant when possible.

Importantly, many topics in global health curricula are not novel concepts in medical education. Some have existed in forms integrated into the core medical curriculum (i.e. tropical medicine and microbiology) and others remain as elective opportunities (i.e. rotations in underserved clinics or abroad). The official branding of these offerings as "global health" may be useful in the process of developing a standardized and complete global health curriculum to train physicians competent to work in a globalized world.

This chapter is not a comprehensive review of all programs, but rather a sampling of opportunities aimed at giving general insight into the current landscape of global health education in U.S. medical schools. The information included in this chapter was difficult to attain, often pieced together from various institutional sources and discussions with students and faculty. A real effort should be made by institutions to consolidate and make available the information, and further study is required for a full examination into the administration, content, competencies, and prevalence of global health opportunities in U.S. medical schools.

References:

1. Novak S. "Taking a More Holistic Approach to Global Health Education". New York Times, Feb 19, 2012.
2. Association of American Medical Colleges. 2011 Medical School Graduation Questionnaire All Schools Report. Washington, DC, Association of American Medical Colleges, 2011.
3. American Medical Student Association. International Health Opportunities Directory. Available at: http://www.amsa.org/global/ih/intllist.cfm. Accessed June 5, 2011.
4. Heck J, Wedemeyer D. A survey of American medical schools to assess their preparation of students for overseas practice. Acad Med. 1991; 66:78-81.
5. Izadnegahdar R, Correia S, Ohata B, Kittler A, ter Kuile S, et al. Global health in Canadian medical education: current practices and opportunities. Acad Med 2008, 83(2): 192-198.
6. Imperato PJ. A third world international health elective for U.S. medical students: the 25-year experience of the State University of New York, Downstate Medical Center. J Community Health. 2004;29:337–373.
7. Moskowitz D, Glasco J, Johnson B, Wang G. Students in the community: an interprofessional student-run free clinic. Journal of Interprofessional Care. 2006, Vol. 20, No. 3 , Pages 254-259
8. Beck E. The UCSD student-run free clinic project: transdisciplinary health professional education. J Healthcare Poor Underserved. 2005;16: 207-219.
9. Bennard B, Wilson JL, Ferguson KP, Slinger C. A student-run outreach clinic for rural communities in Appalachia. Academic Medicine. 2004;79(7):666-671.
10. Peluso MJ, Forrestel AK, Hafler JP, Rohrbaugh R. Structured global health programs in US medical schools: a web-based review of certificates, tracks, and concentrations. Academic Medicine. 2013; 88: 124-180.
11. Suchdev P, Ahrens K, Click E, Macklin L, Evangelista D, Graham E. A model for sustainable short-term international medical trips. Ambulatory Pediatrics. 2007; 7(4):317-320.
12. Chapin E, Doosey S. International short-term medical service trips: guidelines from the literature and perspectives from the field. World Health & Population. 2010;12(2):43-53.
13. ELAM Official Website, "Historia de la ELAM." Available at: http://www.sld.cu/sitios/elam/verpost.php?blog=http://articulos.sld.cu/elam&post_id=22&c=4426&tipo=2&idblog=156&p=1&n=ddn. Accessed June 20, 2012,
14. MINSAP. Curriculum of Studies for Medical School. Havana, Cuba: Higher Institutes of Medicine. Ministry of Public Health, Cuba, 2008
15. Pastors for Peace website, ELAM Curriculum and Plan of Studies. Available at: http://www.ifconews.org/node/353. Accessed June 20, 2012.
16. Medic official website, Latin American Medical School Curriculum. Available at: http://www.medicc.org/ns/index.php?s=10&p=0. Accessed June 20, 2012.
17. "Proyecto Henry Reeve" Presentation by Dr. Jorge Jimenez Armada, Faculty Dr. Salvador Allende, Municipality of Cerro, Havana, Cuba, 5th June 2006.
18. University of Saskatchewan College of Medicine, Making the Links official website. Available at: http://www.medicine.usask.ca/leadership/social-accountability/initiatives/mtl1/index.html. Accessed June 20, 2012.

19. Margolis, C.Z., Deckelbaum, R.J., Henkin, Y, Baram, S., Cooper, P., and Alkan, M.L. A Medical School for International Health Run by International Partners. Academic Medicine. 2004;79:744-751.
20. The Medical School for International Health. Available at: http://www.cumc.columbia.edu/dept/bgcu-md/index.html. Accessed June 20, 2012.
21. Brewer TF, Saba N, Clair V. From boutique to basic: A call for standardised medical education in global health. Med Educ 2009 Oct;43(10):930-3.
22. Low N, Lawlor D, Egger M, Ness A. Global issues in medical education. Lancet 2002 Feb 23;359(9307):713-4.
23. Duvivier R, Brouwer E, Weggemans M. Medical education in global health: Student initiatives in the netherlands. Med Educ 2010 May;44(5):528-9.
24. Vora N, Chang M, Pandya H, Hasham A, Lazarus C. A student-initiated and student facilitated international health elective for preclinical medical students. Med Educ Online 2010 Feb 15;15:10.3402/meo.v15i0.4896.
25. Anderson KC, Slatnik MA, Pereira I, Cheung E, Xu K, Brewer TF. Are we there yet? preparing canadian medical students for global health electives. Acad Med 2012 Feb;87(2):206-9.
26. Dotchin C, van den Ende C, Walker R. Delivering global health teaching: The development of a global health option. Clin Teach 2010 Dec;7(4):271-5.
27. Global Health Curriculum [Internet]: Cornell University. Available from: http://weill.cornell.edu/globalhealth/education/global_health_curriculum_at_weill_cornell/. Accessed June 20, 2013.
28. Certificate in Global Medicine. Yale School of Medicine, Office of International Medical Student Education official website. Available from: http://medicine.yale.edu/globalhealth/yale/certificate.aspx. Accessed June 20, 2012.
29. Yale School of Public Health, Global Health Seminar official website. Available from: http://medicine.yale.edu/ysph/global/curriculum/seminar.aspx. Accessed June 20, 2012.
30. Global Health Concentration [Internet]: Yale University. Available from: http://publichealth.yale.edu/global/curriculum/seminar.aspx. Accessed June 20, 2012.
31. Goldner BW, Bollinger RC. Global health education for medical students: New learning opportunities and strategies. Med Teach 2012;34(1):e58-63.
32. Global Health: Clinical and Community Care [Internet]: University of Arizona. Available from: http://www.globalhealth.arizona.edu/description. Accessed June 20, 2012.
33. Duke University School of Medicine, Office of Curriculum. Official Website. Accessed June 20, 2012: http://medschool.duke.edu/education/office-curriculum-landing-page. Accessed June 20, 2012.
34. University of Pennsylvania School of Medicine, Office of Admission and Financial Aid, The Curriculum Overview and Outcomes. Official Website. Available from: http://www.med.upenn.edu/admiss/curriculum.html. Accessed June 20, 2012.
35. Johns Hopkins Center for Global Health, Global Health Related Courses. Official Website. Available from: http://www.hopkinsglobalhealth.org/events_seminars/courses.html. Accessed June 20, 2012.
36. Brown University Alpert Medical School, Global Health Initiative, Education. Official Website. Available from: http://med.brown.edu/GHI/education. Accessed June 20, 2012.
37. Case Western Reserve University, Center for International Health. Official Website. Available from: http://www.case.edu/orgs/cghd/About.htm. Accessed June 20, 2012.
38. Albert Einstein College of Medicine, Global Health Center, Projects. Official Website. Available from: http://www.einstein.yu.edu/centers/global-health/projects/. Accessed June 20, 2012.

39. Yale School of Public Health, Downs Fellowship. Official Website. Available from: http://publichealth.yale.edu/downs/index.aspx. Accessed June 20, 2012.

40. Supercourse Official Website. Available from: http://www.pitt.edu/~super1/. Accessed June 20, 2012.

41. Dorris Duke Charitable Foundation. Clinical Research Fellowships for Medical Students. Official Website. Available from: http://www.ddcf.org/mrp-crf. Accessed June 20, 2012.

42. Bissonette R, Route C. The education effects of clinical rotations in non-industrialized countries. Fam Med. 1994; 26:226-231.

43. Office of International Medical Student Education. Available from: http://medicine.yale.edu/globalhealth/yale/clinelect/asia.aspx. Accessed June 20, 2012.

44. FACES-STEP Program, UCSF School of Medicine Official Website. Available from: http://www.faces-kenya.org/step/clinical.php. Accessed June 20, 2012.

45. UCSF Latina Health, UCSF School of Medicine, Official Website. Available from: http://www.medschool.ucsf.edu/intlprograms/Programs/Latin_America.aspx. Accessed June 20, 2012.

46. George Washington University - Alexandria University School of Medicine. Official Website. Available from: www.iseo.alexmed.edu.eg. Accessed June 20, 2012.

47. University of Chicago Pritzker School of Medicine. Official Website. Available from: http://pritzker.uchicago.edu/current/students/gmsp/practicum.shtml. Accessed June 20, 2012.

48. Michigan State University College of Human Medicine. Official Website. Available from: http://lmu.msufame.msu.edu/index.php. Accessed June 20, 2012.

49. Tervalon M, Murray-Garcia J. Cultural humility versus cultural competence: a critical distinction in defining physician training outcomes in multicultural education. J Health Care Poor Underserved. 1998; 9: 117-25.

50. Peluso MJ, Encandela J, Hafler JP, Margolis CZ. Guiding principles for the development of global health education curricula in undergraduate medical education. Medical Teacher. 2012; 34: 653-658.

51. Association of American Medical Colleges. Cultural Competence Education. Washington DC, Association of American Medical Colleges, 2005. Available from: https://www.aamc.org/download/54338/data/culturalcomped.pdf. Accessed June 20, 2012.

52. University of Wisconsin Health Sciences, The Training in Urban Medicine and Public Health Official Website. Available from: http://www.med.wisc.edu/education/md/triumph/main/681. Accessed June 20, 2012.

53. University of Wisconsin-Madison, Global Health Institute Official Website. Available from: http://ghi.wisc.edu/wp-content/uploads/2012/02/ourse-Schedule-for-Global-Health-Core-and-Elective.pdf. Accessed June 20, 2012.

54. University School of Medicine, The Center for Cultural Proficiency in Medical Education, Official Website. Available from: http://depts.washington.edu/fammed/predoc/programs/upath. Accessed June 20, 2012.

55. University of Washington School of Medicine Department of Family Medicine, Underserved Pathway Official Website. Available from: http://depts.washington.edu/fammed/predoc/programs/upath. Accessed June 20, 2012.

56. Mentorship Guidelines for Global Health [Internet]: University of California San Francisco. Available from: http://www2.aap.org/sections/ich/toolkit/UCSF%20Documents/UCSF%20Mentorship%20Guidelines%20for%20Global%20Health%20Mentors.doc. Accessed June 20, 2012.

57. Global Health and Disparities Path of Excellence Program [Internet]: University of Michigan. Available from: http://www.med.umich.edu/lrc/ghd/index.html. Accessed June 20, 2012.

58. Global Health Pathway [Internet]: Unviersity of Rochester. Available from: http://www.urmc.rochester.edu/education/md/prospective-students/global-health-pathway.cfm. Accessed June 20, 2012.

59. Emphasis Program [Internet]: Vanderbilt University. Available from: https://medschool.vanderbilt.edu/emphasis-program/. Accessed June 20, 2012.

60. Global Health at the University of Arizona, College of Medicine [Internet]: University of Arizona. Available from: http://www.globalhealth.arizona.edu/. Accessed June 20, 2012.

61. Medical College of Wisconsin. Global Health Pathway. Official website. Available from: http://www.mcw.edu/medicalschool/Curriculum/ScholarlyPathways/GlobalHealth.htm. Accessed June 20, 2012.

62. Steering Committee and Faculty Advisors [Internet]: University of Southern California. Available from: http://medweb.usc.edu/rsp/RSP_steering_committee_and_faculty_advisors_11-12.pdf. Accessed June 20, 2012.

63. Scholarship and Discovery [Internet]: University of Chicago. Available from: http://pritzker.uchicago.edu/md/curriculum/scholardiscovery.shtml. Accessed June 20, 2012.

64. Battat R, Seidman G, Chadi N, Chanda M, et al. Global health competencies and approaches in medical education: a literature review. BMC Medical Education 2010, 10:94.

CHAPTER 4

Competencies and Evaluation

Hrishikesh K. Belani, MPH
MD Candidate
University of Minnesota

Kyle Dempsey, AB
MD Candidate
Harvard University

Geren Stone, MD, DTM&H
Medical Team Liaison , Indiana University-Kenya Program
Visiting Assistant Professor in Clinical Medicine , Indiana University School of Medicine
Visiting Lecturer , Moi University

Editors

Karen E. Gieseker, PhD, MS
Director of Research and Evaluation
Child Family Health International

Kevin Pottie MD CCFP MClSc FCFP
Associate Professor , Departments of Family Medicine, Epidemiology and Community Medicine
University of Ottawa

Lynda. Redwood-Campbell, MD, FCFP, DTM&H, MPH
Association of Faculties of Medicine of Canada Resource Group
Department of Family Medicine
McMaster University

THIS CHAPTER OUTLINES THE CORE competencies and assessment methods that can be used in the development of global health curricula for medical and other health professional students. The aim of this chapter is to assist educators in integrating global health content and assessing students proficiency and preparedness to serve as global healthcare providers.

Introduction

Growing student interest has led to the recent expansion of global health programs within medical education. The Global Consensus for Social Accountability of Medical Schools (GCSA) initiative serves as the call for educational institutions to hold themselves responsible not only for educational programs targeting priority health problems, but also to anticipate society's health and human resource needs and ensure graduates are competent to deliver the services most needed in the areas of greatest need.[1] This group has challenged medical education to become "socially accountable" for addressing a broad set of the 21st century's challenges: improving quality, equity, relevance of effectiveness in health care delivery; reducing the mismatch with societal priorities; redefining roles of health professionals; and providing evidence of impact on people's health status.[1] Incorporated within this challenge is the call for medical education to be focused and responsible for training health care providers with the competencies to meet these challenges. Global health, as an emerging field of practice and work, has been defined as "the goal of improving health for all people by reducing avoidable diseases, disabilities, and deaths"[2] and "an area for study, research, and practice that places a priority on improving health and achieving equity in health for all people worldwide."[3] Highly interdisciplinary and multidisciplinary, global health provides a framework to address many of the challenges delineated by the Global Consensus for Social Accountability of Medical School (GCSA). Moreover, the literature with respect to global health training continues to highlight its benefits with respect to healthcare providers' development.

Global health experiences have been shown to contribute to increased medical knowledge, heightened diagnostic acumen, less reliance on technology, increased sensitivity to and awareness of cost, and improved appreciation for cross-cultural communication.[4,5] Furthermore as globalization continues with people, products, and diseases rapidly moving around the world, Gro Brundtland, the former Director General of the World Health Organization, summarized: "The separation between domestic and international health problems is no longer useful."[2]

In light of these transitions, around the world medical schools are moving to incorporate global health education within their curricula. For instance, nearly all U.S. and Canadian medical schools currently incorporate some form of global health education within their curricula, and, in 2010, over 30% US medical school graduates reported participation in a global health experience during medical school.[6] Similar results were seen in a cross-sectional study of German medical schools in 2007 with 33% of respondents having participated in an international health elective.[6b] The current state of global health programs in medical education, however, has been labeled as "fragmented,"[7] "inconsistent, [and] haphazard,"[8] leading to a "patchwork" of programs[8] without uniform objectives and guidelines across institutions. While acknowledging that variations in educational approaches are an important source of innovation,[7] there has been concern that the variability and lack of consensus among global health experiences could have adverse consequences on students and lead to health practitioners that are unprepared to recognize and meet the healthcare challenges of an increasingly interdependent and global community.[9, 10]

Proponents of global health training have stated, "it is difficult to imagine a pursuit more closely aligned [than global health] with the professional values and visceral instincts of most physicians."[11] Therefore, there has been a call for the development of common standards and core competencies in global health education.[9, 12]

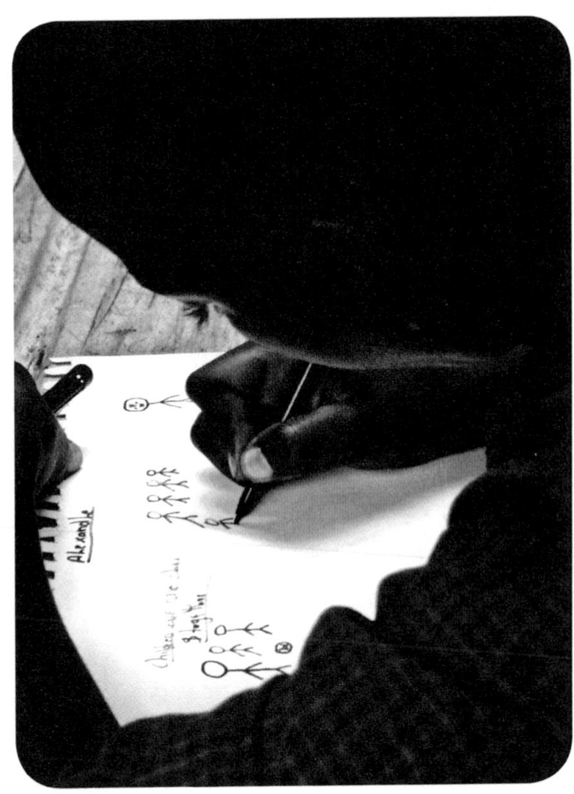

An Ethiopian child draws his version of what life would be like in an ideal world
Photographer: *Kimberly Krauk*

How Can Competencies Improve Integration of Global Health Education?

As defined by Epstein and Hundert, professional competence in health care is considered "the habitual and judicious use of communication, knowledge, technical skills, clinical reasoning, emotions, values, and reflection in daily practice for the benefit of the individual and community being served."[13] Beyond cognitive knowledge, competency encompasses abilities, skills, attitudes and behaviors and their application in service and care. As a number of authors have summarized, competencies encompass the 'know-how,' the 'show-how,' and the consistent practice of 'doing'.[14, 15] Moreover, as it is dynamic and context-dependent, competence is founded upon on continual attentiveness, curiosity, self-awareness, and presence.[13] Competency-based education focuses on desired performance characteristics and the ability of learners to perform to established expectations.[15] It involves "beginning with the end in mind."[16] Rather than focusing on completion of prescribed course work, competency-based education "de-emphasizes time-based training and promises greater accountability, flexibility, and learner-centeredness."[15b] Furthermore, as an independent commission on Education of Health Professionals for the 21st Century led by Julio Frenk and Lincoln Chen wrote,"[by] focusing on the outcomes of education, the [competency-based] approach is more transparent and therefore accountable to learners, policy makers, and stakeholders."[15c] Medical education curricula and accreditation standards around the world in this context have thus moved to adopt a competency-based approach (examples include Tomorrow's Doctor initiative in the UK [15d] and the Netherlands Framework for Undergraduate Medical Education.[15e]

When attempting to define the core competencies of global health training within medical education, there are two different perspectives that are possible. One perspective is to examine what competencies are vital to all students. That is to say: what are the core competencies specific to global health that all students, regardless of interest in global health, should attain. Houpt and others were of the first to recommend three domains of competency in global health for all students: (1) global burden of diseases (2) traveler's medicine (3) immigrant health.[17] The authors called for medical schools to ensure adequate curricular coverage of these three areas either incorporated in existing courses or added as a stand-alone course. Later in 2007, the Association of Faculties of Medicine of Canada (AFMC) Resource Group on Global Health expanded these domains to include a fourth domain, (4) cultural awareness.[18] These recommendations were followed by the development of a Joint US/Canadian Committee on Global Health Core Competencies in 2008-2009. In association with the Global Health Educational Consortium (GHEC) and the AFMC, this committee was tasked with developing common standards for global health training in North American medical schools.[7] Through a review of relevant literature, global health program websites, and expert opinion followed by peer review, the committee developed a list of 7 topic areas and 18 competencies. The 7 topic areas included the (1) global burden of disease; (2) health implications of travel, migration, and displacement; (3) social and economic determinants of health; (4) population, resources, and environment; (5) globalization of health and healthcare; (6) healthcare in low-resource settings; and (7) human rights in global health. Overall these competencies have sought to define the knowledge, skills, and practices particular to global health that are essential to the education of all students.

The second perspective to take when attempting to define the core competencies of global health training is to examine how these experiences and activities support and further student growth in the defined core competency areas of all practitioners such as the Accreditation Council for Graduate Medical Education's (ACGME) 6-core competency areas or the 7 CanMEDS roles. In 1999, the ACGME, which regulates accreditation to graduate medical programs in the United States of America, established six general competencies to assess medical residents: (1) patient care (2) medical knowledge (3) practice-based learning and improvement (4) interpersonal skills (5) professionalism (6) systems-based practice.[19, 20] In Canada, the Royal College of Physicians and Surgeons of Canada has a similar framework of competencies,[16] the seven CanMEDS roles define the different roles fulfilled by physicians from Canada in serving their patients and communities, they include: (1) medical expert (2) communicator (3) collaborator (4) manager (5) health advocate (6) scholar (7) professional. Both the ACGME core competencies and the CanMEDS roles serve as frameworks for competency-based medical education and training with a focus on the end product.

An illustration of this perspective is that taken by American Academy of Pediatrics Section on International Child Health. The working group on resident education has developed a competency model within the framework of the ACGME core competencies.[21] For example, one of the objectives listed within 'systems-based learning' is to understand the WHO's Integrated Management of Childhood Illness (IMCI) as a model of health care interventions in low and middle-income countries. The American Academy of Family Physicians (AAFP) has similar curriculum guidelines for global health which lists competencies relevant to one or multiple ACGME core competency areas.[22] Analogously in Ontario, Canada, a group of global health experts along with experts in medical education curriculum developed an evidence-informed interactive framework for global health education programs within family medicine training programs while aligning the competencies with CanMEDS roles.[23]

An emergency medicine elective in Toronto similarly applied the CanMEDS roles to its program aiming to foster cross-cultural dialogue and use health as bridge to peace.[24] Together these examples demonstrate the means by which global health education can contribute to student growth in the areas of core competencies and support the value of global health training in modern medical education.

The value global health programs add to students, academic institutions, and populations worldwide is tremendous. In order to maximize this value — and not compromise it — it is important for students to meet key competencies during their global health training.

Competencies

This section will utilize the ACGME's core competency framework to demonstrate the various ways training in global health contributes to student growth. The CanMEDS framework or another framework for viewing these proficiencies could be similarly utilized. In certain domains, global health training offers a unique competency such as an understanding of the global burden of disease largely exclusive from other areas of medical education. Yet, in other domains such as physical exam skills, global health plays a complementary role to other areas of medical education. For the purposes of this chapter, attempts are made to identify each of these areas as either specific or complementary competencies respectively. While at times the delineation is difficult and subject to continued conversation, it supports the value of global health training both in what it uniquely adds to medical training and what it complements and enhances within the existing curriculum.

To facilitate further discussions on this complex topic we have developed a listing of competencies agreed upon by regulating bodies and consensus committees or otherwise supported by literature and expert opinion. The 50 competencies listed in Table 1 are grouped into six competency domains, defined below, with relevant citations for each one shown in brackets. Additional citations regarding the development and listing of competencies are provided in Chapter 13.

Patient Care

Global health training with its focus on equity and the health of all encompasses care for the marginalized populations around the world, and yet still embraces the notion that globalization interconnects every person and community. Regardless of the setting today, migration and travel have created a context where every healthcare provider needs to have skills in understanding how these factors may affect the health of patients as well as the ability to provide high quality care to patients of differing cultural backgrounds. Data suggest that over 700 million people travel across international borders annually[25] and up to 8% of travelers seek health care while traveling abroad or upon returning home.[26] Moreover, it is estimated that over 42 million people living in the United States currently (approximately 13% of the population) and over 6 million people in Canada (approximately 20% of the population) were born in another country.[27, 28] Emerging infections such as severe acute respiratory syndrome (SARS), H1N1, and drug-resistant *Mycobacterium* tuberculosis only further the argument of the link between domestic and international health and underlie the need for every healthcare provider to have competencies to care for patients in this context. Additionally, around the globe, the health of patients and populations are shaped by social and economic conditions including poverty, urbanization, education, gender, and ethnicity. As the WHO Commission on Social Determinants of Health states, inequities in health "arise because of the circumstances in which people grow, live, work, and age" and these are "shaped by political, social, and economic forces."[29] Thus, whether a student is preparing to work in an academic tertiary referral hospital in North America or a district hospital in rural sub-Saharan Africa, global health training offers core competencies related to patient care needed for the healthcare providers of today and tomorrow.

Medical Knowledge

Healthcare practitioners need to demonstrate a fundamental knowledge of the established and evolving biomedical, clinical, epidemiological and social-behavioral sciences along with the ability to apply this knowledge to patient care. Beyond the basic curricula, global health training provides students with an introduction to principles of public health and epidemiology. Global health encourages an encompassing understanding of disease starting with a pathogen or a pathophysiological process expanding upwards to a patient, a population, and the entire globe. This perspective encourages an awareness of the social and economic determinants of health along with the resulting inequity and disparity in health burdens, access, and outcomes. Historically, the roots of global health are found in the fields of hygiene and tropical medicine.[3] Undoubtedly, a basic understanding of tropical diseases such as malaria, dengue, tuberculosis, and schistosomiasis are still a part of global health; however, the epidemiologic shifts towards non-communicable and chronic diseases around the world will increasingly lead to a change in healthcare systems' focus towards these public health burdens.

Today noncommunicable diseases (NCDs), mainly cardiovascular disease, cancer, chronic respiratory disease and diabetes mellitus represent a leading threat to human health and development. These four diseases are the most common causes of mortality globally, responsible for 60% of all deaths around the world, with 80% of these deaths occurring in low and middle income countries[30] An understanding of these trends within the global burden of disease and their effects on patients will be vital for the practitioners who will rise to meet the healthcare problems of tomorrow. Global health introduces students to how disease risk varies by world region and how factors such as rapid population growth, global travel and trade, environmental degradation, and pollution affect the health of populations. As the world population recently passed 7 billion and we continue to see rapid population growth in low-income countries, the adverse health impact on populations is nearly inevitable. [31] In this context, students should have an understanding of the relationship of clean water, sanitation, and nutrition to the health of individuals and populations. Students, moreover, should be aware of the inequitable distribution and consumption of resources, and their effects on individuals and communities worldwide.

Lastly, for students participating in experiences in low-resource settings outside of their home situation, they need to demonstrate appropriate preparation to maximize their learning and safety while minimizing the risks of harm to themselves, colleagues, and patients. Thus, as medical education moves to hold itself accountable for addressing and anticipating society's healthcare needs and problems, the medical knowledge gained through global health training will equip healthcare providers to address and meet the healthcare challenges of tomorrow.

Practice-based Learning and Improvement

As an emerging field with a growing body of literature and research, global health offers students the opportunities to grow as life-long learners as they seek to make their own contributions to the health of the populations for whom they care. Global health supports student growth by encouraging students to make a critical examination of their own practices as well as that of others through an increasing body of scientific knowledge. Unfortunately, the history of global health is littered with damages caused by well-intentioned groups to the very populations they were seeking to help. The growth of global health educational initiatives and programs allows for an increased ability of students to learn best practices from past successes and failures in global health. An example of this is Harvard's Global Health Delivery Case Studies where students can examine the issues, themes, and principles in health care delivery from various different countries.[32]

Moreover, there is a growing presence of global health research and articles in the major medical journals. Modern technology allows for the ability to access these resources from nearly anywhere in the world. Furthermore, exposure to other healthcare systems and differences in practices often acts as the stimulus for critical appraisal of both one's personal practices and those of one's home healthcare system. That is to say, exposure to new and different practices often leads students to question why these differences exist and to consider what may be best in each context—whether at home or away— along with a search for supporting evidence. Therefore, in many ways global health training supports and fosters practice-based learning and improvement in students.

Interpersonal Skills

Global health as a field is multidisciplinary and interdisciplinary. Providers frequently function as part of a team or an organization, and they are required be able to communicate and collaborate effectively with other health professionals, health system leaders, public officials, patients, families, and the public. Around the globe, healthcare systems are looking to practices such as task-shifting and community healthcare to meet growing healthcare demands, and students will need to be prepared to work effectively as teachers and leaders in these systems. Cultural differences, particularly around health beliefs and behaviors, can hinder communication, as can differences in education and literacy. Appropriate preparation along with continued self-reflection, humility, and a sense of humor will be invaluable practices allowing for growth and improvement despite the inevitable mistakes. In order to meet future healthcare challenges, healthcare providers need to be able work as members and leaders of teams through effective communication and understanding the value and roles of other team members and the communities that they are serving. Through exposure to different cultures, populations, healthcare practices, and systems, global health training undoubtedly supports and contributes to growth in these skills.

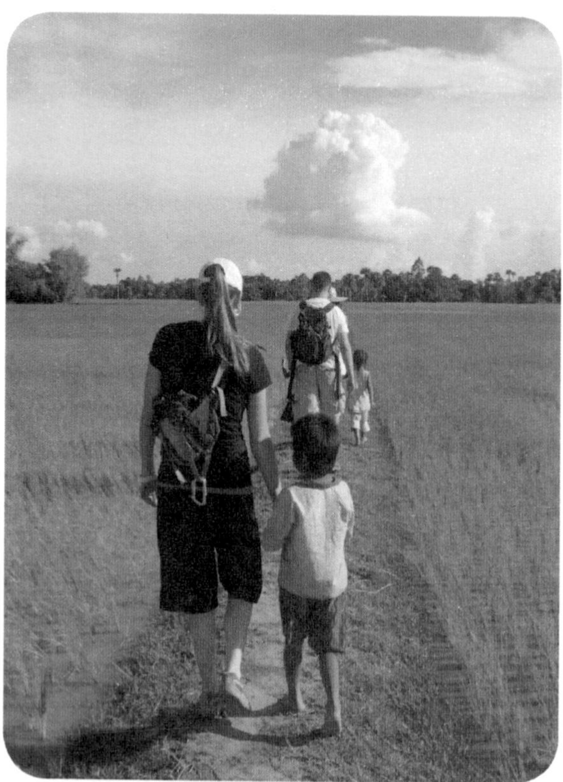

American volunteers walk with Cambodian children through rice paddies from one village to the next
Photographer: *Chelsea Small*

Professionalism

The American Board of Internal Medicine along with other professional organizations has declared, "Professionalism is the basis of medicine's contract with society."[33] Founded on principles of the primacy of patient welfare, patient autonomy, and social justice, professionalism captures those behaviors and commitments that act as a "structurally stabilizing, morally protective force in society."[34] With its priority on improving health and achieving equity in health for all, global health exemplifies these principles of medical professionalism. Encouraging an awareness of structural inequities and social injustice, global health fosters the growth of students as altruistic, compassionate healthcare providers. Research has demonstrated that students and residents who participate in international clinical rotations are more likely to pursue primary care medicine, obtain public health degrees, engage in community service, and practice medicine among underserved and multicultural populations.[5, 29a, 36, 37] Moreover, global health experiences often support increased cultural competency and an evaluation of personal biases. In 2002, Shaywitz and Ausiello called on the medical profession to nurture and encourage students' passionate interest in global health for 2 reasons—first to improve the health of people throughout the world and secondly "to revitalize ourselves while renewing the dignity of our calling."[11] Global health, well aligned with the professional values and calling of medicine, encourages students to grow in compassion, integrity, sensitivity, and responsiveness to all patients, communities, and colleagues.

Systems-based Practice

The final core competency from the ACGME calls on medical education to train health care providers who can "demonstrate an awareness of and responsiveness to the larger context and system of health care, as well as the ability to effectively call on other resources to provide optimal health care."[38] With global health's focus on public health and populations, global health is uniquely situated to provide students with growth in this competency. Through exposure to various different healthcare systems, students are challenged to think critically about healthcare funding, rationing, and priority setting. They are exposed to different models of healthcare delivery including various examples of community-based healthcare and primary care. Moreover, global health encourages students' understanding of multinational efforts such as the United Nations Millennium Development Goals and how governments and organizations are working together to address the health problems of populations around the world. Yet, global health also invites students to examine critically how these efforts along with local forces of economics, culture, politics, conflict, and famine combine to affect the quality and availability of healthcare in various settings. This examination certainly includes an understanding of the global healthcare workforce and global trends in availability and movement. Through this understanding of systems-based learning that global health training offers, students are better equipped to step into their professional roles as healthcare providers, advocates, and leaders for their patients and communities.

Table 1. Global health competencies

	COMPETENCIES
Patient Care	With respect to patients and populations, understand the health risks associated with travel and migration, with emphasis on potential risks and appropriate management, including referrals (17,18,21,22,39,40) Demonstrate an understanding of cultural and ethical issues in working with underserved populations (4,18,21,22,39–41) Demonstrate cross-cultural communication skills including utilization of interpreters or language proficiency (4,18,21,22,39–41) With respect to patients and populations, understand the relationship between health and the social determinants of health, and how these vary across world regions (4,18,21,22,40–43) With respect to patients and populations, identify barriers to health and healthcare locally and internationally (18,21,22,42)* Apply and improve clinical skills (i.e. physical exam skills, procedural skills) and practice in all settings including those with limited resources for diagnosis and treatment (18,21,22,35,44)* Within the cultural context of practice and the resources available, create treatment plans that are cost-effective, evidence-based, patient-centered, and focused on patient-defined quality of life (21,22,40)* Demonstrate understanding of the value of health promotion and disease prevention strategies and how their inclusion or absence impacts individual patient lives and populations (21,40)*

Medical Knowledge	Demonstrate knowledge of the major global causes of morbidity and mortality and how health risks vary by gender and income across regions (17,18,22) Demonstrate a basic understanding of the common diseases endemic to resource poor areas including the presentation, diagnosis, treatment and control measures for conditions including acute respiratory infections, diarrheal diseases, malnutrition, meningitis, tuberculosis, HIV, and parasitic infections such as malaria and helminthic infections (18,21,22,39,40,45) Demonstrate basic understanding of emerging chronic diseases and understand the double impact these diseases pose in countries with concomitant high infectious disease burden (18,22) Demonstrate an awareness of the major causes of maternal, perinatal, and under 5 mortality worldwide (18,40) Demonstrate an awareness of the health issues encountered by vulnerable populations such as immigrants, refugees, internally displaced persons, and those with disabilities (17,18,21,22,39,40,46) Understand how travel and trade contribute to the spread of communicable diseases (17,18,22) Understand the impact of rapid population growth and of unsustainable and inequitable resource consumption on important resources essential to human health, including water, sanitation, and food supply, and know how these resources vary across world regions (18) Describe the relationship between access to clean water, sanitation and nutrition on individual and population health (18,21,22) Describe the relationship between environmental degradation, pollution, and health (18,21)

Medical Knowledge	For students who participate in experiences in low-resource settings outside their home situations, demonstrate appropriate preparation with respect to personal health, travel safety, cultural awareness, expected ethical challenges, and an awareness of the historical, socio-political, economic, and linguistic context in which they will be learning (18,21,22,42) Develop a refined awareness and understanding of the sequela of late-stage presentations of untreated common illnesses and the value of preventive health for individuals and populations (45) Apply and improve clinical skills (i.e. physical exam skills, procedural skills) and practice in all settings including those with limited resources for diagnosis and treatment (21,22,35,44)*
Practice-Based Learning	Appraise the differences in practice across different healthcare systems including critical self-reflection with an understanding of contextual influences and openness to change (21, 22, 29c, 29i) Identify standardized guidelines for diagnosis and treatment of conditions common to low and middle-income countries such the World Health Organization's Integrated Management for Childhood Illness (IMCI) (21,40) Within the cultural context of practice and the resources available, create treatment plans founded on principles of evidence-based medicine that are patient-centered and focused on patient-defined quality of life (21,22,40)* Utilize information technology to support evidence-based patient care by allowing for continual growth and practice changes from the growing body of scientific literature and resources (21,22,40)* Apply and improve clinical skills (i.e. physical exam skills, procedural skills) and practice in all settings including those with limited resources for diagnosis and treatment (21,22,40)*
Practice-Based Learning	Work collaboratively with health care team members to assess, coordinate, and improve patient care practices in settings with limited resources (21,22,40)* Establish individualized learning objectives for global health experiences and strategies for meeting those objectives (21)*

Interpersonal Skills	Demonstrate cross-cultural communication skills including utilization of interpreters or language proficiency (4,21,22,39–41,46) Demonstrate understanding of health beliefs, behaviors, and patient and community expectations specific to the setting (21,22,40) Demonstrate an ability to utilize appropriate strategies and resources to care for specific patient populations including those with lower education and literacy levels (21,22,40,44)* Demonstrate an awareness and recognition of the importance for all roles on the healthcare team, including non-traditional and lay providers, in providing optimal patient care (21,22,40,44)*
Professionalism	With respect to patients and populations, understand the relationship between health and the social determinants of health, and how these vary across world regions (4,18,21,22,40–43) Demonstrate a basic understanding of the relationship between health and human rights (18,22,43,47) Demonstrate an understanding of ethical issues in working with underserved populations (18,21,22,40) Demonstrate an understanding of specific cultural issues in working with underserved populations, including such practices as traditional and complementary medicine (4,18,21,22,40)

Professionalism	Be able to discuss the issues of equity and social justice in the distribution of health services in resource-poor settings (21, 22, 29c, 37b) Develop an understanding of the ethical standards and review processes for research with human subjects carried out on vulnerable populations including those in low and middle-income countries (21)* Reflect and recognize personal biases in caring for patients of diverse populations and different backgrounds and how these biases may affect care and decision-making (21,44)* Demonstrate a commitment to professional behavior while working collaboratively with health care team members and being respectful of differences in knowledge, practices, and culture (21,22,40,44)*
Systems-Based Practice	Understand how global trends in healthcare practice, commerce, and culture contribute to health and the quality and availability of healthcare locally and internationally (18,21,40) Demonstrate an understanding of major multinational efforts to improve health globally such as the Millennium Development Goals (18,21,22,40) Understand and describe general trends and influences in global availability and movement of healthcare workers (18,21,40) Demonstrate an understanding of healthcare delivery strategies in low-resource settings, especially the role of community-based healthcare and primary care models (18,21,22) With respect to patients and populations, identify barriers to health and healthcare locally and internationally (18,21,22)

Systems-Based Practice	With respect to patients and populations, understand the relationship between health and the social determinants of health, and how these vary across world regions (4,18,21,22,40–43) Be able to discuss the issues of equity and social justice in the distribution of health services in resource-poor settings (21,22,43,47)* Be able to knowledgeably discuss priority setting, healthcare rationing and funding for health and health-related research (18,22)* Demonstrate the ability to adapt clinical skills and practice in all settings including those with limited resources for diagnosis and treatment (18,21,22,40)* Demonstrate an understanding of optimal resource management to provide optimal, cost-effective care including task-shifting, algorithm-based care, and use of technology support (21,22,35,44)* Develop an increased understanding of the interdependence of multiple systems involved providing healthcare to patients (21,22,44)*

* *Complementary competencies*

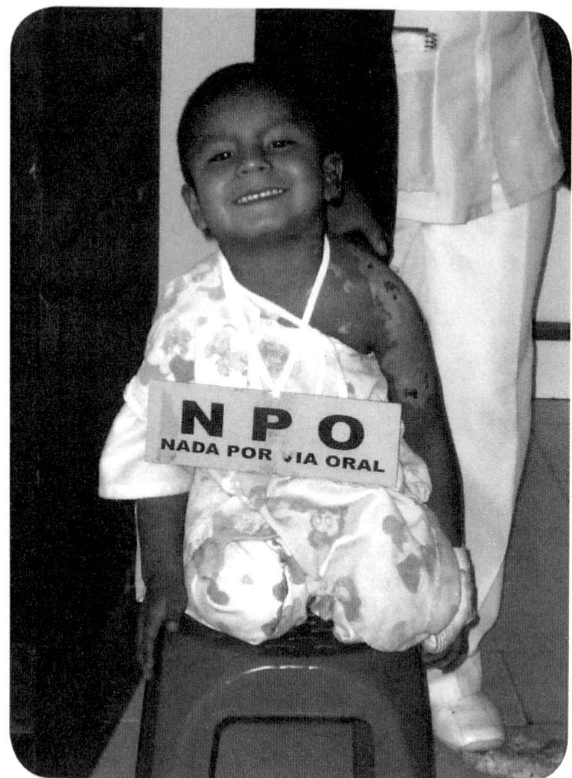

A young patient proudly displays her diet
Photographer: *Meg Steiner*

Assessing Global Health Education Outcomes

This section addresses the means by which the above global health competencies can be assessed for medical and other students. As medical education evolves, with greater focus being placed on concepts and the application of knowledge to clinical decision-making, assessment in medical education also evolves. Dynamic curricula call for equally dynamic assessment modalities to adequately measure performance and achievement. Thus, in undergraduate and graduate medical education, it is common to use multiple methods of assessment, both formative and summative. Moreover, given that no method of assessment is without flaws, use of multiple methods helps to compensate for shortcomings across them.[48]

Formal validation of assessment methods specific to global health programs is lacking and educators need to look more critically at how programs and students are assessed and which methodologies work. Currently, global health programs employ a variety of assessment methods to evaluate their students. Among the different methods used for competency-based assessment, the four most common in practice are: (1) standardized testing (2) 360-degree evaluations (3) scholarly projects (4) self-reflections. These modalities are described below with the corresponding competencies they are best suited to assess highlighted at the end of each sub-section.

Standardized Exams

Scores on standardized exams, such as the USMLE, have been correlated to success rates of specialty-specific certification exams,[49] and are often integral to admission decisions for different training programs. There are currently no validated standardized exams available for global health curricula in medical and other health professional schools. Creating a single standardized exam for global health training is challenging, given country or region specific variations. Standardized exams are also limited in the type of skills and knowledge that they are able to test. For example, empathy, the ability to connect with patients, and a student's overall potential as a global health practitioner are difficult to measure using a summative tool. Additionally, the employment of standardized exams can incentivize students to focus on tested material rather than exploring a wide breadth of knowledge during their training. If available, standardized exams should be used in conjunction with other assessment methods, serving the role of testing discrete knowledge a student should gain from a global health training program.

Global Health Competencies Assessed:

Medical Knowledge competencies 1-9 and 11
Professionalism competencies 1-6
Systems-Based Practice competencies 1-4 and 6

360-degree Evaluations

Also known as multi-source or multi-rater feedback, 360-degree evaluations take many perspectives into account when evaluating a student. Assessors solicit feedback about the student from the students' peers, educators, patients, and other staff with whom the student works. This broad feedback is valuable in helping the student to identify areas for skill and interpersonal development.

Three hundred and sixty-degree evaluations have been used to evaluate the effectiveness of short term medical missions,[50] and have been shown to improve interpersonal and communication skills among medical residents more than traditional evaluations.[51] They are well suited for global health education evaluations, being ideal for assessing cultural sensitivity and effectiveness as a member of a multi-disciplinary team. Additionally, 360-degree evaluations can encourage self-directed improvement.

Global Health Competencies Assessed:

Interpersonal competencies 1-4
Patient Care competency 2
Practice-Based Learning competency 6
Professionalism competency 8

Scholarly Work

Scholarly work consists of abstracts, posters, peer-reviewed publications, narrative literature projects, community-based public service projects, and artistic renditions of medicine, among others.[52] In completing scholarly projects, students integrate a variety of interdisciplinary skills—leadership, creativity, teamwork, interventions to address local needs, statistical methods, advocacy—and the projects help them think more critically about the environments in which they work. Bierer and Chen found medical students who completed broad scope scholarly projects would report that specialty choice, research interest, understanding of the research process and method, and successfully obtaining grant funding had all been influenced by their projects.[53]

In the context of global health programming, scholarly projects can an iterative process that starts by identifying and characterizing host communities' needs and organically leads to new projects that address those needs. This data-driven approach to research helps students develop research and methodological skills that will be helpful throughout the student's career. It is important, however, to ensure that any project reflects local priorities and not be burdensome to host sites.[54]

Designing and executing high quality projects—whether research or otherwise—can be challenging depending on the setting and many factors that are often beyond a student's control. Designating a mentor is key to ensuring the feasibility of a project, with the mentor available to provide feedback and ideas, relay cross-disciplinary expertise (e.g., survey development ideas, statistical analysis, knowledge of the local community). Ideally two mentors, one from the student's home institution and from the student's local host community would be available to engage a diversity of perspectives.

The scope of feasible scholarly projects usually cannot address all of the skill areas that a program deems desirable in its global health graduates. Therefore the scholarly project should be only one component of a competency-based assessment.

Global Health Competencies Assessed:

Patient Care competency 5
Practice-Based Learning competencies 1 and 4
System-Based practice competencies 5, 8, 10, and 11

Self-Reflection

Self-reflection encourages students to be self-aware and self-critical in their learning and can promote humanism within healthcare training. A recent study at Tufts University, for example, used taped patient encounters to review opportunities for compassionate care with medical students finding that the exercise promoted "student reflection on and self-assessment of compassionate care."[55] Additionally, it is thought that self-directed learning in health education can be improved with self-reflection,[56] and there are now requests to explicitly teach self-reflective techniques to enhance students' self-auditing ability.[57]

In 2011, Louise Aronson provided a 12-point system for teaching critical self-reflection in medical education.[58] Aronson emphasizes that "with a better understanding of the conceptual frameworks underlying critical reflection and greater advance planning, medical educators will be able to create exercises and longitudinal curricula that not only enable greater learning from the experience being reflected upon but also develop reflective skills for life-long learning." The 12 points involve: (1) defining reflection, (2) deciding on learning from the reflective exercise, (3) choosing an appropriate instructional method for the reflection, (4) deciding whether to use an unstructured or structured approach, and to create a prompt, (5) making a plan for dealing with ethical and educational concerns, (6) creating a mechanism to follow up on learners' plans, (7) creating a conducive learning environment, (8) teaching learners about reflection before asking them to do it, (9) providing feedback and follow up, (10) assessing the reflection, (11) making the exercise part of a larger curriculum to encourage reflection, and (12) reflecting on the process of teaching reflection.

Recent strides have been made to create validated and standardized self-assessment rubrics,[59] but these are not yet specific to global health training. If in line with Aronson's, or similar guidelines, however, a self-reflection assessment can be a successful competency-based assessment.

Global Health Competencies Assessed:

Medical Knowledge competency 9
Practice-Based Learning competency 7
Professionalism competencies 5 and 7

References:

1. Boelen C. [Global consensus on social accountability of medical schools]. Sante Publique. 2011 Jun;23(3):247–50.
2. Brundtland G. Addressing the challenges of unequal distribution [Internet]. Davos, Switzerland; 2001 [cited 2012 Jun 4]. Available from: http://www.who.int/director- general/speeches/2001/english/20010129_davosunequaldistr.en.html
3. Koplan JP, Bond TC, Merson MH, Reddy KS, Rodriguez MH, Sewankambo NK, et al. Towards a common definition of global health. Lancet. 2009 Jun 6;373(9679):1993–
4. Haq C, Rothenberg D, Gjerde C, Bobula J, Wilson C, Bickley L, et al. New world views: preparing physicians in training for global health work. Fam Med. 2000 Sep;32(8):566–72.
5. Drain PK, Primack A, Hunt DD, Fawzi WW, Holmes KK, Gardner P. Global health in medical education: a call for more training and opportunities. Acad Med. 2007 Mar;82(3):226–30.
6. Medical school graduation questionnaire all schools report. [Internet]. Washington DC: Association of American Medical Colleges; 2011 Oct. Available from: https://www.aamc.org/download/263712/data/gq-2011.pdf
7. Arthur MAM, Battat R, Brewer TF. Teaching the basics: core competencies in global health. Infect. Dis. Clin. North Am. 2011 Jun;25(2):347–58.
8. Izadnegahdar R, Correia S, Ohata B, Kittler A, Ter Kuile S, Vaillancourt S, et al. Global health in Canadian medical education: current practices and opportunities. Acad Med. 2008 Feb;83(2):192–8.
9. Brewer TF, Saba N, Clair V. From boutique to basic: a call for standardised medical education in global health. Med Educ. 2009 Oct;43(10):930–3.
10. Frenk J, Chen L, Bhutta ZA, Cohen J, Crisp N, Evans T, et al. Health professionals for a new century: transforming education to strengthen health systems in an interdependent world. Lancet. 2010 Dec 4;376(9756):1923–58.
11. Shaywitz DA, Ausiello DA. Global health: a chance for Western physicians to give- and receive. Am. J. Med. 2002 Sep;113(4):354–7.
12. Battat R, Seidman G, Chadi N, Chanda MY, Nehme J, Hulme J, et al. Global health competencies and approaches in medical education: a literature review. BMC Med Educ. 2010;10:94.
13. Epstein RM, Hundert EM. Defining and assessing professional competence. JAMA. 2002 Jan 9;287(2):226–35.
14. Battel-Kirk B, Barry MM, Taub A, Lysoby L. A review of the international literature on health promotion competencies: identifying frameworks and core competencies. Glob Health Promot. 2009 Jun;16(2):12–20.
15. Gruppen L, Mangrulkar R, Kolars J. Competency-based education in the health professions: Implications for improving global health [Internet]. University of Michigan; 2010 page 1–25. Available from: http://hdl.handle.net/2027.42/85362
16. Frank J. The CanMEDS 2005 physician competency framework. Better standards. Better physicians. Better care. Ottawa: The Royal College of Physicians and Surgeons of Canada; 2005.
17. Houpt ER, Pearson RD, Hall TL. Three domains of competency in global health education: recommendations for all medical students. Acad Med. 2007 Mar;82(3):222–5.
18. Creating Global Health Curricula for Canadian Medical Students Report of the AFMC Resource Group

on Global Health [Internet]. Association of Faculties of Medicine of Canada Resource Group on Global Health; 2007 Mar. Available from: http://www.afmc.ca/pdf/pdf_2007_global_health_report.pdf

19. Batalden P, Leach D, Swing S, Dreyfus H, Dreyfus S. General competencies and accreditation in graduate medical education. Health Aff (Millwood). 2002 Oct;21(5):103–11.

20. Perina D. The ACGME general competencies challenge--perspective of the Council of Emergency Medicine Residency Directors. Acad Emerg Med. 2002 Nov;9(11):1218– 9.

21. Evert J, Stewart C, Chan K, Rosenberg M, Hall T. Developing Residency Training in Global Health: A Guidebook. San Francisco: Global Health Education Consortium; 2008.

22. Recommended Curriculum Guidelines for Family Medicine Residents Global Health [Internet]. American Academy of Family Physicians; 2011. Available from: http://www.aafp.org/online/etc/medialib/aafp_org/documents/about/rap/curric ulum/globalhealth.Par.0001.File.tmp/Reprint287.pdf

23. Redwood-Campbell L, Pakes B, Rouleau K, MacDonald CJ, Arya N, Purkey E, et al. Developing a curriculum framework for global health in family medicine: emerging principles, competencies, and educational approaches. BMC Medical Education. 2011 Jul 22;11(1):46.

24. Valani R, Sriharan A, Scolnik D. Integrating CanMEDS competencies into global health electives: an innovative elective program. CJEM. 2011 Jan;13(1):34–9.

25. Hill DR. The burden of illness in international travelers. N. Engl. J. Med. 2006 Jan 12;354(2):115–7.

26. Freedman DO, Weld LH, Kozarsky PE, Fisk T, Robins R, Von Sonnenburg F, et al. Spectrum of disease and relation to place of exposure among ill returned travelers. N. Engl. J. Med. 2006 Jan 12;354(2):119–30.

27. International Migration 2009 [Internet]. United Nations Department of Economic and Social Affairs Population Division; 2009. Available from: http://www.un.org/esa/population/publications/2009Migration_Chart/2009IttMi g_chart.htm.

28. 2006 census: immigration in Canada: a portrait of the foreign-born population, 2006: highlights. [Internet]. Statistics Canada; Available from: http://www12.statcan.ca/census-recensement/2006/as-sa/97-557/p1-eng.cfm

29. World Health Organization Commission on Social Determinants of Health. Closing the gap in a generation: health equity through action on the social determinants of health. Geneva, Switzerland: WHO Press; 2008.

30. 2008-2013 Action plan for the global strategy for the prevention and control of noncommunicable diseases [Internet]. World Health Organization; 2009. Available from: http://www.who.int/nmh/publications/9789241597418/en/

31. The Lancet Infectious Diseases. 7 billion of us. Lancet Infect Dis. 2011 Nov;11(11):801.

32. Global Health Deliver Case Studies [Internet]. GHDOnline. [cited 2012 Jun 7]. Available from: http://www.ghdonline.org/cases/

33. Medical professionalism in the new millennium: a physician charter. Ann. Intern. Med. 2002 Feb 5;136(3):243–6.

34. Wynia MK, Latham SR, Kao AC, Berg JW, Emanuel LL. Medical professionalism in society. N. Engl. J. Med. 1999 Nov 18;341(21):1612–6.

35. Gupta AR, Wells CK, Horwitz RI, Bia FJ, Barry M. The International Health Program: the fifteen-year experience with Yale University's Internal Medicine Residency Program. Am. J. Trop. Med. Hyg. 1999 Dec;61(6):1019–23.

36. Miller WC, Corey GR, Lallinger GJ, Durack DT. International health and internal medicine residency training: the Duke University experience. Am. J. Med. 1995 Sep;99(3):291–7.

37. Thompson MJ, Huntington MK, Hunt DD, Pinsky LE, Brodie JJ. Educational effects of international health electives on U.S. and Canadian medical students and residents: a literature review. Acad Med. 2003 Mar;78(3):342–7.

38. Common Program Requirements [Internet]. Accreditation Committee for Graduate Medical Edication; Available from: http://www.acgme.org/acwebsite/navpages/nav_commonpr.asp

39. Margolis CZ, Deckelbaum RJ, Henkin Y, Baram S, Cooper P, Alkan ML. A medical school for international health run by international partners. Acad Med. 2004 Aug;79(8):744–51.

40. Suchdev PS, Shah A, Derby KS, Hall L, Schubert C, Pak-Gorstein S, et al. A proposed model curriculum in global child health for pediatric residents. Acad Pediatr. 2012 May;12(3):229–37.

41. Ramsey AH, Haq C, Gjerde CL, Rothenberg D. Career influence of an international health experience during medical school. Fam Med. 2004 Jun;36(6):412–6.

42. Imperato PJ. A third world international health elective for U.S. medical students: the 25-year experience of the State University of New York, Downstate Medical Center. J Community Health. 2004 Oct;29(5):337–73.

43. Parsi K, List J. Preparing medical students for the world: service learning and global health justice. Medscape J Med. 2008;10(11):268.

44. Gladding S, Zink T, Howard C, Campagna A, Slusher T, John C. International electives at the university of Minnesota global pediatric residency program: opportunities for education in all Accreditation Council for Graduate Medical Education competencies. Acad Pediatr. 2012 May;12(3):245–50.

45. Federico SG, Zachar PA, Oravec CM, Mandler T, Goldson E, Brown J. A successful international child health elective: the University of Colorado Department of Pediatrics' experience. Arch Pediatr Adolesc Med. 2006 Feb;160(2):191–6.

46. Pottie K, Hostland S. Health advocacy for refugees: Medical student primer for competence in cultural matters and global health. Can Fam Physician. 2007 Nov;53(11):1923–6.

47. Association of Schools of Public Health. Global Health Competency Model [Internet]. 2011. Available from: http://www.asph.org/document.cfm?page=1084

48. Epstein RM. Assessment in medical education. N. Engl. J. Med. 2007 Jan 25;356(4):387–96.

49. Thundiyil JG, Modica RF, Silvestri S, Papa L. Do United States Medical Licensing Examination (USMLE) scores predict in-training test performance for emergency medicine residents? J Emerg Med. 2010 Jan;38(1):65–9.

50. Maki J, Qualls M, White B, Kleefield S, Crone R. Health impact assessment and short- term medical missions: a methods study to evaluate quality of care. BMC Health Serv Res. 2008;8:121.

51. Berger J, Pan E, Thomas J. A randomized, controlled crossover study to discern the value of 360-degree versus traditional, faculty-only evaluation for performance improvement of anesthesiology residents. Journal of Education in Perioperative Medicine. 11(2):1–13.

52. Green EP, Borkan JM, Pross SH, Adler SR, Nothnagle M, Parsonnet J, et al. Encouraging scholarship: medical school programs to promote student inquiry beyond the traditional medical curriculum. Acad Med. 2010 Mar;85(3):409–18.

53. Bierer SB, Chen HC. How to measure success: the impact of scholarly concentrations on students--a literature review. Acad Med. 2010 Mar;85(3):438–52.

54. Jones E. Students Going Abroad for Service-Learning Experiences: Questions Considered. The Advisor. 2009 Jun;25–9.

55. Kalish R, Dawiskiba M, Sung Y-C, Blanco M. Raising medical student awareness of compassionate

care through reflection of annotated videotapes of clinical encounters. Educ Health (Abingdon). 2011 Dec;24(3):490.

56. Nothnagle M, Anandarajah G, Goldman RE, Reis S. Struggling to be self-directed: residents' paradoxical beliefs about learning. Acad Med. 2011 Dec;86(12):1539–44.
57. Gagliardi AR, Brouwers MC, Finelli A, Campbell CE, Marlow BA, Silver IL. Physician self-audit: a scoping review. J Contin Educ Health Prof. 2011;31(4):258–64.
58. Aronson L. Twelve tips for teaching reflection at all levels of medical education. Med Teach. 2011;33(3):200–5.
59. Koole S, Dornan T, Aper L, De Wever B, Scherpbier A, Valcke M, et al. Using video- cases to assess student reflection: Development and validation of an instrument. BMC Medical Education. 2012 Apr 20;12(1):22.

CHAPTER 5

Global Health Partnership Building and Collaboration

Rachel A Umoren MB.BCh, MS
Assistant Professor of Clinical Pediatrics
Indiana University School of Medicine

Brian T Montague, DO MS MPH
Faculty, Division of Infectious Disease
Warren Alpert School of Medicine at Brown University

Ndidiamaka L Musa
Associate Professor, Department of Pediatrics
Medical College of Wisconsin

Editor

Mirriam Rafiq Braden MPH
Interim Executive Director
Child Family Health International

True Partnership in Global Health

THE INTEREST IN INTERNATIONAL HEALTH experiences expressed by trainees at all levels of undergraduate and graduate global health education has driven the establishment of many international training programs and partnerships between US/Global North universities and institutions around the world. Reciprocity, the meeting of mutual needs, and the collective sharing of both the tangible and intangible profits of the collaboration characterize true partnerships. Education is increasingly becoming the core objective of many of these global health partnerships, moving beyond a traditional focus on research, consultation, and service. This shift reflects the appreciation of capacity development as a key intervention for better health outcomes and the recognition that ethical institutional partnerships support learning and professional growth on both sides of the collaboration. Global health educational partnership is a broad term. Generally, there are two types of global health education programs and related partnerships—one type aims to educate students from the Global North about global health, the other aims to educate individuals in the Global South utilizing expertise from the Global North. Occasionally programs aim to do both in tandem, although usually the core activities are focused more in one realm or the other.

The increasing body of literature on global health partnerships has focused initially on research collaborations and subsequently on capacity development for research. While there is a current trend towards understanding the nature of such collaborations, there has been little attention paid to the principles specific to educational partnerships. While educational partnerships have some similarities to research partnerships, there are also unique challenges for educators. In this chapter we will outline the key principles to building ethical and sustainable global health education partnerships, discuss some of the challenges and potential pitfalls, and describe approaches to evaluating the success of these partnerships.

International aid workers representing UNICEF collaborate with local communities in Benin and speak to women about the importance of birth registration
Photographer: *Stephanie Cate*

Types of Collaborations

Global health partnerships can be divided into several broad categories based on the types of participants:

North-North partnerships: Universities from the global North collaborate bilaterally on mutually beneficial projects and educational initiatives including the exchange of curricula in global health. As institutions increasingly recognize that global health has local application regardless of where the institution is based, the relevance of these partnerships can be expected to grow. An example of this is the Joint US/Canadian Committee on Global Health Core Competencies that developed the Global Health Essential Core Competencies.

North-South partnerships: These typically involve academic institutions in high-income countries (HIC) partnering with public or private institutions in low- and middle-income countries (LMIC) and typically involve aspects of clinical exchange and/or collaborative research. These partnerships range from simple exchanges based on individual connections between faculty and established collaborations between institutions formalized with a memorandum of understanding. Individual institutions have formed bilateral partnerships for the purposes of research, clinical care and educational development e.g. the Duke-Singapore partnership[1], Muhimbili University-UCSF project[2,3], and the Botswana-University of Pennsylvania partnership (see Case Study 4). This type of partnership is very common, often starting from key relationships formed by one or two founding participants. Though these may expand into broader programs, the scope of these initiatives is often limited. These partnerships may go beyond those between individual institutions and include multiple universities or individuals to form groups that then target the efforts of their partnership towards designated foreign institutions e.g. the AMPATH consortium (see Case Study 3) and the Human Resources for Health Rwanda Initiative (see Case Study 1). These partnerships minimize redundant effort created by multiple individual partnerships with the same institution or professional bend and often allow for a higher level of support and more continuous level of engagement over the course of the year(s).

South-South Partnerships: An important type of partnerships is those involving 2 or more universities/organizations from the Global South. These organizations are uniquely positioned to understand each others' challenges, have similar approaches, and be on an even playing field with regard to power and resources. Examples of such partnerships include those facilitated by Global Health Through Education, Training, and Service (GHETS; www.ghets.org) and the Training for Health Equity Network (www.thenetcommunity.org). As the focus of this guidebook is institutions and individuals in the Global North, these partnerships are not detailed. However, they are a critical component of the global health landscape and provide important lessons for partnerships of all varieties. As global health partnerships evolve it will be important for the Global North consider how they can support and reinforce more peer-to-peer relationships.

Academic-NGO partnerships: Academic institutions from the Global North are often aided in their global health engagement by non-governmental organizations (NGOs). NGOs are often fruitful partners for academic institutions to allow students to work directly with community-based organizations at home and abroad. Campus Compact (www.compact.org) is a national coalition of almost 1,200 colleges and universities that promotes public and community service that develops students' citizenship skills, helps campuses forge effective community partnerships, and provides resources and training for faculty seeking to integrate civic and community-based learning into the curriculum. Commonly, academic institutions partner with non-profit groups to provide international service and/or learning-focused experiences. These groups provide the funding mechanism for regular program visits, comprehensive in-country orientations, emergency safety procedures, and country-specific legal and regulatory compliance. These non-profit groups may be based either in the global North e.g. CFHI-Northwestern University (see Case Study 2) or in the global South as described by Trehan et al[4].

Partnerships with faith-based organizations: A sub-type of NGO, faith-based institutions are often rooted in the community and can help higher institutions engage with families directly, particularly those of low-income or diverse cultural backgrounds. Universities may partner directly with unaffiliated faith-based organizations. In addition, there are universities with affiliations with faith-based organizations such as Loma Linda University and their active international work and partnerships.

Community members line up outside a clinic in Zambia run by a faith-based organization from North Carolina
Will Bynum

Consortia of Universities and Professional Organizations: Through Consortia of universities or professional organizations, partnerships benefit from pooled resources, information sharing, and enhanced advocacy. Consortia of professional organizations may be composed of career-stage individuals, such as WONCA (World Organization of National Colleges, Academies and Academic Associations of General Practitioners/Family Physicians) a network of 300,000 physicians working toward shared global health expansion. They may also be consortia of trainees, such as the International Federation of Medical Students (IFMSA), which is a consortia of medical student membership organizations from over 100 countries, representing over 1.2 million medical students worldwide.

Ethics of Partnering

When engaging in a partnership at any level, ethical considerations are extremely important. This is most true when large power or wealth differentials exist between partners. As the provision of educational activities for trainees has been an integral part of many global health partnerships, particularly those involving universities, there have been calls for a formal set of ethical guidelines for global health training programs[5].

In 2010, the Working Group on Ethics Guidelines for Global Health Training (WEIGHT) group published a set of guidelines to address the needs and roles of the multiple stakeholders involved in global health training. These guidelines are meant to address global health experiences of varying duration and levels of formality, trainees of multiple levels and disciplines, uni- and bi-directional exchanges, and the clinical, public health, research, and educational activities that take place under the umbrella of global health [5,6]. The WEIGHT guidelines for global health training programs represent an important effort to codify ethics and best practices for sending and host institutions, program participants, and sponsors.

Adaptation of these guidelines to focus on partnerships produced eight key principles of reciprocity, starting from the development stage of the partnership with clearly stated program goals that are guided by local needs and priorities, providing trainees with specific pre-departure training, ensuring adequate trainee supervision, seeking ethics board approval of research activities, and finally, assessing the costs and benefits to hosts including collaborative authorship[7]. These principles are outlined in Table 1.

Table 1: Key Principles of Reciprocity for Educational Partnerships (Adapted from the WEIGHT Group Guidelines)	
i)	Harmonization of program goals of both partners or *memorandum of understanding* between partner institutions.
ii)	*Local needs and priorities* guide program activities.
iii)	Trainee activities in host country correspond to level of training and *supervision.*
iv)	*Costs and benefits to the host* partner.
v)	*Pre-departure Training* in language, sociocultural, political, and historical aspects of host community.
vi)	*Adherence to host country licensing standards,* visa policies, research ethics review, training on privacy and security of patient information.
vii)	*Ethics committee approval* for research and appropriate training in international research ethics.
viii)	Adherence to international standards for authorship of publications with input for host faculty and if possible *collaborative authorship.*

Unfortunately, many published program descriptions do not demonstrate these principles. A review of 45 descriptions of global institutional partnerships revealed that partnerships between North American and African institutions are at particular risk of failing to emphasize these principles of reciprocity when compared with descriptions of North American-Asian, or South American institutional partnerships.[7] These findings support a general concern that as global health becomes an increasingly sought-after field, well-intentioned efforts are creating a 21st-century scramble for Africa by US universities in order to boost their standing in a competitive academic environment.[8,9] Structured educational partnerships with devoted human resources and infrastructure foster integrative, supervised trainee exchanges, which in turn may help to mitigate some of the intangible costs of volunteerism.[10,11]

Developing the Partnership

Key steps to take in developing a partnership include: identifying a global health partner, developing a connection and building trust, setting expectations and understanding needs, and incorporating bilateral faculty and student exchanges while recognizing and avoiding potential pitfalls.

Identifying a global health partner

Developing partnerships begins with identifying appropriate global health partners. Sources that are helpful in identifying global health partners include: the office of international affairs, international medical graduates, medical missionaries, colleagues and international meetings. These connections often build from a mutual interest or need on the parts of the collaborating faculty. To be successful, however, this need or interest must be paired with a supportive academic environment that allows allocation of time and resources. Too often time is frequently unfunded in the development of new projects. Developing a relationship beyond the initial individual contact requires institutional buy-in and is crucial for sustaining strong partnerships.

Developing a connection and building trust

The connection should be based on key elements that include a shared common interest. The Swiss Commission's Guide for Transboundary Research Partnerships advanced eleven principles and was updated in 2012 to include 7 questions for research partnerships with developing countries, many of which are equally applicable in the setting of partnerships focused on education.[12] Another approach reported by Kolars et al, [13] originally designed for research collaborations, utilizes ten "learning questions" for designing educational collaborations. Key principles adapted from those outlined for international research collaborations that contribute to building educational global health partnerships are outlined in Table 2 and further discussed below.

Table 2: Key Principles for Building an Effective Educational Global Health Partnership
Deciding on objectives together
Building mutual trust
Sharing of information and developing networks
Sharing responsibilities
Creating transparency
Monitoring and evaluating the collaboration

Deciding on objectives together is an important step in the process. Collaborative decision-making allows both sides to reach mutual agreement on the objectives of the partnership and thus promotes equity in cooperation and shared ownership. Both sides should meet to brainstorm ideas, review barriers, and devise mutually beneficial and sustainable solutions to the problem. There are inherent inequalities between the North and the South with regard to funding, infrastructure, and many other systems. This can be overcome by comprehensive planning: who will do what and how; defining mutually expected outcomes; and listing what requirements need to be fulfilled by each partner to achieve these results.

Building mutual trust is crucial at every stage of the process. It requires a commitment to value each other's cultural perspectives, limitations, and expertise and to reflect critically on what enhances the relationship by building consensus. In addition, effective communication and negotiation are equally important in developing mutual trust and respect. It also requires clarifying roles and responsibilities and ensuring accountability. It is also essential to establish a pattern for solving potential conflicts. A broker acceptable to both parties may become necessary to mediate any potential conflicts.

Sharing of information and developing networks is more applicable in the research setting, however in the context of educational partnerships there are opportunities to share information on how each system works, both advantages and disadvantages, while at the same time looking for common ground. It is also important to form networks that will enhance collaboration. Different groups bring differing expertise to the table, so the partnership is not linked to one donor, recipient, or relationship, but to multiple partners in a consortium.

Sharing responsibilities takes into consideration that each partner will contribute what they are particularly skilled in doing. It is important to identify competencies on each side and share responsibilities according to clear rules and duties. In the initial phase the Northern partner may assume the majority of the responsibility but as time goes on it is important that the Southern partner's responsibility increases. Mutual respect must be maintained, and both partners must see themselves as equals.

Creating transparency is essential at every stage of the process. This should take the form of open lines of communication and regular dialogue regarding unexpected challenges. Each party should feel like they have a voice and should consider themselves as stakeholder in the process. Formal feedback mechanisms allowing for anonymous and direct feedback should be established in order to provide an explicit mechanism for each side to express their opinions. An important aspect of transparency is also financial transparency. Ideally, both sides will not only be justly compensated for their time, efforts, and relative value to the project, but financial dealings will be transparent and independently overseen.

Monitoring and evaluating the collaboration enables both partners to assess whether the stated goals of the partnership are being met and to determine the need, if any, for revision of the terms of a Memorandum of Understanding, Affiliation Agreement or the like. This allows both sides to evaluate both positive and negative outcomes, and to make the case for the partnership to funders and to the general public.

Cambodian children and their family listen intently about hygiene and clean water sanitation needs for their new well
Photographer: *Chelsea Small*

Setting expectations and understanding needs

It is important to define goals and expectations for the partnership that are sustainable and mutually beneficial to both partners. These goals should be feasible and should yield tangible results that can be monitored, evaluated, and sustained. Sometimes funding may be the limiting factor in defining the agenda. The AMPATH consortium (see case study 3) and Human Resources for Health in Rwanda (see case study 1) are examples of a "consortium" type model in which resources can be pooled to alleviate the dependence on a single institution. In order to proceed, all parties must agree on the specific details. Communication across language and cultural barriers is a typical challenge at this stage of the partnership and each side must attempt to overcome this by learning each other's communication style and striving to be as clear and consistent as possible. As described in Case Study 1, extensive communication with all stakeholders and multiple planning meetings are necessary at the start of any collaboration. During this process, a needs assessment or strengths–mapping exercise may be helpful. This may be reinitiated on an ongoing basis to identify the desires of each of the partners so that important and relevant issues are addressed. Asset-based community development (ABCD) is a strategy developed by John McKnight and John Kretzmann, which is used to discover a community's capacities and assets and to mobilize those assets for community improvement. The ABCD process focuses on the strengths of a community and how to bring those strengths to bear in community improvement activities. The importance of conducting a local needs assessment has traditionally been emphasized. ABCD challenges the use of a needs assessment and characterizes it as deficit-based thinking. Where a typical needs assessment may ask, "What is the problem?" ABCD work asks, "How can our community assemble its strengths into new combinations, new structures of opportunity, new sources of income and control, and new possibilities?"[14] The ABCD Institute based at Northwestern University has been developed to specifically focus on this sustainable model for community partnerships and the Child Family Health International-Northwestern University partnership utilizes it for interpreting local needs in a global health setting as discussed in the Case Study 2.

Following this process, an MOU can be developed which expresses the expectations and responsibilities of each partner. Such an agreement sets boundaries for the relationship so that everyone signing the agreement is well aware of the formal terms of engagement, and sets the stage for revisiting the terms of agreement periodically.

Case Study 1: Human Resources for Health Rwanda, a South-Driven Academic Alliance for Medical Education

The Human Resources for Health initiative in Rwanda offers an example of an academic collaboration that developed under the direction of the host country from the global South. The Ministry of Health of Rwanda, together with the Clinton Foundation and Partners in Health, began in 2011 to frame a novel strategy for leveraging partnerships with US universities to support capacity development for health. The project developed from the recognition on the part of the Ministry of Health in Rwanda of the significant personnel shortages across the health system. Because there were few teachers, they were not able to train personnel in sufficient number to fundamentally impact these shortages. Though partnerships had been established independently with a number of US institutions, the decision was made to establish new partnerships around a common goal of promoting long-term placements of US faculty in Rwanda as teaching faculty to expand the number of persons trained and allow a more rapid increase in the Rwandan healthcare workforce. Representatives from participating US universities, the National University of Rwanda, and the Rwandan Ministry of Health convened a series of planning meetings between 2011 and 2012. US universities were identified and selected based on their established experience in global health education and include the Alpert Medical School at Brown University, Geisel School of Medicine at Dartmouth, Duke University Schools of Medicine and Nursing, Harvard Medical School, University of Texas Medical Branch, University of Virginia School of Medicine, Yale School of Medicine and Public Health, Howard University School of Nursing, New York University College of Nursing, University of Maryland School of Nursing, and the University of Illinois at Chicago College of Nursing. Funding for the initiative was obtained through a direct petition by the Ministry of Health of Rwanda to the US Government and includes funding from USAID and the Global Fund.

Faculty members placed in Rwanda include specialists in internal medicine, pediatrics, surgery, emergency medicine, and associated subspecialists together with nurses and health administrators. The program includes the unique goal of high-level involvement by US faculty in the first years of the collaboration, with tapering involvement as newly trained Rwandan specialists join the workforce. The first foreign faculty were placed in August of 2012. Though not yet tested, this collaboration offers a unique example of coordinated effort across multiple US universities in an academic partnership to support medical education and workforce development in a resource limited but significantly developing country. It also demonstrates the importance of establishing buy-in from all participants at the *outset* of the collaboration and the importance of *effective communication in the planning phase* to assure that the goals and expectations for all participants are clear. If successful, this partnership may serve as a model for future educational partnerships established for the purpose of capacity development around the world. For more information, see http://hrhconsortium.moh.gov.rw/

Case Study 2: CFHI-Northwestern University Partnership

Academic institutions in the global North may want to orient their global health education programs within an ethical framework from the initiation of the project, but most lack the human resources and infrastructure to maintain optimum partner relations and quality control. Specifically, they lack funding mechanisms to send their in-house faculty and staff to visit program sites regularly, to meet partners at their institutions in the global South, and to arrange comprehensive in-country orientations, emergency safety procedures, and country-specific legal and regulatory compliance. Despite good intentions, they are often unable to identify appropriate on-site mentors and/or supervisors, troubleshoot and overcome logistical hurdles, and ensure liability and risk management. Indeed, these principles often do not align with their academic mission.

One solution is for Northern universities to partner with third-party organizations to "outsource" risk management, quality control, and an ethical framework of capacity building and professional development opportunities. Child Family Health International (CFHI) is a leading international non-governmental organization (NGO) with 20+ programs in five countries that connect local health care professionals with international students.

CFHI and Northwestern University Feinberg School of Medicine (FSM) Center for Global Health have partnered together to engage FSM students and other health science students in a wide variety of community health projects in resource-limited, international settings. The program places a strong emphasis on cross-cultural competency, language learning, and community engagement by involving students in sustainable healthcare services to underserved communities. CFHI programs match international students with local attending physicians who precept medical students in clinical settings, ensuring that students are able to receive clinical supervision while developing a more thorough understanding of the local community's health status and ongoing public health agenda.

Using an asset-based engagement model, the program capitalizes on existing medical resources and adds to them with integrated community education in order to reflect the strengths and agenda of the host community. This model aims to meet the host community needs, and to empower local health practitioners by making them the experts of their own health-care environment. In addition, partners are compensated for the education they are providing to visiting students. For more information see http://globalhealth.northwestern.edu/MedEd/current-affiliations/CFHI.html

Incorporating bilateral faculty/student exchanges

It is important for the partnership to be bilateral in order to be mutually beneficial. Importantly, benefit may include knowledge acquisition, prestige, financial remuneration, infrastructure, and other perceived benefits. Ensuring adequate benefit for all partners requires a concerted effort from all levels of faculty and trainees. Ensuring mutually beneficial partnership will increase the likelihood of a sustainable long-term relationship that will accomplish the goals of all stakeholders. An example is the AMPATH consortium presented in Case Study 3. This partnership allowed for bilateral exchanges between the faculty and students that made for a robust collaboration that benefited all schools involved from joint research projects, joint applications for funding, student and staff exchanges and a transnational perspective.

Case Study 3: The IU-Kenya Partnership/AMPATH Consortium

In 1989, the Indiana University (IU) School of Medicine and Moi University School of Medicine (MUSM) began the IU-Kenya partnership as a deliberate and formal institutional partnership built on counterpart faculty relationships and with a memorandum of understanding based on mutual trust, respect, and shared goals.[15] Although the IU-Kenya partnership began as an individual institution partnership, it was expanded in 1997 to form a University consortium, with other academic institutions in the U.S. and Canada joining the work of Indiana University in Kenya and establishing what is now known as the Academic Model Providing Access to Healthcare (AMPATH consortium).[16] The key principles in this international partnership are a focus on the development of the local health system, emphasis on equity and mutual respect, and the provision of opportunities for students and faculty of both institutions.

AMPATH has a tripartite academic mission that "leads with care." In other words, the traditional research and education missions are coupled with a sincere and genuine effort to engage in the development of local health system. In this way, local needs and priorities set the goals of the partnership. Mutual respect is emphasized, with the focus on respecting the office or position of the South partner even if the North partner does not necessarily agree with the actions or behaviors of the person in that position.

Participation on the part of clinical and research faculty members is a vital part of the partnership. While many partnerships begin with student-level exchanges, the AMPATH consortium involves regular faculty exchanges for the purposes of training and collaborative research. This approach establishes faculty relationships and engenders collaborative applications for grant funding from public and private sources.

Faculty-level exchanges were followed by student and resident relationships, with the opportunity for a bi-directional student exchange. Each year, the AMPATH consortium hosts Kenyan medical students for 2-month electives, and Kenyan Internal Medicine and Pediatrics Masters of Medicine (MMED) students (registrars), for up to 6-month electives. U.S. medical students and residents receive pre-departure training and adhere to country and institutional requirements for visitors during their 2-month elective in Kenya.

Today, the AMPATH consortium consists of: Indiana University School of Medicine, Indianapolis, Indiana; Warren Alpert School of Medicine at Brown University, Providence, Rhode Island; Duke University School of Medicine, Durham, North Carolina, Lehigh Valley Hospital, Allentown, Pennsylvania; Providence Portland Medical Center, Portland, Oregon; Purdue University, West Lafayette, Indiana; University of Utah School of Medicine, Salt Lake City, Utah; University of Washington, Seattle, Washington; and the University of Toronto School of Medicine, Toronto, Canada; and the list continues to grow. For more details see www.iukenya.org and www.ampathkenya.org

Sustaining Partnership Beyond the Initial Phase

Sustaining a partnership begins with aligning the partnership objectives with the identified needs of the partners. Though the foundation for this is determined as part of the partnership development process, it is important to recognize that these needs may change and the partnership will need to evolve accordingly.

The value of the partnership should be established equally on both sides of the partnership. For universities in resource-plentiful settings, the value is often in the need for academic products or other return on investment. The challenge is to develop these partnerships in a way that empowers the partners from the Global South, often letting them take the lead on key publications. To be sustainable, universities need to recognize the mentorship role played by participating faculty as part of academic review and not focus solely on the academic deliverables of primary authorship, as they recognize the work of faculty in global health partnerships. The indirect value of these mentorship relationships becomes clear as the mentored work develops into new grant proposals and program developments that expand the scope of the collaboration.

For the partners from low- or middle-income countries, the key challenge to sustainability lies in the lack of funding both at the individual and institutional level. At the institutional level, this leads to challenges maintaining engagement in program activities in light of multiple conflicting draws on institutional resources. For participating faculty, low reimbursement for academic and clinical work can cause distraction of faculty attention toward private clinics and other than the partnership. Creating pathways for professional development through activities within the partnership and incentives for those who are able to commit to the partnership is key to maintaining engagement of faculty of both institutions.

Life Cycle of a Partnership

Academic global health partnerships often begin as innovation projects. The funding base for these projects may be quite narrow, either a single grant with or without in-kind contributions from partners. The roots of these partnerships vary, ranging from clinical and educational exchanges to services projects and research collaborations. These initiatives build on this initial relationship, typically defining in clearer terms the relationship between the institutions and establishing the goals and expected outcomes. For funding agencies, the success of these collaborations is defined based on the ability to articulate and achieve these short-term measures.

As programs transition from the initial funded phase, sustaining the partnerships requires leveraging additional funding sources. Within institutions, identification and highlighting of secondary gains to the institutions may provide critical support to sustaining and enhancing in-kind support for the program. Support may include grants and other funding drawn to the institution through the efforts of the collaboration. For many institutions, the collaboration may meet institutional objectives for charitable giving and provide an important incentive towards recruiting top caliber faculty and trainees. It is equally important to create investment in the partnership within the institution from the global South by targeting the ongoing activities of the collaboration to the institution from the global North's academic and service priorities. Alignment of the partnership with program funding from agencies such as PEPFAR, USAID HED, and the Fogarty International Center at the NIH can provide opportunities for sustaining partnerships over longer durations. Equally important is alignment with local needs and the capacity building and incorporation of local leadership. Developing partnerships with local government ministries of health ensures that the objectives of the partnership align with national priorities and encourages visibility, greater public awareness of the partnership's mission, and sustainability.

In order to grow, collaborations must transition from singular funding to programs with multiple concurrent funding streams over the long-term. Frequently this will include some component of institutional support on both sides of the collaboration, new innovation projects fostered within the initial collaboration, research grants, and service grants. The momentum created through these concurrent activities can help support start-up activities for new projects in development, which will in turn help to sustain the collaboration over time—as described in Case Study 4.

Case Study 4: Botswana-UPENN Partnership (BUP)

The University of Pennsylvania-Botswana Partnership developed from a program specifically responding to the epidemic of HIV/AIDS but has evolved and rapidly expanded to include many aspects of clinical care. The African Comprehensive HIV/AIDS Partnership (ACHAP) is a collaboration involving the Government of Botswana, the Bill and Melinda Gates Foundation, and the Merck Company Foundation. In 2001, ACHAP approached University of Pennsylvania Medicine's HIV/AIDS experts with a request to help train local providers as Botswana implemented its HIV treatment and prevention programs.

Although the partnership was initially focused around a specific disease process, it has now evolved to include educational exchanges for University of Botswana undergraduates, nursing students, and faculty. To the initial focus on clinical care, has been added outcomes research that has added benefits for the health system of Botswana. There is a strong focus on developing local capacity through clinical teaching.[17]

This partnership is now in its 11th year and is another example of a successful partnership in which the initiating contact came from the South. The Government of Botswana had decided to make antiretroviral drugs available to its citizens. Doctors with experience using these pharmaceuticals were needed to help train the local health care workers. These circumstances highlight an important principle: partnerships that develop at the invitation of the host country rather than at the request of the North institutions are more likely to succeed. In addition, the partnership was able to successfully transition from the clinical care model to a broad-based and sustainable model incorporating education, research, and clinical care. For more details, see http://www.med.upenn.edu/botswana

Challenges to partnerships:

Challenges to partnership are multifactorial—some are general and are applicable to both partners, whilst others are specific to one partner.

Factors relating to the Global North partner

Imbalance of Power: Educational partnerships may build upon existing global health research models that utilize the imbalance of power between high and low income countries to one's advantage. For example, the "Semicolonial model" ignores ownership, sustainability, and the development of national capacity in health care. This approach promotes a dominant position for visiting health care providers and trainees over the local health care providers. In the extreme version of this, North partners may develop and sustain "Annexed sites" in global South in which the entire operation is led and managed by the high-income partner.[18] In both cases, there is unequal sharing of benefits and risks between the North and South partner, which can lead to resentment and dependence rather than increased capacity.

Trainee preparation: The need for adequate preparation of trainees from either institution to encounter another culture and health system cannot be underestimated.[19, 20] This preparation must include both training in key elements of appropriate clinical practice at the site participants are visiting and training in the sociocultural aspects of life in the host country. Importantly, such preparation should ensure there is clarity around the role, scope of tasks and supervision of the trainee while abroad. Anticipating and preparing participants for the emotional challenges of providing care in under-resourced settings is also critical. An increasing number of institutions arrange some sort of pre-departure preparation, but the effectiveness of these preparation strategies has not been comprehensively evaluated.

Fragmentation: Academic institutions still operate in "silos" and the international efforts of their faculty mirror this trend. To avoid re-inventing the wheel with each partnership, institutions can bring together and coordinate faculty members with similar global health interests under a "Center" or "Institute" for Global Health to.[21] Similarly, multiple institutions from the Global North with separate agendas may partner with an institution in the Global South and compete for limited personnel and resources locally. . The formation of Consortia may help to alleviate this duplication of effort and create economies of scale.

Funding and Infrastructure: Although partnerships can be initiated by a relatively small number of faculty members, support staff and program managers are integral to the harmonization of student activities and program oversight. Many academic institutions lack personnel and infrastructure to manage and maintain relationships. Although the support for research activities can be substantial, educational global health efforts in most cases are not a compensated activity. Junior faculty may be discouraged from participating in this career path due to the traditionally poor recognition and reward from conventional promotion and tenure systems. Trainees may have financial and scheduling constraints and may experience a lack of institutional support. [22,23] Partnering with non-profit organizations to help with logistical support and administrative resources may help academic institutions who may not be able to ensure reliable, ongoing support personnel.

Factors relating to the South partner

Lack of protected time. For clinical faculty, workloads in institutions in the global South tend to be significantly higher. It is often difficult for such stakeholders to gain sufficient protected time to assist fully in the development of the partnerships. This has the potential to create an imbalance in which day to day activities for the partnership are facilitated by personnel from the North. Unless this inequity is specifically addressed it may serve to disempower the partners from the South.

Lack of infrastructure. Establishment and maintenance of an effective collaboration requires infrastructure support at multiple levels. This includes the ability to effectively administer grants and track program expenditures. Many funding sources expect institutions to pay for immediate expenses and submit receipts for future reimbursement. For many institutions from the South, the lack of resources within the institutions makes this a significant barrier to program development.

Unclear management structure. To be successful, clear lines of decision-making are necessary on both sides of the collaboration. The lack of protected time to administer the program combined with the relative newness of international collaborations often makes management within the South partner institution challenging. The most senior person in an institution is often charged with maintaining the collaboration. However, these individuals may be too busy to assure smooth day-to-day operations. Addressing the need for a dedicated management team within the South partner institution with protected time for administration can be critical to assuring the success of these initiatives. In cases where a completely new organization is being put in place, it is possible to establish a management structure in agreement with the host partner, such as The Duke-Singapore partnership in establishing a new medical school in conjunction with the National University of Singapore.[1] When this is not the case, North institutions may establish parallel management structures in-country—an approach which may unintentionally undermine host country systems.

Operational Challenges

Maintaining regular and complete communication. When forming a partnership that includes exchange of trainees and/or clinical faculty, it is important to be aware of the potential for misunderstanding and miscommunication. Personnel are entering systems of care with which they are not familiar. A visitor to the host institution may treat busy staff with multiple responsibilities as though they are "at his disposal." The daily reality of suboptimal clinical outcomes in resource-limited settings due to structural constraints to healthcare poses an emotional challenge to faculty and trainees, particularly those who are visiting these settings for the first time. Their frustration may cause them to withdraw or burnout, undermining the core mission of the partnership. There is also the potential that the responsibility for these outcomes may be misattributed to individuals working within the system. In particular, be aware of the potential for implied judgment on the part of visitor. Anticipating challenges to international exchanges and helping the individuals to understand the broad context of healthcare at the partner site can minimize these risks and improve the experience of participants.

Need for infrastructure: Partnerships that focus on undergraduates and other trainees need to have established structures to support participants in their placements at the international sites. This typically should include onsite mentorship, orientation, monitoring of their status during the time of the placement and a plan to address key emergencies which may arise during their stay. Even a single instance where a student is harmed or experiences a poor medical outcome due to an inadequate support system or emergency response plan can be sufficient to end an exchange. This infrastructure may be provided by a third-party organization that has time and expertise in providing student support in the local context.

Evaluation of Partnerships

The effectiveness of global health partnerships in achieving their goals and the impact of the partnerships' activities on the local community should be evaluated on a regular basis—in collaboration with community stakeholders. Program planners should identify the specific outcomes they seek to produce, what impact they want to contribute, and with whom they need to partner in order to attain desired outcomes and impact. Successful public-private partnerships that target specific global health concerns have been instrumental in advocating for or providing large-scale new financing; raising the profile of their target diseases at the highest political levels globally and nationally; accelerating progress; encouraging the use of evidence-based approaches to public health (such as harm reduction and substitution therapy); providing a means of supporting global public goods; securing substantial economies of scale (e.g. in drug procurement); and in some cases catalyzing innovation. It is important however to note that while individual partnerships may have contributed greatly in specific areas, their collective impact may create or exacerbate a series of problems at country level. This isolated approach can undermine national development plans, distort national priorities, and divert scarce human resources.[24] There is a need for careful self-assessment of global health partnerships that focus specifically on education and capacity building to avoid these pitfalls. Education-focused partnerships must critically evaluate their programs to demonstrate impact (positive or negative), while setting realistic goals and a timeframe to demonstrate tangible impact so important to donors. Outcomes should ideally be demonstrated using rigorous mixed-method qualitative and quantitative measures, though solely qualitative or quantitative data is preferable to none.

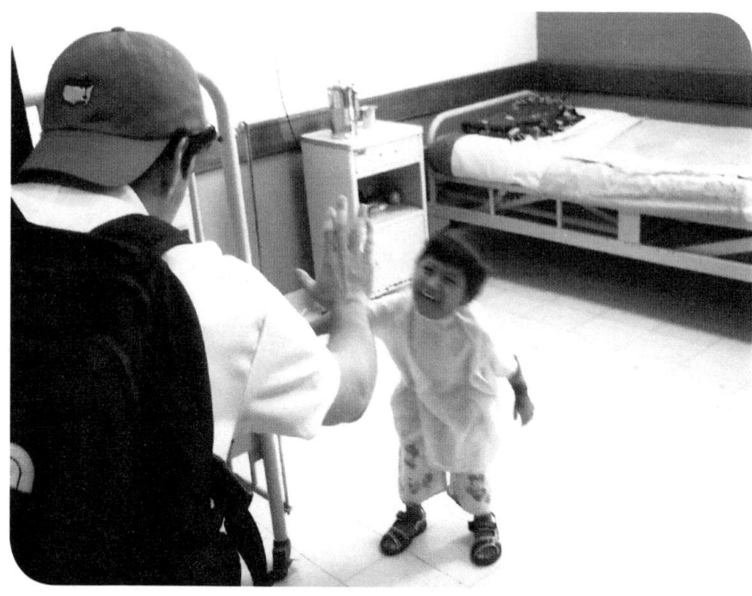

A partnership is forged
Photographer: *Meg Steiner*

Approach to Evaluation

Evaluations of partnerships occur at multiple levels, and both the form and the content of the evaluation will vary based on the goals of the evaluation. The key questions to consider for any evaluation process are the audience (Who is it for?), the projected impact (What are our outcomes?) and the availability of short and long-term data (What is the time-frame?).

Who is it for?

To design a program evaluation, evaluators must first consider their audience. Will the report be for the purposes of internal management or process improvement, local stakeholders, or funders?

What are our outcomes?

Next, evaluators should decide if they wish to demonstrate adherence to planned workflows, reach within the community (number of participants/learners), enhancements in capacity (new skills demonstrated within the institution), and/or improvement in health outcomes. While outcomes studies related to capacity development in undergraduate and graduate medical education are increasing, evidence about the outcome and impact of medical schools on population health and health systems is limited. Research from socio-economic and political sciences is rarely considered. Most institutional performance and accreditation measures are composed of input indicators, such as number and quality of faculty and facilities, or output indicators, such as the number of graduates, skills and knowledge learned, research published and grants received.

While the global health literature holds many descriptions of the educational impact of global health experiences on North institution trainees,[22,25-31] there are relatively few articles on the impact on South institution trainees who participate directly or indirectly in the educational activities of the partnership.[31-34] There is a growing awareness of the need for studies describing the impact of global health partnerships on the local academic institutions, medical practitioners, and the community. Educators and social scientists that are familiar with the cultural norms of these populations and comfortable with both quantitative and qualitative approaches for evaluation, health outcomes, and local health systems are best suited to conduct such studies.

What is the time frame?

Finally, the evaluator must determine the time frame in which the evaluation will occur and whether the evaluation will be conducted prospectively or retrospectively. Short-term evaluations tend to be process-oriented. Intermediate-term evaluations may focus on capacity development, while long-term evaluations focus on health outcomes. Measuring the long-term outcomes and symbiotic effects of education programs on the health system and its beneficiaries can be challenging, as health system outcomes are usually the result of a multiple factors, relationships, and events.[36] One long-standing example of a trans-national group of academic institutions that share a specific focus and approach to community impact evaluation is the collaborative of health professions schools called Training for Health Equity Network (THEnet) described in Case Study 5.

Case Study 5: Training for Health Equity Network (THEnet)

THEnet is a collaborative of socially accountable health professionals schools located in mostly low resouce regions of the globe.[37,38] These schools share a core mission to increase the number, competencies, and commitment of physicians to work in underserved communities around the worldTo accomplish this mission, THEnet institutions have defined their reference or target populations; identified priority health and competency needs and designed their programs accordingly. They work in close collaboration with communities, health services, and health care providers in all aspects of the education enterprise; from student recruitment and governance to evaluation of activities. This work includes graduate tracking and retention research, health workforce modeling, and collaborative health services research with indigenous, rural, and remote populations.[39] Such activities are applicable to the evaluation of educational partnerships in global health.

The approach to program evaluation used by THEnet schools is based on the principles of conceptualization ("How does our school work?"); production ("What do we do?"); and outcomes and impact ("What difference are we making?"). These questions include:

Are our strategies and policies developed through collaboration with our stakeholders and does decision-making involve meaningful participation from all stakeholders?

Do our education programs reflect the priority health and social needs of the communities we serve, as defined by community partnerships, and is this is evident in our programs and the services we provide?

Are our education interventions having the desired effect on the behavior and practice of our graduates?

Do we influence policymakers, education providers, and other stakeholders to transform the health system to increase performance and health equity?

For more details see (http://www.thenetcommunity.org/about-thenet.html)

While quantitative outcomes are an important way of assessing partnerships, it is equally important to examine relationships and processes within the partnership. This assessment can be made by conducting partner interviews, surveys, and practice observation with the targets being compliance with prerequisites and success factors, degree of partnership practice, the outcomes of the partnership relationships, partners' performance, and efficiency.[40] The Partnership Assessment Toolkit (PAT) is an example of an interactive tool to monitor and evaluate the nature of the collaborative relationship in an ongoing manner.[41] Developed for research partnerships by the Canadian Coalition for Global Health Research in conjunction with BRAC (Bangladesh), the Universidad Andina Simon Bolivar (Ecuador), and the Armauer Hansen Research Institute (Ethiopia), it can be adapted for use by educational global health partnerships.

Teaching partnership principles

Global health training should result in the development of competency in multiple areas spanning both discipline-specific domains (such as epidemiology, health policy, and environmental health sciences) and interdisciplinary domains (such as leadership, collaboration, program planning, and systems thinking). Global health partnerships need to develop curricula that will teach students how to build, maintain, and nurture ethical and sustainable global health partnerships as an essential skill.

An example of such a curriculum is the Association of Schools of Public Health (ASPH) Global Health Competency model which provides a baseline overview of the knowledge, skills, and other attributes that are expected of masters-level students in global health programs.[42] While all seven domains contribute to partnership development, the competencies under the domains of Collaborating and partnering; Ethical reasoning and professional practice; Program management; Socio-cultural and political awareness; and Strategic analysis are worthy of special attention. See Table 3 below for definitions of these domains and competencies For more details on ASPH competencies, see http://www.asph.org/.

Table 3: Association of Schools of Public Health Competencies in Global Health Relevant to Global Health Partnerships

Domain	Competency
Collaborating and partnering The ability to select, recruit, and work with a diverse range of global health stakeholders to advance research, policy, and practice goals, and to foster open dialogue and effective communication.	2.1 Develop procedures for managing health partnerships. 2.2 Promote inclusion of representatives of diverse constituencies in partnerships. 2.3 Value commitment to building trust in partnerships. 2.4 Use diplomacy and conflict resolution strategies with partners. 2.5 Communicate lessons learned to community partners and global constituencies. 2.6 Exhibit interpersonal communication skills that demonstrate respect for other perspectives and cultures.
Ethical reasoning and professional practice The ability to identify and respond with integrity to ethical issues in diverse economic, political, and cultural contexts, and promote accountability for the impact of policy decisions upon public health practice at local, national, and international levels.	3.1 Apply the fundamental principles of international standards for the protection of human subjects in diverse cultural settings. 3.2 Analyze ethical and professional issues that arise in responding to public health emergencies. 3.3 Explain the mechanisms used to hold international organizations accountable for public health practice standards. 3.4 Promote integrity in professional practice.
Program management The ability to design, implement, and evaluate global health programs to maximize contributions to effective policy, enhanced practice, and improved and sustainable health outcomes.	5.1 Conduct formative research. 5.2 Apply scientific evidence throughout program planning, implementation, and evaluation. 5.3 Design program work plans based on logic models. 5.4 Develop proposals to secure donor and stakeholder support. 5.5 Plan evidence-based interventions to meet internationally established health targets. 5.6 Develop monitoring and evaluation frameworks to assess programs. 5.7 Utilize project management techniques throughout program planning, implementation, and evaluation. 5.8 Develop context-specific implementation strategies for scaling up best-practice interventions.

Socio-cultural and political awareness The conceptual basis with which to work effectively within diverse cultural settings and across local, regional, national, and international political landscapes.	6.1 Describe the roles and relationships of the entities influencing global health. 6.2 Analyze the impact of transnational movements on population health. 6.3 Analyze context-specific policy making processes that impact health. 6.4 Design health advocacy strategies. 6.5 Describe multi-agency policy-making in response to complex health emergencies. 6.6 Describe the interrelationship of foreign policy and health diplomacy.
Strategic analysis The ability to use systems thinking to analyze a diverse range of complex and interrelated factors shaping health trends to formulate programs at the local, national, and international levels.	7.1 Conduct a situation analysis across a range of cultural, economic, and health contexts. 7.2 Identify the relationships among patterns of morbidity, mortality, and disability with demographic and other factors in shaping the circumstances of the population of a specified community, country, or region. 7.3 Implement a community health needs assessment. 7.4 Conduct comparative analyses of health systems. 7.5 Explain economic analyses drawn from socio-economic and health data. 7.6 Design context-specific health interventions based upon situation analysis.

Other groups such as the American Association of Colleges of Nursing, American Association of Colleges of Osteopathic Medicine, American Association of Colleges of Pharmacy, American Dental Education Association, Association of American Medical Colleges, and Association of Schools of Public Health have developed Core Competencies for Inter-professional Collaborative Practice. Given that global health is inherently interdisciplinary and attracts trainees from multiple disciplines who engage with each other at the global health site, these core competencies for interdisciplinary collaboration are relevant to global health training.[43]

As global health trainees engage with the local population for the purposes of education, project implementation, and research, consideration should also be given to training students from both host and visiting institutions on conducting community needs assessments or asset inventories and on models of community engagement, community involvement, community based participatory research, and participation. In addition, students from both North and South institutions need to know how to conduct a proper evaluation of a global health partnership.

Conclusion

As the number of partnerships between North and South institutions increases, greater attention should be given to ensuring that these partnerships are established not just with good intentions, but deliberately, ethically, and with a focus on outcomes. Moreover, attention should be given to translating the principles of partnership established through collaboration science to global health trainees. Finally, we must ensure that the partnership is sustainable through broad-based support and coordinated faculty and administration involvement.

> *"Success is measured in health outcomes and indicators, not in number of individuals trained or publications. If you train the best in the world but their* [health] *system is dysfunctional, what have you really accomplished? Likewise, if you find the solution to the most vexing problem, but are not able to translate that solution into the health system, what have you really accomplished?"*
>
> —Dr. Robert Einterz, Director of AMPATH

References

1. Williams RS, Casey PJ, Kamei RK, et al. A Global Partnership in Medical Education Between Duke University and the National University of Singapore. *Academic Medicine.* 2008;83(2):122-127 110.1097/ACM.1090b1013e318160b318168bc.
2. Macfarlane SB, Agabian N, Novotny TE, Rutherford GW, Stewart CC, Debas HT. Think globally, act locally, and collaborate internationally: global health sciences at the University of California, San Francisco. *Academic Medicine.* 2008;83(2):173.
3. Taché S, Kaaya E, Omer S, et al. University partnership to address the shortage of healthcare professionals in Africa. *Global Public Health.* 2008;3(2):137-148.
4. Trehan I, Piskur JR, Prystowsky JJ. Collaboration between medical students and NGOs: a new model for international health education. *Medical education.* 2003;37(11):1031-1031.
5. Crump JA, Sugarman J. Ethical considerations for short-term experiences by trainees in global health. *JAMA.* Sep 24 2008;300(12):1456-1458.
6. Crump JA, Sugarman J. Ethics and best practice guidelines for training experiences in global health. *Am J Trop Med Hyg.* Dec 2010;83(6):1178-1182.
7. Umoren RA, James JE, Litzelman DK. Evidence of Reciprocity in Reports on International Partnerships. *Education Research International.* 2012;2012.
8. Macfarlane SB, Jacobs M, Kaaya EE. In the name of global health: trends in academic institutions. *Journal of Public Health Policy.* 2008;29(4):383-401.
9. Crane J. Scrambling for Africa? Universities and global health. *The Lancet.* 2011;377(9775):1388-1390.
10. Heck JE, Bazemore A, Diller P. The Shoulder to Shoulder Model-Channeling Medical Volunteerism Toward Sustainable Health Change. *FAMILY MEDICINE-KANSAS CITY-.* 2007;39(9):644.
11. Powell DL, Gilliss CL, Hewitt HH, Flint EP. Application of a partnership model for transformative and sustainable international development. *Public Health Nursing.* 2010;27(1):54-70.
12. The Swiss Commission for Research Partnerships with Developing Countries. A Guide for Transboundary Research Partnerships. http://www.kfpe.ch/11-Principles. Updated May 23, 2012. Accessed February 20, 2013
13. Kolars JC, Cahill K, Donkor P, et al. Perspective: partnering for medical education in Sub-Saharan Africa: seeking the evidence for effective collaborations. *Acad Med.* Feb 2012;87(2):216-220.
14. Asset-Based Community Development Institute. http://www.abcdinstitute.org/, accessed Jan 20 2013.
15. Einterz RM, Kimaiyo S, Mengech HNK, et al. Responding to the HIV pandemic: the power of an academic medical partnership. *Academic Medicine.* 2007;82(8):812.
16. Oman K, Khwa-Otsyula B, Majoor G, Einterz R, Wasteson A. Working collaboratively to support medical education in developing countries: the case of the Friends of Moi University Faculty of Health Sciences. *Educ Health (Abingdon).* May 2007;20(1):12.
17. Cohn J, Friedman HM. Sustainable International Partnership Building for Academic Medical Centers: Experiences with the Botswana-UPenn Partnership. *Virtual Mentor.* 2010;12(3):179.
18. Costello A, Zumla A. Moving to research partnerships in developing countries. *BMJ.* Sep 2000;321(7264):827-829.
19. Torjesen K, Mandalakas A, Kahn R, Duncan B. International child health electives for pediatric residents. *Archives of Pediatrics and Adolescent Medicine.* 1999;153(12):1297.

20. Heck JE, Wedemeyer D. A survey of American medical schools to assess their preparation of students for overseas practice. *Academic Medicine.* 1991;66(2):78.

21. Haq C, Baumann L, Olsen CW, et al. Creating a center for global health at the University of Wisconsin-Madison. *Academic Medicine.* 2008;83(2):148.

22. Sawatsky AP, Rosenman DJ, Merry SP, McDonald FS. Eight Years of the Mayo International Health Program: What an International Elective Adds to Resident Education2010.

23. Gattey DM, Lauer AK. International ophthalmology in training programs. *Ophthalmology.* 2006;113(12):2379-2380.

24. Caines K. *Best practice principles for global health partnership activities at country level.*

25. Bazemore AW, Goldenhar LM, Lindsell CJ, Diller PM, Huntington MK. An International Health Track Is Associated With Care for Underserved US Populations in Subsequent Clinical Practice. *Journal of Graduate Medical Education.* 2011/06/01 2011;3(2):130-137.

26. Godkin MA, Savageau JA. The effect of medical students' international experiences on attitudes toward serving underserved multicultural populations. *FMCH Publications and Presentations.* 2003:26.

27. Niemantsverdriet S, Majoor GD, Van Der Vleuten CPM, Scherpbier AJJA. 'I found myself to be a down to earth Dutch girl': a qualitative study into learning outcomes from international traineeships. *Medical education.* 2004;38(7):749-757.

28. Jeffrey J, Dumont RA, Kim GY, Kuo T. Effects of International Health Electives on Medical Student Learning and Career Choice. *Family medicine.* 2011;43(1):21-28.

29. Miller WC, Corey GR, Lallinger GJ, Durack DT. International health and internal medicine residency training: the Duke University experience. *American Journal of Medicine.* 1995;99(3):291-297.

30. Gupta A, Wells CK, Horwitz RI, Bia FJ, Barry M. The international health program: the fifteen-year experience with Yale University's internal medicine residency program. *The American journal of tropical medicine and hygiene.* 1999;61(6):1019.

31. Federico SG, Zachar PA, Oravec CM, Mandler T, Goldson E, Brown J. A successful international child health elective: the University of Colorado Department of Pediatrics' experience. *Archives of Pediatrics and Adolescent Medicine.* 2006;160(2):191.

32. Pust R, Dahlman B, Khwa-Otsyula B, Armstrong J, Downing R. Partnerships creating postgraduate family medicine in Kenya. *FAMILY MEDICINE-KANSAS CITY-.* 2006;38(9):661.

33. Gordon G, Vongvichit E, Hansana V, Torjesen K. A model for improving physician performance in developing countries: a three-year postgraduate training program in Laos. *Academic Medicine.* 2006;81(4):399.

34. Fins JJ, Rodríguez del Pozo P. The Hidden and Implicit Curricula in Cultural Context: New Insights From Doha and New York. *Academic Medicine.* 2011;86(3):321-325 310.1097/ACM.1090b1013e318208761d.

35. Airhihenbuwa CO, Shisana O, Zungu N, et al. Research capacity building: a US-South African partnership. *Glob Health Promot.* Jun 2011;18(2):27-35.

36. De Savigny D, Adam T. *Systems thinking for health systems strengthening*: World Health Organization; 2009.

37. Kaufman A, Van Dalen J, Majoor G, Mora Carrasco F. The Network: Towards Unity for Health- 25th anniversary. *Medical education.* 2004;38(12):1214-1217.

38. Schmidt H, Neufeld V, Nooman Z, Ogunbode T. Network of community-oriented educational institutions for the health sciences for the health sciences. *Academic Medicine.* 1991;65:259-263.

39. Kristina T, Majoor G, Van der Vleuten C. A survey validation of generic objectives for community-based

education in undergraduate medical training. *EDUCATION FOR HEALTH-ABINGDON-CARFAX PUBLISHING LIMITED-*. 2006;19(2):189.

40. Brinkerhoff JM. Assessing and improving partnership relationships and outcomes: a proposed framework. *Evaluation and Program Planning*. 2002;25(3):215-231.
41. Afsana K, Habte D, Hatfield J, Murphy J, Neufeld V. Partnership Assessment Toolkit. *Ottawa: Canadian Coalition for Global Health Research*. 2009.
42. Association of Schools of Public Health. www.asph.org/document.cfm?page=1083#Undergraduate, accessed Feb 20, 2013.
43. Core Competencies for Interprofessional Collaborative Practice. www.aacn.nche.edu/education-resources/ipecreport.pdf, accessed Feb 20, 2013.

CHAPTER 6

Advocacy Training and Global Health Education

Timothy Anderson, MD MA
Internal Medicine Resident
Global Health and Underserved Populations Track
University of Pittsburgh Medical Center

Nilo Habibullah
BMS/M.D Combined Degree Candidate
Youth Commission, Lancet-University of Oslo Commission on Global Governance for Health
International Federation of Medical Students' Associations (IFMSA)

Editors

Predrag Stojicic, MD MPH
Community Organizing Coach, ReThink Health
The Fannie E. Rippel Foundation
Executive Director, Serbia on the Move

Ranit Mishori, MD MHS
Associate Professor
Director, Global Health Initiatives
Department of Family Medicine
Georgetown University School of Medicine

Introduction

ADVOCACY IS COMMONLY DEFINED AS a process to influence policies, laws, regulations and the allocation of resources. Earnest et al offered the following definition of physician advocacy: "action by a physician to promote those social, economic, educational, and political changes that ameliorate the suffering and threats to human health and well-being that he or she identifies through his or her professional work and expertise."[1]

Though applied to a physician in this context, it may ring true to many individuals in health-related fields. For those of us in medicine and allied professions, advocacy has often reflected a desire to highlight issues that affect our patients' lives within and beyond the clinic or operating room. For physicians, the role of advocate goes back to Hippocrates' time, when he challenged the profession to keep the sick from harm and injustice. While the idea of physician as patient-advocate has long been accepted, the implementation of advocacy efforts and education has evolved over the past century. It is understood—and often even expected –that a health care professional should advocate on behalf of his or her individual patient. But acceptance of health care professionals' role in advocating for social, educational, political and economic change has been lagging.

Currently we see advocacy in medicine taking many forms: the researcher who pursues laboratory cures for neglected diseases, the trauma surgeon who uses clinical vignettes to advocate for safer driving laws, the medical student who meets with his Congresswoman to tell his patients' stories to urge funding for a threatened government health program, the resident who educates her peers on the ways to reduce wasteful tests and procedures, or the physician who takes a banner to the streets of Washington, DC pushing for increased HIV/AIDS funding at home and abroad. Health advocates now encompass students, researchers, educators, policy-makers, entrepreneurs, and other consciousness-raisers.

Global health education provides an opportune context to incorporate an advocacy curriculum. Global health is no longer a silo of expanded infectious disease training but necessitates an understanding of the economic, political, and social structures that create specific disease burdens across the world. Implementing effective global health programs requires understanding and raising awareness of health, economic and social conditions. Importantly, the same skills of coalition building, communication, and community organizing are equally integral to the success of global clinical projects as they are in advocacy. Whereas individual physicians may be seen as leaders in global health, in reality it is a field best addressed by trans-disciplinary teams and approaches. Advocacy is an essential skill for most, if not all, individuals who wish to be a part of the global health movement. Importantly, as the effectiveness of many Western-centric aid-oriented approaches is questioned, advocacy may become a predominant mechanism for Westerners to contribute to health in the Global South.

In section 1 we develop the background discussion on teaching advocacy in the medical school curriculum. Section 2 offers basic starting principles and steps to developing an advocacy project. Rather than provide a complete guide, we hope to help identify the skills an advocacy curriculum might focus on. In section 3 we highlight medical school and non-profit programs that emphasize advocacy training in the global health context.

A young student reflects quietly in one of three rudimentary schoolrooms in his remote African village
Photographer: *Will Bynum*

Should We Teach Advocacy in Medical Education?

Medical and other health-related professions have wavered on whether advocacy skills should be a formal component of medical education. A special issue of Academic Medicine which presents nine physician views on the necessity of advocacy training in medical education is introduced by editor Stephen Kanter, with the question: "Should physician advocacy be a mandatory part of physician education and practice? If so, what does that mean?"[2] A frequent concern is that teaching advocacy skills is inherently teaching a political agenda and thus advocacy should remain an optional avocation. This view contrasts with the majority of professional society mission statements, as well as many medical school oaths and guiding principles that explicitly place advocacy as part of physician training. Further questions linger, such as should advocacy be taught more empirically, as a skill—much like patient communication—that all physicians must develop? Or should it be taught more theoretically, as a topic to be aware of but not necessarily actively engage in?

Not committing to either side of the debate, the Global Health Education Consortium (GHEC) stated in its mission: we are "*committed to improving the health and human rights of underserved populations worldwide and the ability of the global workforce to meet their needs through improved education and training.*"[3]

Other professional societies have embraced the need for advocacy more fully. The American Medical Association implores a commitment stating physicians must "advocate for the social, economic, educational, and political changes that ameliorate suffering and contribute to human well-being."[4] In graduate medical education, advocacy is increasingly being recognized as an integral part of health provider training. The Accreditation Council for Graduate Medical Education (ACGME) has integrated advocacy into the Common Program Requirements, and many disciplines are now requiring it of their residents.[5] Schools developing or expanding global health curricula will be well-served to incorporate an advocacy training component as both a complement and an alternative to traditional models of clinical services in global health.

It is our view as authors that a global health curriculum lacking instruction in the methods and principles of advocacy, is akin to general medical school curriculum that instructs on treating symptoms but not diagnosing or treating the root causes of disease. Thus in the next section we provide a skeleton of an advocacy project on which to identify the skills and experiences students should have in order to be prepared for future global health experiences.

The Ingredients of an Advocacy Project

Advocacy initiatives can be designed using a wide variety of frameworks. An advocacy curriculum, according to Earnest et al, should include teaching the following basic steps:[1]

1. Identifying a problem amenable to advocacy
2. Defining the problem and its scope
3. Identifying and engaging strategic partners
4. Developing a strategic action plan
5. Communicating a message effectively

Within this framework there are multiple steps and skills that can be taught. These can include, but are not limited to: goal setting, community organizing, coalition building, and tactics for creating change. Change creation strategies may include raising awareness on an issue, obtaining project or community funding, changing institutional or government policies, to name only the most common. Skills for creating change often include instruction in effective public speaking and writing, using the media, organizing public events, and training how to access and lobby institutional, political or public officials.

Below we walk through the steps in developing a plan for an advocacy project.

1. **Identify a problem or define a situation**

   Advocacy begins with identifying an issue that affects an individual, a community or a population. One that you care about and believe needs to be changed. With an problem identified, we must first ask: Why does this problem exist? Is the cause a misunderstanding or lack of knowledge? A result of scare resources or funding? Perhaps of injustice or unintended consequences? For each reason identified continue to ask why until a root problem or cause is identified. Having identified an issue and a root cause, we can seek the best evidence available to frame and highlight the inequities, injustice or maltreatment that you would like to focus on.

2. **Establish goals and objectives.**

   Create clear goals that are SMART (specific, measurable, achievable, realistic, time- bound). Consider short-term and long-term opportunities and barriers. Take into consideration levels of public awareness and understanding of the issue at hand, the political climate, and existing policies. Develop a roadmap of how you will get there and the outcome expected, whilst including milestones and expected barriers.

3. **Identify a target.**

   Think about who you are trying to influence: who are the people whose opinion you'd like to change, who will make the decisions you would like to see taken? Are the decision-makers politicians, legislators, government officials, CEOs, religious leaders, or patients? These will be your primary audience. Also consider your secondary audience: the people or groups who have the power to influence the decision makers (workers, citizens, celebrities, consumer groups, community leaders, etc). Spend time figuring out what will motivate or influence your target audience.

4. **Build partnerships.**

   Consider the support needed to bring about a change—it usually includes building partnerships or a coalition. A coalition is a group of people working on a shared issue and may include diverse viewpoints, agendas and motivations, but can become effective when group members are well informed, respectful, committed and have interdependent roles. Effective coalitions will include members of the target community and may focus on recruiting allies, amassing public support, generating financial leverage, or fostering a sense of belonging towards the shared advocacy cause.

5. **Develop key messages.**

   How you frame your messages will be very important in appealing to your target audience. Your messages should be direct, compelling, concise, clear, free of jargon, consistent and convincing. They should help convince your audience to act, rather than just inform them. When crafting your key messages consider: what do you want to achieve? Who is your main audience? What will motivate them to act? Try to connect to their value and cultural systems, political views and religious leanings. Along the rational and logical, consider the emotional message to appeal to their hearts as well as their heads. Include a call to action.

6. **Develop and implement your advocacy plan.**

   Advocacy campaigns and projects can take many forms and there are many ways of engaging with, and delivering your message to, your target audience. Using a combination of methods may be the most useful. Approaches are often specific to the target change. Changing policy may involve letters, petitions, demonstrations, face-to- face meetings, and media events. Raising awareness may involve op-eds, public events, media utilization, and teaching or marketing an issue. All projects may necessitate the need for further research or investigation on an issue. The method you choose should be appealing and accessible to the target audience.

7. **Monitoring and evaluation.**

   As in any other project you are undertaking, monitoring and evaluation (M&E) is a crucial in advocacy work: you should continuously assess whether your campaign is effective and proceeding according to plan. Questions to ask: am I following my roadmap (process) and meeting my milestones? Are my techniques working? Am I making an impact? Am I reaching the target audience? An M&E plan will help you decide if you need to change your messages, your communication tactics, your logistics; It will help provide feedback to your funders, and assist you in charting a plan for the future of your campaign.

Tools, Approaches, and Resources

The purpose of advocacy training in global health education should be to develop leadership and interpersonal skills of physicians to initiate and participate in advocacy initiatives. This outcome can be achieved without teaching a particular political agenda, allowing medical students to decide what they will advocate for according to their professional, ethical and moral convictions.

There are a variety of approaches to teaching global health advocacy. Pedagogical methods may include didactics, problem-based learning, workshops, role modeling, critical reflections, and experiential and practical applications in a community setting. Whatever method is used, it is of great importance to ensure that students gain some practical hands-on experience and reflect on it, since that is the best way to teach leadership and advocacy skills.

Like any component of global health education, the approach depends on the priorities, expertise, and logistical scope of each institution's program. Here we present only a small sample of formalized medical school programs, non-profit extracurricular student programs, and advocacy curriculum resources.

Street kids in Ethiopia receive teaching on forgiveness, a concept that helps them cope with the difficult circumstances surrounding their lives
Photographer: *Kimberly Krauk*

Medical School Based Global Health Advocacy Training

Brown Alpert Medical School

http://brown.edu/academics/medical/education/concentrations/advocacy-and-activism
Brown offers a concentration in activism and advocacy which aims to develop "an understanding of advocacy and activism on behalf of patients and their communities as an essential part of professionalism," and develop "skills and experience in identifying issues, analyzing issues and policy, organizing advocacy strategies, and advocating for patients and communities with policy makers, stakeholders, with the media, and legislatively." These goals are accomplished through didactics on social justice and experiential opportunities that include working with legislators, community-based organizations and advocacy organizations. The program specifically addresses advocacy across borders and implications for global health.

University of California San Francisco School of Medicine

http://globalhealthsciences.ucsf.edu
The University of California San Francisco offers a Global Health 101 survey course that includes didactics on major global health policy issues including: barriers to development, intellectual property and free trade agreements, refugees and displaced persons. The course uses a Letter to the Editor training as a platform for basic advocacy skill-building.

Harvard Medical School

http://ghsm.hms.harvard.edu/education/courses/#ghsm
Harvard Medical School requires all first year students to complete an Introduction to Social Medicine course and Global Health Delivery seminar. These courses focus on identifying the determinants of disease and health inequalities between populations and over time; how social factors influence medical knowledge and health care; and what must be done to combat and prevent health inequalities in local, national, and global contexts. Students are exposed to didactics and tutorials and asked to develop a tool kit of possible solutions to a challenge encountered in clinical practice.

Global Health Advocacy Training Outside of the Classroom

American Medical Student Association (AMSA)

www.amsa.org
AMSA is a student-governed, national organization committed to representing the concerns of physicians-in-training. AMSA supports chapters and student-led action committees focused on advocacy in global health, AIDS advocacy, health policy, gender & sexuality, and other topics. AMSA has national and regional conferences with training seminars on project development, yearly leadership institutes focused on developing advocacy and leadership skills, national lobby days, and a web-based campaign center to engage students in advocacy projects. AMSA students have been active nationally on health care reform, global HIV/AIDS funding, global health education, and pharmaceutical and international patent law policy.

SocMed

http://www.socmedglobal.org
SocMed is a non-profit organization that advocates for and implements global health curricula. SocMed curriculum focuses on encouraging students to reflect upon their personal experiences with power, privilege, race, class, gender, and sexual orientation as central to effective partnership building in global health. SocMed offers month-long immersion courses in Gulu, Uganda, and Port-au-Prince, Haiti to fourth year medical students with emphasis on inclusion of students from the local site. These courses merge the teaching of traditional clinical tropical medicine with instruction on the socioeconomic, cultural, political, and historical underpinnings of illness.

Courses include student-directed advocacy projects and didactics by local community-based advocacy organizations and government officials.

Physicians for Human Rights (PHR)

http://physiciansforhumanrights.org/students/
Physicians for Human Rights is an organization of physicians and concerned citizens that uses medicine and science to stop mass atrocities and severe human rights violations against individuals. PHR has worked to document and raise awareness on instances of genocide, torture, chemical weapons, and child soldiers. They have successfully advocated for banning landmines and contributed to international human rights investigations. PHR include a student program which fosters advocacy skills and includes many online resources, tool kits and opportunities to become involved in advocacy projects.

Additional Advocacy Curriculum Resources

World Health Organization (WHO)

www.who.int/chp/advocacy/chp.manual.EN-webfinal.pdf
The WHO produced a useful "Practical Guide to Successful Advocacy" which focuses on chronic disease prevention. The underlying principles described in the web-based guide can be applied to other advocacy initiatives.

PATH

http://www.path.org
PATH is an international nonprofit organization that sets out to transform global health through innovation. Their website provides multiple accessible resources including a workbook of strategies and stories on global health advocacy, a web-based training course, and a 10-step approach that can be used as a framework for a curriculum or an advocacy project.

CARE

http://www.care.org/getinvolved/advocacy/tools.asp
CARE is a humanitarian organization focused on fighting global poverty, focusing on community-based efforts and emphasis on working alongside poor women. CARE's provides a useful advocacy toolkit.

ReTHINK HEALTH

http://rippelfoundation.org/rethink-health/learning-opportunities/rethinkinghealth/
The flagship initiative of the Rippel Foundation, ReThink Health serves as an incubator to support

the emergence and application of new ways to accelerate the transformation of American health and health care. Founded in 2007, ReThink Health works to enable a genuine metamorphosis within the health system to occur—one in which seemingly different stakeholder groups come together in unexpected ways to redefine solutions and bring them to action. ReThink Health began as a roundtable conversation among some of the nation's most influential thought-leaders from health, business and energy, including Don Berwick, Amory Lovins, and Elliott Fisher. It is now supported by an array of project and funding partners and has a growing portfolio of initiatives in regions and with partners across the country.

Summary

In summary, advocacy and advocacy training is an increasingly important aspect in global health practice and education. Despite the paucity of formalized, evidence-based curricula, multiple resources that introduce learners to some basic advocacy skills do exist and can be used to begin the process effectively.

Acknowledgement

We are grateful for the inspiration and guidance of Michael Slatnik, MD CCFP.

References

1. Earnest MA, Wong, SL, Federico, SG. "Perspective: Physician Advocacy: What Is It and How Do We Do It?" Academic Medicine 2010; 85: 63-67
2. Kanter SL. "On Physician Advocacy." Academic Medicine 2011; 86: 1059-1060
3. Global Health Education Consortium. About Us. 2013. <http://globalhealtheducation.org/aboutus/Pages/SAC.aspx>.
4. American Medical Association. Declaration of Professional Responsibility. 2013. <http://www.ama-assn.org/ama/pub/physician-resources/medical-ethics/declaration-professional-responsibility.page>.
5. Accreditation Council for Graduate Medical Education. Categorization of Common ProgramRequirements. 2013. <http://www.acgme-na.

CHAPTER 7

Networking in Global Health: Organizations, Meetings and Funding

Jonathan Abelson, MD
Laura Bertani, MD-candidate
William Cherniak, MD
Sarah Kleinfeld, MD-candidate

Editor
Paul K. Drain, MD, MPH

AS WE HAVE SEEN IN the previous chapters, the field of global health is undergoing a period of rapid expansion and growth. Efforts of colleagues across the globe have led to the establishment of numerous organizations with goals of developing new and innovative ways of connecting people and their ideas. As the world has become increasingly more interconnected through advances in travel and communication, the field of global health continues to expand and evolve. Due to this rapid expansion, it is impossible to maintain a comprehensive, current, and accurate list of resources. In this chapter, we outline and describe some of the most prominent organizations, meetings, grants, and scholarships available to the global health community. We encourage you to use this chapter as a starting point to create your own networks and explore the diverse field of global health.

In the section below on organizations, we've included descriptions for prominent governmental and non-governmental organizations that provide on-the-ground medical assistance, advance medical education through curriculum building, facilitate global health research at home and abroad, and/or participate in additional global health activities. As you use this section and search for global health organizations, take time to carefully review an organization's description and mission, and ensure they match your own ideals and goals. Working in and advocating for global health involves dedication and motivation, and aligning with like-minded organizations and people makes the experience easier and more enjoyable. Although we have listed website addresses, a webpage rarely provides a comprehensive overview of an organization. Therefore, we encourage every prospective global health advocate to arrange telephone calls and meetings to make educated decisions about working with any particular global health organization.

After identifying your particular interests in global health, and perhaps aligning with a global health organization, you may wish to seek either grant or scholarship support to obtain more practical field experience. Many grants and scholarship opportunities exist, but the process of locating funding can be daunting. Your home academic institution may be the best place to start. Many universities, medical schools, and graduate programs have established opportunities and designated funding for students to engage in global health activities. General funding sources may often be applied to specific global health work, so we recommended that students first speak with faculty and administrators to help locate these funding opportunities. For individuals without access to institutional assistance, there are a variety of other possible funding venues. Many local private organizations, such as Rotary International or Lions Club International, have multi-national affiliations and contacts, but may also serve as potential sources of funds through direct donations and facilitating fundraising events. If local avenues are unsuccessful, then many national funding opportunities in the form of public grants and scholarships are available to most students. Although these grants often have many well-qualified applicants, they can be extremely valuable and prestigious, while conferring additional benefits, such as developing a network of professional contacts. There are also private grants available, although they are often very competitive and require a great deal of patience. Finally, perhaps the best way to come across funding is to talk to people in your network, such as administrators, professors, professionals, and fellow students, who share your similar interests. In the section on funding in this chapter, we have provided a list of organizations that provide a variety of scholarships and funding opportunities that may help with your search.

Attending a meeting or conference can be an excellent way to expand your global health network. These meetings connect individuals with different backgrounds and experiences through formal presentations and personal interactions. Meetings and conferences on global health occur around the world. In this chapter, we listed many of the global health meetings located across North America and Europe. Global health conferences may cover a wide range of topics, from global health curriculum to specialty-specific research to improving sanitation in low-income nations. Therefore, selectively choosing options that match your particular interests will be most beneficial.

Ultimately, it is through teamwork and collaboration that information will be disseminated to bright minds across the planet. Through this chapter we provide numerous resources to connect with different organizations and individuals that are working along parallel lines of interest. The first section covers a variety of professional and non-governmental organizations involved in the field of global health. The second section of this chapters highlights a variety of fellowship and grant options. The final section is a listing of global health conferences held throughout the year. We hope that this chapter provides a valuable starting point for developing your global health career.

Networking via duck-duck-goose
Photographer: *Kimberly Krauk*

I. Organizations

The following organizations are divided between professional and non-governmental organizations and listed alphabetically. Each organization offers different resources to individuals interested in global health. In order to better organize these resources and make your search easier, we have categorized them as the following when applicable:

- Educational resources: This includes courses (online or in-person), publications, informational resources, fact sheets, reading lists and much more.
- Databases and Links: These may include resources not listed in this chapter, so they are worth perusing.
- Internships and Volunteering: This category includes internship and volunteering opportunities (paid, unpaid, and paid-for), as well as local and international educational experiences. Exchange programs are also included in this category.
- Awards and Fellowships: These are discussed in more depth in the awards and fellowships section, but are briefly mentioned if there is some overlap between organizational opportunities
- Newsletters: Many organizations put forth newsletters listing important global health meetings and opportunities, the current work of the organization, and more!
- Listservs and Forums: A variety of the organizations provide online communities to discuss global health issues. Listservs are also a good way to learn about meetings, grants, and fellowships.

- Employment Opportunities: Some of these organizations list either employment opportunities for their own organization or databases of alternate employment opportunities.
- Leadership Opportunities: This is listed for a few organizations that particularly emphasize this potential on their website, particularly for students.

Professional Organizations

American Academy of Family Physicians

The American Academy of Family Physicians (AAFP) is one of the largest national medical organizations. Its mission is to preserve and promote the science and art of family medicine to ensure high-quality, cost-effective health care for patients of all ages.

Resources:

- Databases and Links: The AAFP has a compiled list of U.S. family medicine residency programs with international rotations available. There is also a database of other websites listing potential international health opportunities, including a separate database for disaster and relief opportunities.
- Newsletters: An email discussion group is available for those interested in international family medicine.
- Website: http://www.aafp.org/online/en/home/aboutus/specialty/international.html

American Academy of Pediatrics

The American Academy of Pediatrics' (AAP) global mission is to attain optimal physical, mental, and social health and well being for all children around the world. To accomplish this mission, the Academy supports the professional needs and interests of its membership to work internationally, identify organizations that can further the international mission of the AAP, and collaborate with them efficiently through its Office of International Affairs (OIA).

Resources:

- Educational Resources: The section on International Child Health includes a Global Health Curriculum Tool Kit, which includes a variety of PDF and word documents to be used as a base for future global health curricula. There is also an article on global health electives for pediatric residents. There are also books on international pediatric health for purchase.
- Newsletters: There is an archive of newsletters available on the AAP's website.
- Website: http://www2.aap.org/international/connect.html

The American Medical Student Association

The American Medical Student Association (AMSA) is committed to improving health care and healthcare delivery to all people; promoting active improvement in medical education; involving its members in the social, moral and ethical obligations of the profession of medicine; assisting in the improvement and understanding of world health problems; contributing to the welfare of medical students, premedical students, interns, residents and post-MD/DO trainees; and advancing the profession of medicine.

Resources:

- Educational Resources: The Global Health Action Committee website provides access to a variety of pertinent global health documents, including information on current policy and policy initiatives and informational publications on global health and global health opportunities. AMSA also has an online international health journal—*Global Pulse.* AMSA's AIDS Advocacy network also has online global health resources, particularly policy and advocacy information as well as resources for local initiatives, including a World AIDS Day Toolkit and presentations on issues such as harm reduction and human sexuality.
- Databases and Links: AMSA's Global Health Action Committee lists a variety of links to pertinent global health organizations as well as a database of international opportunities that can be searched by country, region, opportunity type, and eligibility.
- Internships and Volunteering: As part of the International Federation of Medical Students' Associations, AMSA participates in clinical and research exchanges with other participating international medical student organizations. The program offers clinical medicine and biomedical research opportunities to AMSA members in exchange for providing the same opportunities for foreign students in the U.S.
- Listservs and Forums: AMSA runs a number of listservs in a variety of topics, including global health, the International Federation of Medical Students' Associations, and the AIDS Advocacy Network. These are run through the AMSA member-only social networking site—*Inspiration Exchange.* The listservs share a number of pertinent global health opportunities.
- Leadership Opportunities: AMSA runs at the local and national levels, with many opportunities for medical and premedical students to become involved in the association's various global health related organizations—particularly the Global Health Action Committee, but also the AIDS Advocacy Network. AMSA is the United States' representative to the International Federation of Medical Students' Associations, so there are opportunities for national leadership involvement on the international level.
- Website: www.amsa.org

American Public Health Association

The American Public Health Association (APHA) was one of the first US non-governmental organizations to become involved in the field of public health. The membership organization includes a strong international health section and promotes global health through various programs and projects.

Resources:

» Educational Resources: The website includes a recently published booklet available in PDF entitled *Growth of International Health: An Analysis and History.*
» The website also provides pages on current global health issues and resources.
» Website: http://www.apha.org/programs/globalhealth/

American Society for Tropical Medicine and Hygiene

The American Society for Tropical Medicine and Hygiene (ASTMH) is a worldwide organization of scientists, clinicians and program professionals dedicated to promoting global health through prevention and control of infectious and other diseases disproportionately affecting the global poor.

Resources:

» Educational Resources: The ASTMH website includes a regular clinical quiz with archives of previous quizzes, Herman Zaiman's Pictorial Presentation of Parasites collection, a CTropMed certificate course in clinical tropical medicine and travelers health as well as an intensive update course. The ASTMH also provides resources for medical schools to host a Global Health Career Night. The website offers access to the society's journal *The American Journal of Tropical Medicine and Hygiene.*
» Databases and Links: The website provides several lists of resources, including a recommended list by topic in the publications section, a list of meetings and courses in the field of tropical medicine, and a travel clinic directory. There is also a links section dedicated to travel medicine resources.
» Employment Opportunities: The website has a career center with potential job openings.
» Website: http://www.astmh.org

Association of American Medical Colleges' Global Health Learning Opportunities

The Association of American Medical Colleges (AAMC) is in the process of developing the Global Health Learning Opportunities program, which will offer clinical and research exchanges for final-year medical students. The pilot is set to begin in September 2012 with 10 U.S. universities and 15 international universities participating. Universities set their own tuition rates for these experiences.

Resources:

- Educational Resources: The program will provide electives for final year medical students.
- Newsletters: The program puts out an electronic newsletter
- Website: www.aamc.org/ghlo

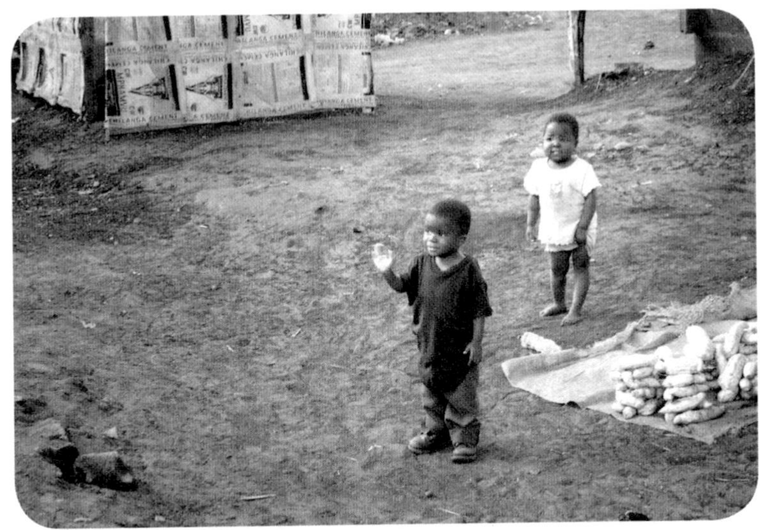

Children wave to a van full of medical personnel as they leave their village
Photographer: *Will Bynum*

Canadian Federation of Medical Students

The Canadian Federation of Medical Students (CFMS) is the representative voice of Canadian medical students to the federal government, public, and national medical organizations. It comprises over 7,500 medical students at 14 Canadian medical schools. It includes within its structure the Global Health Program, which provides global health resources to Canadian membership and represents Canada in the International Federation of Medical Students' Associations.

Resources:

- Educational Resources: CFMS is active in the role of Canadian medical student global health education, particularly in the areas of global health curriculum development, pre-departure training (to prepare for global health experiences), aboriginal health, sexual health, and immigrant and refugee health. There are some reports and documents available from the organization, the most recent from 2009 at time of publication.
- Databases and Links: The CFMS website has a list of links to partner organizations.
- Internships and Volunteering: CFMS participates in the IFMSA international exchange program and makes exchange opportunities in research and clinical experience available to its members.

- » Newsletters: CFMS has a global health blog where officers post pertinent information on global health and CFMS issues. They also have a mailing list.
- » Leadership Opportunities: CFMS is a medical student organization comprised of Canadian medical student officers. There are a variety of leadership roles in their Global Health Program.
- » Website: www.cfms.org

Canadian Paediatric Society

The Canadian Paediatric Society is the Canadian national association of paediatricians committed to advancing the health of children by nurturing excellence in health care, advocacy, education, and research. The Global Child & Youth Health Section acts a subset of the society to network pediatricians interested in working overseas in low and middle-income countries.

Resources:

- » Educational Resources: The website has a global child health curriculum with four different modules, with a trainer's guide to help with those running the curriculum. The society also has an educational partnership with Health Child Uganda. There is also a list of articles, books, and other resources available on the website.
- » Databases and Links: The website provides a list of links and resources for organizations and opportunities in global health.
- » Awards and Fellowships: Members are eligible for the Don & Elizabeth Hilman International Child Health Grant.
- » Listservs and Forums: The Global Child & Youth Health Section has a server for members.
- » Website: http://www.cps.ca/en/sections/section/global-child-youth-health

The International Federation of Medical Students' Associations

The International Federation of Medical Students' Associations (IFMSA) is a non-governmental organization representing associations of medical students. Founded in 1951, the IFMSA currently maintains 106 national member organizations (NMOs) from 99 countries across six continents. It includes six standing committees on medical education professional exchanges research exchanges), public health, reproductive health (including AIDS) and human rights and peace.

Resources:

- » Educational Resources: Each NMO and standing committee produces a variety of materials pertinent to their particular work and interests. These are generally shared via the listserv for the appropriate standing committee.
- » Internships and Volunteering: IFMSA's research and clinical exchange programs offer international clerkships and research opportunities for NMOs (including CFMS and

AMSA) that participate in these exchanges. Additionally, the IFMSA has a relationship with the WHO and occasionally shares internship opportunities, primarily with the WHO, on the national member organization server.

- Listservs and Forums: Each of the IFMSA's regions and standing committees have a listserv where important announcements and documents are shared. These are hosted through yahoo groups. There are also listservs reserved for national officers of certain committees and national member organization presidents.
- Leadership Opportunities: The IFMSA is a student-run organization that has a variety of opportunities for students to get involved locally, nationally, and internationally. In general, students become involved through their respective national member organization in order to become more active on the international level.
- Website: www.ifmsa.org

Society for Academic Emergency Medicine

The Society for Academic Emergency Medicine (SAEM) offers several virtual academies on its website, one of which is the Global Emergency Medicine Academy (GEMA). The academy's mission is two-fold: to improve the global delivery of emergency care through research, education, and mentorship and to enhance SAEM's role as the international emergency medicine organization that augments, supports, and shares advances in global research, education, and mentorship.

Resources:

- Educational Resources: GEMA provides a public library where past meeting minutes, news, and announcements can be accessed.
- Newsletters: GEMA has an online newsletter which can be found on their webpage covering a variety of topics related to international emergency medicine.
- Website: http://www.saem.org/global-emergency-medicine-academy

World Federation of Public Health Associations

The World Federation of Public Health Associations is an international federation of public health associations worldwide, of which the American Public Health Association is a member.

Resources:

- Educational Resources: The federation provides its members with access to the *Journal of Public Health Policy*, which allocates a portion of each issue to the WFPHA, at a reduced price. The website links to the WFPHA articles, which are free of charge.
- Databases and Links: The website provides a small list of links to journal websites and those of other global public health organizations.

- Internships and Volunteering: The federation offers unpaid internships in their office of the secretariat in Geneva, Switzerland.
- Newsletters: The WFPHA puts forth a newsletter available on the website, which can be subscribed to via email. It also provides its annual reports and links to newsletters from certain member public health organizations.
- Website: http://www.wfpha.org/

World Organization of Family Doctors

The World Organization of Family Doctors (WONCA) is a not-for-profit organization with 126 member organizations in 102 countries with a membership of about 300,000 family doctors. WONCA represents and acts as an advocate for its members at the international level.

Resources:

- Educational Resources: The website provides a list of A-Z resources on a variety of topics, along with links to national organizations with further resources. There are also links to relevant clinical apps and journals.
- Databases and Links: Links are scattered throughout the website, for things like literature databases, and general international health links.
- Website: http://www.globalfamilydoctor.com/

Nongovernmental Organizations

American International Health Alliance

The American International Health Alliance's (AIHA) partnerships and projects harness the knowledge and expertise of the U.S. healthcare sector in a coordinated response to public health challenges in developing and transitioning nations around the globe. AIHA provides peer-to-peer exchanges of information, skills-based training, broad-based programmatic management, and technical assistance that helps partner institutions and communities make the best use of limited financial, material, and human resources. It's most prominent program is the HIV/AIDS Twinning Center, which operates its own website that provides additional information and resources.

Resources:

- Educational Resources: The AIHA main resources section provides links to a variety of publications and educational resources. They include publications, manuals, toolkits, clinical practice guidelines, posters, presentations, and the EurasiaHealth Knowledge Network and AIDS Knowledge Network, clearinghouses of resources.
- Website: http://www.aiha.com/en/

American Refugee Committee

The American Refugee Committee (ARC) works with its partners and constituencies to provide opportunities and expertise to refugees, displaced people and host communities. They help people survive conflict and crisis and rebuild lives of dignity, health, security and self-sufficiency.

Resources:

- » Educational Resources: The ARC has an e-newsletter covering refugee news and ARC activity. There are also videos, audio clips and photo essays on ARC's work available on their website. There is a toolkit on gender-based violence prevention and response, as well as other papers and reports the ARC has put together, such as their micro-lending methodology. There is also a suggested reading list on refugee issues.
- » Internships and Volunteering: Information about openings for volunteers/interns is posted on the ARC website.
- » International: Theses positions require a minimum 4 month (ideally 6) commitment. Volunteers must be able to cover the cost of travel to/from the placement and health insurance. The ARC can usually provide group housing and a small living expense stipend. Assignments require volunteers to have a specific skill, and some countries require the ability to speak French.
- » Domestic: Part time or full time volunteer positions are available in Minneapolis, MN. These internships are unpaid, but past volunteers have been able to receive academic credit or have been able to secure sponsorship for their volunteer stay.
- » Employment Opportunities: The ARC lists a few employment opportunities on its website, including a roster of rapid response teams as well as more long term paid positions.
- » Rapid Response Team: This consists of a roster of experienced personnel available for short-term emergency assignments in the cases of human displacements. Relief workers should be able to deploy globally on as short of notice as 48 hours for assignments of 1-3 months. Team members generally conduct initial needs assessments, coordinate with other implementing agencies and design and implement relief projects. Openings in areas as varied as logistics to administration and finance to health and human resources are posted periodically on the site.
- » Website: http://www.arcrelief.org/site/PageServer

The Aspen Institute

The Aspen Institute is an educational and policy studies organization based in Washington, D.C. Its mission is to foster leadership based on enduring values and to provide a nonpartisan venue for discussing and acting on critical issues. The Aspen Institute includes a Global Health Development section, which aims to identify, assess, and support highly innovative strategies for global health and poverty alleviation.

Resources:

- Educational Resources: The Aspen Institute website contains information such as statistical data and a variety of council reports on its primary initiatives –namely reproductive health and health worker migration. There are also pages covering past initiatives. There is a separate section including access to policy briefs produced by the Institute, which can be set to filter strictly for the Global Health and Development publications, or for their other policy documents.
- Website: http://www.aspeninstitute.org/policy-work/global-health-development

The Canadian Coalition for Global Health Research

The Canadian Coalition for Global Health Research (CCGHR) is a not-for-profit organization promoting better and more equitable health worldwide through the production and use of knowledge. They are dedicated to strengthening capacities of individuals, institutions, and systems in Canada and low and middle-income countries to produce and use knowledge, speak as Canada's voice for global health research, build effective, equitable and respectful north-south research partnerships, connect people, ideas and expertise, and learn and communicate from their work.

Resources:

- Educational Resources: The network has made available a number of articles and resources on partnerships and networking, as well as mentorship and leadership. There are also summer institutes for new researchers in global health in Canada or low or middle income countries.
- Internships and Volunteering: Information is posted on the website from one student's experience in Zambia interning with CCGHR.
- Newsletters: Members receive updates and news on funding, job and professional development opportunities, and summary information about funding resources.

Canadian Society for International Health

The Canadian Society for International Health (CSIH) is a Canadian non-governmental organization that works domestically and internationally to reduce global health inequities and strengthen health systems. Founded in 1977, CSIH members share a common interest and commitment to global health, global health research, and international development. Members include individuals and organizations representing a broad spectrum of experience in various disciplines.

Resources:

- Educational Resources: CSIH provides a variety of position papers and power point presentations in its "Public Engagement" section.

- Databases and Links: The "Other Resources" sections on the CSIH website have a variety of links to other global health resources.
- Internships and Volunteering: Paid internships lasting 6-7 months in global health and health systems strengthening in developing countries are available through CSIH.
- Newsletters: Members can sign up to receive news bulletins.
- Employment Opportunities: Members receive news and employment bulletins.
- Leadership Opportunities: Members are eligible to run for leadership positions within CSIH.
- Website: http://www.csih.org/

Three patients wait patiently in line to see American medical personnel
Photographer: *Will Bynum*

Child Family Health International

Child Family Health International (CFHI) is a global family of health professionals and students working at the grassroots level to support international partners through community health projects and global health immersion programs. There are over 20 programs in 5 countries which connect local health professionals with international students to create ethical and sustainable educational experiences.

Resources:

- Listservs and Forums: CFHI has an email list.
- Internships and Volunteering: Although called Global Health Education Programs, we have

listed these in this category because of their similarity to other internship and volunteering opportunities abroad. CFHI has developed socially responsible international experiences by working collaboratively with local healthcare workers in their many international sites, and part of the fees go towards supporting the hosting community. The programs include the Global Health Education programs in Argentina, Bolivia, Ecuador, India, Mexico, and South Africa, as well as Community Health Initiatives in Bolivia, Ecuador, India, Mexico and South Africa focusing on a variety of topics. There are also two Professional Development Programs—a Pediatric Life Support Training in Mexico and Advanced Training in Laparoscopic Surgical Equipment in the San Francisco. The program includes fees that help support the volunteer's stay in their hosting country and to support the host community. There is a wealth of fundraising information and ideas on the website.

» Newsletters: CFHI provides copies of its press releases on its website, as well as informational videos on its programs.
» Website: http://www.cfhi.org/

Consortium of Universities for Global Health (CUGH)

The Consortium of Universities for Global Health (CUGH) is a membership organization committed to building collaboration and exchange of knowledge and experience among interdisciplinary university global health programs across education, research and service. In December 2011 CUGH merged with the Global Health Education Consortium, retaining the identity of CUGH. Membership is institutional, with a list of participating universities listed on the website.

Resources:

» Educational Resources: The organization makes available publications and reports of interest to the global health community, particularly publications put forth by the organization.
» Databases and Links: The "organizations" section of the website lists global health organizations categorized by type of organization.
» Newsletters: The CUGH website also posts newsletters and a variety of upcoming events, including meetings, fellowships and courses. The announcements section often lists available fellowships and job openings in the field of global health. The website also links to the organization's blog.
» Website: http://www.cugh.org

Doctors for Global Health

Doctor's for Global Health (DGH) is a private, not-for-profit organization promoting health, education, art and other human rights throughout the world. The organization is comprised of health professionals, students, educators, artists, attorneys, engineers, retirees and others. It helps bring community-oriented primary care to the communities where it works, as well as education, human rights promotion, and the arts.

Resources:

- Internships and Volunteering: DGH selects volunteers from a variety of professions, including physicians, medical students, physical therapists, social workers, nurses, engineers, teachers, agronomists, artists and lawyers. Volunteer opportunities are a minimum of one month with preference for longer stays. An application process is required. DGH is also looking for volunteer translators to work remotely.
- Leadership Opportunities: Members of DGH can be active in three committees: Human Rights and Advocacy Committee, International Volunteer Committee, and Development and Finance Committee.
- Website: http://www.dghonline.org/

Doctors without Borders

Doctors Without Borders/Médecins Sans Frontières (MSF) is an international medical humanitarian organization that provides independent, impartial assistance in more than 60 countries to people whose survival is threatened by violence, neglect, or catastrophe. MSF provides independent, impartial assistance to those most in need, and reserves the right to speak out to bring attention to neglected crises, challenge inadequacies or abuse of the aid system, and to advocate for improved medical treatments and protocols.

Resources:

- Educational Resources: The Doctors Without Borders website provides access to many of its publications online including research articles, transcripts, special reports, and op-eds. There is also a bookstore to purchase additional publications. Videos, slideshows and aid worker blogs are available on the site.
- Internships and Volunteering: Doctors without Borders has a paid ($10/hour) internship program in their New York Office in the spring, summer, and fall. Interns support the departments of communications, development, program, human resources, and executive departments and receive a basic introduction to international medical humanitarian aid and advocacy. There is also the opportunity for work/study when qualifications are met. Volunteer positions are available at the New York office, even with limited time constraints, generally during regular work hours. These generally involve primarily clerical work, although they can involve more with more active volunteers.
- Employment Opportunities: Doctors Without Borders employs individuals internationally and in the New York office, with positions for the domestic office posted on the website. Field workers must meet a list of general requirements: at least 2 years of relevant work

experience (residency completion for physicians), availability for a minimum of 9 to 12 months (except surgeons, anesthesiologists, nurse anesthetists, and OB/GYNs). Complete details regarding the recruitment process are available on the website.

» Website: http://www.doctorswithoutborders.org/

Foundation for Advancement of International Medical Education and Research

The Foundation for Advancement of International Medical and Research (FAIMER) is a non-profit foundation committed to improving world health through education. It concentrates its efforts in developing regions in Asia, Africa, and Latin America, and focuses on three specific strategies: faculty development, targeted research that informs health workforce policy and practice, and development of data that advances educational quality improvement decisions.

Resources:

» Educational Resources: FAIMER's educational resources vary from the FAIMER institute, a two-year fellowship program for international health professions educators, to access to FAIMER staff publications on a variety of global health and health workforce issues. There are also regional fellowships and modules that can be taken online. All of these programs have tuition costs.

» Databases and Links: FAIMER's website has a directory of the world's medical schools, as well as a section of useful links on global health and health professions education issues.

» Newsletters: FAIMER MedEd is a newsletter for the international medical education community available through the website, as well as archives of previous issues.

» Website: www.faimer.org

Global Health Council

The Global Health Council (GHC), formerly the National Council of International Health, is a U.S.-based nonprofit membership organization that was created in 1972 to identify priority world health problems and to report them to the U.S. public, legislators, international and domestic government agencies, academic institutions and the global health community. In April 2012, the GHC announced that they would be ceasing operations, although it has not dissolved and a group of interested members as well as board members are exploring options for the future of the organization.

Resources:

» Educational Resources: Although the GHC has closed its doors, a variety of publications and digital media are still available on the website. These resources include issues of the GHC's Global Health Magazine, fact sheets on a variety of global health issues, as well as additional published materials. A variety of recorded video presentations are also available.

» Website: http://www.globalhealth.org/

Global Health Education Consortium

Although the Global Health Education Consortium (GHEC) recently merged with CUGH, at the time of publication GHEC still retained its own website with related resources, so we have listed it under its own category. GHEC is a consortium of faculty and health care educators dedicated to global health education in health professions schools and residency programs.

Resources:

- Educational Resources: GHEC has developed and posted a variety of online modules on numerous topics relevant to global health accessed for free on their website. There is also a high yield global health bibliography available for reference.
- Website: http://globalhealtheducation.org/

Global Health through Education, Training and Service

Global Health through Education, Training, and Service (GHETS) is a non-governmental nonprofit organization dedicated to improving health in developing countries through innovations in education and service. It provides startup grants to local training institutions in low-income countries and the technical help to launch and improve programs that prepare and support healthcare workers in rural and poor communities.

Resources:

- Educational Resources: GHETS offers a Women and Health Learning Package with a variety of modules on contraceptive practices, violence against women, and more. There are also publications and resources provided by The Network: TUFH.
- Newsletters: GHETS provides newsletters and program reports on their website.
- Website: http://www.ghets.org/

The HIV/AIDS Twinning Center:

The HIV/AIDS Twinning Center is the most prominent AIHA program, which creates peer-to-peer relationships between organizations working to improve services for people living with or affected by HIV/AIDS.

Resources:

- Educational Resources: The website lists information for potential organizational partners, including funding opportunities, toolkits, and resources on HIV/AIDS.
- Internships and Volunteering: The volunteer arm of the Twinning Center operates in Ethiopia, South Africa, Mozambique and Botswana. The program recruits clinical volunteers as well as a variety of other professions, including epidemiologists, pharmacists, social workers,

nutritionists, information technologists, and more. Volunteer assignments range from three months to two years depending on the hosting institution's needs. Volunteers are provided with basic support such as travel costs, basic housing, and a modest living allowance.

» Website: www.twinningagainstaids.org

Idealist

Idealist is a directory of jobs, organizations, volunteer opportunities, internships, events, programs, resources, and people that aims to connect resources and individuals working to build a world where all people can live free and dignified lives.

Resources:

» Databases and Links: Idealist is a directory of jobs, organizations, volunteer opportunities, internships, events, programs, resources and people. Searches can be refined by type of opportunity, whether or not opportunities are paid, location, area of focus, time commitment, duration, and much more.

» Website: www.idealist.org

International Medical Corps

The International Medical Corps is a global, humanitarian, nonprofit organization dedicated to saving lives and relieving suffering through health care training and relief and development programs. By offering training and health care to local populations and medical assistance to people at highest risk, and with the flexibility to respond rapidly to emergency situations, the International Medical Corps rehabilitates devastated health care systems and helps bring them back to self-reliance.

Resources:

» Internships and Volunteering: The International Medical Corps offers a variety of volunteering programs, both international and domestic. Opportunities are posted on the website as they become available.

» Emergency Response Volunteers: The emergency response team works to minimize loss of life and alleviate suffering in disaster-affected populations across the globe. This team includes highly trained medical staff members that are added to a roster of individuals ready to deploy, often within 72 hours, and for 2 to 8 weeks. Volunteers pay their own flight but are given food allowance, shared housing and medical evacuation insurance on site.

» Non-medical International Volunteers: This opportunity is open to trained professionals in a variety of fields with a minimum two-month window of availability. Volunteers are sometimes eligible for flight costs, and do receive a daily food allowance, shared housing, and emergency medical evacuation insurance.

- Domestic Volunteers: Volunteer positions with the International Medical Corps offices in Los Angeles, Washington D.C., or London are available on a part-time or full-time basis. Compensation or benefits are not offered.
- Graduate Internship Program: This is a highly competitive program designed for graduate students in universities that provide class credit and stipends for internships with international NGOs.
- Job Opportunities: In addition to internships and volunteering, the organization also posts job openings on its website.
- Newsletters: While not exactly newsletters, the organization posts feature stories about their work and the locations where they operate, as well as archives of past stories.
- Website: http://internationalmedicalcorps.org/

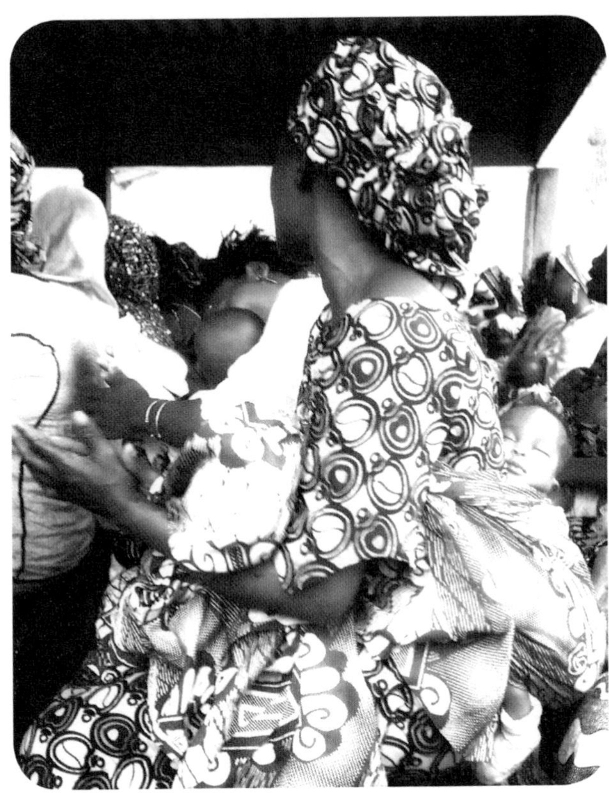

A woman and her child attend an information session on the importance of birth registration in Seme-Podji, Benin
Photographer: *Stephanie Cate*

The Network: Towards Unity for Health

The Network: Towards Unity for Health (The Network: TUFH) is a global network of individuals, institutions and organizations committed to improving the health of the people and their communities. With its longstanding history of over thirty years, The Network: TUFH has played an important role in fostering community-oriented innovations, leading to curriculum reforms in education institutions around the globe. Full members in the United States include FAIMER, Institute of John Snow, Inc., University of Illinois, and University of New Mexico, with the University of Sherbrooke and Northern Ontario School of Medicine as Canadian full members.

Resources:

- Student Network Organization: This is a student network aiming to promote exchange opportunities for students around the globe. Education for Health: The Network:TUFH's journal started in 2007 focusing on global health issues. Access is free, but members get the benefits of alerts for new issues, personal profiles, access to a discussion forum, and the ability to post news items. The journal can be reached directly at www.educationforhealth.net
- Learning Packages: The Women and Health Taskforce has posted several learning packets on a variety of pertinent topics Case Studies: on a variety of topics, some in Spanish
- Listservs and Forums: There is an established forum on the website, but at publication only one topic had been posted.
- Leadership Opportunities: The Network: TUFH has a variety of taskforces, which are most active during the annual meeting, but are also active throughout the year, and are available to all members. Currently listed taskforces include Community-Based Care for the Elderly, Integrating Medicine and Public Health, Interprofessional Education, Social Accountability and Accreditation, and Women and Health.

John Snow, Inc./JSI Research & Training Institute, Inc.

John Snow, Inc. and nonprofit organization JSI Research & Training Institute, Inc. are public health management consulting and research organizations dedicated to improving the health of individuals and communities throughout the world. They collaborate with government agencies, the private sector, and local nonprofit and civil society organizations to achieve change in communities and health systems.

Resources:

- Educational Resources: Along with information on its projects and services and how to contract with them, JSI also makes a number of its publications available on their website. There are links to trainings on a variety of topics such as logistics, family planning, refugee health technical assistance, and more. Some of these trainings are through JSI (although you must create an account to navigate these courses), while others are available through external websites. There are also journal articles available from JHI affiliated research and projects.

- Databases and Links: In the resources section of its website, JSI provides links to websites that it has either developed or supports for its partners and clients, many of which are pertinent global health organizations.
- Newsletters: Not exactly a newsletter, but JSI's blog *The Pump* posts relevant news articles, information, and announcements.
- Website: www.jsi.com

Pan American Health Organization

The Pan American Health Organization (PAHO) is the regional office of the World Health Organization in the Americas and is part of the United Nations systems. It is an international public health agency that has been operating for over 100 years to improve health and living standards in the Americas. PAHO is composed of 34 member states, including the U.S. and Canada.

Resources:

- Educational Resources: PAHO's website offers extensive resources, including access to two peer reviewed journals and a related blog. There is also a multimedia section with a large video gallery and links to PAHO's public health channel on YouTube. A portion of the website is also dedicated to interactive maps which track PAHO projects and offices.
- Databases and Links: Several comprehensive databases exist which are searchable by specific health topic, country/region, or project. There are also links to UNICEF and World Bank statistics.
- Internships and Volunteering: Internships are available for full time university students, while volunteer opportunities are open to non-students. All positions are unpaid and typically last six weeks to three months. They are available in local offices as well as PAHO's headquarters in Washington, D.C.

Partners in Health

Partners in Health (PIH) aims to care for its patients, alleviate the root causes of disease, and share lessons learned with other countries and NGOs. They operate on the principles of providing universal access to primary health care, making healthcare and education free to the poor, hiring and training community health care workers, fighting poverty to fight disease, and partnering with local and national governments.

Resources:

- Educational Resources: PIH's website provides archives of all news announcements and press releases, as well as articles and manuals created by the organization. There is also a list of books related to PIH's work and links to purchase. The website also provides a list of recommended reading, organized by countries where the organization works, or by health issue.

- Internships and Volunteering: PIH provides unpaid internships in Boston for summer, spring, and semester sessions. Interns complete a project with a staff mentor on an issue in social justice and health. There are internship and volunteering opportunities with the office in Boston, as well as occasional international volunteering opportunities, many of which are searching for non-medical professionals, including graphics designers, translators, GIS interns, and more.
- Listservs and Forums: PIH provides a variety of groups and online circles on global health topics through its website.
- Website: http://www.pih.org

Peace Care

Peace Care is a non-profit organization dedicated to enacting sustainable grass roots change in the developing world. They primarily partner with Senegal and other low-income countries.

Resources:

- Internships and Volunteering: There are opportunities for professionals and students wanting to volunteer their services in translation, information technology, literature reviews, grant searching and writing, fundraising, social enterprise assistance, creative writing, and administrative assistance.
- Newsletters: A newsletter is sporadically posted on the website
- Website: www.peacecare.org

Shoulder to Shoulder

Shoulder to Shoulder works in the Intibucá Honduras through long-term relationships with communities to reduce poverty through programs in health, education, nutrition, and environmental hygiene.

Resources:

- Internships and Volunteering: Volunteers can choose to participate in two-week brigades along with health professionals, dentists and teachers. Spanish is not required. Construction and bilingual translators are always needed on these trips. There are also longer-term rotations of a month or more, where Spanish proficiency is required. There are also medical rotations for medical students and residents. Volunteers are required to cover their living expenses and airfare.
- Employment Opportunities: There are open positions posted on a career and long-term

opportunities page on the website. These positions are usually compensated minimally with free housing, a cook and a small stipend to help defray costs and travel.

» Website: www.shouldertoshoulder.org

Unite for Sight

Unite for Sight applies best practices in eye care, public health, volunteerism, and social entrepreneurship to achieve their goal of high quality eye care for all. Unite for Sight partners with local eye clinics to provide year-round comprehensive services including examinations by local eye doctors, diagnosis and care for all treatable conditions, education, and prevention.

Resources:

» Educational Resources: Unite for Sight has established a variety of educational resources in its Global Health University. There are a variety of low-cost certificate programs in numerous global health topics, training workshops, online courses, and social enterprise consulting. Costs and additional information are listed on the website.

» Internships and Volunteering:

» International: Unite for Sight has volunteer sites in Ghana, Honduras, and India. Volunteers include physicians, medical students, undergraduates, other health professional students and non-health professionals who are interested in health and development. Available program dates, which range from 7-30 days, are posted on the website. Volunteers are also eligible to participate in an optional research study, the Global Impact Lab.

» Domestic: High schools, universities and graduate programs can establish local chapters, which collaborate with Unite for Sight staff to develop effective, high-impact projects and programs. These typically include educating and training community members on eye care resources, as well as fundraising activities for Unite for Sight's international outreach services.

» Website: http://www.uniteforsight.org/

United Nations Educational, Scientific and Cultural Organization

The United Nations Educational, Scientific, and Cultural Organization (UNESCO) works to create the conditions for dialogue among civilizations, cultures and peoples, based upon respect for commonly shared values. In addition to education, sustainable development, addressing of social and ethical challenges, and fostering cultural diversity, UNESCO also focuses on HIV and AIDS issues.

Resources:

» Educational Resources: UNESCO is active in a variety of global issues and topics such as education, sustainable development, climate change, responsible research, gender equality,

HIV and AIDS, and much more. The website is divided by category, with each category listing relevant links, publications, toolkits, and guidelines. The EDUCAIDS program by UNESCO provides curricular materials on HIV and AIDS, educator training and support documents, and additional strategy documents. UNESCO also publishes guidelines for research ethics committees.

» Databases and Links: There are a variety of external links pertinent to a specific topic listed in the right-hand panel of many of the topic pages.
» Newsletters: Different subcategories have newsletters linked to on the topic webpage. For example, the HIV and AIDS section has a newsletter.

World Health Organization

The World Health Organization (WHO) is the directing and coordinating authority for health within the United Nations system. It is responsible for providing leadership on global health matters, shaping the health research agenda, setting norms and standards, articulating evidence-based policy options, providing technical support to countries and monitoring and assessing health trends.

Resources:

» Educational Resources: The WHO website has a wealth of data and information for public use. There is general information on a variety of priority health topics, data and information on those topics on a global scale, as well as a variety of reports and analysis on data collected on the various topics, organized by main category. The WHO also makes available weekly podcasts on global public health topics.
» Databases and Links: There are databases of WHO guidelines and publications available on the website.
» Internships and Volunteering: The WHO offers an internship program for graduate students working on a topic in one of the WHO departments. Internships last from 6 weeks to 3 months and are unpaid. There is also a Junior Professional Officer program at regional offices sponsored by respective countries.
» Newsletters: The Media Center section of the website posts news, events, and other pertinent information. There is also the option to receive RSS feed of WHO news. They also have a twitter feed.
» Employment Opportunities: Current vacancies and eligibility are listed on the website.
» Website: http://www.who.int/

A Zambian boy and an American student working in his community
Photographer: *Will Bynum*

II. Fellowships and Grants

The American Society of Tropical Medicine and Hygiene

Several fellowships are offered for medical students, residents, physicians, and scientists to pursue research related to tropical medicine. All fellowships provide various amounts of funding to support travel and living expenses. Links to outside resources for additional grant sources are also provided. Fellowships sponsored entirely by ASTMH include:

- Benjamin H. Kean Traveling Fellowship in Tropical Medicine
- Burroughs Wellcome Fund/ASTMH Postdoctoral Fellowship in Tropical Infectious Diseases
- Centennial Travel Award in Basic Science Tropical Disease Research
- Gorgas Memorial Institute Research Award
- Robert E. Shope International Fellowship in Infectious Disease
- Website: http://www.astmh.org/ASTMH_Sponsored_Fellowships.htm

Boren Awards for International Study

Boren Fellowships provide up to $30,000 to U.S. graduate students to add an important international and language component to their graduate education through specialization in area study, language study, or increased language proficiency. Boren Fellowships support study and research in areas of the world that are critical to U.S. interests. Public health and medical students

have utilized Boren Fellowships to study languages, take health-related coursework, intern with non-governmental organizations, and research issues related to medicine and public health in Africa, Asia, Central & Eastern Europe, Eurasia, Latin America, and the Middle East.
Website: http://www.borenawards.org

Don and Elizabeth Hillman International Child Health Grant

The Don and Elizabeth Hillman International Child Health Grant consists of four $750 grants awarded annually to residents and fellows training in Canadian pediatric postgraduate training programs. The grant may be used to complete a pediatric clinical or research elective in a developing country.
Website: http://www.cps.ca/grants-bourses/details/don-elizabeth-hillman-international-child-health

Fulbright Scholarships

Fulbright-Fogarty Fellowships, offered in partnership between the Fulbright Program and the Fogarty International Center of the U.S. National Institutes of Health, have been established to promote the expansion of research in public health and clinical research in resource-limited settings.
Website: http://us.fulbrightonline.org/about/types-of-grants

Fogarty International Center Scholarship

The Fogarty International Center is dedicated to advancing the mission of the National Institutes of Health by supporting and facilitating global health research conducted by U.S. and international investigators, building partnerships between health research institutions in the U.S. and abroad, and training the next generation of scientists to address global health needs.
Website: http://www.fic.nih.gov/Pages/Default.aspx

Global Health Service Corps

Created as a partnership with the Peace Corps, the Global Health Service Corps will place physicians and nurses in education systems and health institutions to increase capacity and strengthen the quality and sustainability of medical, nursing, and midwifery education and clinical practice. Stipends up to $30,000 will be provided to cover debt repayment of educational loans in addition to a monthly living stipend. The pilot program will launch in summer 2013 and initial assignments will be for one year. Website: http://globalhealthservicecorps.org/

The Global Women's Health Fellowship

This opportunity is offered through Brigham and Women's Hospital, a major teaching hospital of Harvard Medical School, the Harvard Global Health Institute and the Harvard School of Public Health. The fellowship is a two year program for physicians in fields related to women's

health including, but not limited to, anesthesiology, obstetrics and gynecology, family medicine, internal medicine, psychiatry, surgery, and medicine/pediatrics. The program is a collaborative research and training program designed to develop future leaders in the field of global women's health.
Website: http://www.brighamandwomens.org/Departments_and_Services/womenshealth/connorscenter/GWH/default.aspx?sub=2

Hubert Global Health Fellowship

This program is offered through the Centers for Disease Control and available to third and fourth year medical and veterinary students. The fellowship provides the opportunity to complete a 6-12 week field assignment under the mentorship of current CDC researchers working on public health projects in developing countries. Students are provided with a $4,000 stipend for travel and living expenses, and are also funded to attend an orientation session at the CDC's headquarters in Atlanta, GA.
Website: http://www.cdc.gov/hubertfellowship/

Stanford—NBC News Fellowship in Media and Global Health

Beginning in 2011, this fellowship opportunity is a partnership between Stanford University's Center for Innovation in Global Health and NBC News. This year-long program allows successful applicants to work with leaders in global health media and reporting to hone their journalistic and writing skills. Medical students who have completed their first two years of medical school, residents, fellows and faculty are eligible to apply.
Website: http://globalhealth.stanford.edu/strategicinitiatives/gh_media_fellowship.html

USAID Global Health Fellows

USAID Global Health Fellows work in a variety of global health technical areas ranging a variety of topics. Fellows work full time for 2 years at a placement site within USAID or one of its implementing partners, and have the possibility of extending their fellowship an additional 2 years. Placements are made in both Washington, DC and in developing countries. Fellows perform a wide range of duties from monitoring and reporting on trends and developments in the global health field to providing technical assistance, writing content, and making recommendations to USAID on project design. Applicants are required to have a master's degree in a relevant field and US citizenship or US permanent residency status.
Website: www.ghfp.net

Yale/Stanford Johnson and Johnson Global Health Scholars Program

The Yale/Stanford Johnson and Johnson Global Health Scholars Program places highly qualified physicians and residents at partner institutions abroad to work and teach in underserved areas. A

stipend is awarded to cover salary and living expenses. Although most scholars come from Yale or Stanford, highly qualified applicants from outside institutions will also be considered.
Website: http://medicine.yale.edu/intmed/globalhealthscholars/index.aspx

Siblings wait for medical care at a clinic run by medical professionals from the United States
Photographer: *Will Bynum*

III. Meetings and Conferences

- The Mount Sinai Global Health Conference
- Hosted by the Mount Sinai School of Medicine Global Health Center
- Location: New York City
- Month: February
- Website: http://mssm-ghc.org

- Western Regional International Health Conference
- Sponsored by the University of Washington and partner institutions in the Western US and Canada
- Location: Alternates yearly from University of Washington to a partner institution
- Month: April
- Website: http://depts.washington.edu/deptgh/index.php

- Unite for Sight International Health Conference
- Hosted by Unite for Sight
- Location: Rotates within the United States

- Month: April
- Website: http://www.uniteforsight.org

- International Conference on Global Health
- Hosted by the Global Health Council
- Location: Washington D.C.
- Month: May-June
- Website: http://www.globalhealth.org/

- Doctors for Global Health General Assembly
- Hosted by Doctors for Global Health
- Location: Rotates nationally in the United States, next in Los Angeles
- Month: July-August, every two years
- Website: http://www.dghonline.org/182

- International AIDS Conference
- Hosted by the International AIDS Society
- Location: Rotates globally
- Month: July-August
- Website: www.iasociety.org

- WONCA Rural Health Conference
- Sponsored by WONCA—the World Organization of Family Doctors
- Location: Rotates globally
- Month: September
- Website: http://www.globalfamilydoctor.com

- Bay Area Global Health Summit
- Hosted by University of California San Francisco Global Health Sciences Group
- Location: San Francisco
- Month: October
- Website: http://globalhealthsciences.ucsf.edu

- Canadian Conference on Global Health
- Hosted by the Canadian Society for International Health
- Location: Ottawa, Canada
- Month: October-November
- Website: http://www.csih.org

- American Public Health Association Annual Meeting and Exposition

- » Sponsored by the American Public Health Association
- » Location: Rotates in the United States
- » Month: November
- » Website: www.apha.org/meetings

- » Annual Meeting of the American Society for Tropical Medicine and Hygiene
- » Hosted by the American Society for Tropical Medicine and Hygiene
- » Location: Rotating in the United States
- » Month: November
- » Website: www.astmh.org

- » Consortium of Universities for Global Health (CUGH)
- » Hosted by CUGH, with partners GHEC and the Canadian Society for International Health
- » Location: Rotates in Canada and the United States
- » Month: March
- » Website: http://cugh.org/meetings/annual

- » American Association of Family Medicine Global Health Workshop
- » Hosted by the American Association of Family Medicine
- » Location: Rotating in the United States
- » Month: Fall
- » Website: http://www.aafp.org/online/en/home/aboutus/specialty/international/oia/cihi/workshop.html

- » The Network: Towards Unity for Health Annual Meeting
- » Hosted by The Network: Towards Unity for Health
- » Location: Rotating (the organization aims to host it each year in a different WHO region)
- » Month: Fall
- » Website: http://www.the-networktufh.org/conferences

- » World Organization of Family Doctors (WONCA)
- » Hosted by WONCA
- » Location: Rotating (regional and international conferences are offered)
- » Month: The international conference is held every three years
- » Website: http://www.globalfamilydoctor.com/Conferences/WONCAWorldConference2013.aspx

CHAPTER 8

Going Global: Approaching International Medical Electives as an Institution

By Eileen Cheung, Jonathan Abelson and David Matthews
Editor Kelly Anderson

HOW DO ACADEMIC INSTITUTIONS BUILD a socially responsible and accountable framework for students to approach international medical electives (IMEs)? This chapter explores a series of eight necessary questions that institutions must ask themselves in order to create successful, start-to-finish institutional frameworks for students engaging in IMEs. Through these questions, we aim to foster elective programs that are safe, educationally sound, and have mutual and reciprocal benefits for the sending and host institutions and communities.

Students from an American medical institution spend a day at the park with children from an orphanage for recovering burn victims
Photographer: *Strasburger*

Context

Demand for global health education has increased dramatically (Kerry et al. 2011), but many institutions have been slow to implement global health education within their core curriculum (Izadnegahdar et al. 2008). Since formal training in global health is often lacking, students frequently participate in IMEs in low resource settings in order to expand their knowledge and gain practical experience in global health. In 2011, 30.5% of graduating US medical students had participated in a global health experience during their medical training (Association of American Medical Colleges 2011). These experiences are likely beneficial for students (Godkin and Savageau 2003; Mutchnick et al. 2003; Thompson et al. 2003), but there is concern about harm to both learners and host communities from ill-prepared students untrained to deal with completely unfamiliar settings (Hanson et al. 2011). There is also concern about the sustainability of electives that are often organized by students as one-off experiences and which can burden already scarce medical education resources in the host community (Crump et al. 2010).

A growing body of literature has emphasized the responsibility of medical schools to properly prepare students for global health immersion experiences (Shah and Wu 2008; Pinto and Upshur 2009; Anderson et al. 2012). It has been argued that sending institutions in wealthier countries have a fiduciary obligation to ensure that students are safe and learn from their elective. In addition, sending institutions can be seen to have a moral obligation to ensure that patients and host institutions are at a minimum not left worse off as a result of international electives, and arguably have a moral obligation to assist in improving care and service delivery in these communities (Crump and Sugarman 2008).

The Global Consensus for Social Accountability of Medical Schools (2010) challenges academic institutions to "have a vision and mission in education, research, and service delivery principally inspired by the current and prospective needs of society", guided by the "basic values of relevance, equity, quality, responsible application of resources in service to needs, sustainability, innovation and partnership, which should prevail in any health system." Our "society" includes marginalized communities, and in the context of global health, students interact with individuals within these communities as part of their training, whether at home or abroad. Thus, medical schools are accountable to these marginalized communities. IMEs must not be held to a different standard than experiences at home.

Specifically, medical schools have three main responsibilities in regards to IMEs, according to Petrosoniak et al (2010): Firstly, to provide pre-departure training for trainees; secondly, to ensure that IME opportunities have sufficient structure to mitigate the negative effects of medical tourism; and thirdly, to provide opportunities for trainees to conduct self-reflection and to critically assess their global experiences. The Working Group on Ethics Guidelines for Global Health Training (WEIGHT) also provide greater detail on the responsibilities of the host and sending institutions, as well as the students, for ethics and best practices in field-based global health programs (Crump et al. 2010).

Given the pressing institutional responsibilities surrounding IMEs, we suggest that faculty involved in creating IMEs go through the following eight questions. They will not only guide the development of pre-departure and post-return debriefing strategies for IMEs, but will also address the creation of an overarching global health educational programming framework that will underlie safe[1], educationally valuable[2], and socially responsible and accountable[3] experiences for their students.

Critical Questions for Institutions:

Question 1: As an institution, what is our guiding global health philosophy or approach?

In their article on global health ethics for students, Pinto and Upshur (2009) discuss four guiding principles to approaching global health work: humility, introspection, solidarity and social justice. These guiding principles are equally applicable to institutions and faculty engaging in global health work, including the facilitation of learners participating in IMEs. How can institutions build honesty about their motivations, their strengths and level of expertise when deciding to engage in global health initiatives and entering into partnerships? Without careful and thorough examination of these issues, an institution cannot build and support an environment to encourage their learners to do likewise. Learners should understand that the decision to go on an IME, where and with whom, is not one to be taken lightly. Similarly, the responsibility of the sending institution to prepare their medical students for participation in global health work should be taken seriously.

Sharma and Anderson (2012) pose the question, "What is our global health program's underlying philosophy?" What are the goals of the institution's participation in global health work, through IMEs or otherwise? Recognizing your institution's strengths and limitations in the context of these guiding principles and questions can provide insight when evaluating whether new global health opportunities are appropriate for your institution. It can also guide the development of leadership and expertise within your institution to align itself with the institution's goals for global health engagement. Appendix 1 provides a list of questions your institution may wish to consider prior to engaging in new global health initiatives.

Question 2: How do we foster and implement our global health philosophy as an institution?

A comprehensive global health curriculum is vital to framing the attitude with which a learner approaches how he will be engaged with global health work through IMEs and into her future career. Though the majority of global health learning currently takes place during IMEs, we may wish to ask ourselves whether these experiences are justified, or even necessary to learn about global health issues. Jane Philpott (2010) writes:

> *It may be that the demands of students need to be shaped and challenged. These marvellously altruistic young people should be exposed early in their education to a challenging discussion of what really does impact global health outcomes. And many of us may not want to pay the price of addressing the overarching determinants of global health outcomes.*

A more comprehensive global health curriculum should be offered as a foundational navigational tool, forming the base of knowledge should a medical student decide to become involved with IMEs (Battat et al. 2010; Arthur et al. 2011). Relevant curriculum topics are discussed at length elsewhere, but at minimum, it should address global health disparities and their evolution, both amongst nations and within nations, the structural barriers to health and health access, global governance and a brief history of "development" (Sharma and Anderson 2012). It is important for learners to understand that development work comes with "historical baggage," as it is inherently tied to colonialism and mission work. Appendix 2 offers a list of questions that students should be encouraged to reflect upon "pre-engagement" and may be incorporated as part of the above-mentioned global health curriculum.

Question 3: How do we fit IMEs into an overall institutional global health philosophy or approach?

Crump et al. (2010) propose that the best way to ensure that learners' IME experiences reflect the best practices intended by their home institutions is for the IME to be a part of a well-structured program developed by the institutions themselves. The following are recommended components intended to help foster a sensitive and ethics-informed culture around IMEs:

1. Well-structured programs between a sending and host institution (Crump et al. 2010): Global health training opportunities should be designed to serve specific purposes with defined goals and objectives. Roles, responsibilities, duration of partnership and expectations should be discussed and made explicit, with frequent re-evaluation. The priorities and needs of hosting institutions should be at the forefront of a program's formation. In the creation of these programs, it may be helpful to refer to your institution's answers to the questions in Appendix 1 and to ensure that such programs are in keeping with your global health program's philosophy.

2. Long-term, mutually beneficial, equitable and sustainable partnerships (Pinto and Upshur 2009; Crump et al. 2010): Some of the potential harms of short-term IMEs may be mitigated if they are nested within such established partnerships. Partners should seek to invest in each other, with the sending institution bearing in mind the many costs of IMEs to a resource-constrained hosting institution (e.g., financial, human resources, opportunities for local learners). Institutions need

to recognize that building and maintaining such partnerships require investments in the form of human resources, financial resources, and time. When institutions are not in a position to make or sustain such investments, they should consider partnering with non-profit or other institutions that are able to dedicate resources toward fostering and sustaining global partnerships.

3. Development of faculty mentors for learners: Mentors can provide personalized and informal guidance to learners who are considering, preparing for, or on an IME experience. Training and developing mentors within your institution is also a means to maintain interest and activity within the global health program and serve as a feed-forward mechanism to provide sustainability and expansion of global health education initiatives and partnerships.

4. "Local global health" experiences: Consider the marginalized communities in our own backyard. "Global health" has expanded to encompass the health issues faced by marginalized populations, including the homeless, those in the inner city, immigrants, refugees, and Aboriginal populations. In their global health ethics article, Pinto and Upshur (2009) suggest that "Further consideration must be given to the connection between the problems of the developing world, the inner city poor and Aboriginal programs." The "Making the Links" program (http://www.medicine.usask.ca/leadership/social-accountability/mtl/index.html), an innovative service-learning program at the University of Saskatchewan, seeks to do just that. Medical students are selected to participate in a two-year program involving formal global health didactic teaching as well as mandatory experiential learning at inner city clinics, in a First Nations community in remote northern Saskatchewan, and in a rural community in Mozambique (Meili et al. 2011). Other institutions have created structured elective clinical opportunities for students to work with local marginalized communities, including in HIV/AIDS care, care for homeless populations, and with Aboriginal populations. Student-run, physician-supervised clinics have been yet another avenue to engage with marginalized populations. In local approaches to global health and working with marginalized populations at home, the same guiding principles and motivations should be reflected upon as for electives abroad. In parallel, the same care should be given in preparation to work with these populations—gaining an understanding of the history and culture of the community, and pre-departure training (to be discussed in detail below).

Question 4: How do we approach IMEs set up by students themselves, which are not established by our institution?

Institutions may not currently be in a position to offer IMEs to their students within a well-structured program, or students may choose to go on IMEs with different institutions or organizations. Nonetheless, students should be encouraged to work with institutions or organizations that offer IMEs through well-structured programs and those which have long-term partnerships with local institutions or organizations that are mutually beneficial, equitable, and sustainable. Tourism

Concern suggest the following criteria when evaluating an external institution or organization for such guiding principles (Tourism Concern 2012):

1. That the sending organization is clear about their aims, values and ethos
2. That the organization will not make false claims to the efficacy and effects of their programs
3. That the organization's program and placement are based on achievable objectives that have been identified by host partners and communities
4. That the financial costs to host partners and communities are assessed and provision is made to fully meet those costs; and that the organization will provide the information to aid potential volunteers in their decision-making and to learn as much as possible about the requirements of the placement

Tourism Concern also advise students to choose organizations that provide a full breakdown of the costs associated with their specific placement; those which provide clear information, including local contact names, addresses and host organizations with which the learner will be working; and that the organization provide compulsory structured training specific to the placement and country, covering at minimum the topics of cultural awareness, and the roles, responsibilities, and conduct expected of the learner. Institutions should evaluate IMEs for the above criteria and guiding principles when considering whether an IME should be granted for academic credit or funding.

Question 5: How do we select the right candidates for IMEs?

While not always the case, most learners who participate in IMEs will be seeking academic credit or funding from their home institution for such an experience. Institutions can thus take advantage of the application process as another opportunity to facilitate reflection and maximal preparation for a learner's IME. A detailed, standardized application process necessitating explicitly written objectives and plans can help learners evaluate a potential IME for logistical and ethical problems. Appendix 3 contains a template for an IME application and addresses specific considerations for research IMEs. Crump et al. (2010) recommend selecting learners for IMEs who are adaptable, motivated to address global health issues, sensitive to local priorities, willing to listen and learn, whose abilities and experience matches the expectations of the position, and who will be good representatives of their home institution and country. By investing in and implementing socially accountable global health philosophies and frameworks, institutions may be able to foster such qualities in all of their global health learners.

Question 6: How do we adequately prepare students prior to departure on IMEs?

Training taking place prior to departure for an IME is ideally done within the context of a comprehensive global health curriculum and overarching institutional philosophy about global health engagement. Given that these often do not exist, establishing effective pre-departure training (PDT) and post-return debriefing (PRD) is one of the key first steps that medical schools can take in improving their global health programs and addressing some of the ethical and safety issues inherent in IMEs. In this section, we discuss PDT. PRD is addressed below under Question 8.

PDT can be defined as "any preparation that students complete before taking part in a global health elective that has as its goal building trainee competence in the skills necessary to maximize learning while also minimizing harm to themselves and the communities in which they study" (Anderson et al. 2012). Along with concurrent global health curriculum, PDT provides a venue for students to reflect on the type of elective they wish to plan and to understand the benefits as well as harms that can come from this kind of engagement (Philpott 2010). It also encourages students to ask important questions regarding the best timing of their placement as it relates to clinical competency and scope of practice. Without necessary structure, IMEs can result in the serious ethical beech of practicing beyond one's scope of competency (Banatvala and Doyal 1998; Edwards et al. 2004; Crump and Sugarman 2008). Recognizing that ethics training for practice at home is not necessarily applicable or comprehensive enough to include experiences globally, ethics training is an essential precursor to global health work, providing students with the guidance to become reflective global health practitioners (Pinto and Upshur 2009).

The Canadian Federation of Medical Students (CFMS) and the Association of Faculties of Medicine of Canada (AFMC) collaborated to publish a set of national guidelines for PDT in 2008 (AFMC Global Health Resource Group and CFMS Global Health Program 2008). The guidelines outline five core themes in Pre-Departure Training, including personal health, travel safety, cultural competency, language competency and ethical considerations. Along with a concerted lobbying effort, the publication of these guidelines has lead to an increase in the number of Canadian medical schools offering PDT from 11/17 [65%] in 2008 to 16/17 [94%] in 2010. In addition, the number of schools requiring mandatory PDT nearly doubled from 6/17 [35%] to 11/17 [65%] (Anderson et al. 2012). A 2008 online survey of 103 American medical schools indicated that 32 (31.1%) offered a pre-travel preparatory course (McKinley et al. 2008). While these results are encouraging, there is clearly room to expand and improve upon these programs.

A list of topics that should be addressed during PDT can be found in Appendix 4. In addition, the Ethics of International Engagement & Service Learning Project (eIESL), based at the University of British Columbia, have developed an excellent resource kit of practical activities (http://ethicsofisl.ubc.ca/?page_id=1750) addressing cultural competency and ethics of global health engagement, which can be used in PDT training (Ethics of International Engagement and Service-Learning Project 2011).

Question 7: How can we support students during their IMEs?

The first consideration is adequate and effective supervision. Institutions and learners should ensure that supervision appropriate to the learner's level of training is accessible. On the other hand, supervision of IME learners should not occur at a cost to local learners or patient care. Expected scope of practice based on level of training and medical programs often differ internationally. To facilitate learner and patient safety, sending institutions may wish to write a letter to the hosting institution to explicitly define the learner's level of training, as well as scope of practice. This may prevent situations in which students are asked to perform tasks or procedures beyond what is appropriate for their level of training and works to ensure adequate supervision (Crump et al. 2010). In addition, sending institutions must recognize that those equipped to supervise students in the Western context (i.e., US institutional faculty) may not be experts in an international setting. It is important that local faculty and supervisors are given appropriate credit and empowerment as 'experts' within their local health care, cultural, and related realities. Whenever possible and appropriate, students should be learning from local practitioners rather than those imported from foreign institutions.

Secondly, institutions should consider the importance of regular contact with their learner during the IME. Sending institutions should provide an emergency contact that learners may utilize in the case of a crisis, including both logistical and ethical crises that arise during the elective. Consideration may be given to regular liaison between learners and an IME coordinator or mentor to evaluate and review learning goals and objectives as the IME progresses.

Thirdly, institutions should consider logistics, including the development of an emergency evacuation plan for learners in the case of political instability or natural disasters. This is most easily facilitated by purchasing medical, travel and evacuation insurance for the period abroad. Learners and institutions or organizations should both be aware of and in agreement of these plans. Learners should register with the embassy of their home country on arrival at the place of their IME. Institutions or the organizations they work with to facilitate IMEs should consider collecting health histories, current medication lists, and related information from students prior to departure. This will assist in the instance of exacerbations of physical or mental illness that occurs under the stress and exposures encountered during IMEs. In addition, institutions or the organizations they utilize for IMEs should have policies relevant to universal precautions, body fluid exposures, needle stick injuries, and post-exposure prophylaxis.

Finally, institutions should develop a formal code of conduct for IMEs. Expectations and norms of professional conduct should be reviewed with learners prior to their IME. Professional standards of the sending and hosting institutions should be addressed, with special consideration given to differing cultural views (e.g., appropriate dress; differing approaches to communication and conflict resolution, gender roles, etc.) (AFMC Global Health Resource Group and CFMS Global Health Program 2008; Crump et al. 2010).

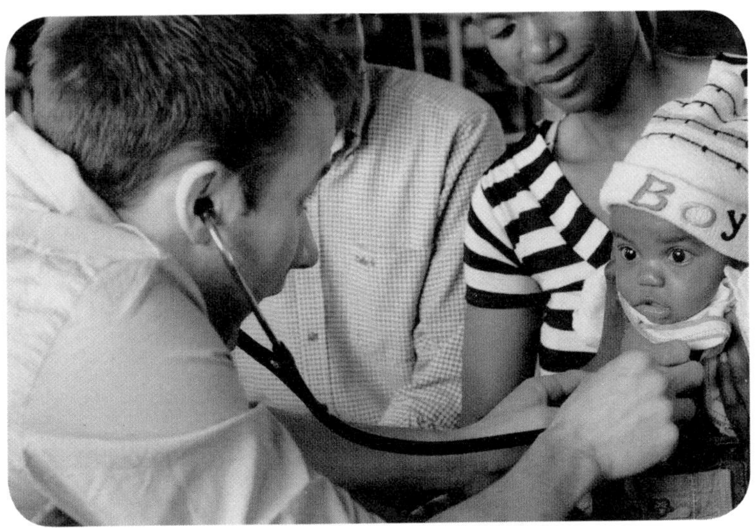

A medical student examines a child in a clinic in rural Africa
Photographer: *Erin Berry*

Question 8: How do we create ideal post-return debriefing (PRD) after IMEs?

Students that return from IMEs are almost certain to have mixed ideas, attitudes and emotions surrounding their experiences. Given the complexity of IMEs, students may experience confusion and possible frustration or disillusionment. It becomes crucial for institutions to develop a PRD program to assist students to process what they observed, mitigate negative effects of moral distress (Lomis et al. 2009) and provide guidance for exploring a career in global health (Lorntz et al. 2008).

As stated previously, medical schools that offer IMEs have a responsibility "to provide opportunities for trainees to conduct self-reflection and to critically assess their [IME] experiences" (Petrosoniak et al. 2010). Lorntz et al. (2008) similarly advocate for incorporating debriefing support as a part of a larger aim of framing each student's work internationally. In fact, there is a general trend to incorporate reflection in all areas of medical education (Aronson et al. 2011), not just in IMEs. According to Aronson et al, reflection is "critical in training physicians who (1) respond creatively to complex health systems, clinical cases, and social situations, (2) participate collaboratively in teams, (3) behave professionally and compassionately in stressful work environments, and (4) have the motivation and skills to continuously improve their practice."

Reflection has many meanings in the medical education literature, but in this discussion, we refer to "the critical analysis of personal experience to enhance learning and improve future behavior and outcomes" (Aronson et al. 2011). Taking it one step further, critical reflection "is the process of analyzing, questioning, and reframing an experience in order to make an assessment of it for the purposes of learning (reflective learning) and/or to improve practice (reflective practice)" (Aronson 2011). Aronson and Niehaus have conceived of a guide for educators to develop a reflective activity at their own institution (Aronson 2011; Aronson et al. 2011).

There are many competing elements to address during a debriefing session. What went well and did not go well for the student? What were the major challenges, and how were they overcome, or not? Were learning objectives met? What could we have done better to prepare the student? Was there adequate supervision or mentorship? What was the perceived impact on the community, and what demand, if any, did the student's presence place upon the community? Would the student continue engagement in this community in the future, or be willing to mentor future students in this process? Is there additional support required by the student following the experience, such as counseling? Is there additional learning required by the student following the IME, such as further reading or local electives?

Offering feedback to the student is a crucial step of the reflection process to enhance learning opportunities, not just in global health, but also in medical education as a whole. According to Branch and Paranjape (2002), "feedback is the heart of medical education." We advocate for formal feedback wherein mentor and mentee set aside at least 30 minutes for discussion. With respect to this chapter's topic, mentors should provide feedback on a number of issues including student performance on IMEs and the content of the student's reflection (Aronson 2011). Branch and Paranjape offer a guide on providing feedback effectively (Branch and Paranjape 2002).

There are many possible structures to a debriefing session. Options include meeting one-on-one with a mentor, or meeting in a group setting with a mentor and other students. Aronson (2011) suggests that shared reflection may be more beneficial than individual reflection. It may be possible for the students to write a reflection, or make a poster presentation, either locally at a school sponsored event, or at a larger global health conference (see Chapter 7 for list of conferences).

Conclusion

While an increasing number of medical students are participating in IMEs, they are often doing so without sufficient formal training to prepare them for the challenges of such ventures. Without proper guidance from institutions or organizations before, during and after the elective, these electives may cause harm for both the student and the host community. This chapter seeks to serve as a guide for institutions to create successful, start-to-finish institutional frameworks for students engaging in IMEs or to pursue rigorously assessed partnerships with organizations that provide sound IMEs. Ideally, institutions that offer IMEs should do so in the setting of a comprehensive global health curriculum to ensure that learners' experiences are safe, educationally valuable, and socially responsible and accountable. Pre-departure training (PDT) and post-return debriefing (PRD) are two integral components of any IME that institutions should develop to strengthen not only the student's experience, but also the partnership between the institution and host community.

Highlighted Resources

Pinto, A. and R. Upshur (2009). "Global health ethics for students." Developing world bioethics **9**(1): 1-10.

Crump, J. A., J. Sugarman and Working Group on Ethics Guidelines for Global Health Training (WEIGHT) (2010). "Ethics and best practice guidelines for training experiences in global health." American journal of tropical medicine and hygeine **83**(6): 1178-1182.

AFMC Global Health Resource Group and CFMS Global Health Program. (2008). "Preparing Medical Students for Electives in Low-Resource Settings: A Template for National Pre-Departure Training." Retrieved March 23, 2012, from http://www.cfms.org/downloads/Pre-Departure Guidelines Final.pdf.

University of Michigan Center for Global Health. (2010). "Student Handbook for Global Engagement." Retrieved May 12, 2012, from http://www.globalhealth.umich.edu/pdf/CGH_standards_handbookV2.pdf.

Ethics of International Engagement and Service-Learning Project. (2011). "Global Praxis: Exploring the ethics of engagement abroad." Retrieved May 12, 2012, from http://ethicsofisl.ubc.ca/downloads/_2011-EIESL-kit-hiRes.pdf.

Appendix 1. **Questions Institutions Should Ask of Themselves** (adapted from Crump et al. (2010), Pinto and Upshur (2009), Boelen and Heck (1995))

Pre-engagement

- What is our global health program's underlying philosophy? (Sharma and Anderson 2012)
- What are the goals of our global health program?
- What are our motivations in engaging in global health work?
- What's in it for our partners? How important is this question to us as an institution?
- What will be the benefits and unintended consequences of global health electives to host institutions and host trainees (Crump et al. 2010)? How will this be measured? What mechanisms will we have in place to respond to unintended consequences?
- Is this work "socially accountable"? (i.e., Is it relevant, high quality, cost-effective, and equitable?) (Boelen and Heck 1995)

Engagement

In regards to partnerships:

- Who are the stakeholders of this endeavour and are all stakeholders involved?
- What are the goals of our partner?
- What are the expectations that the partner institution has?
- What are the benefits for each partner?
- Will this project be sustainable?
- In this partnership, who is setting the agenda? Who defines the goals, objectives, timelines, etc. of the projects within this partnership?

In regards to IMEs:

- Who will benefit?
- What are the costs and who will bear them?
- What are our institution's objectives for IMEs?
- What kind of experiences should receive academic credit?
- What kind of experiences should receive funding?
- How should students logistically prepare for their IME to address safety, meeting educational objectives and social responsibility?
- What kind of pre-engagement and pre-departure training should students receive?

Post-return debriefing

- » How will our institution evaluate the safety, educational value, and social responsibility of IME experiences? What mechanisms will we have in place to act upon these evaluations?
- » What are the mechanisms we have in place to review the progress, goals, and objectives of our partnerships?

Appendix 2. **Pre-Engagement Questions Institutions Should Encourage Students to Ask of Themselves** (adapted from Pinto and Upshur (2009), Philpott (2010), the University of Michigan Student Handbook for Global Engagement (2010))

1. Why do you hope to do this work?
2. What are my motivations?
    a. What are motivations that I would rather suppress?
    b. What are motivations that I can tolerate?
    c. What are motivations that I aspire to?
3. What are your objectives, personal and structural, short and long-term?
4. What are the benefits and who will receive them, and what are the costs, and who will bear them?
5. In the context of very limited resources for global health needs, is your elective justified? What exists close-by?
6. Will this specific rotation meet my objectives?
7. What do you need to do to prepare for your elective, both practical and personal?
    a. Do I currently have the skills to maximize the benefits and minimize the costs/ harms? If not, can I get obtain these skills in time before I go?
    b. Is this the most appropriate time in my training to have this experience?
8. Where are the weaknesses in your plan, specifically?
9. Is the work feasible, cost-effective, necessary, focused, and justified?
10. Will it work to undermine disparity, or actually contribute to it? Will there be a net benefit to the community?
    a. What will be the effect of my being present on patients? On the community? On local health care workers and physicians?
11. Is your work sustainable, and if not, will this leave a negative impact?
12. What do I know and understand about the culture of this community?
13. What are the cultural differences of this community from my experiences and framework at home, and how will this affect my practice?

14. How will resource constraints impact on my practices at home?
15. What do you hope to bring back to your community, and whom will you share it with?

Additional considerations for research projects and research electives

1. Will this research serve the health, social, political and economic goals of the community?
2. Was this research question identified by the hosting community or institution?
3. Who will benefit from the process and from the outcome?
4. How will the research findings be disseminated? Who will have access to the results?
5. What are the motivations of those who are funding this research project?
6. How will I ensure that informed consent is obtained from research participants?

Appendix 3. **IME Application Template** (adapted from the Western University Global Health Funding Committee criteria (2010), and the University of Michigan Student Handbook for Global Engagement (2010))

1. Define clear, realistic learning objectives for your elective experience.
2. Proposed elective details
    a. Elective location
    b. Name of organization/institution and its affiliations
    c. Primary supervisor and his/her appointment
    d. Dates of elective
    e. Expected activities, schedule (and timelines*)
    f. Approval by research ethics review boards of both sending and hosting institution*
3. Expected impact of elective
    a. Potential benefits and harms to applicant
    b. Potential benefits and harms to community
    c. Based on community-identified need*
    d. Sustainability*
4. Deliverables
    a. To the community

i. Dissemination of results*, intellectual property rights* (if applicable)

    b. To the sending (home) institution
5. Travel plans
    a. Travelling to get to elective (air and ground transportation)
    b. Travel plans (for leisure, if applicable)

6. Accommodations
7. Detailed budget
    a. Tuition or program costs
    b. Compensation to site/organisation/supervisor
    c. Sources of funding*
    d. Travel expenses
    e. Health and travel insurance
8. Evidence of attendance of formal pre-departure training

*highlighted as a consideration especially related to research projects

Appendix 4. **Recommendations for Pre-Departure Training** (adapted from AFMC and CFMS (2008), Crump et al. (2010), University of Michigan Student Handbook for Global Engagement (2010))

1. **Personal Health**

This includes a discussion of:

» basic health precautions
» immunizations
» health insurance
» personal protective equipment
» post-exposure prophylaxis
» how and where to access medical care while on elective

2. **Travel Safety**

This includes gaining prior knowledge of:

» local contacts
» transportation options and housing arrangements
» packing requirements
» registration with the embassy of the learner's home country
» local laws and customs
» awareness of the most current travel advisory warnings and how to access this information
» emergency preparedness and evacuation plans

3. **Cultural Competency**

Learners should have an understanding of:

» the concept of culture
» acting with humility
» the specifics of the culture of communities within their placement
» intercultural relationships
» historical trends in the region and community
» religion
» role of traditional healers
» gender norms
» appropriate dress
» the meaning of purchasing and consuming alcohol in the host community
» norms of professionalism of the sending and hosting institutions
» standards of practice of the sending and hosting institutions
» valuing the knowledge and experience of collaborators (both individuals and institutions)
» appropriate conflict resolution and communication skills (in the context of culture)

4. **Language Competencies**
Learners should have an understanding of:

» the language requirements of the IME and the host institution's expectations for level of language competency
» at minimum, language basics

Learners should gain experience working with interpreters, if applicable.

5. **Ethical Considerations**
If not already previously addressed during other global health curriculum, as discussed above, PDT is an opportunity for students to reflect upon the ethical challenges they may encounter on their elective. Discussions should include:

» personal motivations for going on an IME
» an ethical framework to approach various problems
» an expected professional code of conduct
» patient confidentiality (e.g., in light of blogs)
» establishing goals, objectives, level of training and limitations early on with supervisors
» ensuring appropriate and effective supervision and mentorship of IME learners and associated costs to local learners and care provision
» appropriate licensing and privileges for clinical work during the IME
» research-specific considerations
» focuses on interest, priorities, needs and relevance to host
» following research procedures of host and sending institution

» obtain ethics committee approval for the research before initiation of research
» receive appropriate training in research ethics
» follow international standards for authorship of publications
» discuss issues and plans for presentations early in collaborations

References

AFMC Global Health Resource Group and CFMS Global Health Program. (2008). "Preparing medical students for electives in low-resource settings: A template for national pre-departure training." Retrieved March 23, 2012, from http://www.cfms.org/downloads/Pre-Departure Guidelines Final.pdf.

Anderson, K. C., M. A. Slatnik, I. Pereira, E. Cheung, K. Xu and T. F. Brewer (2012). "Are we there yet? Preparing Canadian medical students for global health electives." Academic medicine **87**(2): 206-209.

Aronson, L. (2011). "Twelve tips for teaching reflection at all levels of medical education." Medical teacher **33**(3): 200-205.

Aronson, L., B. Niehaus, J. Lindow, P. A. Robertson and P. S. O'Sullivan (2011). "Development and pilot testing of a reflective learning guide for medical education." Medical teacher **33**(10): e515-521.

Arthur, M. A. M., R. Battat and T. F. Brewer (2011). "Teaching the basics: Core competencies in global health." Infectious disease clinics of North America **25**(2): 347-358.

Association of American Medical Colleges. (2011). "Medical school graduation questionnaire—2011 all schools summary report." Retrieved February 8, 2012, from https://http://www.aamc.org/data/gq/allschoolsreports/.

Banatvala, N. and L. Doyal (1998). "Knowing when to say "no" on the student elective. Students going on electives abroad need clinical guidelines." BMJ **316**(7142): 1404-1405.

Battat, R., G. Seidman, N. Chadi, M. Y. Chanda, J. Nehme, J. Hulme, A. Li, N. Faridi and T. F. Brewer (2010). "Global health competencies and approaches in medical education: a literature review." BMC medical education **10**(2): 347-358.

Boelen, C. and J. Heck. (1995). "Defining and measuring the social accountability of medical schools." Retrieved March 3, 2012, from http://whqlibdoc.who.int/hq/1995/WHO_HRH_95.7.pdf.

Branch, W. T. and A. Paranjape (2002). "Feedback and reflection: teaching methods for clinical settings." Academic medicine **77**(12 Pt 1): 1185-1188.

Crump, J. A. and J. Sugarman (2008). "Ethical considerations for short-term experiences by trainees in global health." JAMA **300**(12): 1456-1458.

Crump, J. A., J. Sugarman and Working Group on Ethics Guidelines for Global Health Training (WEIGHT)

(2010). "Ethics and best practice guidelines for training experiences in global health." American journal of tropical medicine and hygeine **83**(6): 1178-1182.

Edwards, R., J. Piachaud, M. Rowson and J. Miranda (2004). "Understanding global health issues: are international medical electives the answer?" Medical education **38**(7): 688-690.

Ethics of International Engagement and Service-Learning Project. (2011). "Global Praxis: Exploring the ethics of engagement abroad." Retrieved May 12, 2012, from http://ethicsofisl.ubc.ca/downloads/ 2011-EIESL-kit-hiRes.pdf.

Global Consensus for Social Accountability of Medical Schools. (2010). "Global consensus for social accountability of medical schools." Retrieved July 5, 2012, from http://healthsocialaccountability.org/.

Godkin, M. and J. Savageau (2003). "The effect of medical students' international experiences on attitudes toward serving underserved multicultural populations." Family medicine **35**(4): 273-278.

Hanson, L., S. Harms and K. Plamondon (2011). "Undergraduate international medical electives: some ethical and pedagogical considerations." Journal of studies in international education **15**: 171-185.

Izadnegahdar, R., S. Correia, B. Ohata, A. Kittler, S. ter Kuile, S. Vaillancourt, N. Saba and T. F. Brewer (2008). "Global health in Canadian medical education: current practices and opportunities." Academic medicine **83**(2): 192-198.

Kerry, V. B., T. Ndung'u, R. P. Walensky, P. T. Lee, V. F. I. B. Kayanja and D. R. Bangsberg (2011). "Managing the demand for global health education." PLoS medicine **8**(11): e1001118.

Lomis, K. D., R. O. Carpenter and B. M. Miller (2009). "Moral distress in the third year of medical school; a descriptive review of student case reflections." American journal of surgery **197**(1): 107-112.

Lorntz, B., J. R. Boissevain, R. Dillingham, J. Kelly, A. Ballard, W. M. Scheld and R. L. Guerrant (2008). "A trans-university center for global health." Academic medicine **83**(2): 165-172.

McKinley, D. W., S. R. Williams, J. J. Norcini and M. B. Anderson (2008). "International exchange programs and U.S. medical schools." Academic medicine **83**(10 Suppl): S53-57.

Meili, R., D. Fuller and J. Lydiate (2011). "Teaching social accountability by making the links: qualitative evaluation of student experiences in a service-learning project." Medical teacher **33**(8): 659-666.

Mutchnick, I. S., C. A. Moyer and D. T. Stern (2003). "Expanding the boundaries of medical education: evidence for cross-cultural exchanges." Academic medicine **78**(10 Suppl): S1-5.

Petrosoniak, A., A. McCarthy and L. Varpio (2010). "International health electives: thematic results of student and professional interviews." Medical education **44**(7): 683-689.

Philpott, J. (2010). "Training for a global state of mind." Virtual mentor **12**(3): 231-236.

Pinto, A. and R. Upshur (2009). "Global health ethics for students." Developing world bioethics **9**(1): 1-10.

Shah, S. and T. Wu (2008). "The medical student global health experience: professionalism and ethical implications." Journal of medical ethics **34**(5): 375-378.

Sharma, M. and K. Anderson (2012). Approaching global health as a learner. An Introduction to Global Health Ethics (in press).

Thompson, M. J., M. K. Huntington, D. D. Hunt, L. E. Pinsky and J. J. Brodie (2003). "Educational effects of international health electives on U.S. and Canadian medical students and residents: a literature review." Academic medicine **78**(3): 342-347.

Tourism Concern. (2012). "Gap Year & International Volunteerism Standard (GIVS)." Retrieved May 12, 2012, from http://www.tourismconcern.org.uk/givs.html.

University of Michigan Center for Global Health. (2010). "Student handbook for global engagement." Retrieved May 12, 2012, from http://www.globalhealth.umich.edu/pdf/CGH_standards_handbookV2.pdf.

Western University Global Health Office. (2010). "Funding criteria of the Global Health Funding Committee." Retrieved July 9. 2012, from http://www.schulich.uwo.ca/globalhealth/financialassistance/files/documents/GHFCfundingcriteria.pdf.

Defining Principles

1. "Safe" IMEs should include experiences which support the physical, mental and emotional well-being of the learner, the patient, and the community.
2. "Educationally valuable" IMEs should meet a learner's pre-defined goals and objectives for the experience and satisfy the institution's criteria for academic rigour, educational objectives and outcomes, level of supervision and professional standards in line with those expected of other research or clinical experiences.
3. "Socially responsible and accountable" experiences should encourage learners to reflect on the ethics and context of their global health engagement and global citizenship.

CHAPTER 9

Local Health is Global Health

Kate McCalmont MD
Department of Family and Community Medicine
University of New Mexico

Erin Corriveau MD
Department of Family and Community Medicine
University of New Mexico

Tania Rezai MPH
MD Candidate, Stanford University School of Medicine

Lauren Wempe BA
MD Candidate, University of Colorado School of Medicine

Editor

Jack Chase MD
Department of Family and Community Medicine
University of California, San Francisco

Introduction

IN ORDER TO DISCUSS THE interconnectedness of local and international work and demonstrate the shared themes between local health and global health, we must first consider a definition of "global health." Koplan et al propose "global health as an area for study, research, and practice that places a priority on improving health and achieving equity in health for all people worldwide. Global health emphasizes transnational health issues, determinants, and solutions; involves many disciplines within and beyond the health sciences and promotes interdisciplinary collaboration; and is a synthesis of population-based prevention with individual-level clinical care".[1] Koplan et al suggest that global health includes attention to "domestic health disparities as well as cross-border issues".[1] With this perspective and definition, our work to address health disparities and equity at the local level is an integral part of global health.

Global health was born out of public health and international health, and these three disciplines share important themes including "priority on a population-based and preventive focus; concentration on poorer, vulnerable, and underserved populations; multidisciplinary and interdisciplinary approaches; emphasis on health as a public good and the importance of systems and structures; and the participation of several stakeholders."[1] Many of the themes that arise in international work are reflected in our work in home communities.

When discussing the role of medical education in local health and global health, it is important to consider the growing body of literature on social accountability of medical schools. In 1995, the World Health Organization (WHO) defined social accountability for medical schools "as the obligation to direct their education, research and service activities towards addressing the priority health concerns of the community, region, and/or nation they have a mandate to serve. The priority health concerns are to be identified jointly by governments, health care organizations, health professionals and the public".[2] Social accountability involves both the relevance of medical education and the graduate it produces; thus, medical schools must be held accountable for not only producing excellent clinicians, but physicians who are prepared to address community health issues.

Given that local health work is an essential component of global health work and that medical schools must be held accountable for improving the health of society, we must consider how to develop curricula that prepare health science students to address the health needs of local and global communities. A number of medical schools and medical education organizations focus directly on this charge. The Global Health Education Consortium (GHEC) sought to improve "the health and human rights of underserved populations worldwide and the ability of the global workforce to meet their needs through improved education and training".[3] GHEC has now merged with Consortium of Universities for Global Health. The Training for Health Equity Network (THEnet), a group of eleven health professions schools around the world brought together by a GHEC project, strives to "increase the impact of academic institutions on health and the development of equitable health systems".[4] Social accountability and a focus on the underserved are core tenants of THEnet's mission.

The WHO helps to guide the effort toward health equity and training for allied health workers responsive to their communities. The values of social accountability, as defined by the WHO, include relevance, quality, cost-effectiveness and equity.[2] These values can form the basis of how curriculum is created and assessed. To address them, medical schools must constantly update the priority health issues based on the community needs, provide high quality care in the context of cultural expectations, achieve the greatest impact on health while making the best use of their resources, and assure that quality care is available to all people in all countries.[2]

Local health and global health practitioners are one and the same. They must recognize the two-way transfer of knowledge and skills between communities near and far, and apply a keen focus on the members of society carrying the greatest burden of disease. In this chapter, we will demonstrate the connections between local health and global health and we will show that skills health science students gain working in culturally diverse, underserved communities are useful in both local and international settings. The global health competencies outlined in Chapter 4 can be taught and reinforced through work in underserved local or international communities. Additionally, through global collaboration, innovative ways to address inequity and improve care must be shared and applied to the local health or medical education systems.

It is essential that medical schools infuse global health themes throughout the curriculum to provide context for international health experiences that occur in discrete, isolated blocks of time. The incorporation of longitudinal, integrated global health education improves students understanding of the themes relevant to all underserved communities and increases emphasis on preventive health, equity, and social accountability. Furthermore, by developing sustainable long-term local partnerships, health professional schools will have the opportunity to begin to transform the health of our nation by starting with the communities that often face the greatest disparities. An institutional commitment to training health professionals that are conscious of these health disparities and have the skills to address them is essential to creating a new generation of leaders in health care that will be able to tackle the health care challenges seen both locally and globally.

With this definition of global health and the lens of social accountability, we will describe themes that bridge local health work and international work, highlight global health curriculum examples from medical schools, and propose future directions for curriculum development to advance global health and social accountability.

Volunteers repair a house damaged during Hurricane Katrina
Photographer: *Claire Bynum*

Section 1: Universal Themes Connecting Local And Global Health

In this section we will identify seven themes that bridge local and global health experiences. These themes were identified by health science students based on their local and international experiences as key concepts of global health. The same themes are echoed by Koplan et al in their discussion of a common definition of global health[1] and can be found throughout the Global Health Essential Core Competencies developed by a Joint US/Canadian Committee in 2008-09.[5]

Health Disparities: Poor, Underserved, and Marginalized Populations

Health disparities manifest both internationally and domestically. Research published by the WHO cites that lifetime risk of maternal death during or shortly after pregnancy is only 1 in 17,400 in Sweden but it is 1 in 8 in Afghanistan.[6] Similarly, within Australia, life expectancy at birth among indigenous Australians is substantially lower (59.4 for males and 64.8 for females) than that of non-indigenous Australians (76.6 and 82.0, respectively).[6] These statistics demonstrate stark inequities, and highlight the reality that poverty leads to greater prevalence and severity of illness. Both international and domestic comparisons show that the lower a person's socioeconomic status, the worse their health. Thus, when addressing health inequities it is essential to concentrate on the most vulnerable and underserved populations.

The factors that determine health outcomes, or the social determinants of health, are the "circumstances in which people are born, grow up, live, work and age, and the systems put in place to deal with illness."[6] These factors have a variety of influences including economic, social policies, and politics. It is essential that health science students and health professions schools incorporate an understanding of the social determinants of health and the impact of poverty on health factors into the curriculum. The World Health Organization organized a Commission on Social Determinants of Health from 2005-2008 in order to increase awareness of the devastating impact that social determinants have on health.[7] In its summary on closing the health disparity gap, the Commission recommended a focus on the world's most underserved populations, including improvement of daily living conditions, addressing the inequitable distribution of money, power, and resources, quantitative measurement of identified problems and impact assessment of proposed solutions.[7]

The effects of social determinants on health disparities are visible in local communities and international settings where health science students work. To increase social accountability and reinforce the global health competencies, schools must work to address local disparities and involve students in both learning and action. Work in the local community provides an opportunity to better understand poverty and the factors that influence health in diverse settings. Through urban community health centers, homeless shelters, prisons, addiction centers, and schools, students work with patients to understand their circumstances and common health concerns. Training health professionals who work with migrant farm laborers, rural Native American populations, and distant communities develop a more thorough conception of rural life, including the impacts of poverty and geographic isolation on illness and wellness. Such experiences enhance students' knowledge about the social determinants of health.

Public Health Principles: Prevention and Health Education

Global health encompasses the values of both public health and international health. Global health seeks to embrace clinical care of individuals and population-based prevention and treatment. Work on this macroscopic scale provides the opportunity to effect large-scale change, both in local communities and abroad. The following reflection by a medical student demonstrates the important lessons about scope, impact, and the non-physician workforce.

> My global health experiences in both India and Kenya taught me much about public health and working with underserved populations. When I was in India I was lucky enough to take part in a national polio eradication day in which I traveled from house to house administering the polio vaccine to children. Although most of the children we saw did not have access to extensive medical services, in administering the vaccine we were significantly decreasing their risk for this devastating disease as well as the chance that they might transmit the disease to others. The interesting thing to me was that this work, which would have such a significant impact on the health of the country, was done not by physicians but by community health workers. In Kenya I had similar experiences with community health outreach days which focused on vaccinations and nutrition. Here again I was impressed by the breadth of the work done by community health workers and by the impact they made on the health of their community. Back home in New Mexico I found similar principles being implemented on a rotation in which I participated in various outreach events. These outreaches were targeted at underserved and marginalized groups and included administering basic medical care to the homeless and mobile syringe exchanges for injection drug users. Again, the bulk of the work was done by public health workers and the impact was impressive. Ultimately I felt that the work I did on these outreaches had a much greater impact on the health of my community than most of what I had done in the hospital. My experiences abroad and in my own community have made me realize that leaving the hospital to reach out to the underserved by collaborating with those that work in public health will be one of the most effective ways for me to be a physician.
>
> —Leslie Palmerlee, Medical Student,
> University of New Mexico School of Medicine

Before medical school, I worked as a Peace Corps community health volunteer in a rural Andean village in Ecuador. Ellen—a school teacher—had not judged me on my language skills and, instead, had welcomed me into the community. She introduced me as a friend to the families who lived there and taught me how to cook my meals over a little gas stove. Over the next few months, my Spanish improved and our friendship blossomed.

One sunny afternoon, as biting flies nipped my ankles, I started the three-mile walk down the mountain to visit Ellen. She was in the last trimester of her first pregnancy and ready for contractions to come. These labor signs would signal her need to go to the big city hospital several hours away. But she was not there that day. Her time to 'dar la luz'—to give 'light' to a baby had come. I would never see Ellen again. She died at age 22 of post-partum hemorrhage.

Now, as a fourth-year medical student, I live in inner-city Albuquerque, New Mexico. My home is at an inner-city ministry housing development. Drug deals, prostitutes, immigrant families, a community garden, and cracked sidewalks have taken the place of steep slopes and avocado trees in my life. Maria, one of my neighbors here, has end-stage liver disease from Hepatitis C from a contaminated blood transfusion many years ago. Like Ellen, Maria is faced with poverty and lack of access to healthcare.

The stories of these two women are imprinted on my heart. As a human being, as a neighbor, as a future physician it matters that people have access to healthcare. Poverty is crippling enough. It shouldn't determine whether or not you have access to the resources to survive Hepatitis C or childbirth. Local health truly is global health. Whether in Albuquerque, New Mexico or El Airo, Ecuador, there is so much that we can do to improve access to better health.

—Megan Brown, Medical Student,
University of New Mexico School of Medicine

Cost-Effective and Evidence-Based Care: Medical Resources and Clinical Skills

Cost-effective, evidence-based care is crucial for sustainable global and local health initiatives and for improving access, affordability and effectiveness of care. When resources are used wisely, effective care can be provided to a greater number of people. Prevention, including education and screening, is often the most cost effective intervention, and as mentioned previously, prevention must be integrated into medical curriculum and health systems. As the cost of healthcare in the

US and many countries soars upward, it is essential that health science students consider the costs of care and resources necessary to provide excellent care.

Additionally, health science students trained with excellent physical exam and diagnostic skills and an understanding of evidence-based medicine may avoid expensive and unnecessary laboratory tests or imaging studies. These skills are addressed in the global health competencies as well. Learning to skillfully and resourcefully provide care with what is available allows students to provide care in many under-resourced settings locally and globally. There is an increasing role of evidence-based protocols to drive care domestically and internationally.

Health science students may be faced with challenging decisions and limited resources in their work at student run clinics, community health centers, rural clinics, and international sites. In each of these circumstances, health science students must be prepared to evaluate their patients with a thorough history and physical exam, and then decide how to best use the resources available for diagnostic testing or management of the patient's illness. These skills bridge local and international work and are globally applicable as we strive to provide excellent, responsible medical care.

Cultural Competency: Embracing Diversity and Cultural Humility

Today, the movement of people around the globe is increasing at an extraordinary pace. As a result, there is increased diversity of patient populations, as a result health care systems are faced with increased cultural and linguistic challenges. Health science students may see patients from East Africa, Vietnam, Iraq, and Cuba in one afternoon of clinic. Cultural competence must be integral to medical school curricula because students are faced with complex cultural situations in their home communities, even more so when they are working internationally.

Cultural competency involves and openness and a willingness to learn about different cultural beliefs. Health science students must be open to understanding a patient's cultural beliefs about health, illness, and healing. Within this, students must recognize and value alternative systems of healing or traditional medicines. While patients from similar backgrounds may seem to hold the same health beliefs, it is critical to evaluate each patient as an individual with unique perspectives. Thus communication skills are essential to providing culturally competent care, more so than learning general cultural trends. Students must learn to work with interpreters, demonstrate humility and empathy through their communication, feel comfortable with probing and asking clarifying questions about health beliefs, and build trusting relationships with patients of different cultural backgrounds.

Many health systems have worked to involve cultural navigators or community health workers in patient care. These team members are essential in forming a cultural bridge and ensuring that the patient's concerns are heard and understood and that the provider's recommendations are clear and culturally appropriate.

> I spent two years in Mali as an agriculture volunteer with the Peace Corps. My work at the clinic in my market town consisted of helping with prenatal and baby weighing/vaccination visits. While there, before I had any formal medical training

(or any idea that I would end up in medical school), I learned a crucial lesson about how to be an effective provider. I saw that, while confidence in medical knowledge and skills is important, it is equally important to have humility. Humility is a nebulous term but encompasses both knowing your own limits and having genuine respect for patients, which fosters trust. I did not have medical training to offer but patients knew that I genuinely respected them and they in turn felt comfortable being vulnerable with me even though I was not from their community. It was there that I also learned how humbling it could be to see the fortitude of patients themselves who seemed to be facing insurmountable problems.

Humility is not something that can be explicitly taught, but it can be modeled. This quality was strongest in the rural providers that I have observed throughout medical school. It is no revelation that a rural provider must have diverse skills and confidence: confidence to deliver babies without OB backup, to suture a deep laceration, to manage an infant with a fever. But being a cowboy is not enough to make a strong frontier physician. The providers in the Alaskan clinic where I did my Family Medicine clerkship had gained the trust of their patients by being extremely competent but also by admitting their limits to their patients. Patients trusted that these docs knew when it was appropriate to recommend that a woman elect to deliver her baby in Anchorage, when they really needed to make the trip to see a specialist, or when a leg fracture required them to head to town for surgery rather be casted in clinic.

—Emma Wright, Medical Student,
Geisel School of Medicine at Dartmouth College

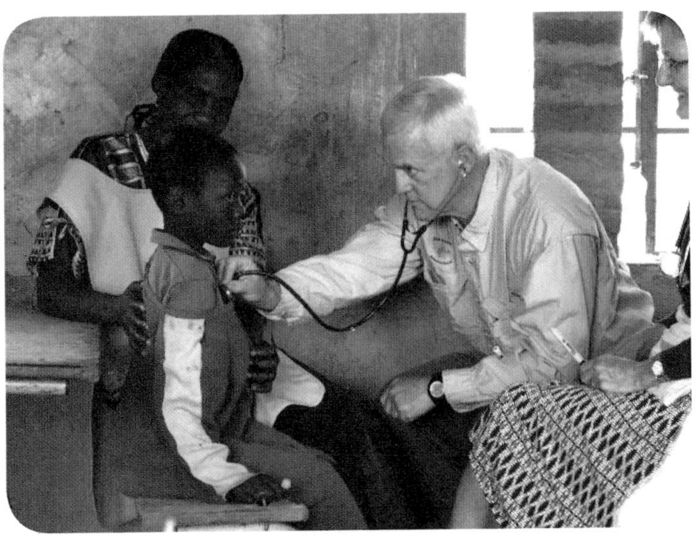

The examination
Photographer: *Will Bynum*

Teamwork: Working on Interprofessional Teams

Multidisciplinary teams are essential to improving the provision of healthcare to patients and populations. The Framework for Action on Interprofessional Education and Collaborative Practice (produced by the World Health Organization Study Group on Interprofessional Education and Collaborative Practice) recognizes that collaborative work will improve health outcomes and play a role in "mitigating the global health workforce crisis."[9] Multidisciplinary education and practice at the local and global level is essential. Incorporating opportunities for local interprofessional work in the medical and health professions curriculum will prepare students to work collaboratively in international settings. Medical schools have begun to create time for health science students to work collaboratively with nursing, physician assistant, social work, nutrition, physical therapy, occupational therapy, and dental students. In the report mentioned above, the WHO acknowledges that "effective interprofessional education enables effective collaborative practice" and that "collaborative practice strengthens health systems and improves health."[8] This is essential to both local and global health.

Health science students must also be exposed to the important role of community health workers (CHWs). CHWs have been utilized to reach patients with limited access to healthcare in developing countries, and there is evidence that when CHWs are carefully selected and supported by their communities, "they can improve access to and coverage of communities with basic health services."[10] Greater numbers of health systems and educational institutions in developed countries have begun to recognize the usefulness of CHWs in extending health services into the community and empowering the community to engage with the local health systems. Research in New Mexico with patients who were high consumers of health resources demonstrated that field-based community health workers improved access to preventive and social services and may reduce resource utilization and cost.[11] This is just one example of how ideas from the developing world can be applied to our local health systems. Often students travel internationally, they recognize innovative ways to address health problems. These strategies can be applied locally to improve the current system.

Connecting to the Community: Working with Local Agencies and Community Partners

Involving the community and engaging with local organizations and service agencies is critical to local health and global health work. This theme overlaps with the ideas of cultural competence and humility and the importance of collaborative practice mentioned above. When entering a new community, whether it be a neighborhood of Chicago or a village in Mali, it is important to understand what services and structures currently exist. One strategy is to work with community members on an asset mapping exercise to understand the strengths and resources of the community. From there, working relationships between organizations and community members can be built. Resources, such as the Asset-based Community Development movement, can be useful to guide this approach.[12]

Knowledge of local agencies and community partners also allows health providers to connect patients to the services that they need and avoid duplication of services. With both local and global health work, it is essential that community partnerships are formed in a manner that is sustainable to avoid depletion of local resources.

Section 2: Teaching Global Health Themes Locally, Curriculum Examples

Having identified seven major themes that are central to local and global health, it is important to consider how medical schools are operationalizing these themes in curriculum. There are a number of institutions that are acutely aware of the issues of social accountability and are addressing global health competencies in their local communities. There are also a number of institutions that are addressing these themes locally, but have yet to connect them to a global context. In this section, we will review innovative curriculum examples from just a few medical schools around the world that are addressing global health themes in their local communities.

THEnet Schools

THEnet is a collaborative group of now eleven medical schools around the world committed to social accountability and working to create innovative models of medical education that truly address the health needs of their communities. By working locally, these institutions are preparing a workforce that understands the social determinants of health and knows how to collaborate with communities.

Ateneo de Zamboanga University School of Medicine in the Philippines has developed a curriculum that "combines competence and problem based instruction with experiential learning in the community, that is responsive to the changing patterns of health care development and the needs of these communities and is sensitive to the social and cultural realities of Western Mindanao".[13] Embracing multiple themes mentioned above, this school prepares graduates to be global health-minded and to focus on the wellness of their local communities.

The Latin American Medical School (ELAM) in Cuba, an institution committed to the principles of social accountability, is dedicated to increasing the global health workforce. ELAM recruits students from underserved communities around the world to study in Cuba—a health system that is founded on the principle that patients have a right to health care and is infused with public health and a biopsychosocial model. ELAM Students commit to returning to their home country to work in underserved communities.[14] This vision of training students with a global health perspective is critical to building a workforce committed to working in poor, remote, marginalized communities.

Northern Ontario School of Medicine embraces the theme of collaboration with communities through its community-engaged educational philosophy. The school has partnerships with over 70 communities in Northern Ontario and students are immersed in rural communities early in the curriculum. Students work locally to learn the important global health principles of population health, cultural competency, and ethics.[15]

TheNET schools are creating a sense of prestige for educational programs in underserved medicine and for practice in low-resource environments. This is in contrast to many university-based medical institutions—which may have small groups of trainees focusing on medicine for underserved communities, but spend the majority of their time, energy, and influence on sub-specialty training and high resource care.

Making the Links: Global Health is Local Health

While the schools mentioned above are working locally to teach social accountability and contribute to global health, the University of Saskatchewan has a unique program called "Making the Links" that immerses medical students in local and global communities and allows them to discover the similarities between local and global healthcare. Students spend time in rural First Nations communities in the northern part of the province, they volunteer at the student run clinic for the homeless in Saskatchewan (SWITCH), and then they travel to Mozambique and spend time working in a community there. One student who participated in the program commented that, "Global health is a way of looking at health care and well-being that understands the connectedness of health. It means understanding that equality is important for the health care of all people and communities."[16] The program immerses students in underserved and marginalized communities, allowing students to develop a commitment to future work in these communities.

Beyond THEnet schools and innovative programs in Saskatchewan, numerous schools in the United States and around the world are expanding their concept of global health and are integrating local experiences, teaching about social inequity, and preparing future healthcare workers to think on a global scale.

Section 3: Institutional Integration Of Local And Global Health Themes And Endeavors

In training health professionals to promote health equity both locally and globally, it is essential to have institutional commitment to these themes. This commitment should be made through three specific avenues:

- Ensuring that the institutional culture is supportive of students with an interest in community health and preventive medicine;
- Providing coursework that highlights the themes that unite local and global health (see Section 1 of this chapter);
- Providing opportunities for students to gain practical experience in applying the principles learned in the classroom.

In this section we will highlight the key components of each of these avenues. It is important to acknowledge that each institution will have unique strengths and challenges when attempting to implement this framework.

Fostering a Supportive Institutional Culture

In order to successfully foster interest and skills in the field of local and global health equity, it is essential to reflect an institutional commitment to this cause. It is essential to have faculty mentors actively engaged with the local community that are available to work with students. Care should be taken to ensure that there are enough faculty and resources to meet the increasing demand and interest in global health among students. When appropriate, institutions should be open to creating partnerships with community-based and other types of organizations that have expertise in aspects of global health and administrative support often lacking in Western academic centers. If possible it is important to establish formal ways of recognizing student efforts in promoting local health equity. This can be through part time community health fellowships, or course credits given to students carrying out community health projects or working in free clinics. Furthermore, integration of local and global health themes throughout the curriculum will help to expose a greater number of students to the challenges they will face in addressing the social determinants impacting patient health.

Providing Coursework Integrating Local Health and Global Health Principles

A number of health professions schools have created time within the curriculum for coursework that addresses the local and global health principles and themes, such as those discussed above. Building curricular time for study of social determinants of health, public health principles, and interdisciplinary work, for example, will serve to increase interest in these areas of health and medicine. At the University of New Mexico School of Medicine, there is curricular time dedicated to the Public Health Certificate program. Medical students study epidemiology, cultural competency, and the impact of poverty on health. Students also have opportunities to integrate this curricular time with practical experiences in the community (see below). A number of health professions schools are creating time for interdisciplinary learning, through tutorial case studies or through interdisciplinary clinical teams. Building these experiences into medical training will serve to increase the skills of future providers in addressing the challenging local and global health issues facing individuals and communities.

Providing Practical Experiences in Community Health

Health professional schools have the opportunity to build long-term sustainable community partnerships that will not only provide valuable educational opportunities to students, but can also serve to enhance the resources available to the local community and promote improvements in local health. Work with community partners should be done in a longitudinal manner; often, because of a lack of time and resources, educational institutions place students in the community in short spurts of time. This high student turnover rate can lead to a greater burden on the community sites and may give only a cursory understanding of the community challenges. Allowing space in the curriculum for students to spend longer periods of time with a single community partner will lead to more positive outcomes for both the student and community partner. In addition, partnering with organizations that can advocate for the community's agenda will lead to more balanced collaboration. Such organizations may be other academic centers, non-profit organizations, faith-based, and others. These organizations may also be able to maintain sustainable administrative support necessary to coordinate logistics, evaluation, and preparation for overseas immersion experiences.

Before beginning the community practicum, students should gain an understanding of the specific needs and priorities of the local community, as well as the strengths of the local community. Key informant interviews with community partners are an invaluable resource for this information. These interviews can help students understand community strengths and needs, and effectively plan sustainable and relevant community-based projects.

Many health professional schools support student efforts in the community by means of research funds. While this does present students with an excellent opportunity to gain skills in community-based research, it is also important to provide support for students that are interested in intervention design and program implementation.

Conclusion

There is incredible work being done around the globe to connect local and global health experiences. Institutions that are preparing healthcare professionals to address global health issues must begin locally and incorporate equity, social determinants, interdisciplinary work, and transnational health issues into the curriculum. Drawing from the themes detailed above, it is clear that local work is an essential component of global health. The social accountability movement in developing medical school curriculum is an innovative perspective that returns the focus to the needs of our local communities and positions educational institutions at the forefront of social and global change.

References

1. Koplan JP et al. Toward a common definition of global health. *Lancet.* 2009; 373: 1993-95.
2. Boelen C, Heck JE. Defining and measuring the social accountability of medical schools. Geneva: World Health Organization, 1995.
3. Global Health Education Consortium, About Us. http://globalhealtheducation.org/aboutus/SitePages/Home.aspx. Accessed May 23, 2012.
4. THEnet: Training for Health Equity, About THEnet. http://thenetcommunity.org/about-thenet.html. Accessed May 23, 2012.
5. Global Health Essential Core Comptencies. Accessed May 24, 2012. http://globalhealtheducation.org.
6. *World Health Organization, Social determinants of health, Key Concepts. Accessed May 24, 2012.* http://www.who.int/social_determinants/thecommission/finalreport/key_concepts/en/index.html.
7. *World Health Organization, Social determinants of health, Commission on Social Determinants of Health, 2005-2008. Accessed May 24, 2012.* http://www.who.int/social_determinants/thecommission/en/.
8. *Anell A & Willis M International comparison of health care systems using resource profiles World Health Organization, 2000. Accessed July 25, 2012. http://www.who.int/bulletin/archives/78(6)770.pdf*
9. Framework for Action on Interprofessional Education & Collaborative Practice. World Health Organization. Produced by the Health Professions Network Nursing and Midwifery Office within the Department of Human Resources for Health. Accessed May 30, 2012. http://www.who.int/hrh/nursing_midwifery/en/.
10. *Lehmann U & Sanders D. Community health workers: What do we know about them? School of Public Health, University of Western Cape and World Health Organization. January 2007.* www.who.int/hrh/documents/community_health_workers.pdf. *Accessed May 31, 2012.*
11. Johnson D et al. Community health workers and Medicaid Managed Care in New Mexico. *J Community Health.* 2012 Jun; 37(3): 563-71.
12. Asset-based Community Development. www.abcd.org. Accessed Jan 1, 2013.
13. Vision and Mission. Ateneo de Zamboanga University School of Medicine. http://som.adzu.edu.ph/info/index.php?page=About%20Us&officeId=2. Accessed June 1, 2012.
14. Cuba & the Global Health Workforce: Training Human Resources. Latin American Medical School-ELAM. http://www.medicc.org/ns/index.php?s=10&p=0. Accessed June 1, 2012.
15. A Distributed Model of Community-Engaged Medical Education. Northern Ontario School of Medicine. http://www.nosm.ca/education/default.aspx. Accessed June 1, 2012.
16. Making the Links: Global Health is Local Health. University of Saskatchewan College of Medicine. http://www.medicine.usask.ca/leadership/social-accountability/news-and-events/making-the-links.html. Accessed June 1, 2012.

CHAPTER 10

Global Health: Health Sciences and Team Based Care

Herica M. Torres, RN, MSN, PhD-candidate
Instructor, University of South Alabama

Natasha Altin, MscOT
Dalhousie University

Baharak Amanzadeh, DDS, MPH
Assistant Clinical Professor
UCSF School of Dentistry

Kaitlin Carlson, DPT
University of Alabama at Birmingham

Benjamin W. Chaffee, DDS, MPH
PhD Candidate
University of California, Berkeley

Marcela Frazier OD, MPH, FAAO
Assistant Professor, University of Alabama at Birmingham

Kerry Adele Gillette, PA-S
PA-Student, Department of Family and Community Medicine
University of Utah

Paula Johns, OD
Optometry Resident, Zuni Indian Hospital

Andrea Johnson, DPT
University of Alabama at Birmingham

Heidi Lauckner, PhD, OT Reg (NS)
Assistant Professor and International Fieldwork Education Coordinator
Dalhousie University

Mazheruddin Mulla, B.S., M.P.H.
Community Educator and Recruiter, Alabama Vaccine Research Clinic
Research Assistant, Center for AIDS Research
Research Assistant, Youth Development Lab
University of Alabama at Birmingham

Shawna O'Hearn, MA, MSc (OT)
Director, Global Health Office
Dalhousie University

Donald M. Pedersen PhD, PA-C
Department of Family and Community Medicine

Professor Emeritus,
University of Utah School of Medicine

Kathy J. Pedersen MPAS, PA-C
Program Manager, Global Partners
Adjunct Assistant Professor, Department of Family and Community Medicine
University of Utah School of Medicine

Sharon E. Shaw, PT, DrPH
Chair, Department of Physical Therapy
University of Alabama at Birmingham

Diane C. Tucker, Ph.D.
Professor of Psychology
Director Science and Technology Honors Program
University of Alabama at Birmingham

Editor

Lynda Wilson, RN, PhD, FAAN
Professor, Assistant Dean for International Affairs
Deputy Director, PAHO/WHO Collaborating Center on International Nursing
University of Alabama at Birmingham School of Nursing

"Team-based health care is the provision of health services to individuals, families, and/or their communities by at least two health providers who work collaboratively with patients and their caregivers to the extent preferred by each patient to accomplish shared goals within and across settings to achieve coordinated, high-quality care."[1]

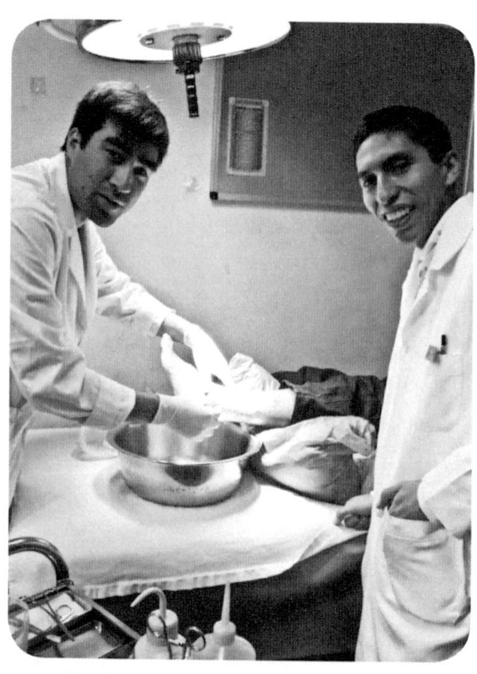

An American medical student works alongside a Bolivian medical resident in a diabetic foot clinic in Cochabamba, Bolivia
Photographer: *Alvin Strasburger*

IN GLOBAL HEALTH, WORKING AS isolated health care providers is an old paradigm that is slowly shifting towards working in teams. Working in disconnect with other healthcare professionals has proven not to work for the benefit of global health, and yet the disciplines in this chapter have made only token efforts to educate students in teamwork.

In order for the team to work efficiently, members need to realize that shared goals, humility, honesty, effective communication, and understanding of roles and responsibilities of each member are vital for achieving positive health care outcomes. Instead of working in relative isolation, health care providers and other professionals can work together towards achieving set goals that are proposed by patients, providers and communities. By acknowledging and understanding the roles and skills that each member brings to the team, duplicating efforts may be avoided and a more effective approach can lead to better health outcomes. Even though competencies tied to different professions may overlap, this could be beneficial if a member of the team is unavailable, so in this way the care of the individual or community will not suffer. The idea that members need to be humble and honest comes from the principle of accepting that no one is perfect or superior to another, that we will all make mistakes, have different strengths, and that we need to be sincere and supportive of each other.[1]

Although some interdisciplinary, team based work has been done in global health, there are monumental challenges to improve health worldwide. It is extremely ineffectual to teach people good nutrition if dental pain prevents them from being able to masticate their food. A health care professional must know when the person needs the complimentary care of other disciplines. The person depressed over the loss of an arm must have occupational therapy to learn to prepare food, with controlled pain, and not simply the ability to consume the diet. It is futile to treat the mind, mouth, muscles, or eyesight, in isolation. The whole person faces the struggles of healthy living for productive lives.

This chapter is a collaborative effort among students and faculty from diverse health professions that include dentistry, nursing, occupational therapy, physical therapy, psychology, physician assistant studies, and optometry. In this section, students and faculty advisors from each discipline address the topics of contributions to global health, education required to become a professional in that discipline, global health content included in each curriculum, and professional linkages. Authors in each section also highlight the importance of working in interdisciplinary teams. As you will see in this chapter, provision of care that is team based is essential to improve global health, but has not been an integral part of the preparation of tomorrow's professionals.

—Mitchell, Pamela, et al. "Core Principles & Values of Effective Team-Based Health Care." Discussion Paper, October, 2012. 6 February 2013 < http://www.iom.edu/Global/Perspectives/2012/-/media/Files/Perspectives-Files/2012/Discussion-Papers/VSRT-Team-Based-Care-Principles-Values.pdf>

Dentistry and Global Oral Health

Global oral health represents an emerging movement to approach the control and prevention of diseases of the teeth, jaws, and oral cavity from a global perspective, taking into account both the biological and socio-environmental context in which these conditions occur. As with other aspects of global health, there is an emphasis on improving oral health among the world's most vulnerable populations, as well as recognition that global oral health issues affect all nations, both wealthy and poor. Although the diagnosis, management, and treatment of oral diseases has traditionally been a role reserved for dentists, a global view reveals the importance of cross-disciplinary and inter-professional collaboration in reducing the burden of oral diseases worldwide.

A variety of diseases affect oral health with differing etiologies, distributions, and potential preventive approaches, all of which can have a profound impact on daily functioning and quality of life.[1] Worldwide, more than 30% of adults age 64-75 report problems with their mouth or teeth.[2] Dental caries, the infectious disease responsible for tooth decay, affects an estimated 60-90% of school age children and is near universal in adulthood.[1] However, much of this decay goes untreated, particularly among lower income populations and in resource poor countries.[3,4] Untreated decay persists despite significant scientific advances in caries prevention and treatment.[5]

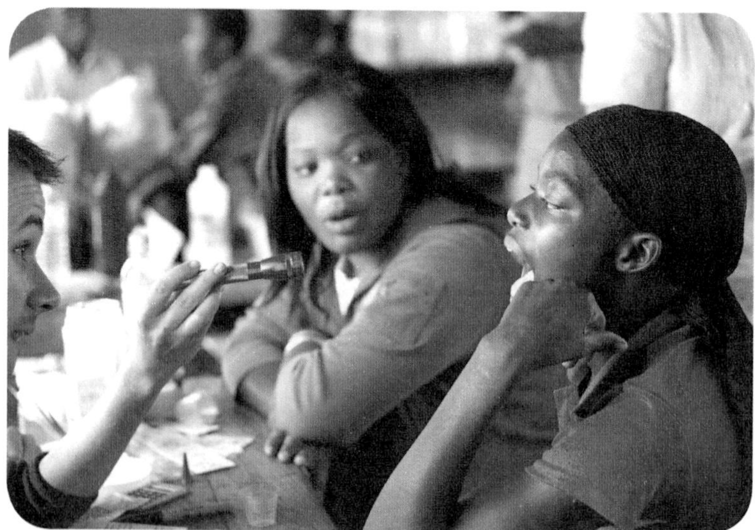

A student performs an exam of a patient's oral cavity in clinic in remote Africa
Photographer: *Erin Berry*

Periodontal disease, an inflammatory disorder of the supporting structures around the teeth, is an important cause of tooth loss. Although global prevalence estimates vary, severe disease may affect 5-20% of adults.[1,6] Cancer of the mouth and pharynx is among the ten most common cancers worldwide,[7] and is the most common cancer among men in India.[8] There are nearly one million adults living with diagnosed oral or pharyngeal cancer,[8] but five year survival rates above 50% are not common.[7] Tuberculosis, sexually transmitted infections, and HIV-associated infections all have important oral health implications.[9]

The treatment of oral diseases is a major expenditure in high income countries, whereas in low and middle income countries oral disease is extensive and a growing problem.[10] There are not only striking inequalities across countries, but also within countries—including wealthy nations. Addressing the social determinants of oral health is a priority in the global oral health research agenda.[10]

Oral Health and Integrated Global Health Promotion

Oral diseases are not purely the result of local processes in the mouth, and they do not occur in isolation from the rest of the body. The oral cavity might present the first signs of nutritional deficiencies, adverse drug reactions, or conditions related to HIV/AIDS. Oral diseases themselves can be detrimental to other aspects of health: tooth loss can impede nutrient intake; oral pain can lead to stress and reduced quality of life; the chronic inflammation of periodontal disease may be related to cardiovascular diseases, poor glycemic control in diabetics, and preterm births.[11] Shared risk factors such as smoking and alcohol use, along with social determinants, contribute to the connections between poor oral health and poor general health.

Developing integrated models in which dentists, physicians, and other health professionals share roles in oral health promotion and research is a key priority. Given the high prevalence of oral diseases, it is virtually assured that any global health practitioner will encounter individuals with oral or dental concerns. Traditionally, dental care services have been delivered separately from medical services and frequently with significant barriers to access and utilization. Thus, in many settings, physicians, nurses, or others might be well positioned to help recognize, address, and ultimately prevent oral disease. Pediatricians have reported a willingness to play a role in caries prevention.[12] However, changing practice behaviors has faced hurdles.[13,14] In a global health setting, developing a team approach will be instrumental in reducing the burden of oral diseases.

Many oral health improvements could be achieved as part of an integrated approach to chronic disease prevention and general health promotion. Efforts to support healthy food choices over processed snacks and sugary beverages, anti-smoking campaigns, and expanded access to clean, fluoridated water are all likely to have oral health benefits. Thus, measuring the success of many types of health and economic interventions should take oral health outcomes into consideration, as well. That said, there remains a pressing need to for effective, targeted interventions to address oral diseases directly and to reduce oral health disparities.[10]

Vignette
Dr. Karen Sokal-Gutierrez and the Children's Oral Health Nutrition Project

In decades working with families around the globe, pediatrician Karen Sokal-Gutierrez reaches out to parents and community members, stressing the importance of a healthy diet for infants and children. She sees good nutrition as essential to support children's healthy growth and development. Recently, she has seen a change in young smiles greeting her in the communities she visits: black and rotten teeth are the norm where once were mostly healthy smiles.

"We're seeing 60-90% of children affected by this. It's really a pandemic," says Sokal-Gutierrez. "When a third to half the baby teeth are decayed, and half the children have mouth pain, I ask, 'How does this affect their overall health?'"

From her work in rural El Salvador, Sokal-Gutierrez notes a startling rise in tooth decay that coincides with an explosion in the availability of soda, chips, and other junk food. In many locations, ownership of a toothbrush is uncommon, and accessing dental services can be difficult and expensive. She sees an ongoing transition from the traditional diet, with more snacking and more baby bottles filled with sweetened drinks like soda or juice. Starchy, sugar-loaded snacks are cheap and omnipresent.

"With something so prevalent, you have to focus on prevention and focus on younger age groups. Treatment is important, but it's not reaching everyone. Preventing disease and suffering is always preferable." Rather than emphasizing fillings and extractions, Sokal-Gutierrez and her team train community health workers to provide counseling in good feeding practices and oral hygiene. The program also helps provide toothbrushes, toothpaste, and fluoride varnish, which makes teeth resistant to decay. She notes that the same nutrition-based messages that can help prevent tooth decay might also help prevent childhood obesity, following a common risk-factor approach supported by the WHO.

She places a high value on working in the local context, joining with national and community stakeholders to coordinate efforts. Investing in local partners helps ensure that community needs are addressed and that intervention efforts are more sustainable. Data collection has proven important for estimating the prevalence and severity of the nutrition and oral health problems among children, and for targeting the intervention toward the communities with the greatest needs. Sharing this information with the local health authorities and the participating communities—including project successes and challenges—has strengthened relationships with collaborators and helped to improve the program.

In El Salvador, Sokal-Gutierrez partners with local non-profit ASAPROSAR (Asociación Salvadoreña Pro-Salud Rural—The Salvadoran Association for Rural Health) (http://www.asaprosar.org) and the Ministry of Health have been developed. She has since expanded the scope of her work to Ecuador, Nepal, Peru, and Vietnam: very different populations, all facing similar nutritional and oral health issues.

"This is a huge problem with severe health consequences for children," Sokal-Gutierrez says. "If the snack food companies have reached every corner of the world, we need to reach just as far with nutrition education and preventive care."

—Karen Sokal-Gutierrez, M.D., M.P.H.
Associate Clinical Professor, UC Berkeley-UCSF Joint Medical Program

Educational Preparation and Global Health Opportunities for Dentists

For those seeking to become a dentist, schools in the United States and Canada offer doctoral-level, professional degree programs that generally require four years of post-secondary education for entry. Graduates from an accredited program may begin clinical practice, contingent on passing the requisite national and state examinations. Many dentists follow their initial training with an optional one-year residency program, while others choose to pursue one of nine American Dental Association (ADA) recognized specialties, such as pediatric dentistry or orthodontics.

Although global oral health is not a formally recognized specialty, dental public health is dedicated to the control, prevention, and treatment of dental diseases at the community rather than individual level. Global oral health similarly embraces applied community research and education of the public. Formal professional education in global oral health has seen some recent growth following calls to increase academic offerings for dental students.[15] Several dental schools have recently incorporated formal global oral health into their education and/or research agendas.

The growth of dental therapist programs is an example of dental education and regulation adapting to successfully address an unmet community need. First put into practice in 1921 in New Zealand and later in dozens of countries, dental therapists are trained mid-level providers of preventive care and limited surgical dental treatments to populations facing poor access to dentists.[16] Similar programs have already been approved or are under consideration in the United States.[17]

Global Health Professional Linkages for Dentists

Several international organizations are dedicated to improving the oral health of all people worldwide. The World Health Organization (WHO) [www.who.int/oral_health], the International Association for Dental Research [www.iadr.com], and the World Dental Federation [www.fdiworldental.org] all have sections devoted to global oral health promotion and/or research. For students wanting to begin a dental career, the American Dental Association [http://www.ada.org] provides information about training in the United States. For current dental students, the International Association of Dental Students [www.iads-web.org] helps foster connections between dental students in multiple countries.

Summary

Oral health is affected by a number of distinct and, in some cases, highly prevalent diseases, which together can have a profound effect on daily functioning and quality of life. Oral diseases do not operate in isolation from the rest of the body, and thus, an integrated health promotion model featuring cross disciplinary, inter-professional collaboration from dentists, physicians, nutritionists and other global health stakeholders is needed to reduce the burden of oral diseases and to address oral health inequalities. Growing interest in global oral health offers opportunities for students, researchers, and practitioners from all backgrounds to make contributions in oral health promotion worldwide.

International Dental Volunteering: A Time for Change?

Dental service delivery systems are weak in many low-income countries, especially in rural areas, leading to considerable suffering from untreated dental infections. For decades, dental non-governmental organizations (NGOs) and volunteer dentists have donated time and equipment for international projects that provide treatment to resource-poor communities.

An opinion article in the *British Dental Journal*, "Dental volunteering—a time for reflection and a time for change," [18] questions the traditional model of dental volunteering. Do volunteer trips provide real benefits to the populations they aim to help or can they result in more harm than good? How can efforts be redirected toward a more appropriate and sustainable contribution to population oral health?

The authors note that dental volunteering can be a valuable experience for the volunteers and can directly address some pressing health needs. Yet, there are concerns whether short-term projects, often stressing tooth extractions for pain relief, can fulfill community oral health needs sustainably. Most often there is little evaluation or accountability associated with volunteer projects. Dental NGOs rarely integrate with the local healthcare system, possibly leading to duplication, competition, or dependence on outside assistance.

Can dental volunteering be improved? Suggested approaches include interfacing with the local healthcare system for capacity building of local partners, a greater emphasis on prevention, and creating a sound evidence base for effectiveness under real-life conditions. Re-thinking the way dental NGOs operate can leverage their considerable capacity for a greater positive impact.

—Benjamin Chaffee DDS MPH, PhD epidemiology student
University of California Berkeley

References

1. Petersen, Poul Erik, et al. "The Global Burden of Oral Diseases and Risks to Oral Health." *Bulletin of the World Health Organization* 83.9 (2005): 661-9.
2. Petersen, Poul Erik, et al. "Global Oral Health of Older People—Call for Public Health Action" *Community Dental Health* 27.2 (2010): 257-68.
3. Yee, Robert, and Aubrey Sheiham. "The Burden of Restorative Dental Treatment for Children in Third World Countries." *International Dental Journal* 52.1 (2002): 1-9.
4. Roberts, Michael W. "Dental Health of Children: Where We Are Today and Remaining Challenges." *The Journal of Clinical Pediatric Dentistry* 32.3 (2008): 231-4.
5. Milgrom, Peter, Domenick T. Zero, and Jason M. Tanzer. "An Examination of the Advances in Science and Technology of Prevention of Tooth Decay in Young Children since the Surgeon General's Report on Oral Health." *Academic Pediatrics* 9.6 (2009): 404-9.
6. Pihlstrom, Bruce L., Bryan S. Michalowicz, and Newell W. Johnson. "Periodontal Diseases." *Lancet* 366.9499 (2005): 1809-20.
7. Johnson, Newell W., et al. "Global Oral Health Inequalities in Incidence and Outcomes for Oral Cancer: Causes and Solutions." *Advances in Dental Research* 23.2 (2011): 237-46.
8. Bray, F., et al. "Global Estimates of Cancer Prevalence for 27 Sites in the Adult Population in 2008." *International Journal of Cancer* 132. 5 (2013):1133-45. doi: 10.1002/ijc.27711.
9. Challacombe, Stephen, et al. "Global Oral Health Inequalities: Oral Infections-Challenges and Approaches." *Advances in Dental Research* 23.2 (2011): 227-36.
10. Williams, David M. "Global Oral Health Inequalities: The Research Agenda." *Journal of Dental Research* 90.5 (2011): 549-51.
11. Cullinan, Mary P., Pauline J. Ford, and Gregory J. Seymour. "Periodontal Disease and Systemic Health: Current Status." *Australian Dental Journal* 54 Suppl 1 (2009): S62-9.
12. Lewis, Charlotte W., et al. "The Role of the Pediatrician in the Oral Health of Children: A National Survey." *Pediatrics* 106.6 (2000): E84.
13. De la Cruz, Georgia G., R. Gary Rozier, and Gary Slade. "Dental Screening and Referral of Young Children by Pediatric Primary Care Providers." *Pediatrics* 114.5 (2004): e642-52.
14. Isong, Inyang A., et al. "Provision of Fluoride Varnish to Medicaid-Enrolled Children by Physicians: The Massachusetts Experience." *Health Services Research* 46.6pt1 (2011): 1843-62.
15. Karim, Asef, Ana Karina Mascarenhas, and Shafik Dharamsi. "A Global Oral Health Course: Isn't it Time?" *Journal of Dental Education* 72.11 (2008): 1238-46.
16. Nash, David A., et al. "Dental Therapists: A Global Perspective." *International Dental Journal* 58.2 (2008): 61-70.
17. Mathu-Muju KR. "Chronicling the Dental Therapist Movement in the United States." *Journal of Public Health Dentistry* 71.4 (2011): 278-88.
18. Holmgren, Christopher, and Habib Benzian. "Dental Volunteering—a Time for Reflection and a Time for Change." *British Dental Journal* 210.11 (2011): 513-6.

Nursing and Global Health

The profession of nursing "encompasses autonomous and collaborative care of individuals of all ages, families, groups and communities, sick or well and in all settings. Nursing includes the promotion of health, prevention of illness, and the care of ill, disabled, and dying people. Advocacy, promotion of a safe environment, research, participation in shaping health policy and patient and health systems management, and education are also key nursing roles".[1] This definition illustrates the contributions nurses can make towards improving the health of individuals and communities worldwide. Nurses care for individuals within a cultural, evidence-based, holistic framework. As the profession with the greatest number of health care providers in the world, nurses can impact the wellbeing of communities by promoting health, preventing disease, providing direct care during illness, conducting research to create evidence to guide practice, and developing health and social policy.[2]

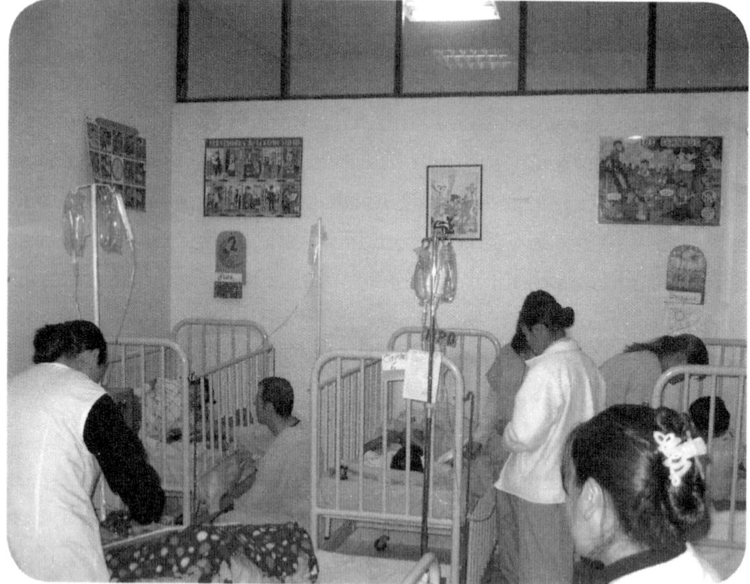

Bolivian nurses care for burned children in a clinic that frequently hosts and teaches visiting nursing students
Photographer: *Will Bynum*

Nursing's Contributions to Global Health

Because nurses throughout the world are first-line health care providers, nurses are key to achieving the United Nations Millennium Development Goals (MDGs), particularly MDGs 4, 5, and 6 which relate specifically to health.[3] Through direct care provision, accurate reporting, research, partnering with local community leaders, and involvement in policy-making, nurses make significant and cost-effective contributions to the health of communities.[3]

Nurses contribute to improving global health outcomes through their work in primary, secondary, and acute care settings, decreasing barriers to health access, and providing high quality care. Nurses work in a variety of settings including hospitals, clinics, health departments, schools, occupational health programs, nursing homes, and rehabilitation facilities. They are prepared to provide care for individual patients, families, and communities, and to coordinate care provided by all members of the health care team.

In the United States, advanced practice nurses, such as nurse midwives, nurse anesthetists, and nurse practitioners, are prepared at the master's level to provide high quality care that includes some types of care more traditionally provided only by physicians including diagnosing medical problems, prescribing medications, and treating problems defined within a specific scope of practice.[4,5] Findings from many studies have demonstrated that outcomes of primary care health services provided by advanced practice nurses are comparable to those provided by physicians.[5]

Vignette
Example of Nurses' Contributions to Global Health in Zambia

Because of the global shortage of health care providers, there has been a growing interest in task shifting to expand the scope of practice of nurses and other health care workers to address global health care needs.[6] Task shifting refers to the redistribution of tasks among members of the health team, so that workers with less education assume roles traditionally reserved for those with more advanced training. A number of studies have indicated that task shifting is cost-effective and contributes to improved population health outcomes.[7,8] It is estimated that nurses comprise by far the largest portion of the professional level global health care workforce, and thus task shifting programs that provide nurses with advanced education and skills can have a significant impact on addressing global health care needs. One such task shifting initiative was launched in 2007 in Zambia, a country with a severe shortage of nurses, doctors, and other health care workers, and a severe health care crisis associated with the HIV/AIDS epidemic. Under the administrative leadership of the General Nursing Council (GNC) of Zambia, numerous partners collaborated to develop the country's first HIV Nurse Practitioner program.[9] The program was designed as a one year diploma program for enrolled and registered nurses who were already working in HIV clinics and who had completed three 5-day training programs provided by the Zambian Ministry of Health to address basic HIV care, pediatric HIV, and treatment of opportunistic infections. The program was initially administered by the Zambian GNC and was subsequently transferred to one of the largest diploma nursing programs in the country (the Lusaka Schools of Nursing and Midwifery). To date, a total of 92 nurses from throughout the country have completed the program, and there are plans to expand the program to other nursing schools and to train additional nurses by 2017. Findings from the preliminary evaluation indicate that the program has been successful in preparing nurses to provide comprehensive care and treatment (including prescribing first line antiretroviral therapy) to patients with HIV and AIDS.[9] In Zambia, as in many other countries, the nurse is often the only health care provider in rural health centers. Task shifting programs such as the HIV Nurse Practitioner program in Zambia, provide nurses with the education and skills needed to ensure that they can provide quality care to address the most pressing health care needs.

—Lynda Law Wilson, RN, PhD, FAAN Professor
Assistant Dean for International Affairs and Deputy Director, PAHO/WHO Collaborating Center on International Nursing; School of Nursing, University of Alabama at Birmingham

Educational Preparation and Global Health Opportunities for Nurses

Nursing educational programs are typically based on holistic frameworks with a strong emphasis on individual and community advocacy. In the United States, there are three different educational pathways for entering the nursing profession: (a) a 4-year baccalaureate degree program; (b) a 2 to 3-year associate degree program; or (c) a 3 to 4-year accelerated master's program for students who have bachelor's degrees in other fields. Graduates of all three of these programs are eligible to sit for the basic registered nurse National Council Licensure Examination (NCLEX).[10] Advanced practice nurses such as nurse anesthetists, clinical nurse specialists, nurse midwives, and nurse practitioners require further education. The educational requirements for basic and advanced nursing practice vary globally, although the WHO has proposed basic standards to guide professional nursing education worldwide.[11] Some schools of nursing partner with schools of public health to offer joint master's degrees in nursing and public health. Other universities offer global health certificates that are open to students in nursing and other health professions. These programs provide excellent preparation for nurses interested in global health careers.

There is a growing interest and involvement of higher education institutions in global health in the United States and throughout the world. Even though nursing faculty agree that global health concepts are important to incorporate in nursing education, a recent survey of nursing schools in the United States showed that, in nursing, the concept of global health is ill defined and its use is not consistent throughout the curricula.[12] Wilson et al. adapted a list of global health competencies that had been developed for medical students by the Association of Faculties of Medicine of Canada (AFMC) Resource Group on Global Health and the Global Health Education Consortium (GHEC), and surveyed nursing faculty in the United States, Canada, Latin America, and Caribbean to determine the extent to which they agreed that the competencies were relevant for nursing students. Results showed that the respondents perceived the modified competencies as important for nurses. Respondents also indicated additional competencies that should be considered. The researchers agreed that more research is needed in order to include other competencies in nursing curricula depending on the level of nursing program.[13]

In many higher education institutions, nursing students have the opportunity to participate in study abroad and service learning programs. Even though there is a limited body of empirical research evaluating the long-term outcomes of these programs, available evidence suggests that these programs help students develop the concepts of self-efficacy, cultural competency, and broaden their views of global nursing.[14] One example is the University of Tennessee Knoxville's

(UTK) "ready for the world program." The main goal of this program is to expose students to "intercultural learning." Students have the opportunity to travel to Panama and Costa Rica and collaborate with local health care providers to provide direct care and health promotion activities. Other intercultural opportunities for nursing students at UTK include placements in inner city settings and Spring break placements in the Appalachian Mountains.[15]

Vignette

Integration of Global Health Content in Nursing Curriculum

My family and I immigrated to the United States from Argentina in the late 80's; my parents were part of the dying middle class in Buenos Aires and anticipated the economic instability, so they moved what little they had to the United States in hopes of their three children gaining a quality education and doing their part to make the world a better place.

Growing up in the Western United States I attended well funded public schools from the elementary through high school levels, and was fortunate to be able to participate in various extracurricular activities, two factors that are not typical for a lower middle class socioeconomic household. At school I was surrounded mostly by peers who knew only the town they were born in and seemed unconnected from the economic flaws affecting many families, including my own. At home I experienced what poverty was in Argentina from my parent's storytelling, I learned about second and third world economics, although I was living in a country with a developed economy. I had a rare upbringing, and as an adolescent I was constantly aware of socioeconomic classes and how money affected every part of an individual's life. This fascination led to my focus on economic studies in undergraduate school, then to my serving as a Peace Corps volunteer and ultimately to my decision to attend nursing school. I learned through my upbringing and living for 2 ½ years as a Peace Corps volunteer in Zambia (one of the poorest countries in world), that the basis of a quality life is health. A community needs to be healthy in order to begin to bring about development, notwithstanding living life with access to medical care when illness presents. Not all individuals have had the global perspectives I have encountered and not all individuals go into nursing with the same motives. For me, however, nursing provides a broad range of opportunities to improve the quality of life.

I am just beginning an accelerated nursing program for students with bachelor's degrees in other fields. So far very few of my classes have addressed global health issues or the link between socioeconomic factors and health in the United States. I believe that nursing programs would be strengthened by including more focus on global health and on the social determinants of health. There are many ways that nursing faculty could introduce these concepts without adding to an already crowded curriculum. For example, during lectures faculty could introduce the similarities and differences in health problems and solutions across the globe. They could also encourage students to participate in global health interest groups, study away courses, and to enroll in global health elective courses. Nursing schools should put a particular amount of focus on economic and social factors affecting individuals as they relate to healthcare by discussing existing situations in local communities, rural and/or urban, city/county/state or national to give students an understanding of a large element of healthcare.

During my still young life I have been a part of lower-, middle- and upper-middle socioeconomic classes in the United States, I have lived amongst Zambia's poorest for over two years, I have worked with underprivileged and privileged populations stateside, and I have studied economies and global health in an academic setting, all have contributed to a heighten awareness of my role as a nurse in any community. The more empathy a nursing student (nurse) can possess, the more compassion she/he will set forth into their practice, into their patient, and into their community.

—Andrea Torre, Accelerated Nursing Student
University of Alabama at Birmingham

Partnerships among health care organizations and nursing educational programs can improve health care outcomes, increase nursing and student global health capacity, and foster health care delivery using evidence-based practice.[16,17] One example of such a collaboration is the partnership between nurses from North Shore University Hospital in Manhasset, New York, and Erebouni Medical Center in Yerevan, Armenia. Through this partnership, nurses are working towards the application of evidence-based practice in the Erebouini Medical Center. Findings from the evaluation of this partnership indicate that it resulted in improved nursing assessments, plans of care, and performance.[16] Another example of a nursing school collaboration aimed at improving global health is the participatory community action research project conducted in Peru by nursing faculty at the University of San Francisco and the Universidad Católica Santo Toribio de Mogrovejo (USAT) in Chiclayo, Peru (see Focus Box).

Global Health Professional Linkages for Nurses

There are numerous nursing organizations that provide resources for nurses interested in global health (see Table 1). One such organization is the Global Network of the 43 WHO Nursing and Midwifery Collaborating Centers that provide support to advance the MDGs and the WHO Strategic Plan for Nursing and Midwifery. Other key resources are the Sigma Theta Tau International (STTI), Honor Society of Nursing, and the International Council of Nurses (ICN). STTI supports the learning and professional development of nurses to impact health worldwide. The ICN promotes quality care and sound health policies globally. Both organizations have active linkages worldwide to host conferences, develop position statements, advance quality nursing and health initiatives, and affect policy. Another resource is The Nightingale Declaration Initiative for Global Health (NIGH). NIGH is an organization that focuses on providing awareness on global health issues to nurses and citizens and it also highlights the contributions of nursing to achieving MDGs. There are also several online listservs or communities of practice that are excellent resources that can promote collaboration and connection for nurses interested in global health. Two examples are the Global Alliance of Nursing and Midwifery (GANM) and the Global Health Nursing & Midwifery online community of practice.

The Center for Communicable Disease (CDC), the WHO, the United States Public Health Service, and the United States Uniformed Services, and many other voluntary and NGOs, employ nurses in global practice, consultative, and administrative positions.

Table 1.

Organization	Website
Sigma Theta Tau International	http://www.nursingsociety.org/default.aspx
WHO Nursing and Midwifery Collaborating Centers	http://www.who.int/hrh/nursing_midwifery/en/
International Council of Nurses	http://www.icn.ch/
Nightingale Declaration Initiative for Global Health	http://www.nightingaledeclaration.net/
Global Alliance of Nursing and Midwifery	http://knowledge-gateway.org/ganm
Global Health Nursing & Midwifery online community of practice	http://www.ghdonline.org/nursing/
International Federation of Nurse Anesthetists	http://www.ifna-int.org/ifna/news.php
International Federation of Perioperative Nurses	http://www.ifpn.org.uk/
Council of International Neonatal Nurses	http://www.coinnurses.org/
European Federation of Nurses Associations	http://www.efnweb.eu/
International Skin Care Nursing Group	http://www.isng.co.uk/
NANDA International	http://www.nanda.org/
World Federation of Critical Care Nurses	http://en.wfccn.org/

Summary

Nurses comprise the greatest number of professional health care providers throughout the world, and have a key role in contributing to achievement of the Millennium Development Goals. Nurses may be educated in 2, 3, or 4-year college programs or pursue advanced degrees for specialist, practitioner, midwifery, or anesthesia practice. Although global health is not addressed consistently in nursing curricula, public/community health content and practice is a part of all accredited programs and many offer additional field experiences in other countries. Several prominent nursing organizations are active in global health issues to promote policy, education, research, and advanced practice. Nursing leadership is critical to addressing global health challenges, and it is imperative that nursing curricula incorporate global health content to prepare nurses to assume these leadership roles.

Environmental Perspectives on Healthy Households in Rural Peru

"Families living in poverty in rural Latin America face staggering challenges in environmental health, including clean air, safe water and even basic sanitation. A participatory action research aimed at changing the living conditions of rural peasant families in the arid desert region of Pacora and Illimo in Northern Perú was conducted by two nurses from the University of San Francisco. Strategies used were drawn from the WHO (1997) approach on primary environmental health, which supports a preventative, participatory action approach that recognizes the human right to live and flourish in a healthy, sustainable environment. A total of 81 families participated in a 3-year project. The nurses conducted a baseline survey to identify community priorities. Some of the most distressing findings were that families were drinking water directly from lakes, using open fields for human waste, and cooking on open fires inside the home. In collaboration with the people of the community, 36 monthly workshops were given on the following topics: forest management, employment opportunities, animal husbandry, and healthy home interventions. The healthy homes program included training environmental health promoters to strengthen the participation and organization of their communities, including latrine and clean cookstove construction. By the end of this project, most of the area homes were using safe cookstoves, covered latrines, and sanitary landfills. Local economic development was markedly increased, including sustainable management of the dry forest, an important feature of this desert region of Perú. The project was executed by the Center for Ecology and Gender (Centro ECO), faculty and students in the School of Nursing at Universidad Católica Santo Toribio de Mogrovejo (USAT) in Chiclayo, Perú and funded by Heifer Project International. Research faculties at USAT and at the School of Nursing at University of California, San Francisco are currently collaborating to conduct a follow-up study to assess sustained community involvement in improving the environmental health of village families."[18]

—Lisa Thompson, RN, PhD, FNP-C
University of California, San Francisco

—Maribel Diaz Vásquez, RN, MS
Escuela de Enfermería Universidad Católica Santo Toribio de Mogrovejo, Chiclayo, Perú

References

1. "Definition of Nursing." *International Council of Nurses.* 2008. 1 June 2012 <http://www.icn.ch/about-icn/icn-definition-of-nursing/>.
2. Dickenson-Hazard, Nancy. "Global Health Issues and Challenges." *Journal of Nursing Scholarship* 36.1 (2004). 36(1): 6-10.
3. Amieva, Shelly, and Stephanie Ferguson. "Moving forward: Nurses are Key to Achieving the United Nations Development Program's Millennium Development Goals." *International Nursing Review* 59.1 (2012): 55-58.
4. Delamaire, Marie-Laure, and Gaetan Lafortune. "Nurses in Advanced Roles: A Description and Evaluation of Experiences in 12 Developed Countries." *OECD Health Working Papers* 54 (2010): 1-106. 4 June 2012 < http://www.oecd-ilibrary.org/social-issues-migration-health/nurses-in-advanced-roles_5kmbrcfms5g7-en>.
5. Horrocks, Sue, Eliabeth B. Anderson, and Chris Salisbury. "Systematic Review of whether Nurse Practitioners Working in Primary Care can Provide Equivalent Care to Doctors." *British Medical Journal* 324.7341 (2002): 819-823.
6. "First Global Conference on Task Shifting." *World Health Organization.* WHO: Geneva, Switzerland, 2008. 7 June 2012 < http://www.who.int/mediacentre/events/meetings/task_shifting/en/>.
7. Huicho, Luis, et al. "How Much Does Quality of Child Care Vary between Health Workers with Differing Durations of Training? An Observational Multicountry Study." *The Lancet* 372.9642 (2008): 910-916.
8. McPake, Barbara, and Kwadwo Mensah. "Task Shifting in Health Care in Resource-Poor Countries." *The Lancet.* 372.9642 (2008): 870-871.
9. Msidi, Eleanor D., et al. "The Zambian HIV Nurse Practitioner Diploma Program: Preliminary Outcomes from First Cohort of Zambian Nurses." *International Journal of Nursing Education Scholarship* 8.1 (2011).
10. Benner, Patricia, Victoria Leonard, and Lisa Day. *Educating Nurses. A Call for Radical Transformation.* Vista Lane, Stanford. California: The Carnegie Foundation for the Advancement of Teaching, 2010.
11. "Global Standards for the Initial Education of Nurses and Midwives." *World Health Organization.* WHO: Geneva, Switzerland, 2009.
12. Carlton, Kay, H., et al. "Integration of Global Health Concepts in Nursing Curricula: A National Study." *Nursing Education Perspectives* 28.3 (2007): 124-129.
13. Wilson, Lynda., et al. "Global Health Competencies for Nurses in the Americas." *Journal of Professional Nursing* 28.4 (2012): 213-222.
14. Edmonds, Michelle L."An Integrative Literature Review of Study Abroad Programs for Nursing Students." *Nursing Education Perspectives* 33.1 (2012): 30-34.
15. Callen, Bonnie L., and Jan L. Lee. "Ready for the World: Preparing Nursing Students for Tomorrow." *Journal of Professional Nursing* 25.5 (2009): 292-298.
16. Bentson, Joanne, et al. "A Nursing Partnership: The Forces of Magnetism Guiding Evidence-Based Practice in the Republic of Armenia." *Journal of Continuing Education in Nursing* 36.4 (2005): 175-179.
17. Lacey-Haun, Lora C., and Tanya D. Whitehead. "Leading Change Through an International Faculty Development programme." *Journal of Nursing Management* 17.8 (2009):. 917-930.
18. Thompson, Lisa. "Environmental Perspectives on Healthy Households in Rural Peru." Global Health Conference, November, 2011, Montreal, Canada. Unpublished conference abstract (2011). 8 June 2012 <http://www.xcdtech.com/ghc2011/27.003.html.

Occupational Therapy and Global Health

Often when people hear the word "occupation," the immediate association is with a job or employment. Although the original focus of occupational therapy in the late 1800s was on the use of remedial activities to help restore an individual's health (often in the realm of work),[1,2] the profession has moved far beyond this original focus to consider all daily activities that can impact a person's health. The demand for and training in the profession of occupational therapy grew substantially following the World Wars when occupational therapists (OTs) were called upon to help injured soldiers adjust to their lives as civilians. Since then, national and international professional associations have developed the education of occupational therapists has progressed to entry level master's training in North America,[1,3] and the focus of the profession has expanded to promoting health through participation in all daily activities.[4]

A local seamstress prepares burn compression suits for children with third degree burns through a program funded by an American NGO
Photographer: *Will Bynum*

Today, occupational therapy is defined as a profession that focuses on enabling engagement and participation in everyday living by changing and/or accommodating aspects of the person, occupation and environments or a combination of all three.[5,6] OTs work in a number of settings, including community agencies, health care organizations (hospitals, chronic care facilities, and rehabilitation centers), schools and social agencies.[6] In these settings, OTs work with individuals or groups who experience difficulty engaging in the daily activities that are important to them due to body structure or function impairments (e.g., a stroke survivor who is unable to cook for himself/ herself because of limited hand functions), or social and physical environments that restrict their participation (e.g., a child with cerebral palsy who is unable to attend the local school because it is inaccessible to her wheelchair and some children at the school tease the child and won't invite her to play in their games).[5] Despite the varied settings and populations with whom OTs work, the core feature of occupational therapy practice common to all settings is promoting engagement in occupations, which refers to all activities people participate in throughout the day (activities of daily living) including productive occupations (e.g., work or volunteering), leisure, or self-care (e.g., taking care of oneself).[4]

Occupational Therapy Contributions to Global Health

Occupational therapy skills and approaches are easily applied in the global health environment since 'activities of daily living' are fundamental to all human existence and development.[7] When supported by cultural awareness, OTs' client-centered approach helps to identify what is important and meaningful for an individual and OTs' clinical skills help to enable an individual to achieve their goals in culturally-relevant ways. OTs adhere to a broader definition of health that goes beyond just the absence of disease and addresses multiple social and environmental determinants that have an inevitable effect on health (e.g., poverty, marginalization, exclusion, inaccessible environments, stigma and gender inequality).[8] As a result, OTs deliver services to marginalized populations and thus contribute to the achievement of MDGs specifically as they pertain to people with disabilities.

According to WHO's World Disability Report in 2011, there are more than one billion people living with disability, with the majority living in the low and middle income countries in conditions of poverty with limited access to 'activities of daily living' such as education, employment and opportunities for social participation.[9] Together with other professionals, OTs working in the global health settings often use the Community Based Rehabilitation (CBR) framework (first introduced by the WHO) that enables them to provide multidisciplinary solutions to address MDGs.[8] CBR is a strategy that focuses on enhancing the quality of life for people with disabilities and their families, meeting basic needs and ensuring inclusion and participation.[9] CBR often involves family members and community workers in providing basic care and education at the community level that will promote the inclusion of people with disabilities in their community. The CBR team includes health care professionals, people with disabilities, their families and the appropriate educational, vocational and social services who work as a team in the community to contribute to the achievement of MDGs.[8] Today occupational therapy practices have gone beyond rehabilitation by drawing on international development principles to address MDGs beyond those that focus on health. Below is one example of how an OT can address MDGs by working with a young girl with cerebral palsy, at various stages of her life.

Vignette

Hannah is a young girl who lives in a rural village in a low and middle-income country (LMIC). She has cerebral palsy and is unable to walk. She wanted to go to primary school with her siblings but faced a number of barriers. Hannah's parents wanted her to stay at home because education requires a financial investment and spending already limited finances on a child with disability is not considered a priority.[10] Teachers at the school were not trained to work with children with disabilities, so they were uncertain how to work with Hannah. In order for Hannah to go to school, she needed a wheelchair and an accessible path from her home to the main road. An occupational therapist used discipline-specific clinical expertise as well as CBR strategy to enhance Hannah`s quality of life, ensure inclusion and participation and to address MDGs.

Often parents are gatekeepers in determining the opportunities their children with disabilities will have.[10] The OT worked with the family to educate family members on the cause of the disability, importance of supporting Hannah`s endeavors and decision making, and the disadvantage of the excessive assistance from families.[10] In order to change attitudes towards people with disabilities, a community often needs to undergo a paradigm shift.[10] The OT worked with a local church to educate the public regarding disability and human rights to decrease social stigma.

The OT also educated the family members about the activities they could do with Hannah to promote development and learning. By doing so, the therapist contributed to the improvement of the child's current health status and also reduced the risk of secondary health issues. For example, education on positioning, exercises and participation in activities can prevent the development of contractures or pressure ulcers.

By recognizing that education is one of the main occupations for a child, the OT addressed *inclusive education* by working with teachers and the school to raise disability awareness and reduce environmental barriers that limited Hannah's ability to attend school. The OT provided disability training to local school teachers by raising awareness regarding disability issues and provided hands on training on how to assist Hannah with learning. The OT liaised with local Disabled People`s Organizations, which in turn were able to donate a used wheelchair for Hannah. Together with a local bicycle repair shop, the therapist constructed extra postural support devices (solid seat and pelvis side pads) to adapt a used wheelchair to suit Hannah`s needs. By raising family and public awareness, the OT focused on empowering Hannah and Hannah`s family, who then mobilized the community to build a path from their house to the main road to enable Hannah to use a wheelchair to get to school. To make sure that Hannah could use the wheelchair at school, a therapist used scrap wood from a local workshop to build a ramp. The OT taught Hannah how to safely use her wheelchair and focused on encouraging Hannah to do as much independently as she could.

When Hannah finished school, she wanted to support herself by working as a seamstress, but did not have enough money to buy a sewing machine. Micro financing development programs has been successful in helping women gain financial independence in many developing countries but many women with disabilities are marginalized and overlooked when it comes to microfinance initiatives.[10] The OT understood the opportunities a micro financing loan could provide for Hannah and together with Hannah and other members of the CBR team, advocated for the micro financing development programs to be more inclusive of women with disabilities. By using the CBR approach, steps were taken towards *gender equality* and reducing *poverty/hunger.*

Natasha Altin, MscOT
Dalhousie University, Halifax, Canada

Educational Preparation and Global Health Opportunities for Occupational Therapists

The educational requirements for entering the occupational therapy profession vary depending on the country's regulations. However, in order to practice in most countries a person must have either a diploma or university degree in occupational therapy. For example, in order to enter the field of OT in North America, one must graduate from an accredited master's degree OT program, complete 1000 hours of supervised fieldwork and pass a national exam.[3,6] Due to the program's intensity and short timeframe, as well as accreditation limitations, students have limited opportunities for elective courses and often the global health content is not explored in depth in the compulsory curriculum. However, many OT academic programs have incorporated global health into the curriculum through international fieldwork (IFW) experience and include discussions of health disparities, social determinants of health, community development approaches, which can all relate to local and global health issues.[7] IFW experience is a valuable opportunity for OT students to learn about and contribute to global health. Students engaging in the IFW identify this experience as a time of personal and professional development with many students reporting greater cultural awareness and a deeper understanding of global health issues.[11,12] Additionally, students form long-lasting global relationships, and can gain an opportunity to work as part of the interdisciplinary team in a global health context.[12]

Because the required OT curriculum does not consistently provide substantial global health education, some Canadian universities provide mandatory training and support to students before, after and during the IFW process. Since students are often working with individuals in the most vulnerable situations, the ethical dilemmas of working internationally are considered before the departure by using cases presentations, videos, discussions and expert opinions from the field. Dalhousie University integrated the global health competencies that were developed by the AFMC and GHEC in preparing students for IFW through discussions on social, cultural and economic determinants of health; understanding the impact of population growth and of unsustainable and inequitable resource consumption and their effects on determining health status; understanding aspects of healthcare in low resource setting; and promoting and protecting health as a human right. The pre-departure preparation also included discussions on the global burden of disease, and health implications of travel, migration and displacement. Prior to embarking on the IFW experience, students should be able to demonstrate an ability to apply these competencies to a practical setting and translate them into a role as an advocate for their patient and health care team. Debriefing after students complete their IFW is essential to solidify their new knowledge as well as to engage in a formal reflective process about the cross cultural experiences that will enhance their personal and professional development.

The sustainability of IFW for OTs requires strong partnerships based on reciprocity, and can be promoted by collaborative research initiatives and professional development programs. Faculty engagement is a critical element within global health. If IFW focuses solely on student experiences, then the opportunity for OTs to expand and support health care systems is limited. Faculty members offer a mentorship role for students as well as clinicians within the partnership institutions. This mentorship can focus on enhanced clinical skills as well as developing evidence-informed practice. Several Canadian universities have expanded their international fieldwork through research programs and development projects (e.g., University of Toronto and Queens University). These initiatives ensure that faculty members are engaged in global health and can support the ethical growth of international fieldwork for OT students.[13]

Global Health Professional Linkages for Occupational Therapists

The contribution of OT to global health is evident through the establishment of the World Federation of Occupational Therapists (WFOT) in 1952. WFOT is the official organization for the promotion of occupational therapy worldwide and accreditations of the educational programs.[14] WFOT had a tremendous impact on global health by collaborating and partnering with multiple international organizations, such as the United Nations (UN), United Nations International Children's Fund (UNICEF), the WHO, and the International Council on Disability.[14] The WFOT has a long-standing collaboration with WHO and provides input on multiple WHO initiatives, including World Report on Disability (2011) which provides evidence to support policies and programs that can improve the lives of people with disabilities.[9] The WFOT contributed to the development of the report by providing technical and political support and expertise regarding the rights of people with disabilities.[15]

Practicing Occupational Therapy in Sierra Leone

Today, many international organizations that are involved in health promotion, social change and poverty reduction recognize the importance of the participation of people in activities that are meaningful for them.[4] For example, many global health initiatives are built around people going to school, working, participating in community events, all of which are considered occupations. This allows for interdisciplinary collaboration amongst OTs and other professions. The following is an example of an OT's interdisciplinary (health care and non-health care professions) effort in global health development in post-civil war Sierra Leone.

In 2002, a Canadian OT with two local NGOs (Forum for African Women Educationalists and Children Affected by War) in Sierra Leone facilitated the socio-economic reintegration of war victims with physical and psychological disabilities. Sierra Leone has endured one of the most brutal civil wars marked by torture, summary executions, child kidnapping, young girls being reduced to sexual slavery and young boys forced into the rebel army. In the war's aftermath the country faced reconstruction on all levels from health to educational systems while having limited resources.

In partnership with the OT, these two non-health care organizations used programs that combined their cultural beliefs with the notion of occupation. Specifically the two organizations used activities of daily living such as gathering water, building homes or starting a business as a therapeutic medium for managing posttraumatic stress disorder. Establishing healthy routines using activities of daily living allowed individuals to regain a long lost sense of control over their lives.[16] Healthy routines and the introduction of appropriate occupations allowed individuals to regain emotional balance, rediscover traditional values and identity, and learn to refocus their energy away from violence and substance abuse with an emphasis on objectives that promote *inclusive education, hunger reduction, gender equality, maternal and child health.*[16]

Natasha Altin, MscOT
Dalhousie University, Halifax, Canada

Summary

OTs work in varied settings and promote engagement in occupations which represent activities people participate in throughout the day (activities of daily living). OT skills and approaches are transferable into the global health environment since 'activities of daily living' are fundamental to all human existence. OTs deliver services to marginalized populations and thus contribute to the achievement of the UN's MDGs, in particular as they relate to people with disabilities. Global health content is not explored in depth in the required occupational therapy curriculum but many occupational therapy academic programs have incorporated global health into the curriculum through international fieldwork. Pre-departure training and debriefing upon return from fieldwork are key essential elements to the personal and professional development of students in the field of global health. The future of international fieldwork depends on strong partnerships based on reciprocity, collaborative research initiatives and professional development programs. The WFOT is the official organization for the promotion of occupational therapy worldwide and accreditation of the educational programs. WFOT has a tremendous impact on global health by collaborating and partnering with multiple international organizations.

References

1. Driver, Muriel. "A Philosophic View of the History of Occupational Therapy in Canada." *Canadian Journal of Occupational Therapy* 35 (1968): 53-60.
2. Punwar, Alice, and Suzanne Peloquin. *Occupational Therapy: Principles and Practice.* Baltimore, Maryland: Lippincott Williams & Wilkins, 2002.
3. "FAQ about the Entry-Level Master's and Doctoral Degrees for Occupational Therapist." *American Occupational Therapy Association.* 10 July 2012 <http://www.aota.org/ Students/Prospective/FAQs/ FAQDegrees.aspx>.
4. Njelesani, Janet, Deb Cameron, and Helene Polatajko. "Occupation for Development: Expanding the Boundaries of Occupational Science into the International Development Agenda." *Journal of Occupational Science* 19.1 (2012): 36-43.
5. "Statement on Occupational Therapy." *World Federation of Occupational Therapists.* 10 July 2012 < http:// www.wfot.org/ResourceCentre.aspx >.
6. "Occupational Therapy." *Canadian Association of Occupational Therapists.* 10 July 2012 < http://www.caot.ca/default.asp?pageid=546>.
7. Barker, Allison, Elizabeth A. Kinsella, and Ann Bosser. "Learning in International Practice Placement Education: A Grounded Theory Study." *British Journal of Occupational Therapy* 73 (2010): 29-37.
8. Lang, Raymond. "Community Based Rehabilitation and Health Professional Practice: Developmental opportunities and challenges in the Global North and South." *Disability and Rehabilitation* 33.2 (2011): 165-173.
9. "World Report on Disability." *World Health Organization*, 2011. 22 July 2012 < http://whqlibdoc.who.int/publications/2011/9789240685215_eng.pdf >.
10. Kiani, Shirin. "Women with Disabilities in the North West Province of Cameroon: Resilient and Deserving of Greater Attention." *Disability and Society* 24 (2009): 517-531.
11. Clampin, Anna. "Overseas Placements: Addressing Our Challenges?" *British Journal of Occupational Therapy* 71 (2008): 354-356.
12. Humbert, Keiter, Allison Burket, Rebecca Deveney, and Katelyn Kennedy. "Occupational Therapy Students 'Perspectives Regarding International Cross-Cultural Experiences." *Australian Occupational Therapy Journal* 59 (2012): 225-234.
13. O'Hearn, Shawna. Personal interview. 27 August 2012.
14. Carswell, Anne. "The World Federation of Occupational Therapists and the Canadian Association of Occupational Therapists: A Collaborative Venture." *Occupational Therapy Now* 13.1 (2011): 22-24.
15. "Concept Note World Report on Disability and Rehabilitation." *World Health Organization,* 2008. 22 Jul 2012 <http://www.who.int/disabilities/publications/dar_world_report_concept_note.pdf>.
16. Tribeault, Rachel. "Occupation and the Rebuilding of Civil Society: Notes from the War". *Journal of Occupational Science* 9 (2002): 38-47

Optometry

Uncorrected refractive error is the most common cause of vision impairment in the world, causing 43% of the estimated 285 million cases of visual impairment.[1-3] The WHO and the International Agency to Prevent Blindness (IAPB) have identified the correction of refractive error as one of the cornerstones of the Vision 2020 initiative.[4] Impaired vision has a significant impact on quality of life limiting many activities of daily living including reading, working, and accessing public transportation.

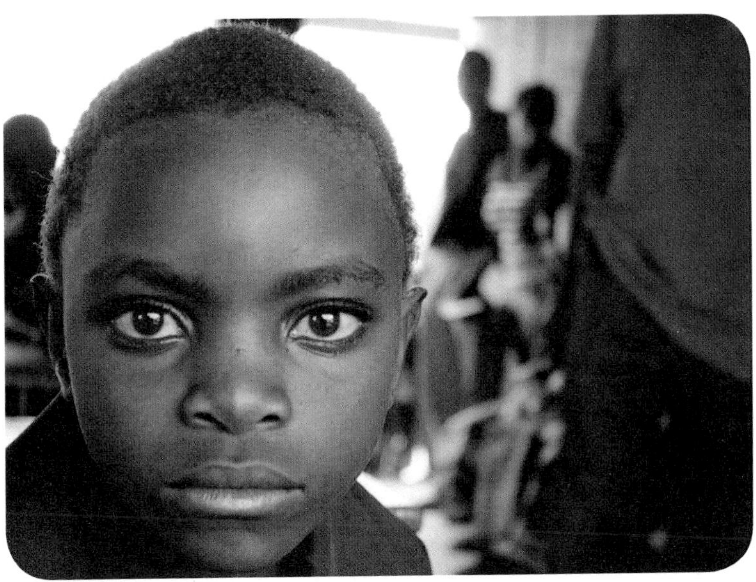

The striking gaze of a patient treated in a rudimentary clinic in rural Africa.
Photographer: *Bynum*

Vignette

A ten-year old, very shy girl who lived in an orphanage in Peru had always been regarded as a blind child. She had no access to eye care in her life, and the orphanage staff could tell that she was not able to see the board at school and had difficulty moving around. A Volunteer Optometric Services to Humanity (VOSH) team came to the orphanage to do eye exams on all the children and found out she was just able to see 1/200 (very large letters at a distance of one foot). Upon measuring her refractive error, the team found the little girl had -15.00 diopters of myopia in each eye, and she had no eye pathology. When she put her glasses on, she smiled and cried and looked around in amazement. She was able to see 20/60 with her glasses! Her mobility and her school performance improved immediately, and even her personality changed. A local optometrist was contacted and agreed to continue to provide care for this little girl. She is now almost finished with high school.

—Marcela Frazier OD, MPH, FAAO
Assistant Professor
University of Alabama at Birmingham

As primary eye care providers, optometrists are uniquely qualified to change thousands of lives in a positive way, simply through prescribing glasses. However, optometrists do more than assessing vision and prescribing glasses. Optometrists are best described as "primary eye care providers." Just as primary care physicians can manage and treat systemic disease, but are also the gateway to specialized care for their patients, optometrists can manage and treat eye disease. When referrals are necessary to specialists (cataract surgeon, glaucoma specialist, etc) an optometrist can make the proper referral. Although the scope of practice in the United States varies from state to state, optometrists are able to diagnose and treat diseases of the eye and adnexa with confidence and skill.

Educational Preparation and Global Health Opportunities for Optometrists

The practice of optometry varies depending on the country of practice, and this can be an issue when an optometrist is practicing or volunteering overseas. In the United States, optometrists must complete an accredited Doctor of Optometry program and receive licensing from a national board, as well as from the state in which they intend to practice. In other countries, such as Malaysia and Taiwan, however, optometry education requires a four-year bachelor's degree.[5] For this reason, practicing and volunteering overseas may sometimes be challenging, depending on the country in which one would like to volunteer.

To become an optometrist in the United States, students must first complete an undergraduate degree and specific prerequisite courses in biology, chemistry, and physics. The doctoral program in optometry is four years in length. Similar to medical school, optometry school begins with mostly classroom work; with more patient care and clinical training being added as students advance through the program. There are opportunities for advanced training after optometry school, with many optometrists electing to complete a one-year residency. Residency offers the chance to hone clinical skills and learn advanced competency in areas of practice. There are residencies offered in primary eye care, contact lens, pediatrics, ocular disease, vision therapy, low vision and various other specialties.

Contributions of Optometrists to Global Health

Optometrists have made significant contributions towards improving global health.[6] Optometrists have been pioneers in identifying and addressing the issue of uncorrected refractive error as a global health concern. Optometry has also made tremendous strides in identifying areas of the world with reduced access to eye care.[6,7] Several optometric organizations continuously provide volunteer clinicians and educators to serve in low resource countries around the world. Optometrists provide direct service as well as education for patients and for health professionals. They provide education on topics ranging from prevention of eye injuries to glaucoma treatment.

Optometrists understand the importance of being part of a multi-disciplinary team. When optometry is practiced as intended, optometrists become the gateway eye care provider, screening out the patients who are visually impaired due to refractive error and making proper referrals for the patients who have other ocular pathology. An optometrist cannot practice in a vacuum. There must be public health efforts to increase the public awareness of eye problems. There must be eye surgeons to treat cataracts and other pathology. As the number of optometrists increases worldwide, the ratio of eye care professionals to patients will hopefully become much more balanced.

To increase the number of eye care professionals in less developed countries, optometric organizations are working with global non-profit organizations to establish self-sustainable training programs in underserved countries. For example, in 2012 the first optometry school in Malawi graduated its inaugural class. As more programs are implemented and developed, national optometrists will continue to function as primary eye care providers, with less need for international mission trips from overseas groups. However, the new schools will always need lecturers and professors.

Global Health Professional Linkages for Optometrists

Student Volunteers in Optometric Service to Humanity (SVOSH)

There are various opportunities to be involved in global health while in optometry school. Most optometry schools in the United States have Student Volunteers in Optometric Service to Humanity (SVOSH) clubs that raise funds and travel overseas on mission trips every year. Another important aspect of SVOSH is to raise awareness of international eye care issues and introduce students to how they can make a difference globally. Getting involved in a school's SVOSH club is a great way to be involved in global health care.

Volunteer Optometric Services to Humanity (VOSH)

When optometry students graduate and begin practicing, they can transition to become a member of a local Volunteer Optometric Services to Humanity (VOSH) group. The primary mission of VOSH is as follows: "To facilitate the provision and the sustainability of vision care worldwide for people who can neither afford nor obtain such care." (www.vosh.org) VOSH chapters endeavor to provide care on both short term and long term trips. VOSH also is working to support sustainable care in the countries in which they work. For more information on VOSH visit www.vosh.org.

International Center for Eyecare Education (ICEE)

The International Center for Eyecare Education (ICEE) is the Public Health part of the Brien Holden Vision Institute, an Australian-based non-profit organization that is working to eliminate vision impairment secondary to uncorrected refractive error worldwide. ICEE estimates that globally, at least 670 million people are blind or vision impaired simply because they don't have access to an eye examination and a pair of glasses. In order to reach their goal, ICEE is heavily involved in training eye care professionals and enhancing infrastructure in many countries. ICEE has opened optometry training programs in Eritrea, Mozambique, Malawi, and other underserved countries. There are opportunities for U.S.-trained optometrists to teach in these schools. For more information on ICEE, please visit http://www.brienholdenvision.org/.

The World Council of Optometry (WCO)

The World Council of Optometry strives to make eye care available to all people. They "facilitate the development of optometry around the world and support optometrists in promoting eye health and vision care as a human right through advocacy, education, policy development and humanitarian outreach."[8] WCO has had tremendous impact in developing data on the current status of eye care in countries around the world, and in creating the partnerships to address the specific needs in eye care for each country. To learn more about WCO, access http://www.worldoptometry.org/.

Summary

Optometrists are uniquely trained and positioned to be a global force for good. Because of their training, optometrists are able to eliminate the most common cause of blindness and visual impairment in the world, uncorrected refractive error. They are also able to manage and treat ocular disease as primary eye care providers. In the global health arena, optometry will become increasingly important as more focus is put onto implementing sustainable training programs in underserved countries.[4,7]

Many new optometry educational programs are being developed will make great contributions to eliminating preventable blindness and visual impairments. There will be a growing need for optometrists and faculty to teach new eye care professionals how to practice. In the developing world, there can be millions of people for each trained eye care professional.[6] As optometry is developed as a profession in underserved countries, optometrists can make a huge impact on people's lives.

Malawi School of Optometry Story

Africa is home to 10% of the world's population, yet this continent claims 19% of the world's blind.[9] Insufficient and poorly distributed personnel, variable qualification levels, limited career paths and fragile health care infrastructures significantly impair eye and vision care. Until recently, just 6 of 57 countries in Africa trained optometrists or refractive personnel at varying competency levels.

Malawi is a small landlocked country in sub-Saharan Africa and is one of the poorest and least developed of all African countries. With the help of several international NGO's, two programs have been created to address the need for primary eye care and refractive correction in a country where access to eye care and even spectacles is not possible for most people.

Mzuzu University, in the northern territory of the country, enrolls 2,500 students, the large majority of which are on government funding. In April 2008, a group of students commenced their studies in a brand new four-year Bachelor of Science degree in Optometry program, under the guidance of foreign optometrist lecturers.

In November 2010, the first group of students was enrolled in a 3-year mid-level eye care diploma course for Optometric Technicians at the Malawi College of Health Sciences in Lilongwe, the capital of Malawi. Once qualified, these Optometric Technicians will be skilled primarily in refraction and basic primary eye care. To ensure equitable distribution of trained eye care personnel, they will be deployed to district hospitals bringing optometric services closer to the majority of citizens.

The provision of affordable and accessible eye care services in Malawi took a big step forward in August 2012 when the first five optometrists graduated from Mzuzu University. These new clinicians will complete a one-year internship, rotating through the various regional hospitals around the country, and will be licensed to practice in the public or private sector. Ultimately, several graduates will return to Mzuzu as educators in the optometry program to ensure proper training and quality eye care will continue to be made available to the people of Malawi, by the people of Malawi.

Along with the success of the degree programs in Malawi, in October 2012 an advanced vision care centre will open, having been constructed as part of the Mzuzu Central Hospital. This centre will be dedicated to primary eye care, offering comprehensive eye exams, refractive services and contact lenses. This vision centre will also function within the greater health care community of the country of Malawi.

The success of the optometric training programs in Malawi has gained international recognition and serves as a model for other countries to develop training programs to bring much needed eye care services to places most in need.

—Sara McGowan OD, MS
Lecturer at Mzuzu University,
2011 Graduate of UAB School of Optometry
2011-2012 Resident Optometrist at Bascom Palmer Eye Institute, Miami, FL

References

1. Dandona, Lalit, et al. "Blindness in the Indian State of Andhra Pradesh." *Investigative Ophthalmology and Visual Science* 42.5 (2001): 908-16.
2. Pascolini, Donatella, and Silvio P. Mariotti. "Global Estimates of Visual Impairment: 2010." *British Journal of Ophthalmology* 96 (2012): 614-18.
3. Resnikoff, Serge, et al. "Global Magnitude of Visual Impairment Caused by Uncorrected Refractive Errors in 2004." *Bulletin of the World Health Organization* 86.1 (2008): 63-70.
4. "What Is VISION 2020?" *Vision 2020: The Right to Sight.* 2011. 08 September 2012 <http://www.vision2020.org/main.cfm?type=WHATVISION2020>.
5. Yap, Maurice, and Vanessa Thai BOptom "Optometry in Asia." *Optometry within the Public Health Community.* Cadyville: Old Post, 2010. 1-27 <http://webpages.charter.net/oldpostpublishing/oldpostpublishing/Section%205,%20World%20Optometry/Section%205,%20Optometry%20in%20Asia%20by%20Thai%20and%20Yap.pdf>.
6. Holden, Brien A., and Serge Resnikoff. "The Role of Optometry in VISION 2020." *Community Eye Health* 15.43 (2002): 33-36.
7. Dandona, Rakhi, and Lalit Dandona. "Refractive Error Blindness." *Bulletin of the World Health Organization* 79.3 (2001): 237-43.
8. "Mission, Vision, and Goals." *World Council of Optometry.* N.d. 22 November 2012 < http://www.worldoptometry.org/en/about-wco/vision-and-mission.cfm>.
9. Naidoo K. "Poverty and Blindness in Africa". *Clinical and Experimental Optometry* 90.6 (2007): 415-21.

Physical Therapy

Physical therapy is the profession that allows licensed therapists to examine, evaluate, and develop intervention programs for patients or clients who experience movement dysfunction secondary to impairments of range of motion, strength, endurance, balance, coordination, or other functional deficits. Physical therapists (PTs) excel in rehabilitative services and also are the preferred healthcare providers to teach individuals and communities how exercise and healthy lifestyles can prevent human movement dysfunction.

PTs serve patients and clients of all ages and with diverse problems such as infants with Down syndrome, high school athletes with knee injuries, or elderly persons recovering from strokes. Common settings in which PTs work include hospitals, schools, home health, outpatient clinics, and inpatient rehabilitation centers. Examples of conditions PTs may treat include but are not limited to pain in joints and muscles, traumatic brain injury, joint replacement, stroke, headaches, impaired posture, wounds, difficulty walking, various neuromuscular disorders, cardiopulmonary impairments, and athletic injuries.

A student volunteer assists a burned patient's rehabilitation efforts
Photographer: *Will Bynum*

The WHO estimates that one billion (approximately 15%) people worldwide live with disabilities,[1] and the majority of these individuals reside in countries with no more than minimal access to rehabilitative services.[2] It is also estimated that between 110-190 million of individuals 15 years and older have severe functional limitations.[1] Due to the health disparities seen across the globe, the PT profession needs to increase its efforts to collaborate with other professions (i.e., physicians, nurses, OTs, speech therapists, pharmacists, engineers, etc.) to meet the needs of communities that have limited access to physical therapy clinics. Some of the challenges that PTs encounter when serving in low resource countries include a high patient-to-therapist ratio, lack of equipment, decreased length of hospital stays, language barriers, and cultural differences.[3] For example, PTs must often utilize close physical contact with patients. However, in certain cultures this contact may be considered unacceptable, especially if a female is treating a male, or vice versa. Therefore, the American Physical Therapy Association (APTA) recommends conducting extensive research of potential international endeavors regarding "all requirements, expectations, risks, and benefits prior to engaging in any volunteer opportunity."[4] The APTA also suggests visiting the United States Department of State's website to learn more about specific countries and cities.[5]

Educational Preparation and Global Health Opportunities for PTs

Ninety-nine percent of physical therapy programs in the United States offer a clinical Doctor of Physical Therapy (D.P.T) degree.[6] Upon graduating from an accredited program and passing the licensure exam, PTs can choose to specialize in a variety of areas such as pediatrics, cardiopulmonary, neurology, orthopedics, sports, women's health, geriatrics, or clinical electrophysiology.[7]

One avenue to improve the involvement of PTs in global health initiatives is to emphasize the importance of global health in academic programs. Several D.P.T programs have incorporated international service learning (ISL) opportunities into their core requirements so that students can begin developing skills to serve in underserved communities. In addition to increasing cultural competence, encouraging students to participate in global health initiatives should advance the physical therapy profession towards practicing autonomously and collaboratively in all practice settings, which is a goal of the APTA Vision 2020 plan.[2,8,9]

In 2006, Pechak and Thompson conducted a research study to assess the number of United States and Canadian physical therapy programs participating in ISL.[8] Ninety-five questionnaires were returned (44.6% response rate). Thirty percent of the programs participated in organized ISL with standard learning objectives, and 43% offered ISL opportunities that were not structured with learning objectives. An additional 15% of respondents indicated they intended to incorporate ISL into their programs over the next two years.[8] There are many benefits to ISL, such as the personal development of students and improving awareness about global problems.[8] However, the logistics of implementing ISL are not always practical given that programs have limited resources. Educators described lack of time and money as the two primary barriers to ISL.[8] Due to some of the barriers found in this study, the authors created a *Resource Guide for International Service in Physical Therapy Education Programs* that is available for members of the APTA Health Policy and Administration Section.[8,10]

Duke University illustrates how an academic institution has acted to incorporate ISL into its physical therapy program. Duke is one of six academic institutions to partner with the First Global Health Leaders (FGHL) program.[11] FGHL was developed to provide "young health professional students, residents, and fellows the opportunity to serve and train abroad in underserved communities for up to one semester."[12] The unique aspect of FGHL is that students continue to receive academic credit while serving overseas.[12] In Spring 2012, four D.P.T students from Duke journeyed to Sri Lanka for a 4-week global health clinical rotation working under the direction of a Sri Lankan physical therapist.[12] Dr. Michel Landry explained, "part of the redesign of the physical therapy division is to seek opportunities to participate in appropriate and sustainable global health initiatives, and the evolution of the partnership between Ruhuna University [Sri Lanka] and the Duke Global Health Institute is an excellent example of sustainable development and academic partnership."[12]

PT programs also incorporate cultural competency training in the classroom to prepare students to appropriately interact with those from other cultures. The Commission for Accreditation of Physical Therapy Education (CAPTE) requires all accredited D.P.T programs to teach students to "identify, respect, and act with consideration for patients'/clients' differences, values, preferences, and expressed needs in all professional activities."[13] The APTA Learning Center offers an online continuing education course developed by Tara Pearce, MHS, PT, called *Professionalism Module 4: Cultural Competency*.[14] This course is available to APTA members, both students and clinicians. The primary objectives for this course include the following: Learn how to assess cultural competency along a continuum, discuss the impact of culture on health beliefs, learn how to utilize Culturally and Linguistically Appropriate Service Standards (CLAS) into clinical practice, identify the impact of health disparities, and discuss methods to communicate with patients with decreased health literacy.[14]

Global Health Professional Linkages for PTs

In addition to opportunities through academic institutions, multiple organizations exist for students and clinicians interested in physical therapy in a global health context. The APTA has a Global Health Special Interest Group within its Health Policy and Administration Section.[15] The APTA also has an "International Volunteer Opportunities and Organizations" page on its website that lists several relevant organizations with which PTs and students may become involved.[4] Global Outreach Physical Therapy Network (GOPTN) is another organization that describes itself as "a social network for physical therapists and nongovernmental organizations who share the goal of helping resource-limited populations get the rehabilitative services they need."[16] Interested students and clinicians can access the website to search for available global health opportunities and several related organizations.[16]

The World Confederation for Physical Therapy (WCPT) is an international organization founded in 1951 to be a resource for PTs and promote physical therapy worldwide.[17] The WCPT includes 106 member organizations and over 350,000 PTs worldwide. It strives to improve global health and advance the physical therapy profession by promoting "high standards of physical therapy research, education, and practice; supporting the exchange of information between WCPT regions and member organizations; and collaborating with national and international organizations."[17] The WCPT website has information regarding a plethora of diverse groups and subgroups ranging from such specialties as sports, animal practice, spinal cord injury, etc.[17]

Summary

PTs offer unique skills related to rehabilitative and preventative healthcare that can help reduce health disparities across the globe. ISL is increasing among D.P.T programs and is an effective avenue to improve students' personal and professional growth, but additional solutions need to be considered to address barriers to implementing ISL among more D.P.T programs.

Multiple organizations (such as the APTA, GOPTN, and WCPT) serve as valuable resources for PTs and students interested in global health opportunities. Students or PTs interested in providing physical therapy services abroad should thoroughly research details related to the location, expectations, logistics, cultural considerations, risks, and benefits well in advance for optimal preparation.

Practicing Physical Therapy in the Dominican Republic

Quisqueya, Dominican Republic, June 2011. Lush, emerald-green foliage adorned with fiery red and orange tropical blossoms provide a stark contrast to the dilapidated, grey cinderblock church building that they envelop. Eighty local residents have walked from their wooden shack homes down a dusty dirt road because they heard a medical team had come to help them free of charge. The health care team consists of physical therapy and medical students from The University of Alabama at Birmingham, along with experienced clinicians in those and related disciplines, involved with the Christian Medical Ministry of Alabama (CMMA).

A nurse calls an elderly man for his turn in the health station inside the church. After she takes his vital signs, she sends him to the physical therapy area. He walks with a large, crooked walking stick and a limp. The student PTs alongside the licensed PTs perform an examination with the help of an interpreter. The man has a sizeable, hardened lump on his misshaped left upper femur. Through the patient interview the team learns the gentleman was in a vehicle collision resulting in a displaced fracture two years ago. Because he did not have the money for corrective surgery or casting, the local hospital had sent him away.

The team decides to first address the fracture. An OT is also a member of the healthcare team, so the PTs ask her to use the available supplies to construct a leg splint. With ingenuity and diligence, the OT, PT students, and PTs work together to better align and splint the gentleman's femur.

Next, the PT students fit him for crutches, demonstrate how to use them, and then train him in how to walk with the crutches. With a big smile, he thanks the rehabilitation team for decreasing his pain, giving him crutches, and helping him to walk. Next, he goes to the medical students and physicians for assessment and medications, and finally to the last station, the spiritual ministry area. When he finishes there, he has a genuine, beaming smile as he thanks everyone for all their help as he leaves, positively impacted by a health team working together.

—Andrea Johnson, DPT
University of Alabama at Birmingham

References

1. "Disability and Health." *World Health Organization*. November 2012 <http://www.who.int/mediacentre/factsheets/fs352/en/index.html>.
2. Pechak, Celia M., and Mary Thompson. "A Conceptual Model of Optimal International Service-Learning and its Application to Global Health Initiatives in Rehabilitation." *Physical Therapy* 89.11 (2009): 1192-1204.
3. Van der Wees, Philip J., et al. "Development of Clinical Guidelines in Physical Therapy: Perspective for International Collaboration." *Physical Therapy* 91.10 (2011): 1551-1563.
4. "International Volunteer Opportunities & Organizations." *American Physical Therapy Association.* 16 April 2012. 25 July 2012 <http://www.apta.org/ProBono/International>.
5. "Background Notes/Country Fact Sheets." *United States Department of State.* May 2012. 25 July 2012 <http://www.state.gov/r/pa/ei/bgn/>.
6. Commission on Accreditation in Physical Therapy Education. "2010-2011 Fact Sheet Physical Therapist Education Programs." *American Physical Therapy Association.* 29 June 2012. 23 July 2012 <http://www.capteonline.org/uploadedFiles/CAPTEorg/About_CAPTE/Resources/Aggregate_Program_Data/AggregateProgramData_PTPrograms.pdf >.
7. "Specialist Certification." *American Board of Physical Therapy Specialties.* 9 February 2011. 23 July 2012 <http://www.abpts.org/Certification/>.
8. Pechak, Celia M., and Mary Thompson. "International Service-Learning and Other International Volunteer Service in Physical Therapist Education Programs in the United States and Canada: An Exploratory Study." *Journal of Physical Therapy Education* 23.1 (2009): 71-79.
9. "Vision 2020." *American Physical Therapy Association.* 3 July 2012. 23 July 2012 <http://www.apta.org/vision2020/>.
10. "Global Health Special Interest Group." *Section on Health Policy and Administration of the American Physical Therapy Association.* July 2012 <http://www.aptahpa.org/displaycommon.cfm?an=1&subarticlenbr=18>.
11. "Duke Physical Therapy Students Embark on Global Health Rotation in Sri Lanka." *Duke Global Health Institute.* 13 March 2012. 23 July 2012 <http://globalhealth.duke.edu/news-events/global-health-news-at-duke/duke-physical-therapy-students-embark-on-global-health-rotation-in-sri-lank/>.
12. "Hope Through Healing Hands." *First Global Health Leaders.* N.d. 23 July 2012 <http://www.hopethroughhealinghands.org/frist-global-health-leaders>.
13. "CAPTE Accreditation Handbook." *Commission on Accreditation in Physical Therapy Education.* 27 Jan. 2012. 23 Aug. 2012 <http://www.capteonline.org/AccreditationHandbook/>.
14. Pearce, Tara. "Professionalism Module 4-Cultural Competence." *APTA Learning Center: Catalog Topic Professional Issues.* N.d. 23 August 2012 <http://learningcenter.apta.org/tp_professionalissues.aspx>.
15. "Section on Health Policy and Administration."*American Physical Therapy Association.* N.d. 25 July 2012 <http://apps.apta.org/custom/wstemplate.cfm?cfmltitle=Chapters%20and%20Sections&cfml=componentsonline/index.cfm&processForm=1&componentType=Sections&specChoice=Y&convertList2Form=yes>.
16. Birmingham, Mary Clare. "Global Outreach Physical Therapy Network." *Global Outreach Physical Therapy Network.* N.d. 25 July 2012 <http://go-pt.net/>.
17. "What is WCPT?" *World Confederation for Physical Therapy.* 21 July 2011. 25 July 2012 <http://www.wcpt.org/what-is>.

Physician Assistants

The physician assistant (PA) profession, based on a commitment to the physician-led team, is viewed as a strategic conduit for expanding access to healthcare, reducing national healthcare costs, and championing the teamwork model for providing healthcare. With estimated physician shortages of over 60,000 in the United States by 2015 and unsustainable national healthcare costs, it is not surprising that the physician assistant will be the second-fastest growing profession in America between now and 2018.[1] Forbes magazine fittingly listed the PA profession as the top master's degree rated by "best long-term opportunities, based on salary and employment outlook".[2] The 2010 Lancet Global Independent Commission Report on "Transforming Health Education to Strengthen Health Systems in an Interdependent World" emphasized connection and collaboration among healthcare professions as a central global goal going forward.[3] The conclusions in the Lancet report underscore the potential leadership of PAs in fostering widespread teamwork within the healthcare system since collaboration is a fundamental principle of the PA profession, training and identity. In addition, the 45 year-old profession is a cost-effective strategy for producing competent medical providers in a fraction of the time it takes to complete medical school. It is remarkable to see that in light of these realities, the PA profession has been ahead of its time for many years. The professional identity of PAs is team practice.

PAs are supported by organized medicine, with endorsements from the American College of Physicians (ACP) and American Academy of Family Physicians (AAFP). PAs are a solution to healthcare shortages in terms of access, quality, and affordability of care. For these reasons the PA profession has flourished in the United States and around the world. This paper will discuss the PA profession, the physician/PA team, inter-professional collaboration, global health curriculum in PA schools, and resources for students.

PAs are nationally certified and state-licensed to practice medicine. They order and interpret diagnostic tests, perform physical exams, prescribe medications and other therapeutic interventions, create treatment plans, perform procedures, assist in surgeries, round on hospital patients, and provide preventive and chronic disease care in a variety of medical settings in partnership with a physician. Created by physicians, PAs are trained in the medical model. With roots in primary care and underserved communities, PAs can be found in all areas of medicine such as rural clinics, private practices, community health centers, specialty and surgical care.[4] They do not have to specialize, ensuring the flexibility to adapt to current healthcare needs and demands. PAs are not a substitute for physicians; rather, their role is to enhance and extend the reach of physicians via teamwork and partnership.

For example, the patient-centered medical home utilizing PAs is coordinated and integrated across disciplines, with enhanced patient access and maximization of the skills of the team members, ideally with the ability to work at the top of all licenses. PAs augment and work in partnership with physicians to deliver medical care appropriate to need, for better care, better health, and reduced cost per patient. PAs are deeply committed to the concept of the physician led team and uniquely equipped to partner with physicians to address health care challenges, providing high quality team centered medicine.

Physician/PA supervision takes different forms based on setting, specialty, state, the preferences of the physician, the experience of the PA, and how long the team has worked together, and is "ultimately a function of shared expectations and trust".[5] Physicians provide reasonable supervision in order to "adequately serve the health care needs of the practice population and ensure that the patient's health, safety, and welfare will not be adversely compromised".[6] Therefore, PAs exercise judgment within a scope of practice that provides a physician standard of care.

An example of successful team partnership is represented in a study done in 2011 in a Fast Track Emergency Room for patients receiving more than four or six hours of emergency care. This study looked at outcomes for patients of this level of medical complexity and risk and whether they could be safely evaluated under the care of PAs. In conclusion, the authors stated that PAs cared effectively for patients suffering from chest pain and trauma in the emergency department observation unit.[7]

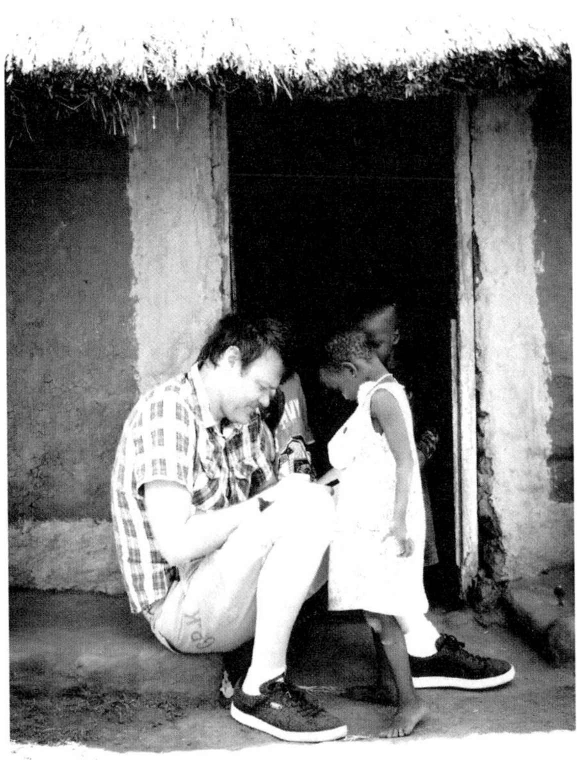

An American volunteer helps a child in Uganda learn how to tell her story on a portable chalkboard
Photographer: *Kimberly Krauk*

Educational Preparation and Global Health Opportunities for PAs

Achieving PA licensure in the United States requires a master's degree, fulfillment of required prerequisites, completion of an accredited PA program, and a passing score on the PA national certification exam. Matriculating PA classes typically include students with previous preparation as nurses, x-ray technicians, EMT/paramedics, lab technicians, dieticians, physical therapists, athletic trainers and other professionals since a prerequisite is significant patient care experience. The majority of the 170 accredited PA programs in the United States grant master's degrees (master of physician assistant studies, master of health science, or master of medical sciences). Programs average 27 months and model medical school curricula. The didactic curriculum focuses on anatomy, physiology, pathophysiology, pharmacology, history and physical exam skills, diagnostics, medical ethics, among other topics. The clinical year involves 2,000 hours in full-time rotations in family medicine, pediatrics, obstetrics and gynecology, psychiatry, general surgery, emergency medicine, internal medicine, and electives. Some programs also offer international rotations. PA programs focus on primary care, family practice, and the under-served populations of the United States with most programs requiring students to serve at least one clinical rotation in an under-served setting. PAs recertify via the national exam every six years, ensuring that their knowledge is up to date in all areas of medicine regardless of the area in which they practice. Every two years PAs need to earn 100 continuing medical education hours.[4] PAs working in emergency medicine, cardiovascular and thoracic surgery, nephrology, orthopedic surgery and psychiatry can elect to take an additional exam in their area of expertise to earn Specialty Certificates of Added Qualifications, in order to demonstrate their additional skills and experience.[8]

The United States is not the only country that has recognized the value of developing PAs and PA-like providers.[9] Over 20 countries have programs based on the United States PA model, including the United Kingdom, the Netherlands, Canada, South Africa, Australia and others. The PA model is adaptable to high income, middle income, and low-income countries.

Many PA programs send students to international rotations, often considered a "life changing" experience that inspires them to consider working in under-served or international communities during their careers.[9,10] The American Academy of Physician Assistants (AAPA) created ethical guidelines for PAs working or volunteering abroad addressing supervision, scope of practice, legal issues, and cross cultural sensitivity in these settings.[11] PAs serve internationally for governmental and non-governmental organizations such as disaster relief agencies, the United States military, the State Department, humanitarian organizations, and the Peace Corps. They provide direct service and also participate in research and educational programs. PAs expand their global impact by collaboration with countries crafting the PA profession, advocating for international awareness of the value of PAs and their role in achieving the MDGs. Twinning projects between PA programs and PA-analogue programs, such as in South Africa, are examples of PAs expanding their global impact.

Interprofessional collaboration between healthcare disciplines includes academic courses involving multiple disciplines;[4] a strategy enacted at George Washington University and Oregon Health Sciences University, or interdisciplinary teamwork activities such as the "Clinical Team

Experience" at the University of Utah[12] and the Interdisciplinary Student Community-Oriented Prevention Enhancement Service (ISCOPES) project at George Washington University.[13] Service learning can include multidisciplinary students in providing patient care, such as the Good Samaritan Health Clinic project at Emory University,[14] and the Junior League Care Fair project at the University of Utah. Student interest groups such as the Student Global Health Initiative at the University of Utah involve students from different programs working together to develop global health events and avenues for students and the community.

Vignette
Interdisciplinary Fieldwork Thai/Burma Border

The state of Utah accepts a large number of international refugees annually for resettlement including the large-scale resettlement of displaced Burmese citizens in 2005. In 2008, the University of Utah Neighborhood Partners Resettlement group, a university-community partnership, approached the School of Medicine Utah Physician Assistant program to conduct field research in Thailand with the end goal of providing better services to the Burmese upon arrival in Utah. A multidisciplinary team of University of Utah faculty embarked to Thailand, led by the Thailand International Elective (TIE) coordinator.[15] The group visited some of the nine refugee camps, their resource agencies and leadership and support groups along the Thai-Burma border.

TIE, established in 2003 at the University of Utah Physician Assistant program, provided the infrastructure needed for the Utah-based resettlement group to accomplish the goal of better understanding the needs of the refugee population from Eastern Burma. TIE provides a multidisciplinary global health offering for physician assistant, pharmacy, public health, nursing, medical students, medical residents, and faculty. Since its inception, TIE has expanded to other academic centers and across other disciplines. Several doctor of pharmacy, master of public health, schools of social work and occupational therapy and others have instituted TIE electives.

For example, during the 2008 University of Utah resettlement field research trip, the OT worked with individuals suffering from land mine injuries and stroke. The OT also assessed refugees' skills for life in Utah. She now leads the Immigration and Resettlement Community Fieldwork Program for several universities. TIE annual and biannual trips of various interprofessional students and faculty provide life skills training and community support to immigrant and refugee populations. The Utah PA Program coordinates with Dr. Cynthia Maung, whose selfless contributions to displaced ethnic minority Burmese at the Mae Tao Clinic in Mae Sot, Thailand resulted in a nomination for the 2002 Nobel Peace Prize. Activities include providing PA curriculum for training a Burmese PA analog: the Backpack Medics who stealthily provide healthcare to villagers hiding in the jungles of Burma, and the Refugee Medics who provide the bulk of treatment to the camps along the Thai/Burma border. PA faculty have also been active in trying to helping these Medics attain legal recognition in hopes of attaining jobs when the climate in Burma becomes safe for repatriation.

—Donald M. Pedersen, PhD, PA-C
Professor Emeritus, University of Utah

Movement towards a core global health curriculum has been advanced in recent years in many health disciplines. In current PA curricula, global health topics are often addressed in classes related to public health, infectious disease, laboratory science, and diversity. Some programs provide a global health core curriculum (e.g., the dual master's programs in Public Health and PA Studies at Touro University, Des Moines University, Yale University, and others). The Consortium of Universities for Global Health, www.cugh.org, has open-source global health educational modules.

The PA profession is positioned to have a significantly positive impact on the United States and potentially the world. If educational institutions seriously consider the goals set out by the Lancet Report,[3] and governments pursue the WHO task shifting strategies,[16] the PA will help lead the way in filling in the gaps in underserved healthcare, and in cultivating an atmosphere of cooperation and interdependence within the healthcare professions. The potential outcomes of providing better care, more efficiently, to more people are goals on which all can agree.

Global Health Professional Linkages for PAs

The AAPA <www.aapa.org> hosts an International Symposium at their annual conference to engage and support those workforce leaders developing the PA profession locally. The International Academy of Physician Associate Educators (IAPAE) <www.iapae.org/> exists to promote the education of physician associates worldwide. Physician Assistants for Global Health (PAGH) <www.pagh.org> and the Fellowship of Christian PAs (FCPA) www.fcpa.net/ are caucuses of the American Academy of Physician Assistants (AAPA) involved in the delivery of international health care. Other international resources are available for members at <www.aapa.org>. The IAPAE is cataloguing the wide array of strategies, initiatives and information utilizing PAs around the world in tackling healthcare problems.[17]

Canadian Association of Physician Assistants

"The PA profession is a rapidly growing and rewarding one filled with dynamic people. In a very short time we have evolved from an organization that existed only in the Canadian Forces [for over 40 years] to one that has four university level programs and dedicated professionals working in four provinces. Physician Assistants (PAs) have improved access to care in surgery, emergency departments, and family health care teams and we continue to make inroads into a multitude of disciplines. PAs believe in, and thrive in, a patient centric team approach to health care, partnering with other disciplines with one focus; improving patient care. In the fiscal reality of today's economy, the PA model is more pertinent than ever. We can help to bring quality health care to all Canadians and make a positive difference in patients' lives."[18]

—Tim Ralph, MPAS, CCPA
National President, CAPA-ACAM

References

1. United States Department of Labor. Bureau of Labor Statistics. *Occupational Outlook Handbook.* U.S. Bureau of Labor Statistics, 2012. 24 July 2012 <http://www.bls.gov/ooh/Healthcare/Physician-assistants.htm>.
2. Smith, Jacquelyn. "The Best and Worst Master's Degrees for Jobs." *Forbes* 08 June 2012. Web. 24 July 2012 <http://www.forbes.com/sites/jacquelynsmith/2012/06/08/the-best-and-worst-masters-degrees-for-jobs-2/>.
3. Frenk, Julio, et al. "Health Professionals for a New Century: Transforming Education to Strengthen Health Systems in an Interdependent World." *The Lancet* 376.9756 (2010): 1923-958.
4. "What Is a PA?" *American Academy of Physician Assistants.* N.d. 24 July 2012 <http://www.aapa.org/the_pa_profession/what_is_a_pa.aspx>.
5. Danielsen, Randy, Ruth Ballweg, Linda Vorvick, and Donald Sefcik. *The Preceptor's Handbook for Supervising Physician Assistants.* Massachusetts: Jones and Bartlett Learning, 2012.
6. "Working Relationship and Delegation of Duties". R156-70a. Physician Assistant Practice Act Rule. Utah Administrative Code. Division of Administrative Rules. State of Utah. 30 July 2012 *<http://www.rules.utah.gov/publicat/code/r156/r156-70a.htm#T>*
7. Sherwood, Kelly, Raymond Price, Thomas White, Mark Stevens, and Don H Van Boerum. A Role in Trauma Care for Advanced Practice Clinicians. EDOU Staffing by PAs: What Are the Effects on Patient Outcomes? Journal of the American Academy of Physician Assistants 24.8 (August 2011): 31-37.
8. "Specialty Certificates of Added Qualifications (CAQs)." NCCPA: Specialty CAQs. *National Commission on Certification of Physician Assistants*, 2012. 24 July 2012 <http://www.nccpa.net/SpecialtyCAQs.aspx>.
9. Pedersen, Kathy. "Physician Assistants and Global Health". *Global Health Training in Medical Education: A Guidebook.* 2nd ed. Ed. Jack Chase and Jessica Evert. Global Health Education Consortium, 2011.
10. Luce, David, Nicole Stewart, and Meredith Davison. "Physician Assistant Students' Attitudes toward International Experiences." *Journal of Physician Assistant Education* 18.2 (2007): 14-20.
11. "Guidelines for PAs Working Internationally." *American Academy of Physician Assistants.* N.d. <www.aapa.org>.
12. "Clinical Team Experience—Interdisciplinary Course, Spring 2012—University of Utah Health Sciences Center." *Spencer S. Eccles Health Sciences Library,* 3 November 2003. 24 July 2012 <http://library.med.utah.edu/cte/>.
13. Pedersen Donald, Doug Barker, Verapan Santitamrongpan Kathy Pedersen, and Han Kim. "Thailand International Elective: A Model Curriculum in International Health and Cross- Cultural Experience. Global Perspectives." *Journal of Physician Assistant Education* 17.3 (2006): 51-55.
14. "GWU—Interdisciplinary Student Community-Oriented Prevention Enhancement Service." *GWU—ISCOPES.* George Washington University, 15 June 2012. 24 July 2012 <http://www.gwumc.edu/iscopes/>.
15. "Community Involvement." *Emory Physician Assistant Division.* Emory University. N.d. Web. 24 July 2012 <http://www.emorypa.org/community_involvement.htm>.
16. "Task Shifting: Rational Redistribution of Tasks among Health Workforce Teams." (PDF File). *World Health Organization.* WHO: Geneva, Switzerland, 2008.
17. "About IAPAE." *International Academy of Physician Associate Educators.* N.d. 24 July 2012 <http://iapae.org/About_IAPAE>.
18. Ralph, Tim. President's Message. *Canadian Association of Physician Assistants.* 5 August 2012 <http://capa-acam.ca/en/>.

Psychology

The field of psychology applies the scientific method to the study of mental function and behavior. As such, it aims to understand mental processes and predict behavioral phenomena based on principles established through empirical investigation.[1] Professionals in the field may engage directly in this task as psychological scientists, conducting research using a range of methodologies. For example, social psychologists examine the influence of other individuals and social situations on thoughts and actions, while cognitive psychologists focus on the role of mental processes such as memory and perception in behavior. Psychologists may teach and conduct research in colleges and universities, work as integral members of teams that design educational and health care interventions and set public policy, or work as practitioners, applying the findings of psychological science in clinical settings. Although there is great potential for psychology to contribute to the success of global health initiatives, psychology has not yet had a prominent position in most global health initiatives. With regard to the treatment of mental health issues, stigma and shame are common barriers to both the reporting of mental illness and the use of treatment services in many countries, leading to a lack of the epidemiological data that is necessary to win government investment in mental health services.[2] Depression is an example of a highly treatable condition that is frequently undiagnosed. It is estimated that in 2000, inadequately treated depression cost the United States over 83 billion dollars in lost productivity, increased medical expenses, and premature death.[3] No reliable estimates of the "costs" of untreated depression are available in developing countries.

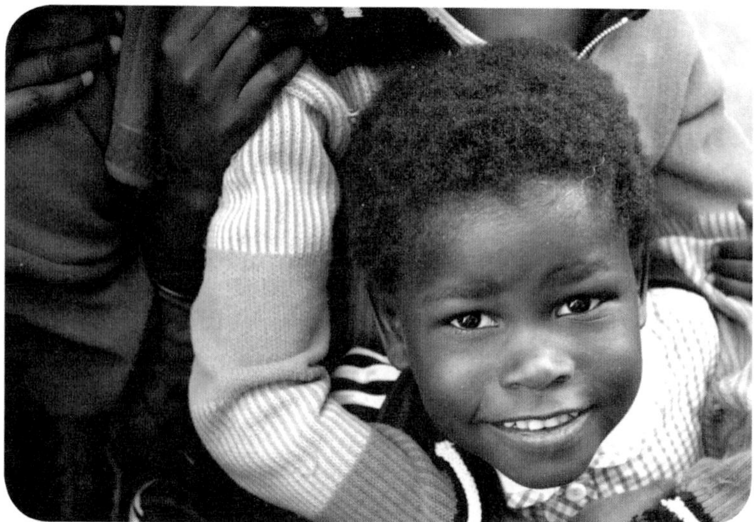

A Zambian child receives loving support from members of her community.
Photographer: *Will Bynum*

Contribution of Psychology to Global Health

In the context of global health initiatives, treatment of mental health concerns has been secondary to more life threatening concerns such as infectious disease or chronic physical health problems. The integration of psychological science into programs geared towards physical health offers the potential of great benefit by facilitating consistent preventive behaviors (e.g., use of bed nets in malaria endemic areas) or consistent adherence to treatment (e.g., for conditions such as HIV infection). Psychological research on adherence to treatment, perceptions of wellness and illness, decisions about seeking care, and many other behavioral and cognitive factors is highly relevant to optimally addressing health concerns, both in low and high countries.

In a global health setting, the cultural context of health concerns must be considered when interventions are developed. The field of social psychology studies the effects of cultural context on factors such as stigma, social barriers and facilitators, and perceived susceptibility to and severity of health threats. Health psychology provides valuable insight into perceptions of health risks and related behaviors such as smoking, diet, exercise, and high-risk sexual practices. The field of cognitive psychology delves more deeply into the abstract and conceptual processes such as decision-making and behavioral economics underlying health behaviors.

Several major global health initiatives have employed psychological sciences to address behavioral aspects of major health issues. For instance, behavior-change interventions in Africa have played a major role in decreasing rates of malaria—a disease responsible for approximately 655,000 deaths in 2010, most of which occurred in Africa.[4] Although bed nets, an effective means of preventing bites from disease carrying mosquitoes, have been affordable and widely available for some time, widespread use by at-risk locals only increased after implementation of behavioral change campaigns aimed at individual, community, and institutional levels of influence. As a result of the behavior change campaigns, bed net ownership more than doubled between 2004 and 2010 in nine countries, while malaria rates concurrently decreased.[5] Programs targeting health issues related to more complex risk behaviors have also been successful. With regard to HIV, a disease reported to affect approximately 33.3 million people worldwide in 2009,[6] over 40 prevention models have been identified to date by the CDC as being significantly efficacious in reducing HIV risk behaviors.[5] Several relatively recent meta-analyses have demonstrated the efficacy of HIV prevention models in affecting the behavior of high-risk populations. For example in 16 of 22 studies conducted in low and middle income countries, the WHO determined that school-based HIV prevention education significantly delayed initiation of sexual intercourse, reduced frequency of sex, reduced number of sexual partners, increased use of condoms and contraceptives, and decreased frequency of unprotected sex.[7]

Recent work by Schwebel and colleagues demonstrates the potential for behavioral interventions to influence the incidence of unintentional child injury.[8] Focusing on the high incidence of kerosene (paraffin) poisoning and burn-related injuries in communities that use kerosene for cooking and lighting,[9] he demonstrated the efficacy of a "train the trainer" model for increasing community residents' knowledge about safe storage and use practices. In this study, professionals educated community leaders who delivered the educational intervention within the community. The intervention increased knowledge about kerosene safety and reduced the hazardous conditions in the homes revealed by home inspection. In the area of injury prevention, legislation has proven highly effective in preventing the conditions which allow injury (e.g., car seats, child proof caps on medication and toxic home care substances) and should be considered as one component of injury prevention.

Psychology is also highly relevant to addressing chronic health problems with strong lifestyle components. Worldwide rates of non-communicable diseases such as heart disease, lung disease, cancer and diabetes continue to rise.[10] Behavior plays an important role in both the development and treatment of these conditions. Reducing high-risk behaviors, such as excessive calorie consumption and smoking, and facilitating the initiation and maintenance of healthy behaviors, such as healthy diet and exercise, is crucial to the prevention and promotion aspects of disease control. Treatment and rehabilitation are also strongly influenced by behavior; even the most effective treatment regimens may be useless if individuals do not adhere to them. Thus, increasing the extent to which psychology is applied in global health programs could contribute greatly to the prevention, promotion, treatment and rehab components of controlling and reducing the global health impact of these diseases.

Given these current and potential contributions, the integration of psychology in global health practice is relevant to several of the MDGs. With regard to the goal of promoting gender equality and empowering women, social psychology may play an important role in identifying and addressing social and cultural barriers to improving women's status and wellbeing. For example, recent research on intimate partner violence has shown that male perceptions of social norms have a significant influence on the perpetration of violence against women, and that addressing these norms holds potential for increasing the efficacy of interventions.[11] As for the goals of reducing child mortality and improving maternal health, the application of health psychology in maternal and child health programs will be vital in order to effectively foster better childcare practices as well as personal health behaviors among mothers. A recent randomized controlled trial of an intervention to improve the quality of maternal-infant relationships in a socioeconomically deprived community in South Africa found that mothers who received guidance on parenting practices from trained community workers were more sensitive during infant interaction at 18 months, and infants of those mothers were more likely to display secure attachment at 18 months—factors known to positively influence child development.[12] In terms of combating HIV/AIDS, malaria, and other diseases, the value of psychology has and will continue to be an integral component of prevention and treatment via interventions that reduce risk-related behaviors and increase adherence to treatment.

The integration of psychological interventions into global health practice is at an early stage, and currently faces many challenges. In addition to cultural differences that affect the perception and manifestations of psychiatric disorders, economic factors and stigma against mental health treatment present barriers that reduce the "demand" for mental health services in many areas of the world. Thus, conditions such as depression and anxiety are often not recognized and treated. Professionals in the field face the challenge of reducing the negative perceptions of using mental health services. Integration of mental and physical health interventions has considerable promise in a global health context, but will require active cross-disciplinary collaboration to be realized.

Educational Preparation and Global Health Opportunities for Psychologists

Given the intricacies of the issues psychologists must deal with both in global and domestic practice, a substantial level of education in the discipline is required for professional practice. Psychological practitioners, such as clinical or industrial/organizational psychologists must have a PhD (the terminal degree in the discipline) or PsyD in their respective field, which typically requires five years. However, some types of counseling and therapy such as school counseling only require a master's degree to practice.

Due to a burgeoning movement to internationalize psychology education promoted by the American Psychological Association (APA),[13] opportunities for psychology training specializing in global health have increased in recent years. Several universities in the United States and abroad offer graduate level psychology programs in global mental health, including the Massachusetts School of Professional Psychology, which offers a master's of arts in counseling psychology and global mental health, and the University of Melbourne's Centre for International Mental Health, which offers a number of courses on global mental health. The Centre for Global Mental Health (CGMH) in London in association with the London School of Hygiene and Tropical Medicine and the Institute of Psychiatry also offers a recently launched master's of science program in global mental health, as well as doctoral level positions for research on global mental health topics. Numerous schools also offer programs in public health, international health, or medicine with specialty tracks in behavioral science and/or curriculum in psychology. Other educational opportunities include professional conferences such as the Annual APA convention and the International Congress of Psychology that hold presentations on psychology and global health.[14] Links to resources for students interested in professional training in psychology and global health are provided on both the APA and Movement for Global Mental Health websites.

Professional Global Health Linkages for Psychologists

The WHO has a substantial focus on behavioral interventions to improve health and on global issues in mental health (www.who.int). The International Union of Psychological Science (http://www.iupsys.net/) publishes the International Journal of Psychology that serves as an academic outlet for researchers in this field.

Summary

The field of psychology relates to global health practice in two ways: directly in the form of mental health care, and indirectly as a component of broader physical health programs. Both of these functions bear their own set of unique challenges and merits. Cultural factors such as stigma and shame as well as economic impoverishment are obstacles to the implementation and advancement of mental health care in many regions in which the need for it is great. The integration of psychological research on health-related behaviors and behavior change in global health programs remains limited, yet understanding the psychological factors associated with the use, compliance, and adherence to these programs is crucial to their success. Addressing such issues and expanding the application of psychology in global health practice will require a great deal of creativity, yet the importance of doing so is becoming increasingly clear. As a science uniquely suited to address the critical social and behavioral aspects of global health issues, psychology comprises a valuable facet of the interdisciplinary approach that will be required to meet the global health challenges of the 21st century. The expertise of psychology in facilitating and maintaining behavioral change has important implications for designing and implementing effective global health initiatives. Psychologists study the environmental contingencies that support behavior and can assist in developing programs that support positive health behaviors.

Research on injury prevention illustrates the effectiveness of establishing policies and laws in supporting public health. The research basis provided by psychology is key to justifying these legal measures. Treatment of mental health problems as part of global health initiatives is at an early stage and represents an area where considerable benefit is possible, given the highly treatable nature of conditions such as anxiety and depression which when left untreated compromise productivity and contribute to physical health problems. Although several psychology training programs include a global health focus, this is an underdeveloped training area.

The Role of Behavioral Science in Clinical Trials of Biomedical HIV Prevention Interventions

Throughout this section we have discussed the various ways in which psychological research on health-related behaviors applies to programs that address physical health issues. Perhaps less apparent, however, is its significant role in the preliminary research upon which these programs are built. Behavioral factors such as participation and adherence are not only relevant to the implementation phase of health programs, but may also influence the ability of clinical trials to accurately detect efficacious interventions, and thus are important to consider even in the context of biomedical interventions.[12] A prominent research initiative that demonstrates the valuable role of behavioral science in clinical trials of experimental interventions is the HIV Vaccine Trials Network (HVTN)—an international effort funded by the National Institutes of Health to test and find a safe and effective vaccine against HIV infection. In a recent publication the HVTN outlined several critical ways in which behavioral science has been used in clinical trials of HIV vaccines,[12] including:

» Investigation of contextual factors at the dyadic, situational and community levels that influence participation, retention, and adherence in clinical trials, as well as risk of HIV exposure.

- » Providing important insights into recruitment of men who have sex with men and transgender women into vaccine trials through investigation of barriers and facilitators to participation.
- » Behavioral investigations to determine if disparities in HIV acquisition among subgroups of vaccine recipients relative to placebo recipients could be explained by differences in HIV exposure, rather than being attributable to the effect of a vaccine.

These contributions reflect the truth that "biomedical and social-behavioral sciences, often perceived as opposites, are, in essence, complementary and interactive within a greater whole".[12] The example of HIV vaccine trials provides a poignant illustration value of incorporating social and behavioral science in the early stages of study design and idea generation in even seemingly disparate areas of health research as part of an interdisciplinary approach that ensures the integration of important insights.

Mazheruddin Mulla, B.S., M.P.H
University of Alabama at Birmingham

References

1. Fernald, Dodge. *Psychology: Six perspectives.* Thousand Oaks, CA: Sage Publications, 2008.
2. Afkhami, Amir. "Looking for Sexy: The Disparity of Mental Health in Global Public Health." *Psychology Today* (2010): N. pag. 8 July 2012 <http://www.psychologytoday.com/blog/global-mental-health/201002/looking-sexy-the-disparity-mental-health-in-global-public-health>.
3. Han, Donald, and Edward C. Wang. "Remission from Depression: A Review of Venlafaxine Clinical and Economic Evidence." *Pharmacoeconomics* (2005): 567-81. 28 July 2012 <http://www.ncbi.nlm.nih.gov/pubmed/15960553>.
4. "World Malaria Report: 2011." *World Health Organization.* WHO: Geneva, Switzerland. 2011
5. "Compendium of HIV Prevention Interventions with Evidence of Effectiveness." *Centers for Disease Control and Prevention's HIV/AIDS Prevention Research Synthesis Project.* Atlanta, GA: Centers for Disease Control and Prevention. November 1999, Revised.
6. "UNAIDS Report on the Global AIDS Epidemic 2010." *Joint United Nations Programme on HIV/AIDS (UNAIDS).* 2010.
7. "Preventing HIV/AIDS in Young People: A Systematic Review of the Evidence from Developing Countries." *World Health Organization.* WHO Technical Report Series #938. Switzerland: WHO Press, 2006.
8. Schwebel, David C., et al. "An Intervention to Reduce Kerosene-related Burns and Poisonings in Low-income South African Communities." *Health Psychology* (2009): 493-500.
9. Schwebel, David C., et al. "Paraffin-related Injury in Low-income South African Communities: Knowledge, Practice and Perceived Risk." *Bulletin of the World Health Organization* (2009):700–706.
10. Weir, Kirsten. "Improving Health, Worldwide". *Monitor on Psychology* 43.5 (May 2012). 10 July 2012 <http://www.apa.org/monitor/2012/05/improving-health.aspx>.
11. Witte, Tricia, and Mazheruddin Mulla. "Social Norms for Intimate Partner Violence in Situations Involving Victim Infidelity." *Journal of Interpersonal Violence* (2012). 25 July 2012 <http://jiv.sagepub.com/content/early/2012/05/15/0886260512445381. abstract>.
12. Cooper, Peter J., et al. "Improving Quality of Mother-Infant Relationship and Infant Attachment in Socioeconomically Deprived Community in South Africa: Randomized Controlled Trial." *British Medical Journal* (2009): 338. 24 July 2012 <http://www.ncbi.nlm.nih.gov/pubmed/19366752>.
13. Belar, Cynthia. "Internationalizing Psychology Education." *Monitor on Psychology* 39.7 (July 2008). 26 July 2012 <http://www.apa.org/monitor/2008/07-08/soe.aspx>.
14. O'Donnell, Kelly. "Global Mental Health: Finding your Niches and Networks." *Psychology International* (March 2012). 27 July 2012 <http://www.apa.org/international/pi/2012/03/global-health.aspx>.

CHAPTER 11

Interdisciplinary Global Health: Contributions Beyond the Health Sciences

Laura Pascoe, MS, PhD-candidate
Leann Andrews, MLA
Sudan Bolton MS, MSCE, PhD
Meaghan Bond, PhD-candidate
Michael S. Cordray, BS
Zachary Crannell, PhD-candidate
Allan Davison, BSc, MS, PhD
Johanna Gusman, MS, JD
Rachel Hanle, BSW-candidate
Tate Lowrey, MPH
Cathy McElderry
Jorge Alarcon Piscoya, BArch
Kate W. Read, PhD
Rebecca Richards-Kortum, PhD
Brittany Rohrman, BA
Pamela Runestad
Ben Spencer, MLA, March
Michael Windle, MPH-candidate, JD-candidate

Editor
Bob Huish, PhD

THE FOLLOWING CHAPTER OFFERS A critical yet often underrepresented perspective of global health from academic and professional disciplines typically perceived by clinicians as "non-medical", including engineering, geography, nutrition, and law. The goal of this chapter is to provide perspectives and voices from disciplines not always encompassed in "global health" as a means of demonstrating the importance of preventive, infrastructural, and social science-related research and interventions as essential to the advancement of healthy populations and global health generally. In all cases there is a call for greater inter-sectorial and collaborative work with clinical global health practitioners. In addition, this chapter seeks to showcase experiences, reflections, lessons learned, and successes and failures of working in the field of "global health" in what is often at the structural level rather than at the clinical level. The challenges for true inter-disciplinary global health scholarship arise when working in isolation from clinical disciplines as well as through interdisciplinary and collaborative projects.

As this chapter was developed, the contributing authors struggled to identify both what term to use collectively for our disciplines in relation to global health (e.g. Non-medical? Non-clinical? Health-related?), as well as how to frame these disciplines in relation to this book and global health more broadly (e.g. Perspectives/Voices from? Role of?). While seemingly insignificant, these debates illustrate the ongoing difficulty of situating these disciplines integral to global health but nonetheless underrepresented in global health literature. In an effort to fill this gap, this chapter includes contributions from nine disciplines, with cases studies from select disciplines to highlight contributions to global health through these disciplines. Health economics and business are represented in a complimentary chapter within this volume. In order to ensure equal representation of the disciplines included here, this chapter is organized alphabetically.

Finally, for the purpose of clarification, this chapter will use the term "non-medical" to describe disciplines that are not specifically "medical" or "clinical", despite the term's inadequacy of encompassing the invaluable contributions and burgeoning expertise in health within these disciplines. Despite the broad spectrum of disciplines included in this chapter, it is important to note that there are many non-medical disciplines equally as important to global health—such as sociology, ecology, agricultural development, environmental sciences, and cultural studies—that are not covered here. Nevertheless, this chapter will demonstrate that there is much more to global health than what happens in a clinic; between a doctor and patient; or with the physical health of bodies. Indeed, improving the health and well-being of populations worldwide requires building the capacity and enlisting the help of those who can both address immediate and long-term concerns; micro and macro-level barriers; preventive and palliative care; and social and structural constraints to health.

This chapter includes the following disciplines:

1. Anthropology (+case study)
2. Design and Architecture (+case study)
3. Engineering (+case study)
4. Gender Studies
5. Geography (+case study)
6. Law
7. Nutrition and Food Security
8. Public Health
9. Social Work

1. Anthropology

Contributing Author: *Pamela Runestad*

Goals of Anthropology and Medical Anthropology

Anthropology is a relatively young discipline, and its purposes have shifted considerably in the past one hundred and fifty years. The goals have moved from 1) recording "vanishing cultures" and explaining why "primitives" were at a earlier developmental stage than "civilized" people in the 19th century; 2) to comparing cultures as a way of understanding people at the individual or societal levels (in American and British anthropology, respectively) in the first half of the 20th century; and 3) to understanding human diversity locally and globally in cultural context through study of their historical, biological, social, and economic realities in more recent years.[8] Medicine has always been a part of these endeavors, and medical anthropology, a sub-discipline of anthropology, began developing in its own right after World War II—around the same time that major efforts were being made to establish programs in international public health. Currently, the primary goal of medical anthropology is to understand the factors that influence health and illness, epidemiological patterns of disease, prevention and treatment methods, healing processes, the social relations of therapy management, and the cultural significance of using multiple medical systems simultaneously.[1]

Caption: *A desolate street scene in a thriving but impoverished neighborhood in the Zambian capital of Lusaka*
Photographer: *Bynum*

The Origins and Scope of Medical Anthropology

The foundations for these goals are often attributed to Rudolph Virchow, W.H.R. Rivers and Erwin Ackerknecht.[2] Virchow, a German pathologist, is considered the "father of social medicine" due to his attention to the relationship between ill-health and poverty in the 19th century. In the 1920s, Rivers, drawing from his experiences on the Torres Straits Expedition in 1898, asserted that medical practices among "primitive" peoples are rational, not disconnected, behaviors. Ackerknecht extended this argument in the 1940s and 50s to state that as functions of culture, medical behaviors reflect and reinforce culture and social structure.[1] Thus, medical anthropologists approach medicine as a resource people access, and prevention and treatment behaviors as explainable through a person's socio-cultural logic. Biomedicine is not a discipline that is excluded from this epistemology. Therefore, medical anthropologists such as Joan Cassell, who examines how female surgeons in the United States shaped and are shaped by the discipline, also explore the socio-cultural contingencies of biomedicine.

The ways anthropologists apply these premises have shifted, just as the goals of anthropology have shifted. Roughly, this has happened in three stages: 1) researchers such as Rivers explained medical practices of "others" as logical to his countrymen; 2) researchers such as Clare DuBois mediated interactions between "others" and health organizations to improve adherence to international health initiatives post-WWII; and 3) researchers, some of whom are also clinicians such as Paul Farmer, have worked directly with those in poor health to find out what they need and how to use existing systems to deliver these services. In other words, medical anthropology has shifted to become more applied; it has also been increasingly concerned with engaging target group members as active participants in health programs that are supposed to be directed at them.

Public Health, International Public Health, Global Health?

From the standpoint of medical anthropology, the goals of these three fields are, at the core, the same: public health, international public health, and global health programs are designed to improve human health and well-being. But the rationale for each field, including who is helping whom, what constitutes a health problem and who puts whom under surveillance, differs depending on the historical and socio-political contexts in which they began and continue to develop. Practical issues such as "protecting" a population from a disease (or another population that supposedly harbors a disease) and maintaining economically as well as reproductively healthy populations underlie each discipline. Each of these disciplines, including anthropology, is linked to colonialism and governance of "others." It is beyond the scope of this section to detail the history of each of these, but put simply, they can be described in these ways:

1. Public Health (PH): Beginning in the middle of 19th century, local health problems in the United States and Britain were solved by local officials with the idea that a healthy population is a productive population—both in terms of labor and reproduction. Organized programs in the US and the UK prompted similar programs in colonies.
2. International Public Health (IPH): From the interwar period, health problems in "developing" countries were solved by researchers and officials from "developed" nations who initiated treatment and prevention programs, and taught local people how to prevent disease. These projects were often motivated by desires to increase worker productivity for outside companies.

3. Global Health (GH): The HIV pandemic in the 1980s forced people to recognize that illnesses do not respect borders, and have the ability to transcend geography, socioeconomic status, ethnicity, and sexual orientation. In other words, particular illnesses pose global health problems and therefore require everyone's attention. The interaction between local and outside practitioners has generally been more equal than in the past, but power hierarchies are still key to project implementation.

Medical Anthropology vis-à-vis PH/IPH/GH

Public health no doubt led to the development of IPH; moreover, global health and some brands of applied medical anthropology developed, to some degree, out of IPH programs. For example, global health seems to have sprung directly from IPH with the emergence of the HIV pandemic, and the first applied medical anthropologists began to consult on IPH projects following World War II when Clara Dubois was hired by the World Health Organization.[3] But global health and medical anthropology diverge where researchers choose to emphasize biomedicine and biomedical campaigns or the importance of local systems of knowledge in their research. Therefore, each yield different ways of conceiving a problem, relies on different sources of evidence, and employs different methods of analysis and inference.[4]

Global health retains the zeal for epidemiological data, evidence-based medicine, surveillance, and the delivery of biomedical interventions (natural science-based theory, method and practice) that comprise public health. Although these methods are critical for diagnosing and treating illness, this perspective allows practitioners to forget that biomedical knowledge (and science in general) itself is a product of what questions are asked by whom, how hypotheses are tested, and how results applied to who by whom—things that are culturally contingent, not necessarily purely "scientifically driven." Therefore, this standpoint makes it difficult to see that health maintenance is done differently in different countries, and that behaviors that look "unscientific" are not "illogical." This forgetfulness can result in misunderstandings during well-meaning health initiatives such as maternal health campaigns, vaccination projects, and drug trials.

Medical anthropologists ask different questions, see and evaluate illness episodes differently, and propose different solutions because of their roots in social science.[4] During an epidemic, for example, they ask, "Why is this person sick and not that person?" This question allows them to explore the socio-economic and cultural factors of an epidemic, which is difficult to do if the question is simply, "Why are these people sick?" In addition, they ask "Why do people think this treatment is effective, and what power does belief have?" instead of focusing on what medicine can cure the illness. Participant-observation is to medical anthropology what surveillance[9] is to public and global health: a way of ascertaining what is happening in communities, and what might be needed as a result. And while public and global health workers strive to deliver appropriate biological interventions, medical anthropologists tend to work as cultural brokers and advocates.

For health programs to be successful, cooperation between social and natural scientists is essential. There are numerous examples of medical anthropologists who have illuminated socio-cultural difficulties in health initiatives: Kaufert and O'Neil show that childbirth was considered "dangerous" by Canadian biomedical practitioners and "natural" by Inuit mothers, leading practitioners to create hospital-based birth plans that mothers circumvented because hospital births required them to leave their communities.[5] Similarly, Renne notes that northern Nigerians refused to participate in vaccine campaigns for reasons ranging from anger that vaccinated children still got sick, conspiracy theories that the vaccines contained HIV or birth control, to frustration that polio vaccines were free but measles vaccines were not—even though mortality from measles was high.[6] Further, Saethre and Stadler describe how South African women participating in clinical trials for a HIV-preventive gel asserted that that specific gel had cleansing and healing properties and thus improved their lives although they knew "clinically efficacy" had not yet been proven—and some were thus disappointed when the trial finished and they could no longer access the product.[7]

Challenges to link Public Health, Global Health and Medical Anthropology

"Global Health," as in health for all, is a tall order for any discipline considering human diversity and the sheer number of humans on Earth; perhaps it is even more so for anthropology, which emphasizes thick description[10] of individuals and small groups. Yet many medical anthropologists, some of whom are physicians or medical practitioners as well, have made significant contributions to global health by using case studies to delink culture and illness, thereby illustrating that poverty and access to resources are often the foundations of epidemics and pandemics. When physician-medical anthropologist Paul Farmer illustrates that political economics and poverty underscore the high rates of HIV/AIDS, tuberculosis and other infections in Haiti and calls for people to consider Haiti's history of oppression by the United States, he is not straying too far from Virchow's assertions that physicians need to be the advocates of the poor. The case studies by Kaufert and O'Neil, Renne, and Saethre and Stadler highlighted above could also be used as references by those in public and global health. In other words, some of the most powerful contributions medical anthropologists make is to illustrate how culture *is not* the reason for poor health: rather, poverty, lack access to resources, and side-effects of globalization such as pollution and lack of access to one's homelands tend to cause or be factors for poor health.

My challenge to public health, global health and medical anthropology is this: work together. From my standpoint, public health needs to consider how local epidemics are pandemics writ small; global health needs to consider how pandemics are epidemics writ large; and medical anthropology needs to work harder to make these trends readily visible and suggest concrete solutions. My case study in HIV/AIDS in Japan provides an example.

Resources for Medical Anthropology and Global Health Journals

Anthropology and Medicine
Body and Society
Culture, Medicine and Psychiatry
Journal of Medical Humanities Social Studies of Science and Technology
Medical Anthropology Quarterly
Social Science and Medicine
Social Studies of Science
Social Theory and Health

Organizations

Society for Applied Anthropology
Society for Medical Anthropology

Academic Programs:

Case Western Reserve University
Creighton University
Duke University
Harvard University
McGill University
University of California at Berkeley
University of Chicago
University of Hawai`i at Mānoa
University of Washington
Yale University

References

1. Wiley, Andrea S. and John S. Allen. 2009. Medical Anthropology: A Biocultural Approach. Oxford University Press: New York.
2. Good, Byron J., Michael M. J. Fischer, Sarah S. Willen, and Mary-Jo Delvecchio Good, eds. 2010. A Reader in Medical Anthropology: Theoretical Trajectories, Emergent Realities. Wiley-Blackwell: Malden.
3. Singer, Merrill and Hans Baer. 2012. Introducing Medical Anthropology. 2nd Edition. Rowman and Littlefield Publishers, Inc: New York.
4. Hahn, Robert A. 1995. Sickness and Healing: an anthropological perspective. Yale University Press: New Haven.
5. Kaufert, Patricia A. and O'Neil, John (1993) "Analysis of a Dialogue on Risks in Childbirth: Clinicians Epidemiologists, and Inuit Women" in *Knowledge, Power and Practice: The Anthropology of Medicine and Everyday Life,* edited by Shirley Lindenbaum and Margaret Lock. University of California Press: Berkeley, LA, and London.
6. Renne, Elisha. 2006. "Perspectives on polio and immunization in Northern Nigeria." *Social Science & Medicine,* Volume 63, issue 7, pages 1857-1869.
7. Saethre, Eirik J. and Jonathan Stadler. 2010. "Gelling medical knowledge: innovative pharmaceuticals, experience, and perceptions of efficacy." *Anthropology and Medicine.* Volume 17, issue 1, pages 99-111.
8. For more on the history of anthropology, see the writings of George W. Stocking.
9. As Michel Foucault has argued, surveillance can be used to create discourses of "normalcy" and "deviance" which can then be used as a means of social control. The concept of surveillance is useful for discussions regarding global health programs because when the range of what constitutes "normal" is narrow, "outliers" (such nations with high rates of a particular illness) become foci for health programs aimed at helping them fit international norms. These programs can then become points of contention based on who is observing and administering care for whom and for what purposes.
10. Thick description, coined by Clifford Geertz, refers to elucidating the complex cultural context of an event or set of signs in an effort to highlight the subjects' humanity ***as well as*** their particularity (see his 1973 essay, "Thick description: toward an interpretive theory of culture").

Case Study: When Museum Exhibits Meet Medical Anthropology and Global Health

Pamela Runestad

Introduction

As noted in the medical anthropology section, medical anthropology has become increasingly more applied. One example of applied medical anthropology is to provide feedback on the ways in which a particular population is portrayed and represented in heath program materials or in public exhibits. Typical questions are, 1) "Why are these people the focus, and not others?"; 2) "Why are these people portrayed in this manner by these sponsors/photographers?"; and 3) "How much power do the people portrayed have in their portrayal, and are there any ways to improve power imbalances?" By asking questions such as these, we can pinpoint representations that may unintentionally reproduce power inequalities, and thus lead viewers to come away with stereotyped impressions of who is susceptible to specific illnesses and who is not. Put another way, exhibitors are challenged to capture both the specifics of particular epidemics while at the same time contextualizing such epidemics globally—and do so in a manner that minimizes power imbalances and strives to make such epidemics significant to audience members (people who *are not* being represented in the exhibit) so that they do not get the impression that the issue is cultural, or only relevant to the "Other", or an issue that simply does not concern them. While no exhibit is perfect, improvements can always be made.

This case study provides a description of a temporary, traveling museum exhibit and some suggestions for how such exhibits could be improved based on the medical anthropology-informed questions above. The analysis the author's alone.

Project Description

The *Access to Life* exhibit is co-sponsored by The Global Fund to Stop HIV, Tuberculosis and Malaria ("The Global Fund") and Magnum Photos. The Global Fund is an international, collaborative venture begun by G-8 nations in 2002 to direct finances for HIV/AIDS, TB and malaria relief into areas of intense need. Large-scale donors such as federal governments and philanthropic foundations supply funds. Organizations in global South nations apply for funds to support HIV/AIDS, tuberculosis and malaria programs. Magnum Photos was founded in 1947 at the Museum of Modern Art in New York with its goal to "chronicle the world and interpret its people, events, issues, and personalities with empathy".[1]

Access to Life Goals and Contents

Access to Life is a temporary, traveling exhibit aimed at demonstrating visually how anti-retrovirals (ARVs) can give people "access to life," and encouraging nations in the global North to donate funds that can be channeled to the global South. The exhibit contains photographs of thirty people living with HIV/AIDS (PLWHA) from Haiti, India, Mali, Peru, Russia, Rwanda, South Africa, Swaziland and Vietnam taken by eight photographers from wealthy nations. The general trend was to portray people before they started ARV therapy as weak and without hope (solitary, facing away, and often in black and white), and during ARV therapy as engaged in everyday life with others and with smiling faces (often in color). The exhibit began in Washington DC in 2008 and has traveled to Paris, Madrid, Oslo, Rome, Oakland, Tokyo and Seoul since. It was shown in Tokyo in September 2010. Admission was free. Approximately three thousand people viewed the Tokyo exhibit, including then-Prime Minister Kan, several other politicians and bureaucrats, members from the medical community, and members of the general public.

Although shown in Japan, no mention was made of the local HIV/AIDS epidemic even though the number of new HIV and AIDS cases there continues to increase. No comparison to global trends was made, even though marginalized populations comprise the majority of new cases around the world, regardless of a country's GDP (although who comprises these marginalized populations, of course, differs from place to place). In other words, the global and local contexts were not addressed, and the focus remained on countries in the global South in which HIV/AIDS prevalence and incidence are comparatively high.

General Outcomes

The primary goal in bringing this exhibit to Japan was to convince the Japanese government, then-Prime Minister Naoto Kan in particular, to continue to contribute to the Global Fund. Other goals included promoting the Global Fund and educating Japanese about ARVs. The exhibit was considered a success because Kan pledged support.

Outcomes From a Medical Anthropological Perspective

Photographing, displaying and explaining PLWHA from the global South to sponsors in the global North should sound familiar: anthropologists focused on photographing, displaying and explaining "primitive others" to their countrymen one hundred years ago. Even though the actions of The Global Fund and Magnum Photos are well-intentioned, an element of "us vs. them" and, by extension "we're better off and thus need to help them" is apparent in the photographs, which portray exotic "Others" from the global South. Many are poor, and many have used illicit drugs. Some have worked as sex workers. Some have been incarcerated. Some have sexual identities different from the majority of viewers. The people in the photographs are very different from the viewers who absorb them, and without the global-local contextualization, it is easy for people to associate HIV/AIDS with categories of "Other" people: the poor, drug addicts, sex workers, criminals, sexual "deviants." The alternate, unintended messages, then, become that HIV is a problem for *those* people that can be solved with "*our*" money, and "we" do not have HIV/drug/prostitution/crime problems. In trying to narrow the focus on garnering funds for ARVs, HIV/AIDS can be read as a "cultural" problem by viewers—something that neither The Global Fund nor Magnum Photos intends.

From a medical anthropological perspective, there are ways to remedy this.

First, the colonial—and, arguable, the "global North"—pattern of "us" portraying "them" for "us" could perhaps be broken if PLWHA themselves, rather than professional photographers, submit photographs to The Global Fund. Photography of PLWHA by PLWHA is already common: Tenanesh Kifyalew, a young girl in Addis Ababa who was instructed in photography and eventually died from AIDS, used photography to document her life playing with family members, toys, and the like in addition to her difficulties in living with HIV/AIDS.[2] Her photography is no less moving than the photographs taken by Magnum's professionals. Given that The Global Fund already requires local organizations (which often include PLWHA) to submit grants for program funding, it seems a logical step to ask local people to represent themselves pictorially.

Second, integrating global and local HIV contexts can remind viewers that the issue is not simply "someone else's" problem. For example, an introduction about the general trends about HIV epidemics and a "Local Focus" conclusion (locally relevant for each exhibit venue) would provide visitors the chance to grapple with social issues in their own areas and see how they are similar to or different from global trends, and give them ideas to become involved in local treatment and prevention initiatives.

Conclusions

In this case study, we can see the difficulty in transitioning from an International Public Health perspective (that focuses on "us" helping "them") to a Global Health perspective in which epidemics are viewed as issues that affect us all. In terms of garnering funding for HIV/AIDS on the global scale, the focus is still "the global North needs to help the global South." Unfortunately, this means that the emphasis is on particular places with large comparative rates of incidence and prevalence, which often obscure local data such as increasing rates of HIV/AIDS in Japan which appear small in comparison.[3] In other words, problems in the global North get forgotten, which both obscures the reality of the global North while at the same time reproducing power inequalities. To make sure that this exhibit and others like it adhere to the ideals of global health, we need to be able to see each one as a piece of a comprehensive, global HIV/AIDS plan. It is difficult, but it is possible—and exhibits are getting better all the time. [a]

Websites for Reference:

Access to Life Homepage: http://www.theglobalfund.org/accesstolife/en/
Magnum Photos Homepage: http://www.magnumphotos.com/
The Global Fund Homepage: http://www.theglobalfund.org/en/mediacenter/campaigns/

References

1. *Access to Life* website, accessed December 2011.

2. Bleiker, Roland and Amy Kay. 2007. "Representing HIV/AIDS in Africa: Pluralist Photography and Local Empowerment." *International Studies Quarterly.* Volume 51, pp 139-163.

3. Runestad, Pamela. 2010. "What People Think Matters: The Relationship Between Perceptions and Epidemiology in the Japanese HIV Epidemic." *International Journal of Interdisciplinary Social Sciences,* Volume 5, Issue 4, pp.331-344.

a The Global Fund continues to improve the Access to Life website. As of fall 2012, the online photo gallery was converted into photo essays complete with the audio recordings of the people photographed speaking in their native languages (with English subtitles). These essays are much more personal and powerful than displaying the photographs alone.

2. Design and Architecture

Contributing Authors: *Leann Andrews and Ben Spencer*

Design Disciplines

This section gives a brief overview of the integral role of the design professions in addressing complex health issues. These disciplines include:

» *Architecture:* the research and design of buildings and building systems
» *Landscape Architecture:* the research, planning, design and management of both natural and built environments; design outside a building
» *Urban Planning:* the research and design of the layout, function and policies in cities, their infrastructure and environment
» *Urban Design:* the research and design of cities and urban systems; specialized design profession that often includes architects, landscape architects, and urban planners
» *Ecological Design:* the research and design of landscape systems that improve biological integrity to address both human needs and the health of natural systems

The Built Environment and Health

Most people spend their entire lives in the built environment. The *built environment* is designed, created and maintained by humans and includes buildings, neighborhoods, plazas, playgrounds, roadways, parks, and their supporting infrastructure. It has a profound effect on physical, mental, social, environmental and economic health and wellbeing and can heavily influence human behavior, daily choices, and life opportunities that lead to (un)healthy living.[1] In fact, more than twenty five percent of the global disease burden stems from environmental factors closely related to the conditions of the built environment.[2] Because of its enormous influence on human lives, a well designed and operated built environment can act as preemptive medicine, preventing diseases, illnesses and disabilities long before they occur.[3]

The built environment can have powerful negative health consequences, especially for vulnerable populations with underserved attributes (e.g. age and disability) and social constructs (e.g. race, ethnicity, gender and poverty). Environmental exposures such as precarious housing, incomplete transportation systems, or inaccessible buildings may lead to adverse health effects, especially for those who do not have access to economic or social support networks. Noisy, crowded and dangerous places may have negative mental and psychological health impacts such as stress, anxiety disorders, depression, and even violent behavior.[1] The strength and redundancy of ecological and man-made infrastructure present in a community may play a large part in protection and recovery from natural disasters.[4] Disasters that hit neighborhoods that have inadequate preparedness planning, poor ecological and building design, and weak social networks may damage the community past the point of recovery.

The built environment can also positively affect the way we lead our lives. For example, it can influence how much physical activity we have the opportunity to engage in, and therefore prevent numerous adverse physical and mental health conditions. Bike trails, sidewalks, and parks provide opportunities to exercise. Access to a wider variety of fresh foods at grocery stores, farmers markets, and community gardens may provide healthier food choices, decreasing body mass and the probability of getting chronic diseases, such as diabetes. Reducing air pollution through carefully designed roadways and alternative transportation systems may decrease the effects of asthma and the risk of lung or other chronic diseases. Transit injuries--one of the leading causes of death worldwide--may be prevented through modifications of the environment to reduce risk and increase safety, such as safe crosswalks or pedestrian/vehicular buffers.[1] The design of the built environment can impact how storm and wastewater flows throughout a community and how pollutants impact critical ecosystems and the food we consume. Decentralized ecological infrastructure such as rain gardens, wetlands and storm water ponds can reduce the load on pipes and storm water treatment plants, lessening exposure to flooding, mold, and fecal matter and in turn reducing air and waterborne diseases, and ecological degradation. Public spaces, community centers and parks draw people together and thus support the development of social ties and enhance the development of social capital, supporting mental health and well-being. Natural day lighting, views of natural settings, acoustic comfort, air circulation, temperature controls, and other aspects of indoor environmental quality (IEQ) positively influence mental and physical wellbeing in schools, hospitals, workplaces, homes and other buildings. [1] Day lit classrooms, for example, improve student performance, concentration and cooperation and provide long-term positive impacts on physical development. Similarly, day lighting in workplace settings boosts productivity while reducing worker absenteeism, depression and stress. Hospital rooms designed to maximize views of natural settings increase pain tolerance and speed patient recovery times. Buildings designed to optimize indoor air quality through the specification of non-toxic, non-off gassing materials and optimal ventilation lead to reductions in illnesses such as asthma and respiratory allergies.[1]

The Role of Design in Global Health

In the global South, the relationship between the built environment and health is often much more dramatic than in the global North due to rapid urban expansion, the presence of tropical diseases, and a lack of resources and planning. For example, an estimated twenty percent of those in global South countries--1.1 billion people--do not have access to safe drinking water[5], compared to less than five percent in most global North countries.[6] Diarrheal diseases attributable to a lack of access to safe drinking water causes 1.6 million deaths each year, mostly in Global South countries.[5] Global South countries have very few resources to treat illnesses, and a shortage of medical professionals. Design is one way to address the underlying causes of global health issues. Well-designed buildings, landscapes, infrastructure and cities have positive "upstream" health effects at a large scale and over long periods. For example, the design of low cost and sustainable sanitation systems could reduce exposure to water and vector borne diseases, therefore reducing the burden on medical staff, clinics and hospitals, and the costs of treatment. While still rare, interdisciplinary design-health teams are becoming a growing practice in global health. Successful global health-design interventions seek low cost, environmentally sustainable and culturally and socially appropriate solutions rooted in research, evaluation and community engagement. It is critical to recognize local context and the need for adaptable designs and materials to create sustainable and smart living environments in order to maximize community health.

Ecological Infrastructure, Climate Change and Global Health

Many global South countries are upgrading or implementing new infrastructural systems in response to rapid urban migration and population expansion. Pursuing design interventions that promote health as part of such infrastructural projects is critical to prevent future hardships and increase quality of life. Well-designed sanitary and water systems can prevent water borne diseases; carefully planned transportation can increase financial security, reduce air pollution and lung diseases and prevent injuries related to vehicular accidents; and housing plans mindful of future growth and natural disasters can increase community resilience to environmental, social and economic challenges.

Designers and researchers are becoming more and more aware of the importance of ecological "green" infrastructure in community planning and design. Green infrastructure is the incorporation of natural systems in urban areas to provide widespread ecosystem services that increase human and environmental health. This ecological layer includes preservation planning, decentralized "soft" storm and wastewater management, floodplain and coastal protection and community green space.

Researchers have found that ecological destruction is correlated with poor mental and physical health and contributes to climate change, which is predicted to have wide-ranging impacts on human health and wellbeing.[7] The World Health Organization states that climate change will likely increase the frequency of tropical disease epidemics and the intensity of weather and natural disasters causing injury and illness. Design of the built environment is one way to address climate change. The severity of climate change impacts will depend, in large part, upon our ability to design the built environment to mitigate and adapt to these changing conditions.[8] Ecological infrastructure reduces carbon emissions, provides carbon sequestration, regulates temperatures, reduces air pollution, retains water, promotes biodiversity, grows local food, and even reduces stress and increases mental wellbeing.[7] Working together, designers and health professionals can help alleviate current and future health threats related to climate change.

Critical Collaboration Between Medical and Design Schools + Professionals

It is important that collaboration between designers and medical professionals take place in both academic and professional settings. Neither discipline has significant exposure to the others' expertise and there is a growing need for research to help educate professions, as well as decision-makers and the public. In-field research is critical to understanding design's impact on global health. Design interventions should be entirely transparent to (and even driven by) the community, and include follow-up monitoring to determine successes and adaptive management needs.

Many universities have recently established programs that integrate health and design through interdisciplinary global health work. The University of Washington, for example, created a Global Health Certificate/Minor for graduate and undergraduate students in any profession, requiring international work experience. Cross-disciplinary classes in planning and public health are offered and students in the design professions have several opportunities to work on design-build global health projects. The Escuela Ecologica Saludable Initiative, is one such project (see case study). It promotes long-term partnerships with international communities and the design and construction of interventions that affect health.

Conclusion: Looking Ahead in Design and Health

The urgency and volume of health matters worldwide accentuated by the looming threat of climate change calls for more proactive measures to address health issues at the source. Unfortunately, the cross-fertilization of the health and design disciplines remains limited. Interdisciplinary collaboration leveraging the expertise of health professionals and design as preventive medicine may be the most cost effective and sustainable way to address the current and future health issues we face together as a global population.

References

1. Dannenberg, A. L., Frumkin, H., & Jackson, R. *Making Healthy Places: Designing and Building for Health, Well-being, and Sustainability.* Washington, D.C: Island Press, 2011.
2. Smith, K. R., Corvalán, C. F., & Kjellström, T. "How Much Global Ill Health Is Attributable to Environmental Factors?" *Epidemiology* 1 Sept. 1999: *10,* 5.)
3. Frumkin, H. Lecture on Climate Change and Health—Impacts and Advocacy. University of Washington. 27 Apr. 2011.
4. Montenegro, Maywa. "Urban Resilience." *Landscape Architecture.* 100.7 (2010).
5. World Health Organization. Water, Sanitation and Health. *Health through safe drinking water and basic sanitation.* 1 Sept. 2012 <http://www.who.int/water_sanitation_health/mdgl/en/print.html>.
6. WHO/UNICEF Joint Monitoring Programme. Millennium Development Goals. *Progress on Drinking Water and Sanitation: 2012 Update,* 2012. United States, 2012.
7. Nurse, J, D Basher, A Bone, and W Bird. "An Ecological Approach to Promoting Population Mental Health and Well-Being—a Response to the Challenge of Climate Change." *Perspectives in Public Health.* 130.1 (2010): 27-33.
8. Spencer, Ben. "Climate Change Adaption and the Built Environment." Unpublished manuscript. Ant. 2012

Interdisciplinary Design Case Study: Escuela Ecológica Saludable Initiative

(The Healthy Ecological School Initiative)

Ben Spencer
Leann Andrews

Location:

Lomas de Zapallal, Lima Peru

Dates:

2010—Present

Project Partners:

Pitágoras Primary and Secondary School
The Universidad Nacional Mayor de San Marcos
University of Washington (UW) Department of Global Health
UW College of Built Environments
UW School of Environmental and Forest Sciences

The Healthy Ecological School Initiative

Three million people, or more than thirty percent of Lima's population live in slums without dependable clean water, sanitation, structurally sound housing or basic public services. Lima receives less than ten mm of rainfall per year and has the lowest green space per capita of any South American capital. Urban expansion has resulted in the destruction of local habitat, erosion, air pollution and increasing temperatures. As Lima's population continues to grow and its water supplies decrease with the melting of the Andean glaciers, the city's slum dwellers will face increasing hardship. Poor living conditions and environmental degradation are likely to exacerbate health problems including tuberculosis, digestive diseases, malnutrition and stress

The Escuela Ecologica Saludable Initative (EESI) (Healthy Ecological School Initiative) responds to these conditions. Based at the Pitágoras School in Lomas de Zapallal (LdZ), an urban slum of 27,000 in northern Lima, the EESI is a community-driven, design activism initiative that brings together professionals, researchers and activists from multiple disciplines including landscape architecture, architecture, engineering, planning, medicine, public health, and environmental science. Several EESI projects, including health assessment and promotion programs and health related interventions in the built environment have been completed or are now underway. A few of the Initiative's built environment projects are outlined below

Lomas de Zapallal Inventory

In the summer of 2010, a professor and students from the University of Washington conducted an inventory of LdZ's built environment. Data collected included access to water and sanitation, durability of housing materials, precarious site conditions, green space access, and community amenities. This information was synthesized in GIS maps and serves as a baseline measurement for ongoing development in LdZ and the impacts that EESI projects have within the community.

The Eliseo Collazos neighborhood in Lomas de Zapalla
Photographer: *Ben Spencer*

Parque Primaria Pitágoras

In the summer of 2011, an interdisciplinary group of eight University of Washington students worked closely with the community to design and construct the Parque Primaria Pitágoras, a 600 m^2 park at the Pitágoras School. Students were both graduate and undergraduates with backgrounds in public health, engineering, pre-med, environmental science, landscape architecture and community planning. The green space was installed to give Pitágoras' 2,000 students (K-12) a play and gathering place, a quiet area to sit and think, a place to experience and learn about nature and ecologies, and shelter from the dust and sun.

The park's design includes vital access between the school's central gathering area and the primary school, green space in an otherwise barren desert landscape and an innovative grey water recycling system that addresses the looming threat of water scarcity in Lima. The project relied heavily upon community investment and served as a platform for community mobilization at an impressive scale. It was constructed in two weeks for under $5,000. Over 300 parents participated in its design and implementation.

This project won the American Society for Landscape Architects (ASLA) National Honor Award in Community Service, the Social Environmental Economic Design (SEED) International Design Award, and the Environmental Design and Research Association (EDRA) Great Places Design Award.

Photo displaying existing conditions of the play area at Pitagoras School
Photographer: *Leann Andrews*

Photo displaying the completed green space including stone paths, seating areas, plantings and educational signage. The landscaping will fill in with time.
Photographer: *Leann Andrews*

Pitágoras Secondary School Classrooms

Many of the secondary classrooms originally constructed at the Pitágoras School expose students and teachers to multiple health hazards. Earthquakes occur frequently and the classroom structures were not seismically stable. Their interior temperatures often exceeded 42° C (107° F) in summer and dipped down to an uncomfortable 12° C (53.6° F) in winter. Lack of air circulation, poor lighting and extreme temperatures contribute to the spread of respiratory illnesses and detract from learning. New classrooms designed as part of the EESI take advantage of natural ventilation and day lighting to create a low energy, comfortable and healthy learning atmosphere. The first of these classrooms was completed in January of 2013.

Existing conditions of the classrooms at the Pitágoras School, 2010
Photographer: *Ben Spencer*

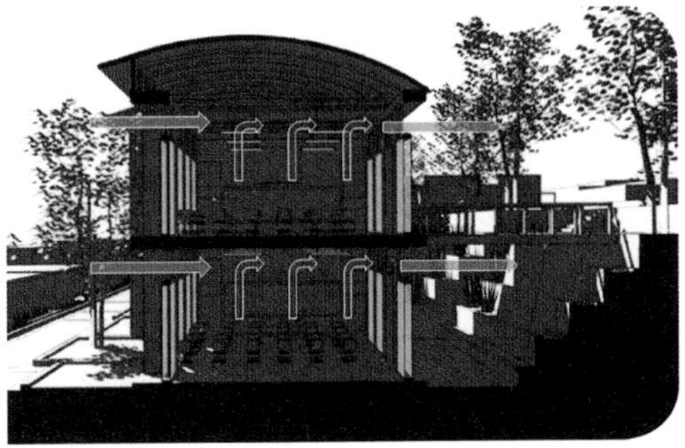

Architectural renderings depicting the proposed classrooms
Photographer: *Coco Alarcon*

Pilot classroom construction Sept 2012-January 2013
Photographer: *Coco Alarcon*

Ongoing Work

Several EESI projects are under development. These include a school-based health center at the Pitágoras School, and household container gardens that will provide food to residents of LdZ's Eliseo Collazos neighborhood. Monitoring and evaluation of completed projects will provide feedback on the EESI's successes and challenges. It is the long term goal of the EESI to construct parks throughout LdZ that provide neighborhood recreational amenities, reduce air pollution, moderate local temperatures, and serve as habitat for local bird and insect species.

Interdisciplinary and Community Collaborations

The EESI provides tangible evidence of the value of interdisciplinary collaboration in addressing complex health issues that stem from the conditions of the built environment. Critical to the success of the initiative is the close involvement and communication with the community. A thorough participatory design process allows the public to envision what *they* want in their community, and deep public involvement during the construction process contributes to local pride, community empowerment, stewardship and independence.

Project Challenges + Lessons Learned

Since the inception of the EESI, a number of challenges have emerged. At times, cultural differences impeded the effective communication with community participants. Misunderstandings about the daily activities of parents, teachers and students at the Pitágoras School, for example, led to participatory meetings with poor attendance. Through ongoing collaboration with community members, EESI project leaders are gaining insights into the cultural and political dynamics of the school and are becoming increasingly effective at facilitating community-driven initiatives. Bureaucratic obstacles and changes in school leadership also contributed to the disruption of progress towards project goals. The three month suspension of the mayor, for example, led to significant delays in permitting the classroom project. These delays, in turn, led to the withdrawal of the classroom's contractor. A taxing nine month search for another contractor willing to take on a project in the community eventually resulted in the classroom's construction. These challenges highlight the importance of working in communities over the long term, learning from past mistakes and remaining flexible in the face of dynamic circumstances.

Further Information

For more information on design activism studios and seminars offered at The University of Washington: http://larch.be.washington.edu/features/activism/designactivism.php

For more information on the Escuela Ecologica Saludable Initiative:
http://globalhealth.washington.edu/sites/default/files/uploads/documents/ParquePrimaria
Pitagoras.pdf

Or contact:
Ben Spencer, UW Assistant Professor, Landscape Architecture, bspen@uw.edu
Susan Bolton, UW Professor, School of Environmental and Forest Sciences, sbolton@uw.edu
Joe Zunt, UW Associate Professor, Global Health, jzunt@uw.edu

3. Engineering

Contributing Authors: *Michael S. Cordray and Brittany Rohrman*

What is Engineering?

Engineering is a discipline based on applying rigorous scientific and mathematic knowledge to solve specific problems. These solutions can include designing and building new devices, refining or improving existing devices, or developing new processes. Engineering is generally broken down into sub-disciplines based on the field of scientific knowledge and the types of problems that the engineer is expected to solve. Some of the principle sub-disciplines of engineering include: chemical engineering, which focuses on developing new methods of chemical synthesis, often on an industrial scale; mechanical engineering, which involves development of physical and mechanical systems as well as the application of novel material properties; electrical engineering, which designs and develops new electronic devices, electrical infrastructure, and optical systems; and civil engineering, which uses engineering principles to design and construct infrastructure such as dams and bridges. Besides these traditional engineering sub-disciplines, there are a large number of other engineering fields including optical engineering, computer engineering, and bioengineering. Although practitioners of many engineering disciplines may be involved in addressing global health problems, civil, environmental, electrical, bio-, and chemical engineers are most likely to develop global health technologies.

Engineers play a critical role in addressing global health challenges by crafting appropriate technologies to improve health worldwide. Throughout history engineers have undertaken projects to improve the health and well-being of their communities. Examples include the development of the sewer system to improve sanitation, the development of the artificial pacemaker, and development of new pharmaceutical compounds. Although engineering has been applied to health problems since antiquity, the role of engineering in global health has changed as the world has become more diverse and interconnected. The challenge of engineering for global health is to extend the standards of health available in rich nations to low- and middle-income countries. Global health engineers accomplish this goal by using the engineering design process to create new technologies or modify existing ones in ways that are affordable and scalable in the face of limited resources and infrastructure.[1]

How is Engineering Applied to Global Health?

The first step in engineering for global health is to identify a need or problem that requires a technical response. Ideally, this is done by consulting community members and medical professionals in the setting where the solution is needed. Once a need has been identified, the engineer begins developing possible solutions, using scientific principles to prove that these solutions are feasible. As in all types of engineering, engineers working to solve global health problems use the iterative design process. This process involves rigorously testing a solution, identifying remaining problems, and generating a new design that incorporates the lessons from the previous iteration. The entire cycle is repeated until the design meets the appropriate criteria set forth to solve the problem.

Global health engineers often find that many of the advances, which have improved the standard of health in wealthy countries, require significant infrastructure that is absent in many locations around the world. In many cases engineers seek to 'leap-frog' these infrastructure requirements by adapting solutions used in resource-rich settings for low-resource environments. Examples of this sort of solution include: low-cost, portable versions of medical equipment such as x-ray machines; new infrastructure such as durable, reliable wells and small-scale water purification systems in rural villages; new synthesis pathways to create effective pharmaceuticals more cheaply; and simple, easy-to-use tests to diagnose infectious diseases.[2]

Global health education and research is often incorporated into the relatively new field of bioengineering, which draws from knowledge of the other disciplines and applies them to biological and medical challenges.[3] Many colleges around the country now offer courses and degrees in bioengineering. Some of these programs have begun offering classes that focus on the engineering needs of the global health community. There is also an increased interest in giving students an opportunity to work directly on global health problems either through projects and trips organized by the school, or through organizations such as Engineers Without Borders and Engineering World Health, although these trips run up against similar ethical and other dilemmas of global health projects stemming from the global North, as explored in Chapter 2 ("Ethics") of this volume.[4] Such programs often emphasize the unique challenges of designing solutions for resource-limited settings, and many of these opportunities focus on the fact that addressing global health challenges often requires inter-disciplinary collaboration.

The Role of Engineering in Global Health Projects

Global health projects often involve collaborations between engineers and people in other disciplines.[5] For example, engineers may communicate with health practitioners and public health experts to learn about what problems need new solutions and to test new solutions in a clinical setting. Sociologists or other social scientists may help engineers understand whether an innovative health technology is culturally acceptable in the society where it is needed. Entrepreneurs may commercialize the technology developed by engineers to manufacture and distribute the product at prices that are affordable for the end user (although too often products remain too costly and patients must rely on hand-me-downs from resource-rich countries). Non-governmental and nonprofit organizations may provide funding and expertise to support implementation and scale-up of promising new solutions. Partnerships between companies, academics, government, and non-governmental organizations are often essential for fully addressing public health challenges.

The development of the vaccine vial monitor (VVM) is an example of how multi-disciplinary collaboration can help solve a global health problem.[5] The VVM is a heat-sensitive sticker that changes color when exposed to heat over an extended period of time. When attached to vials of vaccines, the VVM indicates whether or not the vaccine was exposed to unacceptably high temperatures during storage and transport. The World Health Organization (WHO) first identified the need for a tool like the VVM. Then, scientists and engineers at the Program for Appropriate Technology in Health (PATH) developed the VVM based on a technology licensed from industry partners. Finally, government health ministries in Africa tested the VVM, and the UN scaled up its widespread implementation. This example illustrates the importance of multi-disciplinary cooperation in addressing global health needs.

As engineering plays an increasingly important role in global health, health practitioners would benefit from learning about the contributions of engineering to this discipline. A possible way to incorporate engineering into medical curricula would be to teach medical students and health workers about some of the medical tools developed by engineers, such as prosthetic joints, pacemakers, and drug-eluting stents. Case studies of successful (and failed) global health engineering projects may also illustrate how technological solutions are proposed, tested, and redesigned during the engineering process to address a particular problem. For a more hands-on learning experience, educators may ask health practitioners to design a solution to an existing medical problem using the engineering process. Proposing and designing a technology requires little engineering background but provides an engaging way for students to understand how engineers contribute to global health.

Selected Global Health Training Programs and Organizations

- Beyond Traditional Borders (BTB), Rice University Houston, TX, beyondtraditionalborders.rice.edu
- Center of Innovation in Global Health Technologies (CIGHT), Northwestern University, Evanston, IL, cight.northwestern.edu
- Duke Global Health Institute, Duke University, Durham, NC, globalhealth.duke.edu
- Program for Appropriate Technology in Health (PATH), Seattle, WA, path.org
- Engineering World Health (EWH), Durham, NC, ewh.org

References

1. Richards-Kortum, Rebecca. *Biomedical Engineering for Global Health.* Cambridge Texts in Biomedical Engineering. Cambridge, UK ; New York: Cambridge University Press, 2010. Print.
2. Yager, P, GJ Domingo, and J Gerdes. "Point-of-Care Diagnostics for Global Health." *Annual Review of Biomedical Engineering* 10 (2008): 107-44. Print.
3. Saltzman, W. Mark. *Biomedical Engineering : Bridging Medicine and Technology.* Cambridge Texts in Biomedical Engineering. Cambridge ; New York: Cambridge University Press, 2009. Print.
4. Oden, M., et al. "Engaging Undergraduates to Solve Global Health Challenges: A New Approach Based on Bioengineering Design." *Ann Biomed Eng* 38.9 (2010): 3031-41. Print.
5. Frost, Laura J., Michael Reich, and Harvard Center for Population and Development Studies. *Access : How Do Good Health Technologies Get to Poor People in Poor Countries?* Harvard Series on Population

and International Health. Cambridge, Mass.: Harvard Center for Population and Development Studies : Distributed by Harvard University Press, 2008. Print.

Engineering Case Study

Zachary Crannell
Meaghan Bond

In developing regions of Africa, where HIV prevalence is high, accurate dosing of liquid antiretroviral medication for HIV-positive infants and children is crucial: low doses may be insufficient to combat the virus, but high doses can be toxic to the child. Even with oral dosing syringes, measuring liquid medications can be difficult for untrained, elderly, or illiterate caregivers. Clinicians in these areas asked biomedical engineers for a simple solution to help these caregivers deliver accurate doses of liquid antiretroviral medication.

Engineers began discussions with the products' users: parents and caregivers with a wide range of educational backgrounds and health literacy and numeracy skills. These caregivers needed a simple device that required little or no training to deliver the right dose of medicine to the children. Clinicians helped decide what doses of medicine the dosing-aid should be able to dispense, and dictated that the device be affordable, accurate, small, simple to use, and require no power.

An initial prototype resembled a hand-soap pump and regulated the amount of medication dispensed with each pump. Though this device was accurate, small, and required no power, clinicians felt it was too complicated for field use. The cost of the proposed device also put it out of the reach of its intended users.

With the next prototype, the engineers simplified their approach. They developed a plastic clip that slips into the barrel of a commercially available oral-dosing syringe. The clip physically prevents the syringe plunger drawing up more than the allowable volume of medication. With various sized clips that can be prescribed for different doses, engineers were able to come up with a solution that transformed a variable dosing syringe into a fixed dosing syringe, which reduced the likelihood of user error. Prototypes of these "DoseRight" clips were created on a 3D printer and tested extensively in the lab for accuracy and ease of use. The clips were then tested in Swaziland where they received enthusiastic support from clinicians and patients. Ultimately, DoseRight was licensed to a private company, who has begun distributing over 200,000 clips in Swaziland through the nationwide scale-up of the Prevention of Mother to Child Transmission of HIV/AIDS program.

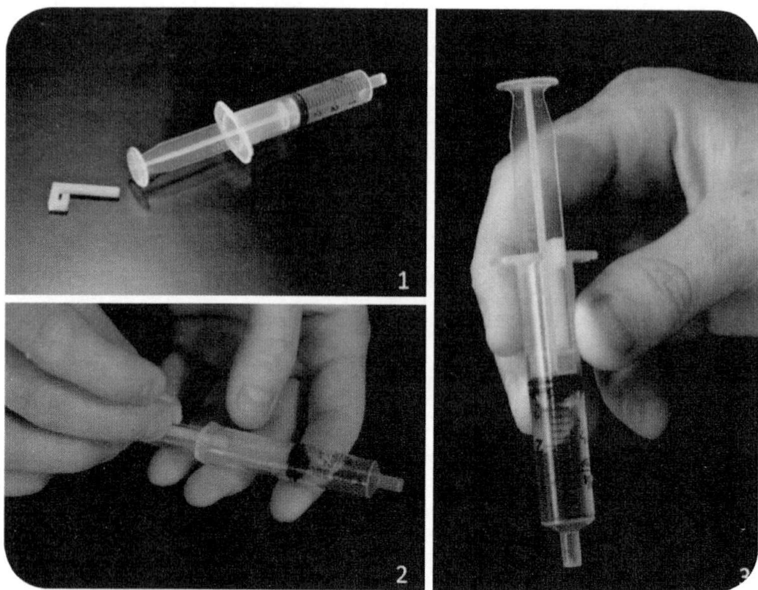

(1) DoseRight clip and oral dosing syringe, (2) inserting the clip into the syringe, (3) clip stopping plunger from withdrawing too large a volume.
Photographer: *Zachary Crannell*

When engineers partner with clinicians, it is important to work together early to define the user needs and the design criteria so the right solution is developed. With the first attempt at the dosing-aid, the design criteria were too broad to direct engineers to develop a suitable solution. The engineers weren't able to develop the simple clips until they realized exactly what the users were looking for. The DoseRight clips also revealed how effective simple solutions can be for difficult problems—and how easy they are to overlook. Ultimately, the plastic clips were innovative, simple, and effective.

Combining the iterative engineering approach of design, testing, and redesign with clinician's on-the-ground expertise can allow engineers and clinicians to produce powerful solutions to some of the biggest global health problems and increase access to medical care.

4. Gender Studies

Contributing Author: Kate W. Read

Gender Studies: A Brief Overview

Also known as "Women's Studies" or "Women and Gender Studies," this relatively young discipline emerged in the 1970s as an expansion of feminist movements, which sought to end sexist oppression. The history of feminism is generally understood to be separated into three "waves" in the global North: the first wave focusing on women's suffrage, the second wave challenging the gendered division of labor, and the third wave advancing a more holistic understanding of oppression that includes not just gender but also race, class, sexuality, and able body-ness. As the second wave feminist movement gained more political influence in the late 1960s and early 1970s, female academics who felt that knowledge production in academic institutions made women invisible and ignored gendered power relations in society sought their own discipline. Eventually, Women and Gender Studies expanded to include gender interactions with other axes of identity such as race, ethnicity, class, sexuality, age, citizenship, and able bodied-ness. This line of thinking was called "intersectional theory".[1,2] More recently, and in addition to the studies of sexualities and men and masculinities, Women and Gender Studies has also expanded to encompass the LGBTQI (Lesbian, Gay, Bisexual, Transgender and Transsexual, Queer, and Intersex) experience as a way of examining problematic structures of patriarchy and capitalism and, more generally, the social, historical, and cultural constructions of gender and power.

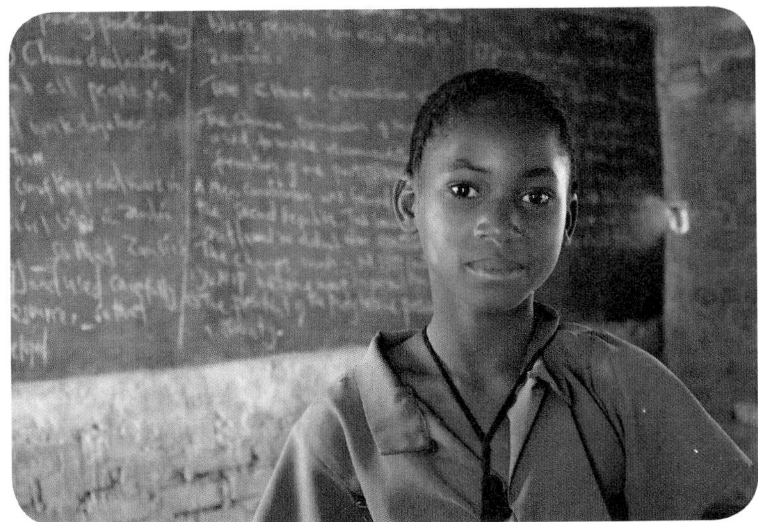

A determined young woman, having recently returned to school with the help of an NGO, poses in her classroom
Photographer: *Will Bynum*

Today, Women and Gender Studies is a well-established interdisciplinary field of study that draws on knowledge largely from the humanities and the social sciences. Some scholars also use Women and Gender Studies to provide a critical lens for the natural sciences and the history of medicine. Regardless of which field or discipline Women and Gender Studies is applied within, it is critical to note that the aim of this discipline is much more than simply to examine constructions of gender. Rather, its goal is to generate a new field of knowledge production that accounts for the synergistic effects of multiple fields of "power" and "identity" that may lead to inequality (including age, race, class, and gender), with specific interest in challenging mainstream and dominant discourses that may not take into account these perspectives. In doing so, Women and Gender Studies scholars facilitate more opportunities for the voices and perspectives of marginalized populations to be heard and valued so that disparities and inequalities can be more accurately and efficiently addressed. This is critical in addressing health disparities and understanding the health and well-being of populations worldwide.

The History of Health in Gender Studies

Health is an important arena that Women and Gender Studies scholars have been engaging with since the beginning of Women and Gender Studies programs. Because Women and Gender Studies initially evolved as a way for women to gain voice in academia and science, an emphasis was placed on women's medical, sexual, and reproductive rights as key indicators of their health and well-being. Beyond taking a more holistic understanding of health that conceptualizes health as more than the mere absence of disease (a definition also eventually adopted by the World Health Organization), Women and Gender Studies scholars have also inspired those within the field of global health more generally to focus on women's health and human rights, gender-based violence, structural violence, and gender equity.[3,4] In addition to bringing a critical focus to women and their health, Women and Gender Studies scholars have also drawn attention to the health needs of those identifying as non-heterosexual and/or non-gender conforming (i.e. LGBTQI). Further, Women and Gender Studies has been instrumental in shedding light on the detrimental effects of gender inequality and problematic notions of masculinity on the health and well-being of men and boys.[5]

With a focus on interdisciplinarity, Women and Gender Studies scholars often explore many contemporary health issues, including (though not limited to): reproductive rights; technology and reproductive health; sexual health; (the medicalization of) sexual pleasure; infectious disease, including HIV & AIDS; violence and warfare; mental and behavioral health; water and food security; LGBTQI sexual minority health disparities/ relational violence; globalization and economic development; migration and trafficking; and occupational health.

Women and Gender Studies in the Global Arena

One defining characteristic of Women and Gender Studies is its emphasis on *power* and *inequality*, particularly as it relates to a critique of public health work, theories, and methods. For example, anyone who incorporates a gendered lens will undoubtedly recognize that power dynamics at the micro-level of the household impact health; however, far fewer scholars recognize the lasting impact of post-colonial power dynamics between nation states. Additionally, feminist scholars have also been somewhat divided in terms of how they portray women in the global South, and many feminist scholars (particularly those from a Western context) have been critiqued for carrying on the legacy of inequality that portrays non-industrialized peoples as "victims," "backward," and "in need of saving," particularly when research relates to gender dynamics and women's rights. However, efforts to bridge the gap between the global North and global South have been made by many feminists. These efforts continue through transnational feminism and significant strides have been made in key areas, with women from local contexts sought as primary stakeholders with the capability to define their own local priorities in health.

Women and Gender Studies and its Contributions to Global Health

Women and Gender Studies have already made important contributions to the global health field. For example, gender and women's health experts and feminist methodologies have helped establish how to differentiate between *sex* (defined as the biological and physiological characteristics that define males and females) and *gender* (defined as the socially constructed roles, behaviors, activities, and attributes that a given society determines is appropriate for men and women, girls and boys) as a way to better understand the social and biological determinants of health. An individual's health status is primarily determined by who (personal attributes) does what (work), where (place), when, and how; correspondingly, who does what, where, when, and how this is influenced, to a strong degree, by gender roles and expectations. This, in turn, is formulated according to cultural norms and traditions. Utilizing this understanding, Women and Gender Studies experts have helped the global health field explore how gender differences and inequalities impact health disparities.

Just as important, Women and Gender Studies can help achieve the goals of global health by exploring the overarching influences of gender, culture, nationality, and related social structures on health. By doing so, Women and Gender Studies is critical to expanding the disease-oriented, biomedical model of global health into a more holistic understanding of health and well-being that incorporates multiple contributing factors to health that might be overlooked without such a perspective. In addition, the focus that Women and Gender Studies places on population/community health, health disparities, and the social inequalities underlying these disparities—namely social divisions by gender, class, race/ethnicity, sexual identity, able bodied-ness, and age—is philosophically rooted in a commitment to social justice. For example, Women and Gender Studies emphasizes the need for a better understanding of how social norms, discrimination, and stigma impact the health and well-being of men, women, and those who identify as LGBTQI. Utilizing an intersectional framework is especially important in terms of global health because it catalyzes important questions such as: In what ways does class, race, gender, sexuality, citizenship, and employment status or occupation influence one's access to health care? To understanding one's body and sexuality? To reproductive rights? How do specific communities access health care? What prevents specific communities or individuals from seeking health care? What larger social/

political/cultural structures impede such access? Students interested in these ideas would benefit greatly from courses in Women and Gender Studies.

Women and Gender Studies and feminism also offer critical contributions to the ethics of global health more broadly. As students, faculty, health professionals, and community partners alike continue to raise questions and concerns about the ways in which global health is conceptualized, developed, and engaged in, the emphasis that Women and Gender Studies places on power dynamics and reflexivity will be invaluable to the enrichment of this discussion. In addition to critiquing the role of the U.S. (and the global North more broadly) in shaping global health (past and present), the perspectives offered by Women and Gender Studies can also be used to examine the (often inequitable) power dynamics within global North and global South academic, institutional, and governmental partnerships. Furthermore, Women and Gender Studies provides a lens through which global health scholars and practitioners can question the production, dissemination, and ownership of knowledge around global health. This includes questions about how research agendas are chosen (i.e. based on grant requirements, community needs, pre-arranged agreements with in-country institution), what methodologies are used to obtain data and the implications of these choices, and who benefits from this research and knowledge.

Unfortunately, Women and Gender Studies programs in the U.S. tend to focus more on U.S. issues (including health); far fewer take a more global or transnational perspective, although this is beginning to change. Global health scholars could have a significant impact on work done by U.S. Women and Gender Studies scholars by collaborating with them on issues of cross-cutting relevance and social change. By incorporating the expertise of Women and Gender Studies scholars on the social and cultural issues around gender-based health disparities, global health scholars could develop a broader, multi-faceted approach to health intervention programming that grapples with social complexities. Correspondingly, Women and Gender Studies scholars, regardless of their geographic area of interest, have much to offer global health scholars. Opportunities to co-author grants and research studies, publications, and textbook materials should be sought by those in both settings to improve channels of communication between the two.

Portrait of a beautiful woman, one of the pillars of her remote African community
Photographer: *Will Bynum*

Global Health Training Opportunities in Gender Studies

While there are currently no Gender and Global Health degrees offered, many universities offer Ph.D. programs in Gender and/or Global Health, as well as majors, minors, and certificate programs in either. To better understand the connection between Women and Gender Studies and global health, students can take specialized coursework within Women and Gender Studies programs with a global health focus, or take coursework within Global Health programs that are focused on gender such as the University of California Global Health Institute's Global Women's Health and Empowerment Summer Institute: (http://www.summer.ucla.edu/institutes/womenshealth/overview.htm).

Other Resources

If students' universities do not offer such courses, students can access field training opportunities and internships at various Non-Governmental Organizations (NGOs) such as:

The Population Council:
http://www.youtube.com/watch?v=hgCqz3l33kU

The World Medical Fund:
http://www.worldmedicalfund-usa.org/

Project Inform:
http://www.projectinform.org/

The Well Project:
http://www.thewellproject.org/en_US/

The Global Fund for Women:
http://www.globalfundforwomen.org/

Interagency Gender Working Group:
http://www.igwg.org/

Change: Center for Health and Gender Equality
http://www.genderhealth.org/the_issues/us_foreign_policy/global_health_initiative/

Students can also utilize a growing assortment of reference materials and edited collections on women's global health and human rights, as well as seek opportunities at various conferences that host panels on gender and global health such as:

National Women's Studies Association:
http://082511c.membershipsoftware.org/content.asp?pl=19&contentid=19

American Anthropological Association:
http://www.aaanet.org/

Inaugural Conference on Global Health, Gender and Human Rights:
http://www.wcl.american.edu/secle/founders/2012/20120321.cfm

Women Deliver:
http://www.womendeliver.org/conferences/

Gender and Health Meetings and Conferences:
http://www.researchraven.com/conferences/category/gender-and-health.aspx

References

1. Crenshaw, Kimberlé. "Demarginalizing the Intersection of Race and Sex: A Black Feminist Critique of

Antidiscrimination Doctrine, Feminist Theory, and Antiracist Politics." *University of Chicago Legal Forum*, 1989.

2. Crenshaw, Kimberlé. "Mapping the Margins: Intersectionality, Identity Politics, and
3. Violence against Women of Color." *Stanford Law Review* 43 (1991): 1241-1279.
4. Birn, Anne-Emanualle, et al., eds. *Textbook of International Health: Global Health in a Dynamic World.* 3rd ed. UK: Oxford University Press, 2009.
5. Murthy, Padmini and Clyde Lanford Smith. *Women's Global Health and Human Rights.* Mass: Jones & Bartlett Publishers, 2009.
6. Connell, R.W. *Masculinities.* Berkeley: University of California Press, 2005.

5. Geography

Contributing Author: *Laura Pascoe*

Geography: in brief

Geography is a diverse discipline that includes the study of both the physical and human elements of the earth, including physical landscapes, their features, natural phenomena, climate and atmospheric studies. Geography is ultimately about the relationship between people and place. It utilizes uniquely human characteristics such as culture, language, and religion to inform the ways in which people interact with the earth. Within the two main branches of geography--physical and human--there exist many subfields. Within physical geography, this includes biogeography, geomorphology, ecology, and climatology. Human geography includes political geography, geopolitics, environmental geography, cultural geography, economic geography, regional geography, and health geography. While all of these subfields of geography may be used to address health concerns, the subdiscipline of health geography is specifically geared towards building a substantive body of knowledge around health and reducing health disparities.

A medical volunteer takes in the beautiful landscape surrounding the South American community he serves
Photographer: *Bynum*

Health Geography

Koplan and colleagues, as quoted in an article by well-known health geographers Tim Brown and Graham Moon[1], described global health in the following way:

> "Global health...places a priority on improving health and achieving equity in health for all people worldwide. Global health emphasizes transnational health

> issues, determinants, and solutions; involves many disciplines within and beyond the health sciences and promotes interdisciplinary collaboration; and is a synthesis of population-based prevention and individual-clinical care."

As Brown and Moon go on to argue in their article, this definition seems similar to the ways in which health-related research by geographers is now defined and approached. Health geography did not always conceptualize health in such expansive terms, however. Similar to the ways in which global health has increasingly widened its scope of how it defines and addresses both "global" and "health" over the last few decades, "health geography" is an evolved sub discipline that originated as "medical geography" in the 1960s. Medical geographers were traditionally focused on two main areas of health: disease ecology and mapping health care provision.[2] Approaches to medical geography also tended to be based on biomedical frameworks and quantitative methodologies. In the early 1990s, however, geography scholars recognized the need to look beyond disease and health services, and re-conceptualized the field to include a more holistic understanding of disease, health and well-being.[3] In doing so, scholars also expanded their approach to their work towards a more 'socioecological' model of health, utilizing mixed and qualitative methods and questioning the biomedical frameworks they traditionally had employed.[4] This "health geography", also referred to as "geography of health and health care", is now understood to encompass a broad scope of research that links health, disease, and health care with understandings of place and space. Health geography builds understanding of the relationship between people, place, public health, and one's health experience. It acknowledges that both place and space are significant factors in health inequalities through social and environmental determinants of health. Health and life expectancy, for example, can often be predicted by what neighborhood, region, and/or country one lives in.

Geography: Relevant to Global Health?

Pulling from other subfields in geography as well as from a variety of other disciplines, health geography allows us to explore a wide range of health-related concerns that take a particular interest in the relationship between health and place and space. Some areas of interest include[6]:

- The link between HIV/AIDS and mobility and migration for HIV positive individuals;
- Increasing levels of air travel and the global spread of disease;
- Rising rates of medical tourism and the effects on both home and destination countries;
- The political economy of a given country and its influence on health decision-making;
- Health implications of environmental change, including the effects of rising oceans on coastal villages, illnesses as a result of pesticide usage, or lead poisoning from materials left at abandoned factories in Mexico;
- Relationship between food production and delivery and the living conditions of those who produce the food;

- The health implications of livestock and human populations co-existing in limited spatial environments and the spatial analysis of animal-borne diseases;
- Harmful (i.e. coal mines) or toxic (i.e. run-off from factories) places verses healing (i.e. hot springs) or therapeutic (i.e. remote wilderness, day spa) places, and who inhabits those spaces or is excluded/has exclusive access to them;
- Disabled bodies and their mobility in rural verses urban spaces;
- The body, understood as a "place" with its own "geography", the relationship between the mind and body, and ways in which this relationship informs individual experience of health.

As this brief list suggests, geography is a diverse discipline that is critical to the advancement of global health; and the skills, techniques, and perspectives that are used by geographers can be invaluable to addressing health inequities. Geographic Information Systems (GIS), such as ArcGIS or open source applications such Quantum GIS (QGIS)[7], for example, can track, analyze, and map health-related concerns such as access to health care or the spread of disease. HIV/AIDS, for example, can be depicted through three "generations" of mapping: it was first examined by rates by location; then on its diffusion within and across nations; and then by linking diffusion of HIV/AIDS to both the underlying behavior of the risk groups as well as to socioeconomic context in which these risk-taking behaviors took place.[5]

Geographers are also well situated to pay particular attention to the relationship between people and their surrounding environment, whether that "environment" is understood as their home, their peers, their neighborhood, their city, their water sources, their national forests, or their national economic system. Health geographers, as they tend to engage in their work today, perceive health not as something to be measured solely by the rate of disease or the degree of health care in a given region, but as a complex interplay of variables (such as socioeconomic status, education, employment opportunities, safe public spaces, transportation, stable economy) that inform the ability of a given population to achieve their utmost capacity in health and well-being.

Geography and Global Health: Thinking Ahead

Still, there are many areas of health-related research that geographers must continue to expand. These are also areas that would contribute greatly to the field of global health. For one, there is a need for more large-scale comparative research across countries, particularly in order to address the relationship between globalization, security, and health.[1] Global health projects are also often isolated by geographic area, or unconnected to national health care systems or public health interventions. Understanding global health practices and projects through geography allows us to think about how we might challenge the problematic verticalization of services—as opposed to an integrated or "one-stop shop" style of services—in the global South and instead think regionally, nationally, and globally about our strategies for addressing and providing quality and accessible health care services.

Similar to other global health disciplines, geography is also a discipline that has its roots primarily among Anglo scholars and practitioners from the West. Early geographical accounts of the world outside of Europe are closely linked with colonialism and notions of the "exotic Other". This is important to mention because, just like global health, geography is a discipline that still has a long way to come in supporting and producing contemporary literature and research originating from the global South. For example, there is a notable lack of scholarship in the global South compared to the health geography research in the global North. In terms of health geography more specifically, it is also imperative to acknowledge that the needs of Western countries are often very different from those in the global South. In Western countries for example, pressing health issues may be focused around chronic illnesses. In the global South, by comparison, there remains an urgency to address infectious diseases (while some low- to middle income countries are finding an increasing overlap in both infectious and chronic diseases) and there is a greater likelihood of health emergencies that require different research, different resources, and different actions than in Western countries. In both of these contexts, however, it is noteworthy that addressing these health issues and managing disease is often done through biomedical frameworks (as opposed to other frameworks for health) and may be influenced with questions about surveillance and control through medicine (such as Michel Foucault's theory of "biopower", or the notion that governments exert power over its population by disciplining *bodies*, such as controlling birth, death, illness, and reproduction, that pertained mostly to 19th century Europe). As such, it is important to be cautious and aware of how health interventions may be interpreted in different contexts and communities.

Developing Global Health Expertise in Geography

As the sub discipline of health geography continues to grow, albeit slowly, there are an increasing number of opportunities to examine health from a geographical perspective. In addition to specifically "medical" or "health" geography courses, student interested in developing their global health expertise within geography would seek geography courses that examine the impact of development, the environment, landscapes, cultures, bodies, or politics on people. McGill University, for example, has various courses offered in areas such as Environment and Environmental Change and Global Health, and Global Land and Water Resources (http://www.geog.mcgill.ca/courses.html). Queen's University in Kingston Ontario has a strong tradition of health geography, and critical health geography scholarship. www.geog.queensu.ca. The University of Washington also has a Minor in Global Health offered to Geography undergraduates that opened in 2011 (http://depts.washington.edu/geog/2011/01/new-minor-in-global-health/).

Other Geography and Global Health Entities

The Royal Geographical Society's Geography of Health Research Group
(http://ghrg.wordpress.com/about/)

Conclusion

Geography, by its history and by its nature, lends itself to interdisciplinary work. Much of the work geographers do is an amalgamation of areas of interest, research methods, scholarship, and frameworks from within the subfields of geography and across a wealth of other disciplines. This interdisciplinary approach has been critical to the production of substantive knowledge and expertise in geography around a wide array of topics. In health geography, there is a growing body of literature produced by health geographers that contributes to better understandings of health and to reducing health disparities. Like many other disciplines, geography still has a long way to go to incorporate knowledge and perspectives produced from within the global South, rather than primarily the global North. Nevertheless, health geography is well aligned with global health and shares the same values of improving health and achieving equity in health for all populations. In addition, health geography, and geography more generally, exemplifies the importance of continuing to build collaborations and partnerships within and across disciplines so that we can better address the pressing needs of today's world.

References

1. Brown, Tim, and Graham Moon. "Geography and Global Health." *The Geographical Journal,* 178.1 (2012): 13-17.
2. Kearns, Robin A., and Wilbert M. Gesler, eds. *Putting Health into Place: Landscape, Identity, and Well-being,* Syracuse, New York, Syracuse University Press, 1998.
3. Andrews, Gavin J., and Graham Moon. "Space, place, and the evidence base: part I—An introduction to health geography." *Worldviews On Evidence-Based Nursing,* 2.2 (2005): 55-62.
4. Kearns, Robin A., and Graham Moon. "From medical to health geography: novelty, place and theory after a decade of change." *Progress in Human Geography,* 26.5 (2002): 605-625.
5. Rosenberg, Mark W. "Medical or Health Geography? Populations, Peoples, and Places." *International Journal of Population Geography,* 4 (1998): 211-226.
6. These are taken from references including: Brown and Moon, 2012; Kearns and Gesler, 1998.
7. For more information on QGIS, visit http://www.qgis.org.

Case study: HealthNow and the Intersection of Geography and Global Health

Laura Pascoe

The following case study seeks to demonstrate the application of geography in global health and the value of engaging a multi-disciplinary approach to global health. While parts of this case study are based on real events, this case study is a hypothetical example; not a factual project.

A health-related organization in an urban city in South Africa, called "HealthNow" had been doing HIV testing using mobile clinics in a black township for two years. At this time, HealthNow staff realized there was a need to expand its services in this township, and the organization felt prepared to fulfill this need. In order to ensure the additional services were both necessary and utilized, however, HealthNow wanted to know what services the community had and was aware of in their area; what additional services people wanted; and what barriers community members perceived in accessing those services. HealthNow partnered with geography graduate students at both a South African university as well as a U.S. university to conduct the research needed to address these questions.

Research conducted included participatory mapping workshops with community members to see what health-related services (i.e. clinics, housing, dentists, nutritionists) they knew of; where they were in their community; and how "accessible" community members rated each of these services based on location, opening times, convenience, and quality of services. The South African and U.S. geography students also conducted focus groups and interviews with men and women between the ages of 18-44. These revealed attitudes and beliefs individuals had about the various health-related resources in their community, and expanded on identifying and exploring logistical barriers, such as hours of operation and transportation, as well as concerns that people experienced in accessing these services (i.e. What's the point of having a nutritionist if there are no places to buy fresh fruit and vegetables in the area?; How am I supposed to take my child to the clinic and wait for hours when I will lose my job if I miss a day of work?). While the clinicians were able to assess what services they could feasibly add to their existing services, the geography students were able to bring the spatial and logistical challenges of individuals in this community into focus, and illuminate the possible ways that HealthNow could improve access to health care by taking these issues into consideration.

Results of the project:

Responding to the identified needs and barriers experienced by community members, "HealthNow" expanded its mobile clinic services to include:

- Basic cold and flu check ups and services (in addition to HIV testing already provided);
- More evening and weekend hours as well as stops at locations that were identified as needing the services by community members;
- In order to provide more fresh fruit and vegetables to the community, HealthNow also partnered with a local spaza (informal grocery store) and began bringing fresh fruit and vegetables as part of their mobile clinic services twice a month;
- HealthNow compiled the information gathered from the participatory mapping workshop into a resource binder of all the health-related services in the community that is now available at multiple locations in the community

Successes of this project:

This project proved quite successful in utilizing collaborative efforts to both identify and address needs and barriers in the community. It engaged an interdisciplinary approach that allowed fruitful partnerships between HealthNow staff, clinicians, and geographers. While other social scientists would also be useful in a project similar to this, geographers were able to put a particular focus on the spatial elements of health access for this community. That is, geographers used their expertise in understanding space, place, and mobility to highlight the limitations this community had in accessing health care, fresh fruit and vegetables, and moving between work, home, and health clinics. This project also built on existing infrastructure rather than creating a new project or organization, and built pride around existing infrastructures in the community. Further, this project tapped into local knowledge as the primary source of expertise. Finally, this project maximized the efficiency of the mobile clinic that went around, and worked with the clinicians so they became intimate with the needs of the community.

Challenges of this project:

As in any global health project, this project was not without challenges, misunderstandings, and even missed opportunities. For example, researchers did not recognize the importance of engaging religious leaders and organizations in the community, and as a result ran into some delays with getting people to agree to interviews and focus groups. Similar projects in such settings would benefit from spending more time identifying local community and religious leaders in the community to approach before jumping into the project.

6. Law and Global Health

Contributing Authors: *Johanna Gusman & Michael Windle*[8]

The importance of the social determinants of health as well as the necessity of collaboration between nations, disciplines, and institutions in overcoming global health challenges is increasingly apparent, particularly in a progressively interdependent world. Inequality is at the root of the economic, human, and environmental causes of health disparities. Addressing these disparities requires an interdisciplinary approach to strengthening health systems that focuses on reducing inequalities and expanding rights. Keeping this in mind, this section aims to discuss the relationship between law and global health, expound on how the two practices inform each other, highlight certain critiques of law in global health, and describe the future of law and global health education with an eye towards advancing health and human rights.

The Relationship Between Law and Global Health

Law is one tool that can be used to end global inequalities in health. Law is largely an attempt to impose a social order on a community, whether that be at the local, national, regional, or global level. This attempt tends to be reinforced by the tacit or explicit threat of coercive deprivation, be it of money or of freedom. Alone, such threats are generally considered morally unacceptable, and such laws need an extrinsic justification. That is, there needs to be a reason it is permissible to deprive someone of their liberty or confiscate their property beyond the fact that the law states as much. Typically, such laws are justified by reference to well-being, be it of an individual or of a community. In an era when health is understood to be a state of complete physical, mental, and social well-being, is not surprising, then, to find consonance in the aims of law and global health.[1]

The relationship between the disciplines of law and global health is bidirectional. In one direction, legal practice can be used explicitly to the benefit of global health aims. Human rights, intellectual property, and immigration are some of the areas of legal practice with clear global health applications. In the other direction, the skills acquired in global health education have applications in the legal sphere. Where a law concerns well-being, and well-being is necessary to health, it can be said that a key feature of that law is that it has a health outcome. The methodologies of global health, conveniently, are preoccupied almost entirely with investigating health outcomes and promulgating well-being. Finally, it is important to remember that law's effect on global health is not necessarily always a positive one. The manner in which international intellectual property law has restricted access to antiretroviral therapy is perhaps paradigmatic. Law has often been inimical to well-being, be it through malicious intent or a lack of reflection on the part of legal actors. It is, then, important to approach law and its usages critically.

Law and Its Role in Global Health

The practice of law is essentially that of one person (or entity) advocating on behalf of another.

Within the context of global health, lawyers often play competing roles. On the one hand, certain lawyers serve the purpose of advancing global health aims and play a critical role in advocating for public policies that can address the most urgent global health challenges. As this chapter highlights, resolving global health challenges—which are embedded in complex relationships between social, biological, economic, political, and environmental determinants—requires a diversity of expertise. Within this context, law can be particularly critical in answering difficult questions such as: Who is culpable for a botched vaccine provided to a developing country from a donor country? What standards should be used for international research between a home country and a host country with differing ethical norms? Who bears the burden of containing infectious diseases that may spread rapidly from one country to another? These questions, along with many others, are indicative of the growing and ongoing need for lawyers to more fully engage with the field of global health.

On the other hand, unfortunately, there are certain lawyers that serve an opposing purpose and drastically set back global health initiatives. This group of lawyers advocate for policies that reduce the social contract and promote schemes that make health inaccessible, such as the maintenance of costly pharmaceuticals. In fact, many of the well-known global health law cases have involved allegations of serious human rights violations. Take, for example, *Abdullah v. Pfizer, Inc.* (the lawsuit that inspired the 2005 movie "The Constant Gardener") regarding the 1996 clinical trial of the antibiotic Trovan on children during an outbreak of bacterial meningitis in Nigeria.[2] According to the trial participants, eleven children died and many others were badly injured. They allege that *Pfizer* deviated from its clinical protocol and failed to inform the children or their guardians of Trovan's life-threating side effects, or that Médecins Sans Frontiéres (Doctors Without Borders) was providing the conventional, proven treatment for bacterial meningitis for free at the same site. Furthermore, *Pfizer* deliberately reduced the standard dosage of the proven drug and the lead investigator of the research falsified documents for ethics approval. *Pfizer* has denied any wrongdoing and as of 2010, the United States Supreme Court has denied review of the case.

Additionally, globalization and the advancement of public health and medicine have contributed to a proliferation in global health interventions aimed at the eradication of disease. However, only ten percent of the worldwide expenditure on health research and development is devoted to problems that primarily affect the poorest ninety percent of the world's population—a statistic that is often referred to as the "10/90 Gap." Addressing this disparity requires redirecting resources—and opportunities to be heard in a court of law—to populations most in need. The recognition of health as a fundamental human right, indispensible for the exercise of many other human rights and necessary for living a life in dignity, is key in actually addressing inequality. It helps to establish the redistribution necessary to address the needs of poverty-stricken communities unable to advocate for such change—and it is this precise intersection where lawyers can make a difference.

Global Health and Its Role in Law

Where laws are justified in reference to well-being, it would seem useful to have some method of quantifying or evaluating this well-being. The standard legal education does not necessarily provide the methodologies appropriate to the task, but metrics and nuanced policy analysis are two primary benefits of global health education. These can be of use to a lawyer. First, the quantitative methodologies developed by public health researchers can provide new ways of evaluating laws. Second, a global health education can provide a lawyer with certain policy analysis and research skills, which will allow her to examine laws beyond a simply legal context, be it domestically or internationally.

A global health education is one way to gain familiarity with the quantitative methodologies a law student might not otherwise study, including basic competencies in statistical methods. Epidemiological and bio statistical methodologies may in turn provide a more robust means of comparing the outcomes of laws. For example, it might be possible to calculate the risk of rejection attributable to a lack of representation in asylum cases, using regression analysis to control for the merits of a case.

Policy research and analysis skills are an additional benefit of a global health education, and useful to any lawyer concerned with the human costs of a law's operation. As with quantitative methodologies, such training may be neglected in the course of a standard legal education. The impact of laws can fall far outside the scope or concern of traditional legal practice.[3] Laws, of course, have health outcomes. In some cases, these are obvious. Portugal recognized this when it cited public health concerns as its motivation for decriminalizing recreational drug use.[4] Differing constructions of constitutional doctrines might have a more oblique effect on health. The Canadian understanding of constitutional doctrines of equity may have rendered it impossible to legally exclude abortion from publicly provided healthcare services.[5] The U.S. Constitution, on the other hand, has been understood to offer no such right, despite apparent similarities in language.[6] A global health education will better acquaint a law student with the outcomes of these legal determinants of global health, and correspondingly permit a more informed policy analysis.

Law schools or courses offered on law specialize in providing students with the skills to understand the technical aspects of legal analysis and the operation of legal ecosystems. A global health education augments that with the ability to contextualize legal systems according to their impact on communities. Society-wide changes clearly require mending much more than the law itself. Nevertheless, laws and regulations provide formal architecture of our social systems, and a critical point of intervention.

Critiques of Law in Global Health

Legal mechanisms, just like most things created by people, are not without some sort of moral agenda, which is why the "law" is often discordant with the "just." That is, if the law can be helpful in the context of global health, it can also be problematic. While the law putatively promotes well-being, in fact, law often operates to the well-being of a privileged few. This is as apparent in the context of global health as it is elsewhere. Intellectual property laws, both domestic and international, serve as an excellent example. Intellectual property treaties have traditionally functioned to protect property rights holders. Ostensibly, this is to the benefit of all, allowing these rights holders to recoup profits, which are then invested in further medical research. In truth, it can be argued, the law has prevented the manufacture of life saving medications at a sustainable cost, primarily to the benefit of corporate shareholders.

Furthermore, law may permit or legitimate war, which is a consummate public health concern. The combination of immigration law and trade policies can deprive communities of traditional incomes while prohibiting migration to find new work, perpetuating those communities into poverty. Drug laws tend to be punitive rather than therapeutic and, as evidenced by the fallout in Mexico from the domestic drug policies of the United States, can impact health far outside their jurisdiction. As a result, the health outcomes of laws are often rather poor.

Moving Forward: Legal and Global Health Education

The conceptualization of global health within the legal discipline is still underway. Many leaders in the field consider the practice to be in its infancy. Much of the discourse related to law and global health has evolved from a need to regulate health-related businesses, such as pharmaceutical companies, as well as protect vulnerable populations from health-related discrimination, whether through law or policy. This has included focusing public health efforts on the communities most in need, as discrimination is often attributed to the social, economic, and environmental inequalities that keep those communities vulnerable. This is precisely why "health and human rights" describes the proper intersection of global health and law and the type of education students in the field need.

Students interested in the intersection of law and global health should focus their studies on international law related to health, such as courses on health and human rights. They should also take science courses grounded in public health policy, such as courses on emerging diseases and community health. Furthermore, demonstrating the interdisciplinary nature of global health, studies in epidemiology and biostatistics will help to establish the science background needed to properly and meaningfully engage in the technical discourse surrounding global health policy. Formal concurrent study programs are still nascent, but the advantage of the current informality is that it affords students a greater degree of freedom and an opportunity to affect the shape of emerging programs. As the field develops, it will provide students with exciting new avenues to challenge the global inequities in law and health.

Students interesting in pursuing a law degree with an emphasis on global health will probably find that they need to do some of the work in putting together a concurrent degree. With this in mind, the prospective student of law and global health should evaluate a law school (and its faculty) for its willingness and commitment to working with other disciplines. While global health strives for interdisciplinarity, it is probably noncontroversial to say that the study of law has in many ways been a walled garden.[7] The degree to which this remains the case can vary widely between schools.

Law & Global Health Programs

Many schools offer concurrent programs in general public health and law, but few offer programs in global health and law specifically. Using the 2012 rankings of the U.S. News & World Report's List of the Best Healthcare Law courses (as well as the authors' own knowledge of existing programs) and determining which universities offer programs specific to global health, the following is a small sampling of schools with courses, initiatives or projects available across each field:

- Boston University
- Case Western Reserve University
- Emory University
- Georgetown University
- Harvard University
- Indiana University
- Loyola University Chicago
- Seton Hall University
- The University of California, Berkeley
- The University of Houston
- The University of Maryland (Carey Campus)
- The University of Minnesota, Twin Cities
- The University of Washington

Law & Global Health References

The following references serve as excellent resources for further reading on the intersection between law and global health as well as its conceptualization within the legal field:

- Obijiofor Aginam, *Global Health Governance: International Law and Public Health In A Divided World* (University of Toronto Press, 2005)
- Andrew Clapham et. al., *Realizing the Right to Health: Swiss Human Rights Book* (Ruffer & Rub Vol. III, 2009)
- Tracy Kidder, *Mountains Beyond Mountains: The Quest of Dr. Paul Famer, A Man Who Would Cure the World* (Random House, 2004).
- Anne-Emmanuelle Birn. *Textbook of International Health: Global Health in a Dynamic World* (2006).
- The Honorable Claire L'Heureux-Dubé. *It Takes A Vision: The Constitutionalization of Equality in Canada*, 14 Yale J.L. & Feminism 363 (2002).

Law & Global Health Opportunities

The following is a list of conferences, continuing legal education (CLE) programs, training programs, internships/externships and fellowships in the field of law and global health for interested parties:

- The O'Neill Institute for National and Global Health Law—Fellowship Program
- Partners In Health (PIH)—Internship Program
- World Health Organization—Internship Program
- Bill & Melinda Gates Foundation—Grand Challenges in Global Health Initiative
- Global Health and Innovation Conference—at Yale University annually.

Conclusion

The health and human rights framework is the nexus upon which global health and law should strive to interact. This framework provides three major benefits specific to the dialogue of this book: (1) it allows for a greater emphasis on law in the education of health practitioners and vice versa; (2) it helps achieve the goals of global health in general; and (3) it contributes to the multidisciplinary efforts in global health creating a common link between the more traditional global health fields, like medicine and public health, to the all other disciplines. In other words, resolving the world's complex problems requires complex solutions. Too often, the knowledge and information that makes such innovative solutions possible is siloed instead of shared; compartmentalized instead of universalized; and privatized instead of publicized. Interdisciplinary learning between global health and law is absolutely necessary for a well-rounded and complete education in both areas. It is this exchange of ideas that allows for progress in the field as a whole and the improvement of the health and well-being of populations worldwide. Advocating the right to health provides an avenue for building the bridges that can allow for participatory, rights-based interactions between all global health fields and the communities they serve.

References

1. Preamble to the Constitution of the World Health Organization as adopted by the International Health Conference, New York, 19 June—22 July 1946; signed on 22 July 1946 by the representatives of 61 States (Official Records of the World Health Organization, no. 2, p. 100) and entered into force on 7 April 1948.
2. Abdullah v. Pfizer, Inc. 562 F.3d 163 (2d Cir. 2009). Federal Court of the United States of America. *Westlaw*. Web. 17 Jan. 2013.
3. Birn, Anne-Emanuelle, Pillay, Yogan and Holtz, Tim. *Textbook of International Health: Global Health in a Dynamic World*, 3rd edition. Oxford University Press, 2009.
4. European Monitoring Centre for Drugs and Drug Addiction (2011). *Drug Policy Profiles: Portugal*. Lisbon, Portugal: Publications Office of the European Union, 2011. Available at: http://www.emcdda.europa.eu/publications/drug-policy-profiles/portugal.

5. Erdman, Joanna N. "In the Back Alleys of Healthcare: Abortion, Equality, and Community in Canada." *Emory Law Journal* (2007): 1093-1155.
6. Harris v. McRae. 448 U.S. 917. Supreme Court of the United States. 1980. *Westlaw.* Web. 17 Jan. 2013.
7. Kennedy, Duncan. "Legal Education and the Reproduction of Hierarchy." *Journal of Legal Education* (1983): 591-615.
8. The authors are both William H. Gates Public Service Law Scholars at the University of Washington School of Law. The views described in this section are from the perspectives of an international health worker and a domestic public health worker turned law students and the lessons learned along the way. We do not claim to have global health law expertise nor do we assert the authority to speak on behalf of our entire discipline. We are merely sharing our thoughts as students hoping to practice in this field.

7. Nutrition and Food Security

Contributing Author: *Allan Davison*

The goals and concerns of nutrition

The importance of nutrition is imprinted on global health personnel during their first encounter with a community disadvantaged to the point of starvation. In high-income countries, most nutritionists lack any comparable contact to see their discipline in global context. Their main concerns are, appropriately, those of the location in which they work. These range widely. They may be: bench researchers in the metabolism of nutrients in cultured cells; public health nutritionists; dieticians in a hospital settings or retirement homes; teachers of nutrition or health promotion. Nutrition is also taught in agricultural schools, often in departments of Food Science and Nutrition. Those closest to the global health skillset are community nutritionists who, even in high-income settings, see malnourished clients from time to time. Their main concerns then, not surprisingly, are those in the location in which they practice. The number of nutritionists in low-income countries is woefully inadequate. This is slowly changing. Options to study in disadvantaged situations have long been available to medical students and are now increasingly available in nutrition programs, although it is important to consider the ethics around these opportunities, as discussed in Chapter 2 of this volume. Moreover, low- and middle-income countries are training their own health personnel in growing numbers.

Promisingly, many community nutritionists now describe their focus as "food security", a term that emphasizes long-term sustainability in both high and low-income settings. It refers to "a steady supply of nutritionally adequate and safe foods, obtainable by socially acceptable means". The determinants of food security closely match the broad socioeconomic determinants of global health. Neither can be met in the absence of the other and, as we already know, poverty is the main determinant of both. Where malnutrition is widespread, it is difficult—if not impossible—to access the ladder of development. In addition to malnutrition, however, there are the additional food-related risk factors that contribute to poverty and therefore poor health, such as the non-agricultural uses of foods; pestilence and disease; resource appropriation; climatic or social disruption; and economic exploitation.

The first year of the 21st Century marked a milestone for the merging of nutrition and global health, with the announcement of the Millennium Development Goals (MDGs). The "first and primary" of the eight goals is the "elimination of extreme poverty and hunger". The goals were approved and ratified by 189 member states of the UN with funding pledged by high-income nations. Most, if not all, of the goals have malnutrition as a co-determinant: perinatal mortality, immune function, infections, physical and cognitive stunting, and school attendance.[1] For example, MDG#4 (to decrease under-five mortality by sixty six percent). Children's deaths are categorized as due to three main causes: pneumonia (18%), diarrhea (11%), malaria (7%).[2] The resulting statistics understate the role of malnutrition, which by weakening the immune system "allows" these infections to kill. It is estimated that nutrition is the underlying cause of over thirty percent of under-five mortality. An overview of global nutrition provides a framework for much of what follows.[3]

The most important nutrient deficiencies that remain are: drinkable water, proteins, and total calories available. Following close behind are micronutrient deficiencies: iron, vitamin A, iodine, and folic acid. Among these, the micronutrient initiative focuses on iron, vitamin A, iodine, zinc, and folic acid as giving the most health benefit for cost. One of the most impressive of the improvements made over the past ten years has been the mitigation of micronutrient deficiency.

Children wait patiently for lunch provided by a program that offers nutritionally sound meals at their school
Photographer: *Will Bynum*

Recent shifts in global health change the roadmap, including the role of nutrition

Paradoxically, the hungry no longer live mainly in low-income countries. Three quarters of the hungry live in *previously* poor countries that have now achieved middle-income status.[4] More than half live in India or China, two countries undergoing rapid development and poverty reduction. Nutrition, however, lags behind economic development, because market economies lack mechanisms to bring food security to the poorest of the poor. Moreover in most low-income countries, hunger is decreasing, largely in Southeast Asia, Latin America and North Africa. However, in some high-income countries in North America and the European Union, where wealth is growing, malnutrition too is increasing—particularly among rural aboriginal peoples, urban homeless communities, and those newly unemployed. Food security and development policy have been redefined to include all marginalized communities regardless of where they occur.

Conversely, obesity is no longer confined to high-income countries. Worldwide, average life expectancy has increased from 56.4 years in 1970 to 67.7 years in 2010 for males (and to 73.3 years for females), paralleling declining deaths from malnutrition and infectious diseases. Worldwide, diabetes has become an epidemic and chronic diseases have replaced infectious diseases as the major cause of death, followed by non-communicable diseases including Alzheimer's.

Finally, food security is fragile; and emergency aid and development aid must complement each other and operate as mutually beneficial to one another. This means including capacity building through agriculture, food security planning, training local community health workers in complementary local food groups, perinatal counseling, and sustainable agriculture. This interdependence is erasing the distinction between relief aid and development aid. For emergencies, care must be taken not to miss invisible malnutrition or subclinical deficiencies. Thus, nutritional assessment can be crucial to a timely warning of a problem that might otherwise go unnoticed. For development aid it means reserve capacity for future emergencies that might disrupt the food supply. Information is increasingly disaggregated so village-by-village risk assessments can be used to assess cushioning needed to protect against famine.

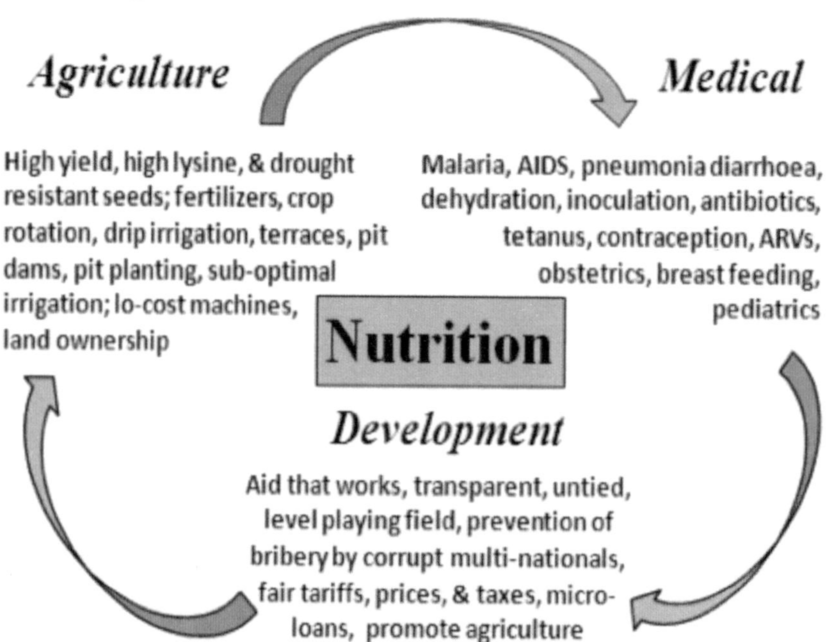

Possibilities for synergism between nutrition and global health

The most respected agencies for global health agree that better coordination between the diverse agents of change is urgent. Those that operate on a large scale, like the UNICEF, the Millennium Villages, World Food Program (WFP) and the MDG initiative have already implemented multi-faceted approaches that strongly incorporate nutrition. To increase effectiveness, the Food and Agricultural Organization along with WFP are sponsoring resources for collaboration between experts in global nutrition, global agriculture, and global development.[5] As examples, local nutritional knowledge can help agriculturists selecting crops and seed varieties and, in turn, the kind of seeds selected, such as high-lysine or drought-resistant seeds. These decisions will impact what physicians will encounter if there is a crop failure. Development decisions regarding irrigation may impact whether drip irrigation or drought-resistant seeds will provide a larger or more nutritious crop yield. The annual reports of the Bill and Melinda Gates Foundation are rich in examples of the benefits of such collaboration.

Another synergism that involves nutrition is the utilizing village or community health workers. South Africa, with assistance from Cuba, is deploying teams of community health workers, including nutritionists on a larger scale, as are Zimbabwe, Zambia, Kenya, Bhutan, Guatemala, and the Philippines. These are wonderful examples of synergism between approaches that interface with nutrition. There is now a vast range of nutritional information on the web and as multimedia—see the Resources section below for more information. More and more low income countries have the expertise to develop for themselves materials that employ local perspectives, and locally relevant solutions to their specific needs. The government of Uganda, for example, has developed exemplary training materials for their initiatives village health teams (VHTs). The illustrations are excellent, providing nutritional guidance where it is relevant in the context of malaria, aids, disorders of pregnancy and early life and healthy eating guidelines. In regions with a scarcity of conventionally trained health professionals, VHTs can have a dramatic impact. While assessments of progress reveal successes, it also shows problems. Some nutritional have quick solutions like supplementation, others, like underfunding, or failures of trickle-down, or capacity building require long term change. As the infrastructure improves, additional skills can be added, such as the ability to use growth charts to follow child development. Many workers are unpaid and selected from volunteers. This makes them extremely cost-effective but, not surprisingly, these have a higher dropout rate and may not ultimately be as beneficial to those carrying out the work as might be intended.

Towards a smooth interface between nutrition and the practice of global health

The remaining gulfs that separate global health and nutrition rise in the adaptations of curriculum to local needs. Thus, the global North emphasizes diabetes, metabolic syndrome, hyperlipidemias, obesity, and anemia—in other words; problems that have not reached the same levels of urgency in the South. Optional courses for global health nutritionists could have a curriculum closer to that in Sub-Saharan Africa, where scurvy, kwashiorkor (protein deficiency), marasmus, pellagra, xerophthalmia, and beriberi, and multiple deficiencies are core. Universities in Canada, the US, Netherlands, Norway, Australia, and other countries already encourage nutrition students to spend a semester in a location where they will encounter inequities.

What does the future hold?

There is an opportunity for nutritionists from the global North to be part of the profound change that is happening in the global South. There is corresponding opportunity for physicians and other global health practitioners to use nutritionists to free up their time for treating disease, rather than learning the differential diagnosis of multiple deficiencies. If nutritionists are not adequately trained and integrated appropriately into these settings, physicians with MSF and others will handle nutritional deficiencies themselves, using upper arm circumference for triage, micronutrient sprinkles, rehydration solutes, and ready-to-use foods as first solutions, rather than specific nutritional assessments and treatments. The nutritional expertise for low-income settings will be increasingly provided by members of the VHTs with nutritional training from local training centers. As knowledge accumulates there will be evolutionary pressure from those providing funds for accountability and the use of evidence-based practices in achieving goals. This lends optimism to the emergence of best practices over time. Those who take part, whether from nutrition or the medical side, will gain the satisfactions that come from making a unique difference.

Conclusion

Change is difficult, especially when one is beset on every side with urgent needs. However, the urgent vision of a world without hunger in three or four decades is a powerful incentive. Physicians and public health practitioners will increasingly work in collaboration with experts in nutrition, agriculture, and community development. With most poverty in middle-income countries, the teams will be trained in the country they work in. The diversity of these teams will balance short and long term needs, coordinate local across national and international resources. As knowledge grows, broad resources will be harnessed to increasingly specific local needs. The mission of aid workers is to become unnecessary by helping to build capacity locally. The next few years provide an opportunity to be part of the solution; and the horrors of delay are reason to increase our efforts.

Progress toward achieving the MDGs is steady, but too slow for complacency. Adequate nutrition and food security now widely recognized, along with agriculture, as core elements for achieving MDGs. Opportunities exist for global health workers to put nutrition and agriculture to work at the things they do well. A career in nutrition offers many ways to contribute to global objectives through research, policy development, program implementation, direct provision of services, communication, and education. The best collaborations will be in teams where the members' expertise lies in complementary, but overlapping, fields.

Resources for further information

"MOOCs" are free Massive Open Online Courses. They represent a huge step towards democratizing education by some of the most elite universities. At http://www.class-central.com/ you can search about 500 links for "global" or "nutrition" and you will find some that are appropriate. About 90 courses are starting in first 4 weeks of 2013. Another institution offering free accredited courses is NextGenU, which plans to release a course in Nutrition for Public and International Health. All these are examined, for credit courses. The universities mainly charge for credit, but most instructors will provide you with a signed letter indicate that you took the course and earned the grade you received The Bill and Melinda Gates Foundation are funding these.

Select Courses:

Cornell University's Nutritionworks collection is a spectacular resource of courses at the interface of nutrition and global health, for web delivery, intended for professionals. *http://www.nutritionworks.cornell.edu/features/index.cfm?Action=Catalog&SubCatalog=1&Order=3*

Courses can be taken free, or for $15 per credit if Continuing Medical Education credit is needed. It includes the first in a series of UNICEF training programs: *http://www.nutritionworks.cornell.edu/UNICEF/about/* the course is on "... Infant and Young Child Feeding".

The Global Health Educational Consortium has a vast collection of refereed teaching modules, including

- **Nutrition in global health**—a supplement the medical curriculum and in nutrition courses: *http://globalhealtheducation.org/Modules/Pages/56_Nutrition_In_Global_Health.aspx*
- **Acute malnutrition**: *http://globalhealtheducation.org/Modules/Pages/48_Acute_Malnutrition.aspx*

With the GHEC merger with the Consortium of Universities for Global Health these will shortly be moved to http://www.cugh.org/programs/educational-programs. Together these will comprise a collection of refereed materials to help with training of global health professions

The Nutrition in Medicine system is a fascinating free web outlet for knowledge in clinical aspects of nutrition. It is also a superbly polished example of self-paced problem-centered learning for anyone designing web-based courses. The link is *http://www.nutritioninmedicine.net/* and located at the University of North Carolina

Resources for Village Health teams. Uganda has produced excellent manuals for instructional purposes: Training manual *http://www.omnimed.org/clients/omnimed/docs/VHTHybridManual.pdf*

Aids to use in the villages *http://www.malariaconsortium.org/inscale/downloads/uganda/VHT-job-aids.pdf*

UNICEF along with the World Food Program: *http://www.unscn.org/*

Institute of Nutrition of Central America and Panama (INCAP) materials (also in Spanish translation Instituto de Nutrición de Centro América y Panamá): http://www.incap.org.gt/index.php/en/

Global health training programs that include a nutritional focus—a selection

The Consortium of Universities for Global Health CUGH has a listing of about 150 global health programs. http://www.cugh.org/sites/default/files/content/resources/modules/To Post Trainees/GH Online_links.pdf Moreover, its list of member universities may be more current and has well over 100 universities almost all with global health programs. You can access it at http://www.cugh.org/membership/members. Increasingly nutrition options are being added and these may take some time to locate. Cornell, Emory, UC Davis, and Tufts, have well-established and well-respected global health programs with integrated nutrition options. In Europe, the London School of Hygiene and Tropical Medicine and the U of Copenhagen also have global health nutrition programs. In Canada nutritional interests are emerging in global health programs, and a few courses, but at the time of writing no evidence of real integration was found. Completing a PhD can be a good choice. If your supervisor shares your perspective, you can pursue one subject in depth or several including global nutrition, and the degree is marketable should you choose an academic career.

References

1. Darnton-Hill, Ian, Martin M. Bloema and Mickey Chopra. "Achieving the millennium development goals through mainstreaming nutrition, speaking with one voice." Public Health Nutrition 9 (2006) 537-539 print.
2. United Nations. "Committing to Child Survival: A Promise Renewed." *Progress Report of the Children's Fund* (UNICEF) 2012 Web 23 January 2013
3. Davison, Allan J "Global Nutrition in the 21st Century: Opportunities and Challenges for the Developed and Developing Worlds", (Simon Fraser University) Published in: *Public Health in the 21st Century* (2011) Ed. Madelon Finkel Vol 1 of 3 *Global Issues in Public Health* p91-107 **Santa Barbara** Praeger Press, Print. 21st Century Perspectives
4. Chandy, Laurence and Geoffrey Gertz "Two Trends in Global Poverty" (2011) *Brookings Institute* Web23 January 2013
5. United Nations. Nutrition, agriculture, development. Coordination and integration FAO https://www.securenutritionplatform.org/Lists/Events/DispForm.aspx?ID=114 (2012) New York: UN, 2012 Web23 January 2013.

8. Public Health

Author: *Tate Lowrey*

Introduction

Public health has played a vital role in the creation and evolution of the current conception of global health.[1] Global health is increasingly more relevant in medicine as the role of the modern health professional extends both beyond his or her community, as well as the clinic walls. New infections, environmental concerns, and behavioral risks transcend national boundaries. Therefore, it is imperative that we continue to understand and engage with public health and the interdisciplinary opportunities that exist between public health, global health and medicine. Not only will this lead to medical practitioners better equipped to address the health and security of all citizens, global or local, it will also facilitate stronger and much-needed collaborations across disciplines.

Zambian children watch the dedication ceremony for a clean-water well recently installed in their remote village
Photographer: *Will Bynum*

Public Health: The Fundamentals

Public health is not a product solely of Western society. Origins of public health interventions, such as urban public water, sewage systems and infection containment, trace back to ancient cultures in Greece and imperial Rome as well as in 8th century Islamic societies.[2] However, the modern conception of public health, especially that of collective official action, came from the mid-19th century and namely from England, continental Europe and the USA. It emerged as a result of two catalysts: as part of social reform movements and as part of a desire to deepen understandings of biological and medical developments, particularly those dealing with causation and management of infectious disease.[1] According to Koplan et al.[1], the discipline of public health was established on the basis of four main tenets: (1) data and evidence form the basis from which decisions area made (such as biostatistics, disease surveillance and outbreak investigations, laboratory science); (2) the unit of focus as populations rather than individuals; (3) the quest for equity and social justice as a fundamental philosophical value; and (4) priority given to preventing illness rather than curative care.

A definition of public health put forth by Winslow[3] nearly ninety years ago still stands as one of the best and most comprehensive descriptions of public health:

> "Public health is the science and art of preventing disease, prolonging life and promoting physical health and efficacy through organized community efforts for the sanitation of the environment, the control of communicable infections, the education of the individual in personal hygiene, the organization of medical and nursing services for the early diagnosis and preventive treatment of disease, and the development of social machinery which will ensure every individual in the community a standard of living adequate for the maintenance of health; so organizing these benefits in such a fashion as to enable every citizen to realize his birthright and longevity."

According to Brown[4], what public health aims to achieve, in practice, can be reduced to five main strategies:

- *Protection*: The first mission of public health is to protect the population from contracting diseases transmitted person-to-person or from the environment. This includes developing and enforcing legislation and regulations.
- *Prevention*: Public health works to identify and halt threats to health before they happen. The strategies employed for example are vaccinations, education and health screenings.
- *Promotion*: Increasingly, public health is moving beyond traditional preventative strategies to keep people well. This encompasses promoting healthy behaviors while engaging with a multitude of health determinates that assure conditions where people can be healthy. Such interventions could include campaigns that encourage consumption of more fruits and vegetables as well as public-private partnerships that influence the locations of stores that sell fresh food.
- *Prognosis*: Public health professionals work to predict and estimate potential threats to health. Common techniques used are disease surveillance and monitoring thus making Health Information Systems a core element of a public health system.
- *Provision*: A strong national public health system ensures adequate health care is accessible, efficient and appropriate to all citizens whether that is through government public health institutions or through private practices. Consequently, public health plays a vital role the

conversations around financing of health care as well as in the education of health care practitioners.

The Role of Public Health in Global Health

Public health is a discipline that can help address and solve the health disparities between the global North and the global South as well as the growing inequities in affluent societies.[2] Health practitioners who apply core public health elements and experiences such as population-based and preventative strategies are better equipped to help improve the health of their patients. For centuries, sanitation and hygiene, the building of aqueducts for clean water, ensuring uncontaminated and nutritious food, improving living conditions—all of which are public health measures—have proven more influential in controlling disease outbreaks than biomedical interventions (such as vaccinations) alone.

Public health seeks to know what health risks are present in society, how they are distributed, and why. Historically, quantifying disease and its distribution and analyzing the data to uncover correlations has been a hallmark of public health. In the last thirty years, however, a new public health has emerged; one that is more suited to address the scope of problems facing our interconnected world. Now public health uses sociological and anthropological frameworks and tools to investigate the determinants and distribution of health. Public health today engages with human behavior and political activity, uses multidisciplinary efforts in fields such as engineering and economics, and makes both ethical considerations and human rights a priority.[2] Global health challenges arise from interdependent causes that require international coordination to align resources, pool expertise, and share technological advances and experiences.[5] Public health principles can direct needed multi-sectoral and system-wide solutions. Public health also offers diversity and comprehensiveness in its approach that assures health security for all. This is critical to integrate into the work of any health-related discipline.

An example of engaging public health principles and experiences to improve global health can be seen in the recent initiative by the World Health Organization (WHO) to strengthen health systems.[6] Because systems and structures are critical to building long lasting and successful approaches to health, public health places a high priority on these. According to the WHO, "a health system consists of all organizations, people and actions whose primary intent is to promote, restore or maintain health."[6] As the WHO points out, in a time of great technological and biomedical advances for curing disease and prolonging life, the chasm in health outcomes between countries (and within countries) is only widening. And even though many of the interventions currently available are affordable and effective; unprecedented levels of illness, premature death, and suffering continue to exist. The WHO asserts that if the power of modern interventions was matched by a correspondingly powerful health system to deliver the intervention, health inequities, fragmented care and insufficient scope would not be such a dire global problem.[6] For this reason, it is important to broaden the role of health practitioners beyond treating individuals to encompass improving the performance of the whole health system.

Public and Global Health Focus in Medical Education

Redesigning the education of health professionals to strongly integrate public health principles and knowledge will produce health practitioners and global health practitioners alike that better understand health determinants and are therefore more responsive to evolving health needs. It is important to broaden the education of physicians to understand the biological as well as the social contexts in which health is created and destroyed. When medical and public health practitioners combine forces, their ability to achieve their mission in education, research and practice is strengthened; "the two sectors are able to achieve benefits that none of them can accomplish alone."[7]

Prominent health scholars calling for reforms in medical education offer several ideas on how to broaden the scope and impact of medical practitioners:[8]

1. Adopt a curricula based on the acquisition of competencies that are better respond to changing needs instead of being dominated by static coursework.
2. Promote interprofessional and trans-professional education that enhances collaborative and non-hierarchical relationships in effective teams.
3. Harness global resources and adapt them locally in a way that improves capacity to flexibly address local challenges while using global knowledge, experience, and shared resources. Resources could include faculty, curriculum, materials, and students linked internationally through exchange programs.
4. Expand academic centers to be academic systems, expanding the conventional discovery-care-education continuum in schools and hospitals into primary care settings and communities. Supplement this with external collaboration with other disciplines to create a more responsive and dynamic professional education system.
5. Connect through networks, and alliances between educational institutions worldwide and across to related actors, i.e. governments, civil society organizations, business, and media. This help could break down the ways academic institutions tend to be stand-alone entities, removed from the system around them.

Resources for Public Health, Global Health and Medical Education Collaborations

A monograph named "Medicine and Public Health: The Power of Collaboration", published by the American Medical Association and the American Public Health Association in 1997, is an indispensible resource for any future health practitioner interested in how to better collaborate with public health. It offers a wealth of expertise, examples and case studies, and recommendations on how these two disciplines can be more synergistic. Additional resources include:

World Health Organization. *Framework for action on interprofessional education & collaborative practice.* Geneva: World Health Organization, 2010. Can be accessed at http://whqlibdoc.who.int/hq/2010/WHO_HRH_HPN_10.3_eng.pdf

Interprofessional Education Collaborative Experts Panel. *Core competencies for interprofessional collaborative practice: Report of an expert panel.* Washington, D.C.: Interprofessional Education Collaborative, 2011. Can be accessed at https://www.aamc.org/download/186750/data/core_competencies.pdf

Beaglehole, Robert. "Global partnerships for health." *The European Journal of Public Health* 15.2(2005): 113-114. http://eurpub.oxfordjournals.org/cgi/content/extract/15/2/113

Buse, Kent and Andrew M. Harmer. "Seven habits of highly effective global public-private health partnerships: Practice and potential." *Social Science & Medicine*, 64.2(2007): 259-271. http://www.sciencedirect.com/science/article/pii/S0277953606004631

Health System Action Network (HSAN)--HSAN is a global network of professionals whose goal is to improve access to information on strategies that work in making stronger health systems and to avoid duplication of efforts that have been found to be less effective in strengthening health systems. www.hsanet.org

Training for Health Equity Network (THEnet)—THEnet collaborates with 11 schools committed to prioritizing health equity at the center of global health policy and helping other schools reduce health inequities in their regions. They seek to create innovative approaches to increase access and quality of care. Member schools strive to ensure that learning, research and service activities address priority health needs with a particular focus on the underserved. They aim for health practitioners to become more socially accountable. http://www.thenetcommunity.org/

Schools of Medicine and Global Health/Public Health Partnerships

Johns Hopkins School of Medicine works with the Johns Hopkins Bloomberg School of Public Health and its Department of International Health to offer opportunities for medical students desiring to gain experience in global health. http://www.hopkinsglobalhealth.org/

The University of Washington Department of Global Health connects the schools of Medicine and Public Health, "with a mandate to harness the expertise and interdisciplinary power of all 16 UW schools and colleges." http://globalhealth.washington.edu/

The Hubert Department of Global Health at the Rollins School of Public Health at Emory University offers dual degree programs with The School of Medicine and opportunities to take part in international fieldwork as a part of their program. Field experiences involve a wide range of program, research, and service opportunities. http://www.sph.emory.edu/cms/departments_centers/gh/index.html

The University of North Carolina Gillings's School of Global Public Health "supports faculty, staff, and students in their efforts to improve the health of the world's populations and facilitate interdisciplinary global health research, teaching, and practice across all departments and programs in the School."

http://www.sph.unc.edu/globalhealth/

References

1. Koplan et al. "Towards a common definition of global health." *The Lancet* 373 (2009): 1993-1995.
2. Leeder, Stephen. "The scope, mission and method of contemporary public health." *Health Policy* 32.6(2007): 505-508.
3. Winslow, Charles-Edward Amory. "The untilled field of public health." *Modern Medicine,* 2 (1920): 183–91.
4. Brown, Lawrence D. "The political face of public health." *Public Health Reviews* 32 (2010): 155-173.
5. World Health Organization. *Everybody business: strengthening health systems to improve health outcomes: WHO's framework for action.* Geneva: World Health Organization, 2007.
6. World Health Organization. *The world health report 2006: working together for health.* Geneva: World Health Organization, 2006.
7. Lasker, Roz D. and the Committee on Medicine and Public Health. *Medicine & public health: the power of collaboration.* New York, New York: The New York Academy of Medicine, 1997.
8. Frenk, Julio et al. "Health professionals for a new century: transforming education to strengthen health systems in an interdependent world." *The Lancet,* 376 (2010): 1923-58.

9. Social Work

Contributing Authors: *Rachel Hanle, Dr. Cathy McElderry*

Social Work: Introduction

Social work has led the way in efforts to address the social and economic needs of society and to bring social problems to the attention of the public. The profession is committed to improving the welfare of individuals and communities—particularly the most vulnerable—through empowerment and increased access to resources. Social work is actively engaged in addressing difficult social problems and mobilizing resources to enhance human well-being. Professional social workers are dedicated to promoting social development, facilitating cooperation, and advocating for social justice on a local, national, and global level.[1]

The National Association of Social Workers (NASW) has identified the following areas of social work practice: adolescent health; aging; behavioral health; bereavement/end of life care; children, youth, and families; diversity and equity; health; HIV/AIDS; international; peace and social justice; and school social work.[2] Regardless of the area of practice, all social workers share a set of common goals and values that unify the profession.

Background and Values of Social Work

As a profession whose early efforts focused primarily on poverty, social work practitioners work extensively with the poor and other vulnerable groups such as women, children, the aging, persons with disabilities and mental illnesses, refugees, and people who have been discriminated against based on gender, ethnicity, sexual orientation, socioeconomic status, and/or religious beliefs. Recognizing that poverty and social injustices contribute to the poor health and well-being of much of the world's population, social workers are committed to "supporting, influencing, and enabling structures and systems that positively address the root causes of oppression and inequality."[3]

Social workers are guided by six core values: service, social justice, dignity and worth of the person, importance of human relationships, integrity, and competence. These values guide social work education and practice in all settings. As one of the core values of the profession, social justice binds social workers to an ethical responsibility to advocate for fair, non-oppressive and equitable access to information, services, and resources.[1] Social justice is a concept based on the idea that each individual is endowed with certain rights and responsibilities. Along with these rights and responsibilities, each person is also worthy of being treated with dignity and respect. It is through commitment to social and distributive justice that international social work practice contributes to global health.

In addition to its core values, one of many characteristics that set social work apart from other helping professions is its unique focus on the essential link between humanity and nature. That is, social work seeks to understand the individual within the context of his/her environment, rather than just as an individual sitting alone in an office. This ecological perspective examines all levels of intervention or client systems: micro level (the individual), mezzo level (families and small groups such as schools or neighborhoods), and macro level (organizations, systems of care, and communities). Once these environments have been assessed, social workers can create a comprehensive plan or intervention based on available resources. The practice of social work requires knowledge of human development and behavior, social, cultural and economic factors that impinge on individuals and their environment.

In addition to engaging an ecological perspective, social workers pay special attention to the strengths that the client can mobilize to address the challenges that affect the client and his or her community. Such a strength-based perspective is indicative of the ability of social workers to recognize and respect the capacity and capabilities of clients to effect positive change for themselves and their surrounding environment. The process of identifying and verbalizing these strengths—a key component of what social workers seek to do—is empowering to both clients and their support systems. When a client recognizes their own strengths, he or she can use them as a foundation for positive change. Thus, the application of social work values, principles, and techniques are employed to achieve one or more of the following objectives:[2]

1. Assisting individuals to obtain tangible services (e.g., food, clothing, housing, etc.);
2. Counseling and psychotherapy with individuals, families, and groups;
3. Helping communities or groups provide or improve social and health services;
4. Participating in and supporting the legislative process on important social issues.

Continuum of Social Work Careers

The Council on Social Work Education (CSWE) is the governing body that accredits bachelor's and master's programs in social work education. To be eligible for licensure or certification, many states require graduation from an accredited program. In the United States there are currently 482 accredited baccalaureate (BSW) programs and 209 master's (MSW) programs.[4] Social workers who earn doctorate degrees, either a Ph.D. (Doctor of Philosophy) or DSW (Doctor of Social Work) are qualified to teach at the college level, conduct research, assume administrative positions, or enter private practice. The Association of Social Work Boards (ASWB) is responsible for licensing examinations for social workers. All states, the District of Columbia, Puerto Rico, and the Virgin Islands define and regulate social work practice. In addition to licensure, the National Association of Social Workers establishes and promotes additional credentials, such as advanced practice specialty certifications.[5]

International Social Work

Increasingly aware of the interconnection of critical social issues confronting populations across the globe, social work education has made a significant effort to become more internationally focused. There are three major international social work entities that focus on global issues and the profession. The International Association of Schools of Social Work (IASSW) promotes human rights and social development through policy and advocacy initiatives, as well as provides a forum for international exchange among social work educators. The International Federation of Social Workers (IFSW) promotes social work as a global profession committed to human rights and social justice throughout the world. The third major organization, the International Council on Social Welfare (ICSW) is an interdisciplinary organization that serves as a liaison to the United Nations on social welfare and social development issues. Because many of the world's greatest health problems are directly and/or indirectly related to the social issues communities face, collaboration among helping professions is critical to address health issues at their origin. Social workers contribute to global health by addressing social justice and social welfare issues by collaborating with other health and helping professions at different levels of policy and practice.

The International Federation of Social Workers collaborates with other international entities, such as the World Health Organization, the Office of the United Nations High Commissioner for Refugees, and the Office of the United Nations High Commissioner for Human Rights to accomplish eight specific goals established by the International Council for Social Work Education in 2010· These goals are used as a framework for professional programs of social work education. The international social work goals compliment many of the United Nation's Millennium Development Goals, such as the aim to eliminate poverty and empower women. Working together with other entities, social work professionals collaborate to identify mutual goals in the quest to improve global health.

International Social Work and Global Health

According to the NASW Standards for Social Work Practice, "Health is a matter of both economics and social well-being. Both domestically and internationally, health care social workers strive to gain knowledge about health care: behavior, expenditures, reforms, systems, teams, insurance, health maintenance organizations, health protective behaviors, and more."[6] When clients do not have access to health care services, whether for economic or social reasons, social workers act as resource brokers, social advocates, and mediators to address the challenges clients face. As health care professionals, social workers arrange services for individual clients, such as access to community resources and social support. Social work practitioners also function as advocates for social change by promoting broader community-wide change as well as policies that support social justice and human rights.

While social justice and human rights are important components of social work, respecting the dignity and worth of each person is just as important. A professional focus on distributive justice means that social workers have an ethical responsibility to ensure that individuals are treated with respect and that they have access to needed resources regardless of ethnicity, gender, religion, education level, socioeconomic status, or sexual orientation. From a global health stand point, social workers believe and advocate that clients and communities should have access to basic health services that take into consideration cultural and religious beliefs. Cultural competent health interventions are important, especially in communities with strong traditional values. As part of the profession's core value of self-determination, social workers acknowledge that individuals are the experts in their lives; they know their situations better than any other person. Cultural practices and beliefs about maintaining good health vary throughout the world; working within communities is critical in achieving the goal of basic health care in a global context.

Social workers have an important and unique role in addressing the global health challenges that significantly impact large segments of the world. As identified by the United Nations' Millennium Development Goals (MDG), for example, combating the spread of HIV/AIDS and improving AIDS treatment are major health challenges globally. Over the past three decades social work professionals have become leaders in supporting community-based responses to HIV/AIDS. The International Federation of Social Workers supports an approach that addresses the complex issues associated with the prevention and treatment of HIV/AIDS as a continuum of care. The ideal approach offers "sexual and psychosocial health education, prophylactic means of prevention, adequate testing, and treatment, counseling, and support" upon diagnosis, for both patient and others affected by the disease.[1] Dedicated to promoting social development, facilitating cooperation, and advocating for social justice on a local, national, and global level, social work professionals play a variety of roles in the fight to prevent and treat HIV/AIDS.

To facilitate cooperation and advocate for social justice, social work professionals collaborate with professionals from other disciplines to conduct research on the effectiveness of HIV/AIDS programs and provide information on interpersonal and social issues confronting individuals and communities affected by HIV/AIDS. An important issue that has arisen from the AIDS pandemic is the pervasiveness of gender-based violence. Some women, for example, have become HIV-positive as a result of sexual violence. In addition, there is evidence that some women fear disclosing their HIV status to their partners out of fear of facing physical abuse and/or abandonment.[7] In order to address this concern in Kenya, for example, social work and public health professionals from the University of Alabama at Birmingham (UAB) are working alongside professors of at the University of Nairobi to investigate the extent of gender-based violence among HIV positive women in Kenya. Gathering more information on the relationship between HIV/AIDS and gender-based violence is useful in implementing programs to promote social justice for all people affected by the AIDS.

In HIV/AIDS care and treatment, social workers act as case managers for individual clients and their support systems. A diagnosis of HIV/AIDS is often the beginning of many changes in the lives of individuals and their families. Social workers can organize concrete services (e.g., medication assistance, nutrition counseling, substance abuse treatment, etc.) and mobilize emotional support. Emotional and spiritual supports are important aspects of HIV/AIDS treatment. Professional social workers "can provide therapy and counseling for concerns such as new diagnosis, disclosure, intimate partner violence, depression, fertility, anxiety, relationships (intimate and familial), grief and loss, and addictions."[8]

There are increasing opportunities for social work students who wish to focus on health and international social work. Several universities offer joint degrees in social work and public health to prepare professional social workers. Some social work programs offer international internships, as well as international placement for practicum. In these settings, social work students learn how to approach challenges faced by individuals in the global south, such as poverty and shortage of resources, which negatively impact health and well-being.

Conclusion

Social work is a major player in the pursuit of social and political action to ensure greater equity in access to resources and opportunities. Through various initiatives and partnership, social workers are actively engaged in efforts to promote social justice and improve human conditions. The scope of global poverty, ethnic conflict, human trafficking, HIV/AIDS and other contagious diseases are global challenges that require action on many levels by many disciplines. Nevertheless, these are problems that are directly related to social work ethical responsibilities and expertise:

> "From the most basic duty to advocate fundamental rights, through lobbying for effective and compassionate social and health policy, to advocating just and equitable protocols for research and collaboration, there is much work to be done. Human rights, social work education, social and health policy, research and partnerships—all relate one to the other. May this provide a catalyst to greater action and a standard against which we can measure ourselves."[1]

Resources for Social Work and Global Health Education

NASW Standards of Social Work Practice in Health Care Settings—http://www.socialworkers.org/practice/standards/naswhealthcarestandards.pdf
The International Federation of Social Work -http://ifsw.org/
Council on Social Work Education—http://www.cswe.org/
International Council for Social Welfare—http://www.icsw.org/
National Association of Social Workers—http://www.socialworkers.org/
Social Work Across Nations (SWAN)—http://socialworkers.org/nasw/swan/default.asp

References:

1. "Code of Ethics of the National Association of Social Workers" National Association of Social Workers. 1996. http://www.socialworkers.org/pubs/code/code.asp
2. National Association of Social Workers (NASW). Retrieved 01/18/13 from https://www.socialworkers.org/practice/default.asp
3. The Global Agenda For Social Work and Social Development Commitment to Action. The International Federation of Social Workers, the International Association of Schools of Social Work, and the International Council on Social Welfare. 2012.
4. Council on Social Work Education. (2012). Retrieved 01/18/13 from http://www.cswe.org/.
5. Kirst-Ashman, Karen, *Introduction to Social Work & Social Welfare*. Belmont, CA: Brooks/Cole. 2013.

6. "NASW Standards for social work practice in health care settings." (2005). National Association of Social Workers. http://www.socialworkers.org/practice/standards/naswhealthcarestandards.pdf
7. McDonnell, Gielen, and O'Campo. "Does HIV status make a difference in the experience of lifetime abuse? Descriptions of lifetime abuse and its context among low-income urban women." *J Urban Health*, 80(3):494-509. 2003.
8. Schultz, Cheryl. Social work practice in HIV/AIDS. Canadian Association of Social Work. 2012. <http://www.casw-acts.ca/en/social-work-practice-hivaids>

Chapter Conclusion

As this chapter has demonstrated, there are many players and critical disciplines beyond the clinical setting that contribute to global health. There are many important skills, research endeavors, collaborations, and projects that can and should happen across disciplines, and that are indeed essential in developing preventive and infrastructural approaches within global health. As the engineering case study illustrated, there is a great importance for flexibility and adaptability in developing tools that are locally relevant and user-friendly. The section on nutrition showed the invaluable contributions that nutritionists make to global health in addressing both emergency and long-term needs associated with good nutrition and food security. The gender studies section argued for the need to engage women and gender studies scholars and feminist-informed perspectives in addressing inequality as well as in negotiating the ethics of working in the field of global health. The design and architecture section provided concrete examples for how one's built environment is both critical to one's health and can be crafted to positively impact individual and community health.

Despite this wealth of skills and expertise that each discipline contributes to global health, there is one critical skill that is necessary for all of our work and must be ubiquitous across all disciplines, and that is to listen. It is a skill individuals in all disciplines have, and it is a skill that individuals across all disciplines must continue to hone and use. Before an expert of law decides what policies are most important to develop, or a social scientist focuses on the pressing needs of a given community, or a public health practitioner identifies what interventions are "best" for a clinic, community, or country; first, we must listen. We must listen to those we are working with; we must listen to the subtle and often unspoken cues that are present in any social context or environment; and we must listen to ourselves so that we might increase our chances of engaging in relevant and useful work that develops meaningful collaborations across disciplines and creates beneficial and preventive approaches within global health. It is only through a willingness to critically engage in our work and keep our eyes and ears open that we may hope to truly build the capacity for long-term improvements to the health and well-being of populations worldwide.

CHAPTER 12

Health Economics, Business, and Global Health

Mary MacLennan, MSc, BA&Sc
Health Economist
International Centre for Diarrhoeal Disease Research, Bangladesh

Amy Lockwood, MBA, MS
Deputy Director, Center for Innovation in Global Health
Stanford University

Editor
Paul Drain, MD, MPH
Mass General, Brigham & Women's Hospital
Harvard Medical School

SUPPOSE FOR A MOMENT THAT you are the Minister of Health in your country. How would you allocate your health budget? Would you divide it by region? By health facility? By type of health coverage? Once you realize you can pay for everything, how will you decide which health interventions give the largest benefit for the lowest cost? Can service delivery be made more efficient or more effective? Can some health services include charges to increase revenue, which would enable providing more services, and encourage more prudent use of resources while not discouraging appropriate utilization? These are some of the questions that can be addressed from a variety of perspectives, but health economics can help to inform these decisions.

Economics is a social science that addresses how goods and services are produced, allocated and consumed. Economists analyze the choices of individuals and societies, and when resources are limited, can help prioritize those choices to maximize benefits or outcomes.[1] Health economists apply the concepts of scarcity, choice, and prioritization to the lives of individual patients, health practitioners, and health policy makers. The field of global health economics has been rapidly growing within the last several decades. Because healthcare systems worldwide have been unable to provide adequate health care due to insufficient resources, health economists have increasingly worked in reducing health care disparities. In addition, health economists have illuminated how economic influences such as international trade agreements or market trends have affected the health outcomes of populations.

This section begins with several examples of how the field of health economics can improve health outcomes for people in resource-limited settings. We then provide information about various training opportunities in health economics, and conclude with observations about the likely contributions of health economics to improvement in global health.

Televisions sit idly by, unable to be used due to lack of electricity in this thriving but impoverished global neighborhood
Photographer: *Will Bynum*

The Role of an Economist in Health Services

There are numerous ways in which economic analyses can facilitate decision-making in health services delivery. Four of the more important ways are the following: 1) measuring national health expenditure and health financing; 2) performing economic evaluation; 3) facilitating innovative financing mechanisms; and 4) understanding the two-way relationship between economic growth and health.

1) National health expenditures and health sector financing

National health accounts allow policymakers to categorize the income sources and amounts, as well as the expenditures, for a health sector. The accounts normally cover both the public and private sectors. If prepared using a standardized approach, then cross-national comparisons can be made, which further enhances the value of these accounts. Using national health accounts to improve resource allocation can promote a more efficient and equitable delivery of health care services, particularly as many countries are trying to attain universal coverage for their population.

In 2010, the *World Health Report* highlighted the need to raise global health funds, make better use of financing, reduce reliance on direct payment by patients, and make health service delivery more efficient and equitable.[2] As many countries move closer to providing universal health coverage, many additional questions will arise. Global health economists will continue to play a major role in addressing these questions.

2) Economic evaluation

Economists use economic evaluations to compare the likely benefits and costs that could result from health care policies. These analyses play a fundamental role in decision-making and are especially useful in resource-limited settings. Cost-effectiveness analysis has been used to inform various decisions, such as implementing a new vaccine, diagnostic test or treatment modality. The studies are adjusted to suit different epidemiological and economic situations. For example, recent cost-effectiveness analyses have shown point-of-care tests to be of good value for routine HIV screening[3] and new diagnostic methods for TB diagnosis.[4]

Many developed countries have created health analytical units at national and subnational levels to conduct these types of analyses, which can directly inform policy decisions. While these units may vary in size, scope and authority, the core objectives of a health economist remain the same—to improve the efficiency and effectiveness of the health system, which in turn will improve patients' lives.

3) Innovative financing mechanisms

Recent decades have seen large increases in philanthropic, bilateral and multilateral funding for global health. Though initially focused on stemming the HIV/AIDS epidemic, these funds are now allocated to broadly improve health sector performance and address the needs of vulnerable populations. These developments have led countries and donor organizations to experiment with innovative financing mechanisms that could attract, absorb and effectively utilize these resources.

One example is UNITAID, an international body created in part to lower the costs and increase the availability of diagnostics and treatments for HIV/AIDS, tuberculosis, and malaria. UNITAID has helped shaped the market for pediatric anti-retrovirals by pooling the purchases of multiple countries and programs. By placing much larger purchase orders for fixed-dose drug combinations designed for children, UNITAID has substantially lower costs of care for HIV-infected children in resource-limited settings. UNITAID receives seventy percent of its funding from small add-on taxes on airline tickets for flights leaving from countries (e.g., Brazil, Norway, France) that participate in the UNITAID program.

4) Relationship between economic growth and health.

Economic growth and health are closely related and dependent on each other. In 2001, the WHO released findings from the Commission on Macroeconomics and Health, which addressed the relationship between health status and economic growth.[5] The Report provided robust evidence that the relationship between health and wealth was a clearly two-way process. More wealth clearly contributes to better health but improved health is a powerful promoter to economic development. This report played a pivotal role in shifting attention toward the Millennium Development Goals and increasing funding for health services. More recently, health economists have also been concerned with understanding the degree to which social determinants, such as income, education and social environment, are correlated with health.

Learning Opportunities in Global Health Economics

Training and research related to global health economics was originally offered in relatively few institutions, and primarily those with strong graduate level public health programs concerned with health policy and administration. With the increasing recognition of the centrality of economics to health policies and programs, training opportunities for global health economics have rapidly expanded. In addition, economic programs are devoting more time and teaching to imparting economics skills for relevance to resource-limited settings. Universities that have given particular attention to addressing the needs of people in resource-limited settings include Johns Hopkins University, Harvard University, Duke University, the London School of Hygiene and Tropical Medicine, the Nuffield Centre, the University of Leeds, the University of Sussex, the Karolinska Institute and Queen Margaret College.

Most graduate and postgraduate programs that specialize explicitly in health economics have tended to focus on issues facing high-income countries. However, students increasingly are wanting to address economic and health issues of resource-limited settings. In addition, graduate and postgraduate health economics courses are now being offered in some low- and middle-income countries, such as the University of Cape Town in South Africa and Chulalongkorn University in Thailand. Another opportunity for training in health economics is via distance learning, which is an increasingly popular educational resource.

The Evolution and Future of Global Health Economics

Interest in the economic aspects of health, both nationally and globally, have increased greatly in the past few decades. In rich countries, health services are costly, and cost increases often exceed the rate of inflation. In low-income countries, health resources are often inadequate to meet the needs of the population. Meanwhile, more research is being conducted related to determinants of health in both settings.[6]

A few key developments over the last thirty or so years have helped to greatly increase the interest of economists and the relevance of their expertise in the field of global health. First, the World Bank started to include health, population and nutrition in its portfolio. Spending billions of dollars in these areas required different approaches and metrics to those traditionally used in economic development. Second, economic evaluations were gradually integrated into health planning in many high-income countries and soon demonstrated their utility. This also gave rise to cost-effectiveness analysis. Third, the Global Burden of Disease Project, which uses disability-adjusted life years (DALYs) analysis to quantify and compare health burdens, and *Investing in Health*[6] from World Bank Report of 1993, highlighted the usefulness of economic evaluation in the decision-making. Fourth, with the large increments in funding available for global health activities over the past 10 years has promoted studies on the flow of funds and the impact of aid. The Institute for Health Metrics and Evaluation at the University of Washington has developed a great deal of expertise in this area, and makes its information freely accessible to policy makers. Finally, there has been a marked improvement in the economic data generated by low- and middle-income countries, which greatly facilitates economic analysis.

With all these developments and more, the need for global health economists is not only important today, but will be greatly needed in the future. Global health economists will play a vital role in the further improvements of both global health and economic development.

Resources for further information:

» Drummond M, Sculpher MJ, Torrance GW, O'Brien BJ, and Stoddart GL. *Methods for economic evaluation of health care programmes.* New York: Oxford University Press, 2005.
» Folland S, Goodman A and Stano M. *The Economics of Health and Healthcare.* 6th Ed. Upper Saddle River: Prentice Hall, 2004.
» Gunnarsson A, Smith CS, and Zollner H. *Health Economics as a Tool for Leaders.* World Health Organization, 2003.

Business and Global Health

If the goal of global health is *achieving equity in health for all people worldwide,*[8] then a variety of stakeholders from diverse disciplines must be involved. Medical professionals are often the first discipline to be considered due to the primacy of their relationship with patients and the healthcare system. However, achieving and maintaining good health also requires sound policies, products, infrastructure, data, and technology. Business professionals apply systems and methods to allow health programs to run more efficiently, so medical professionals can focus on their patients. Thus, implementing sound business practices are central to improving global health.

The traditional definition of business has been an enterprise with a driving motivation to make a financial profit for its owners. Recently, however, a broader definition has taken root. From this new perspective, business includes a variety of enterprises, including non-profit organizations, that add social goals to achieving financial gain. All organizations, regardless of their goals, deal with resource limitations. Health care systems around the world use business practices when building a new hospital, ordering drugs and other supplies, hiring doctors and nurses, collecting payments for patients, as well as myriad other elements that contribute to health care.

How Can Business Principles be Applied to Global Health?

When business principles are applied to global health, care must be taken so that the tools and principles traditionally used to increase profits are applied in a context in which profit is not the goal. They are instead used only to reach the desired goal for global health: achieving equity in access and delivery of quality healthcare. If the underlying philosophy—managing resources to achieve goals in the most efficient and effective manner—is maintained, the outcome may be programs that address global health issues successfully and sustainably. Some of the specific ways to do this are presented below in Table 1.

Table 1. Applying business principles in global health programs.

Strategy	Analyzing the environment in which the organization does or will work; developing tactics, products and services that will be delivered to achieve these; and measuring progress in the form of key performance indicators.
Finance	Analyzing operations to understand the financial investment required and interfacing with donors in order to raise funds.
Accounting	Monitoring financial obligations and activities in order to collect and make payments.
Product Development	Researching the knowledge, awareness, and practices of current and potential beneficiaries and designing products or services to address these.
Marketing	Creating communication materials to be used with beneficiaries, donors, and governments to generate demand for needed products/materials/projects and advocate for the organization's mission.
Sales	Identifying organizations and individuals for partnership or channels to deliver the tactics, products, and services.
Administration	Defining and managing the infrastructure, supply chain, Information Technology (IT), and human resources of the organization in order to create, deliver, and monitor the products and services of the organization.
Legal	Ensuring the organization adheres to local and international laws, regulatory requirements, and accepted professional protocols.

Market Analysis and Customer Research

An increased emphasis on understanding both the needs of beneficiaries and the contexts in which global health programs are delivered reflect several business principles. In the business context, these activities are traditionally known as market analysis and customer research. When applied to global health they can be used to understand the needs of patients or health care providers to inform the design of medical devices, services, or technologies.

In global health, multiple parties are involved in the selection, implementation, and use of health care products and services. For example, the World Health Organization (WHO) may suggest treatment guidelines and approve suppliers for drugs, and a national Ministry of Health may use this input to develop local treatment protocols. Meanwhile, donor agencies may provide or fund products *they* prefer, which may be different from the government's formulary. Local health care providers treat patients with the products available to them, and patients will ultimately decide whether to use these products. By using research techniques including qualitative and quantitative methods to understand the needs of each party involved, the relationships between them, and their sociopolitical context, more successful and sustainable solutions may be developed.

Monitoring and Evaluation

Collecting data and performing analysis of project implementation progress and outcomes provides evidence of whether or not an intervention is achieving its goals. A performance management system, which presents data on both what has been done and what impact it has had, is a valuable management tool to understand if a program has achieved its goals. In addition, management tools can proactively inform decisions that may improve results. For example, a global health program designed to reduce malaria deaths by distributing insecticide treated bednets through community health centers could measure process related the following performance indicators:

1. The number of health centers enrolled in the program;
2. The number the number of nets procured and delivered to health centers;
3. The number of nets distributed to families by the health centers;
4. The percentage of distributed nets properly in use in the community.

They may measure the following outcome-related performance indicators:

1. The number of cases of malaria reported;
2. The number of cases of malaria treated;
3. The number of deaths attributed to malaria.

Developing such a system requires defining key performance indicators, determining methods to collect data, and creating processes for interpreting results. A key feature of the most successful performance management systems is the ability to rapidly understand if programs are achieving desired outcomes. This can lead to implementing changes quickly, which will conserve resources and optimize impact.

Case Study: Reducing Costs to Increase Access to HIV Treatment

The Clinton Foundation is known for bringing a business approach to some of the biggest challenges in global health. One of the best examples of this is the Clinton Health Access Initiative (CHAI) program, which focuses on increasing access to essential medicines and diagnostics. In 2002, CHAI began its drug access program with the goal of increasing the number of people receiving life-saving treatment for HIV/AIDS. There were several factors that contributed to the gap between the number of people infected with HIV and those on treatment, including lack of awareness, limited access to healthcare centers, insufficient number of trained healthcare providers, socioeconomic barriers, and stigma. Since the expense of the antiretroviral (ARV) drugs—which was over $10,000 per patient per year—was clearly a major obstacle, the CHAI program focused on reducing the cost of ARVs. They started by understanding the challenges on both the supply and demand side of the issue.

While it was clear that there was a big need for ARVs, it had not been translated into demand because people were not able to purchase the drugs. Initially, it was unclear how many people needed ARVs, which specific ARVs were needed, and how those numbers changed over time. Purchases were made in small batches because governments and organizations had limited funding. In addition, health systems often lacked the infrastructure to diagnose, treat, and provide reliable information. The resulting small and inconsistent orders forced the suppliers to charge higher prices and require longer delivery times because they were making smaller batches and were unable to maintain a regular manufacturing schedule.

This low-volume and high-cost model persisted until CHAI began working with manufacturers and governments to better understand demand, aggregate it across multiple countries, and place large orders—secured by guarantees of payment—with manufacturers. Over time, the market transitioned to a high-volume, low-cost model. Due largely to addressing the cost of ARVs through a business model, the annual cost of ARVs is now between $100 and $200 per patient in many countries.

Models of Scale and Sustainability

Global health programs need to demonstrate an ability to operate across multiple markets and without reliance on philanthropic funding. While all programs strive to operate efficiently, philanthropic funding is generally available only in situations when markets fail and often for a limited amount of time, due to the restricted nature of these resources, it is critical that their impact be optimized. Many programs seek to solve global problems that require large-scale implementations. Taking a program from the initial stages to full-scale operation in multiple geographies often requires reassessing the market environment, drivers of demand, and financial and operational requirements.

As a program scales-up, so too does its costs. Initial funding sources may not be able to cover larger expenses, and funding for global health programs are often time-limited. Often times, it is critical for programs to investigate multiple sources of funding, including revenue generation. Generating revenue does not imply that a program will become motivated entirely by profits, but it does require a keen understanding of market dynamics and operations so that the program is able to use the revenue to achieve its stated goals and improve health outcomes.

What training opportunities exist in Business for Global Health?

Business school curricula have focused on teaching the functions of business (e.g. strategy, finance, economics, marketing, operations, organizational behavior, sales and distribution), in addition to offering classes on particular industries. Traditionally, global health has not been included as an industry. However, several programs now offer relevant courses in health care industry, social enterprises, and public management. Many students also choose to pursue dual degree programs, combining business with public health, public policy, or international relations. There are also programs that offer degrees in health administration and management, which although often domestically focused may include courses on international settings and global health issues.

While it is impossible to fully prepare for the multitude of global health challenges, business training can equip students with the analytic and management tools to improve global health. Additional resources, including some of the organizations that have applied business principles to global health, are listed below.

Organizations

» The Acumen Fund—http://www.acumenfund.org
» The Clinton Health Access Initiative—http://www.clintonhealthaccess.org
» PATH—http://www.path.org
» The Global Fund—http://www.theglobalfund.org/en/
» The Gates Foundation—http://www.gatesfoundation.org
» The Global Business Coalition—http://www.gbchealth.org
» McKinsey& Company—http://www.mckinsey.com/client_service/social_sector
» FSG—http://www.fsg.org
» BCG—http://www.bcg.com/about_bcg/social_impact/global_health/default.aspx

Resources

» The Global Health Innovation Project by the Program in Healthcare Innovation at Stanford University—http://www.gsb.stanford.edu/phi/research/project-healthinnovation.html
» International Partnership for Innovative Healthcare Delivery—http://www.seaatduke.org/

» The Global Health Delivery Project at Harvard University—http://globalhealthdelivery.org/
» Global Health at MIT—http://globalhealth.mit.edu/mini-studies-business-models4gh/
» McKinsey on Society—http://mckinseyonsociety.com/topics/global-public-health/

Acknowledgements

We would like to thank Dr. Lorna Guinness at the London School of Hygiene and Tropical Medicine for her valuable assistance with the Health Economics section.

References

1. Haycox, A. "What is Health Economics?", 2009. Found on January 16, 2013 at http://www.whatisseries.co.uk/whatis/
2. Walensky R.P., Wood R., Fofana M.O., et al. The clinical impact and cost-effectiveness of routine, voluntary HIV screening in South Africa. *Journal of Acquired Immune Deficiency Syndromes* 56 (2010): 26-35.
3. World Health Organization. *Health Systems Financing: the path to universal coverage*, Geneva: WHO Press, 2011.
4. Dowdy D.W., O'Brien M.A., Bishai D. Cost-effectiveness of novel diagnostic tools for the diagnosis of tuberculosis. *International Journal of Tuberculosis and Lung Disease* 12 (2008): 1021-29.
5. World Health Organization. *Macroeconomics and Health: Investing in Health for Economic Development*. Geneva: WHO Press 2001.
6. Wagstaff A., and Culyer A.J. "Four Decades of health economics through a bibliometric lens" *Journal of Health Economics* 31.2 (2011): 406-439.
7. World Bank. *World Development Report.1993 Investing in Health*. New York: Oxford University Press, 1993.
8. http://www.kaiseredu.org/Issue-Modules/Global-Health/Background-Brief.aspx, accessed December 2012.

CHAPTER 13

Global Health Education: Bibliography and other Resources

Alfonso J. Rodriguez-Morales (Universidad Tecnológica de Pereira, Pereira, Colombia)

Daniel Tobón-García (Universidad Tecnológica de Pereira, Pereira, Colombia)

Editor

Thomas Hall (UCSF)

THIS CHAPTER IS INTENDED TO be a reasonably comprehensive list of resources broadly relevant to Global Health education. Though by no means exhaustive, the list demonstrates the breadth of global health and can help individuals become familiar with the topics, research, programs and organizations—present and future—of global health. To help readers sort among the more than 300 resources listed we have grouped them under five broad, somewhat overlapping categories:

» GLOBAL HEALTH BOOKS AND REPORTS
» GLOBAL HEALTH SKILLS, NEEDS, PRIORITIES
» GLOBAL HEALTH COURSES, CURRICULA AND COMPETENCIES
» GLOBAL HEALTH FIELD TRAINING AND PARTNERSHIPS
» GLOBAL HEALTH RESOURCES ON THE INTERNET

A young boy listens as government leaders discuss health and sanitation issues with the local community
Photographer: *Will Bynum*

Global Health Books And Reports

Birn A-E, Pillay Y, Holtz TH (2009), 3rd edition. Textbook of International Health. 806 pp. New York, Oxford Univ. Press.

Brauman, R. (2005) "Controversies within Health and Human Rights." Carnegie Council on Ethics and International Affairs. January 2005.

Drain, P., Huffman, S., Pirtle, S., and Chan, K. (2008). Caring for the World: A Guidebook to Global Health Opportunities. Univ. of Toronto Press.

Gofin, J., and Gofin, R. (2011). Essentials of Global Community Health. 269 pp., Jones and Bartlett publishers.

Gwatkin, D. R. (2000). "Health inequalities and the health of the poor: what do we know? What can we do?" Bulletin of the World Health Organization. 78(1): 3-18.

Holtz, C. (2008). Global Health Care: Issues and Policies. Jones and Barlett Publishers.

Institute of Medicine (1997). Summary. America's Vital Interest in Global Health. Institute of Medicine. Washington, DC, National Academy Press.

Jacobsen KH, Sudbury (2008) Introduction to global health. 366 pp., Jones and Bartlett Publishers.

Johnson, J., and Stoskopf, C. (2009). Comparative Health Systems: Global Perspectives. 451 pp., Jones and Bartlett publishers.

Lindstrand A, Bergstrom S, Rosling H, et al. (2006), Global health, an introductory textbook. Denmark, Studentlitteratur, 2006, 310 pp.

Markle W.H., Fisher M. Smego R. (2007) Understanding global health. Columbus, McGraw Hill, 2007, 361 pp.

Merson, MH, RE Black and AJ Mills (2012). Global Health, 3rd edition, 936 pp. Sudbury, MA, Jones and Bartlett, Publishers.

Millennium Development Goals. www.develomentgoals.org

Murray, CJ, Lopez AD et al. (1996). Summary: The Global Burden of Disease. Cambridge, MA, published by Harvard School of Public Health on behalf of the WHO and World Bank. Additional and more recent publications will also be found under the Global Burden of Disease title.

O'Neil, Jr., E. (2006). A Practical Guide to Global Health Service. American Medical Association.

Ogunseitan O (General Editor). (2011). Green Health—An A-to-Z Guide [Encyclopedia]. Robbins P (Series Editor). The SAGE Reference Series on Green Society Toward a Sustainable Future. SAGE Publications, California, USA.

Osborn, G. and P. Ohmans. (2005) Finding Work in Global Health. Saint Paul, Minnesota, Health Advocates Press.

Seear M. (2007). An introduction to international health. Toronto, Canadian Scholars

Seltzer, J. R. (2002). The Origins and Evolution of Family Planning Programs in Developing Countries. J. R. Seltzer, Rand Corporation. Population Matters (Project). Santa Monica, CA, Rand.

Sen, G., A. George, and P. Ostlin (2002). Engendering International Health: The Challenge of Equity. Cambridge, Mass., MIT Press.

Skolnik R. (2012) Global Health 101, 2nd edition. 434 pp., Jones and Bartlett Learning, publishers.

Skolnik, R. (2008). Essentials of Global Health. 322 pp., Jones and Bartlett publishers.

Wikler, D. and R. Cash (2003). Global Public Health: A New Era. R. Beaglehole. Oxford, New York, Oxford Univ. Press.

World Health Organization (WHO) (2003). International Conference on Primary Health Care, Alma-Ata: twenty-fifth anniversary report by the Secretariat.

World Health Organization and UNICEF (1978). Primary Health Care: Report of the International Conference on Primary Care, Alma-Ata, USSR, 6-12 September, 1978. Geneva, Switzerland.

Zhang Y (Editor). (2008) Encyclopedia of Global Health. SAGE Publications, California, USA.

Global Health Skills, Needs, Priorities

Battat R, Seidman G, Chadi N et al. Global health competencies and approaches in medical education: a literature review. BMC Med Educ 2010;10:94.

Beaglehole R, Bonita R. Global public health: a scorecard. Lancet 2008;372(9654):1988-1996.

Blakely T, Hales S, Kieft C, Wilson N, Woodward A. The global distribution of risk factors by poverty level. Bull World Health Organ 2005;83(2):118-126.

Bloland P, Simone P, Burkholder B, Slutsker L, De Cock KM. The role of public health institutions in global health system strengthening efforts: the US CDC's perspective. PLoS Med 2012;9(4):e1001199.

Brown TM, Cueto M, Fee E. The World Health Organization and the transition from "international" to "global" public health. Am J Public Health 2006;96(1):62-72.

Bunyavanich S, Walkup RB. US public health leaders shift toward a new paradigm of global health. Am J Public Health 2001;91(10):1556-1558.

Caceres CF, Mendoza W. Changing care and prevention needs for global public health: In pursuit of a comprehensive perspective. Glob Public Health 2012.

Cavalli A, Bamba SI, Traore MN et al. Interactions between Global Health Initiatives and country health systems: the case of a neglected tropical diseases control program in Mali. PLoS Negl Trop Dis 2010;4(8):e798.

Cohn J, Russell A, Baker B, Kayongo A, Wanjiku E, Davis P. Using global health initiatives to strengthen health systems: a civil society perspective. Glob Public Health 2011;6(7):687-702.

Daulaire N. Beyond trade: taking globalization to the health sector. New Solut 2003;13(1):67-71.

Davies SE. What contribution can international relations make to the evolving global health agenda? Int Aff 2010;86(5):1167-1190.

Di RE, Zarowsky C, Frank J et al. Coordinating Canada's research response to global health challenges: the Global Health Research Initiative. Can J Public Health 2006;97(1):29-31.

Doyle C, Patel P. Civil society organisations and global health initiatives: problems of legitimacy. Soc Sci Med 2008;66(9):1928-1938.

Doyle J, Waters E, Yach D et al. Global priority setting for Cochrane systematic reviews of health promotion and public health research. J Epidemiol Community Health 2005;59(3):193-197.

Drain PK, Primack A, Hunt DD, Fawzi WW, Holmes KK, Gardner P. Global health in medical education: a call for more training and opportunities. Acad Med 2007;82(3):226-230.

Eckhert NL. The global pipeline: too narrow, too wide or just right? Med Educ 2002;36(7):606-613.

Eichler M, Burke MA. The BIAS FREE Framework: a new analytical tool for global health research. Can J Public Health 2006;97(1):63-68.

Eng TR. Population health technologies: emerging innovations for the health of the public. Am J Prev Med 2004;26(3):237-242.

Free C, Phillips G, Felix L, Galli L, Patel V, Edwards P. The effectiveness of M-health technologies for improving health and health services: a systematic review protocol. BMC Res Notes 2010;3:250.

Friedman EA, Gostin LO. Pillars for progress on the right to health: Harnessing the potential of human rights through a Framework Convention on Global Health. Health Hum Rights 2012;14(1):E4-E19.

Gellert GA. Global health interdependence and the international physicians' movement. JAMA 1990;264(5):610-613.

Guzman P, Schecter WP. Global health opportunities in surgery: a guide for medical students and faculty. J Surg Educ 2008;65(5):384-387.

Haq C, Rothenberg D, Gjerde C et al. New world views: preparing physicians in training for global health work. Fam Med 2000;32(8):566-572.

Hilson M. Advocacy for a new global health development paradigm: building alliances for global public health. Promot Educ 2005;Suppl 3:65-67.

Hogan H, Haines A. Global health: a positive addition to public health training? J Public Health (Oxf) 2011;33(2):317-318.

Hotez PJ. Should we establish a North American school of global health sciences? Am J Med Sci 2004;328(2):71-77.

Inhorn MC, Janes CR. The behavioural research agenda in global health: an advocate's legacy. Glob Public Health 2007;2(3):294-312.

Katz A. The Sachs report: investing in health for economic development--or increasing the size of the crumbs from the rich man's table? Part II. Int J Health Serv 2005;35(1):171-188.

Kerry VB, Ndung'u T, Walensky RP, Lee PT, Kayanja VF, Bangsberg DR. Managing the demand for global health education. PLoS Med 2011;8(11):e1001118.

Kickbusch I. Mapping the future of public health: action on global health. Can J Public Health 2006;97(1):6-8.

Kim JY, Rhatigan J, Jain SH, Weintraub R, Porter ME. From a declaration of values to the creation of value in global health: a report from Harvard Univ.'s Global Health Delivery Project. Glob Public Health 2010;5(2):181-188.

Kruk ME. Globalisation and global health governance: Implications for public health. Glob Public Health 2012.

Kun LG. Telehealth and the global health network in the 21st century. From homecare to public health informatics. Comput Methods Programs Biomed 2001;64(3):155-167.

Labonte R, Mohindra K, Schrecker T. The growing impact of globalization for health and public health practice. Annu Rev Public Health 2011;32:263-283.

Lairumbi GM, Parker M, Fitzpatrick R, English MC. Forms of benefit sharing in global health research undertaken in resource poor settings: a qualitative study of stakeholders' views in Kenya. Philos Ethics Humanit Med 2012;7:7.

Leeder SR, Raymond SU, Greenberg HM. The need for leadership in global health. Med J Aust 2007;187(9):532-535.

L'hirondel A, Yach D. Develop and strengthen public health law. World Health Stat Q 1998;51(1):79-87.

Manabe YC, Jacob ST, Thomas D et al. Resurrecting the triple threat: academic social responsibility in the context of global health research. Clin Infect Dis 2009;48(10):1420-1422.

McCarthy M. European health research and globalisation: is the public-private balance right? Global Health 2011;7:5.

McCoy D, Kembhavi G, Patel J, Luintel A. The Bill & Melinda Gates Foundation's grant-making programme for global health. Lancet 2009;373(9675):1645-1653.

McCoy D, Labonte R, Orbinski J. Global Health Watch Canada? Mobilizing the Canadian public health community around a global health advocacy agenda. Can J Public Health 2006;97(2):142-144.

McKimm J, McLean M. Developing a global health practitioner: time to act? Med Teach 2011;33(8):626-631.

Meier BM, Cabrera OA, Ayala A, Gostin LO. Bridging international law and rights-based litigation: Mapping health-related rights through the development of the Global Health and Human Rights Database. Health Hum Rights 2012;14(1):E20-E35.

Muchukuri E, Grenier FR. Social determinants of health and health inequities in Nakuru (Kenya). Int J Equity Health 2009;8:16.

Mykhalovskiy E, Weir L. The Global Public Health Intelligence Network and early warning outbreak detection: a Canadian contribution to global public health. Can J Public Health 2006;97(1):42-44.

Neusy AJ, Palsdottir B. A roundtable of innovative leaders in medical education. MEDICC Rev 2008;10(4):20-24.

Orman L. Making the case for human rights in global health education, research and policy. Can J Public Health 2011;102(3):207-209.

Palamountain KM, Stewart KA, Krauss A, Kelso D, Diermeier D. Univ. leadership for innovation in global health and HIV/AIDS diagnostics. Glob Public Health 2010;5(2):189-196.

Patel V. Mental health in low- and middle-income countries. Br Med Bull 2007;81-82:81-96.

Ravishankar N, Gubbins P, Cooley RJ et al. Financing of global health: tracking development assistance for health from 1990 to 2007. Lancet 2009;373(9681):2113-2124.

Reardon S. Public health. Experts debate polypill: a single pill for global health. Science 2011;333(6051):1813.

Ridde V, Mohindra KS, LaBossiere F. Driving the global public health research agenda forward by promoting the participation of students and new researchers: perspectives from Quebec. Can J Public Health 2008;99(6):460-465.

Risquez A, Echezuria L, Rodriguez-Morales AJ. Epidemiological transition in Venezuela: Relationships between infectious diarrheas, ischemic heart diseases and transportation accidents mortalities and the human development index (HDI) in Venezuela, 2005-2007. J Infect Public Health 2010; 3(3):95-97.

Rodríguez-Morales AJ, Castañeda-Hernández DM. Relationships Between Morbidity and Mortality from Tuberculosis and the Human Development Index (HDI) in Venezuela, 1998-2008. Int J Infect Dis 2012; 16(9): e704-e705.

Rodríguez-Morales AJ, Von A, Franco-Paredes C. Achievements and challenges in controlling Chagas disease. Bol Med Hosp Infant Mex 2011; 68(2):101-109.

Sadana R, Chowdhury AM, Chowdhury R, Petrakova A. Strengthening public health education and training to improve global health. Bull World Health Organ 2007;85(3):163.

Schrecker T. Multiple crises and global health: new and necessary frontiers of health politics. Glob Public Health 2012;7(6):557-573.

Seror AC. A case analysis of INFOMED: the Cuban national health care telecommunications network and portal. J Med Internet Res 2006;8(1):e1.

Sridhar D, Batniji R. Misfinancing global health: a case for transparency in disbursements and decision making. Lancet 2008;372(9644):1185-1191.

Tindana PO, Singh JA, Tracy CS et al. Grand challenges in global health: community engagement in research in developing countries. PLoS Med 2007;4(9):e273.

Varmus H, Klausner R, Zerhouni E, Acharya T, Daar AS, Singer PA. Public health. Grand Challenges in Global Health. Science 2003;302(5644):398-399.

Velji A. Editorial: Transforming global health, global health education, infectious disease, and chronic conditions in the 21st century. Infect Dis Clin North Am 2011;25(3):485-98, vii.

Velji A. Global Health Education Consortium: 20 years of leadership in global health and global health education. Infect Dis Clin North Am 2011;25(2):323-335.

Velji A. Global health, global health education, and infectious disease: the new millennium, Part II. Infect Dis Clin North Am 2011;25(3):xiii-xxii.

Velji A. Global health, global health education, and infectious disease: the new millennium, part I. Infect Dis Clin North Am 2011;25(2):xiii-xxxi.

Waitzkin H, Jasso-Aguilar R, Landwehr A, Mountain C. Global trade, public health, and health services: stakeholders' constructions of the key issues. Soc Sci Med 2005;61(5):893-906.

West GR, Clapp SP, Averill EM, Cates W, Jr. Defining and assessing evidence for the effectiveness of technical assistance in furthering global health. Glob Public Health 2012.

Willis BM, Levy BS. Child prostitution: global health burden, research needs, and interventions. Lancet 2002;359(9315):1417-1422.

Zinsstag J, Schelling E, Waltner-Toews D, Tanner M. From "one medicine" to "one health" and systemic approaches to health and well-being. Prev Vet Med 2011;101(3-4):148-156.

Global Health Courses, Curricula And Competencies

Anspacher M, Frintner MP, Denno D et al. Global health education for pediatric residents: a national survey. Pediatrics 2011;128(4):e959-e965.

Arthur MA, Battat R, Brewer TF. Teaching the basics: core competencies in global health. Infect Dis Clin North Am 2011;25(2):347-358.

Asgary R, Price J, Ripp J. Global health training starts at home: a unique US-based global health clinical elective for residents. Med Teach 2012;34(6):e445-e451.

Barbiero VK. Global health for undergraduates: "we are not alone". Am J Prev Med 2008;35(3):269-272.

Battat R, Seidman G, Chadi N et al. Global health competencies and approaches in medical education: a literature review. BMC Med Educ 2010;10:94.

Bjorklund AB, Cook BA, Hendel-Paterson BR, Walker PF, Stauffer WM, Boulware DR. Impact of global health residency training on medical knowledge of immigrant health. Am J Trop Med Hyg 2011;85(3):405-408.

Bollinger RC, McKenzie-White J, Gupta A. Building a global health education network for clinical care and research. The benefits and challenges of distance learning tools. Lessons learned from the Hopkins Center for Clinical Global Health Education. Infect Dis Clin North Am 2011;25(2):385-398.

Bozorgmehr K, Schubert K, Menzel-Severing J, Tinnemann P. Global Health Education: a cross-sectional study among German medical students to identify needs, deficits and potential benefits (Part 1 of 2: Mobility patterns & educational needs and demands). BMC Med Educ 2010;10:66.

Bozorgmehr K, Menzel-Severing J, Schubert K, Tinnemann P. Global Health Education: a cross-sectional study among German medical students to identify needs, deficits and potential benefits (Part 2 of 2: Knowledge gaps and potential benefits). BMC Med Educ 2010;10:67.

Bruno S, Silvestrini G, Carovillano S et al. [Global health education in Italian medical schools: survey from 2007 to 2010]. Ann Ig 2011;23(5):357-365.

Calhoun JG, Spencer HC, Buekens P. Competencies for global heath graduate education. Infect Dis Clin North Am 2011;25(3):575-92, viii.

Castillo J, Castillo H, Ayoub-Rodriguez L et al. The resident decision-making process in global health education: appraising factors influencing participation. Clin Pediatr (Phila) 2012;51(5):462-467.

Castillo J, Goldenhar LM, Baker RC, Kahn RS, Dewitt TG. Reflective practice and competencies in global health training: lesson for serving diverse patient populations. J Grad Med Educ 2010;2(3):449-455.

Cole DC, Davison C, Hanson L et al. Being global in public health practice and research: complementary competencies are needed. Can J Public Health 2011;102(5):394-397.

Conrad PA, Mazet JA, Clifford D, Scott C, Wilkes M. Evolution of a transdisciplinary "One Medicine-One Health" approach to global health education at the Univ. of California, Davis. Prev Vet Med 2009;92(4):268-274.

Crandall ML. Integrating population health into a general surgical residency curriculum. Am J Prev Med 2011;41(4 Suppl 3):S276-S282.

Di SA. World optometry: the challenges of leadership for the new millennium. Optometry 2002;73(6):339-350.

Dotchin C, van den Ende C, Walker R. Delivering global health teaching: the development of a global health option. Clin Teach 2010;7(4):271-275.

Doyle J, Waters E, Yach D et al. Global priority setting for Cochrane systematic reviews of health promotion and public health research. J Epidemiol Community Health 2005;59(3):193-197.

Drain PK, Holmes KK, Skeff KM, Hall TL, Gardner P. Global health training and international clinical rotations during residency: current status, needs, and opportunities. Acad Med 2009;84(3):320-325.

Eaton DM, Redmond A, Bax N. Training healthcare professionals for the future: internationalism and effective inclusion of global health training. Med Teach 2011;33(7):562-569.

Evert J, Bazemore A, Hixon A, Withy K. Going global: considerations for introducing global health into family medicine training programs. Fam Med 2007;39(9):659-665.

Finch TH, Chae SR, Shafaee MN et al. Role of students in global health delivery. Mt Sinai J Med 2011;78(3):373-381.

Gillam S, Maudsley G. Public health education for medical students: rising to the professional challenge. J Public Health (Oxf) 2010;32(1):125-131.

Gladding S, Zink T, Howard C, Campagna A, Slusher T, John C. International electives at the Univ. of Minnesota global pediatric residency program: opportunities for education in all accreditation council for graduate medical education competencies. Acad Pediatr 2012;12(3):245-250.

Goldner BW, Bollinger RC. Global health education for medical students: New learning opportunities and strategies. Med Teach 2012;34(1):e58-e63.

Gupta A, Talavlikar R, Ng V et al. Global health curriculum in family medicine: resident perspective. Can Fam Physician 2012;58(2):143-146.

Hill DR, Ainsworth RM, Partap U. Teaching global public health in the undergraduate liberal arts: a survey of 50 colleges. Am J Trop Med Hyg 2012;87(1):11-15.

Holmes D, Zayas LE, Koyfman A. Student Objectives and Learning Experiences in a Global Health Elective. J Community Health 2012.

Houpt ER, Pearson RD, Hall TL. Three domains of competency in global health education: recommendations for all medical students. Acad Med 2007;82(3):222-225.

Howard CR, Gladding SP, Kiguli S, Andrews JS, John CC. Development of a competency-based curriculum in global child health. Acad Med 2011;86(4):521-528.

Izadnegahdar R, Correia S, Ohata B et al. Global health in Canadian medical education: current practices and opportunities. Acad Med 2008;83(2):192-198.

Jayaraman SP, Ayzengart AL, Goetz LH, Ozgediz D, Farmer DL. Global health in general surgery residency: a national survey. J Am Coll Surg 2009;208(3):426-433.

Johnson O, Bailey SL, Willott C et al. Global health learning outcomes for medical students in the UK. Lancet 2012;379(9831):2033-2035.

Lahey T. Perspective: a proposed medical school curriculum to help students recognize and resolve ethical issues of global health outreach work. Acad Med 2012;87(2):210-215.

Laven G, Newbury JW. Global health education for medical undergraduates. Rural Remote Health 2011;11(2):1705.

Leggat SG, Tse N. The role of teaching and research hospitals in improving global health (in a globalized world). Health Pap 2003;4(2):34-38.

Leow JJ, Cheng DR, Burkle FM, Jr. Doctors and global health: tips for medical students and junior doctors. Med J Aust 2011;195(11-12):657-659.

Leow JJ, Groen RS, Kingham TP, Casey KM, Hardy MA, Kushner AL. A preparation guide for surgical resident and student rotations to underserved regions. Surgery 2012;151(6):770-778.

Leow JJ, Kingham TP, Casey KM, Kushner AL. Global surgery: thoughts on an emerging surgical subspecialty for students and residents. J Surg Educ 2010;67(3):143-148.

Magarik J, Kavolus J, Louis R. An American medical student's experience in global neurosurgery: both in their infancy. World Neurosurg 2012;77(1):28-31.

Merridew N, Wilkinson D. Expanded partnerships between medical faculty and medical students: Developing a Global Health curriculum as an example of 'student-led learning' at the Univ. of Queensland, Australia. Med Teach 2010;32(11):919-925.

Murdoch-Eaton D, Green A. The contribution and challenges of electives in the development of social accountability in medical students. Med Teach 2011;33(8):643-648.

Nelson BD, Saltzman A, Lee PT. Bridging the global health training gap: Design and evaluation of a new clinical global health course at Harvard Medical School. Med Teach 2012;34(1):45-51.

Ozgediz D, Chu K, Ford N et al. Surgery in global health delivery. Mt Sinai J Med 2011;78(3):327-341.

Palsdottir B, Neusy AJ, Reed G. Building the evidence base: networking innovative socially accountable medical education programs. Educ Health (Abingdon) 2008;21(2):177.

Parsi K, List J. Preparing medical students for the world: service learning and global health justice. Medscape J Med 2008;10(11):268.

Peel M, Berlin A, Piachaud J, James E. Contemplating a one child world. Medical students should be taught to appraise evidence on global health issues. BMJ 1996;312(7035):907-908.

Pinto AD, Upshur RE. Global health ethics for students. Dev World Bioeth 2009;9(1):1-10.

Pottie K, Hostland S. Health advocacy for refugees: Medical student primer for competence in cultural matters and global health. Can Fam Physician 2007;53(11):1923-1926.

Provenzano AM, Graber LK, Elansary M, Khoshnood K, Rastegar A, Barry M. Short-term global health research projects by US medical students: ethical challenges for partnerships. Am J Trop Med Hyg 2010;83(2):211-214.

Redwood-Campbell L, Pakes B, Rouleau K et al. Developing a curriculum framework for global health in family medicine: emerging principles, competencies, and educational approaches. BMC Med Educ 2011;11:46.

Reza NG. A model for offering an International Medicine Seminar Course for US medical students: the 13-year experience of the New Jersey Medical School. J Natl Med Assoc 1999;91(10):573-577.

Riviello R, Ozgediz D, Hsia RY, Azzie G, Newton M, Tarpley J. Role of collaborative academic partnerships in surgical training, education, and provision. World J Surg 2010;34(3):459-465.

Shah S, Wu T. The medical student global health experience: professionalism and ethical implications. J Med Ethics 2008;34(5):375-378.

Shishani K, Allen C, Shubnikov E, Salman K, Laporte RE, Linkov F. Nurse educators establishing new venues in global nursing education. J Prof Nurs 2012;28(2):132-134.

Simpson WM, Shepard BM, Rushing JW, Schuman SH. An agromedicine initiative for first-year medical students, 1998-2004: biochemistry seminar proves feasible. J Agromedicine 2006;11(1):69-74.

Stanton B, Huang CC, Armstrong RW et al. Global health training for pediatric residents. Pediatr Ann 2008;37(12):786.

Stapleton FB, Wahl PW, Norris TE, Ramsey PG. Addressing global health through the marriage of public health and medicine: developing the Univ. of Washington department of global health. Acad Med 2006;81(10):897-901.

Tamashiro H, Oshima T, Takahashi S, Laporte RE, Sekikawa A, Satoh T. [An Internet-based "distance" learning for health, environment and sustainable development "distance learning without a frontier"]. Nihon Koshu Eisei Zasshi 1999;46(2):130-133.

Urkin J, Morad M, Merrick J, Henkin Y. Cross-cultural medicine in the Middle East at the start of the 21st century: where East and West meet. Scientific World Journal 2006;6:2170-2176.

Valani R, Sriharan A, Scolnik D. Integrating CanMEDS competencies into global health electives: an innovative elective program. CJEM 2011;13(1):34-39.

VanRooyen MJ, Townes DA, Hart RG, Willoughby P. International Health Fellowship: a proposed curriculum for emergency physicians. J Emerg Med 1997;15(2):249-252.

Vora N, Chang M, Pandya H, Hasham A, Lazarus C. A student-initiated and student-facilitated international health elective for preclinical medical students. Med Educ Online 2010;15.

Wendland CL. Moral maps and medical imaginaries: clinical tourism at Malawi's College of Medicine. Am Anthropol 2012;114(1):108-122.

Yudkin JS, Bayley O, Elnour S, Willott C, Miranda JJ. Introducing medical students to global health issues: a Bachelor of Science degree in international health. Lancet 2003;362(9386):822-824.

Global Health Field Training And Partnerships

Abedini NC, Gruppen LD, Kolars JC, Kumagai AK. Understanding the Effects of Short-Term International Service-Learning Trips on Medical Students. Acad Med 2012;87(6):820-828.

Anderson KC, Slatnik MA, Pereira I, Cheung E, Xu K, Brewer TF. Are we there yet? Preparing Canadian medical students for global health electives. Acad Med 2012;87(2):206-209.

Angelini P, Arora B, Kurkure P, Bouffet E, Punnett A. Commentary: critical reflections on subspecialty fellowships in low-income countries. Acad Med 2012;87(2):139-141.

Bosworth TL, Haloburdo EP, Hetrick C, Patchett K, Thompson MA, Welch M. International partnerships to promote quality care: faculty groundwork, student projects, and outcomes. J Contin Educ Nurs 2006;37(1):32-38.

Chin-Quee A, White L, Leeds I, MacLeod J, Master VA. Medical student surgery elective in rural Haiti: a novel approach to satisfying clerkship requirements while providing surgical care to an underserved population. World J Surg 2011;35(4):739-744.

Corbin JH, Mittelmark MB, Lie GT. Scaling-up and rooting-down: a case study of North-South partnerships for health from Tanzania. Glob Health Action 2012;5.

Khan OA, Pietroni M, Cravioto A. Global health education: international collaboration at ICDDR,B. J Health Popul Nutr 2010;28(6):533-536.

Magee M. Qualities of enduring cross-sector partnerships in public health. Am J Surg 2003;185(1):26-29.

McKinley DW, Williams SR, Norcini JJ, Anderson MB. International exchange programs and U.S. medical schools. Acad Med 2008;83(10 Suppl):S53-S57.

Powell DL, Gilliss CL, Hewitt HH, Flint EP. Application of a partnership model for transformative and sustainable international development. Public Health Nurs 2010;27(1):54-70.

Sharafeldin E, Soonawala D, Vandenbroucke JP, Hack E, Visser LG. Health risks encountered by Dutch medical students during an elective in the tropics and the quality and comprehensiveness of pre-and post-travel care. BMC Med Educ 2010;10:89.

Suchdev P, Ahrens K, Click E, Macklin L, Evangelista D, Graham E. A model for sustainable short-term international medical trips. Ambul Pediatr 2007;7(4):317-320.

Vora N, Chang M, Pandya H, Hasham A, Lazarus C. A student-initiated and student-facilitated international health elective for preclinical medical students. Med Educ Online 2010;15. Press, 2007, 352 pp.

Global Health Resources On The Internet

Organizations And Their Resources

Action for Global Health, www.actionforglobalhealth.eu

American Medical Student Association, http://www.amsa.org

BIO Ventures for Global Health, www.bvgh.org/

Canadian Federation of Medical Students, http://www.cfms.org/

Canadian Society for International Health (CSIH), www.csih.org

Child and Family Health International, www.cfhi.org

Consortium of Universities for Global Health's website. www.cugh.org See "Resources" for a wide variety of GH educational resources, including more than 100 modules and documents originally on the Global Health Education Consortium website, now inactive.

Doctors Without Borders, www.doctorswithoutborders.org/

End 7 Diseases by 2020, www.end7.org

FHI360—The Science of Improving Lives, www.fhi360.org

Gapminder, for a wealth of global data, http://www.gapminder.org/

Global Health—Center for Disease Control and Prevention, www.cdc.gov/globalhealth

Global Health—United States Department of Health and Human Services, www.globalhealth.gov

Global Health eLearning Center, www.globalhealthlearning.org

Global Health Facts—Kaiser Family Foundation, www.globalhealthfacts.org/

Global Health Observatory—World Health Organisation, www.who.int/gho/en/

Global Health Program—Bill and Melinda Gates Foundation, www.gatesfoundation.org/global-health

Global Health Watch, www.ghwatch.org/

Health Policy Explained—Kaiser Family Foundation, www.kaiseredu.org

Healthy People 2020—Improving the Health of Americans, www.healthypeople.gov

Instituto de Salud Global—Barcelona (Global Health Institute—Barcelona), www.isglobal.org/

International Federation of Medical Students' Associations—IFMSA, www.ifmsa.org/

International Federation of Pharmaceutical Manufacturers & Associations, www.ifpma.org/

IPAS—Protecting Women's Health, Advancing Women's Reproductive Rights, www.ipas.org

Joint United Nations Programme on HIV/AIDS, www.unaids.org

JSI Research & Training Institute, Inc.—Promoting and Improving Health, www.jsi.com

Knoema, Key world statistics at your fingertips, knoema.com/

Medical Care Development, www.mcd.org

National Institutes of Health, www.nih.gov/

Partners In Health, www.pih.org/

PATH—Program for Appropriate Technology in Health, www.path.org/

Population Council—Research that Makes a Difference, www.popcouncil.org/

Programa de Salud Global del Instituto Nacional de Salud Pública de México (Global Health Program of Mexico's Public Health National Institute), www.saludglobalinsp.mx/

Research Triangle Institute, www.rti.org/

The Canadian Coalition for Global Health Research (CCGHR), www.ccghr.ca

The Commonwealth Fund, www.commonwealthfund.org

The Global Fund to Fight AIDS, Tuberculosis and Malaria, www.theglobalfund.org

The Global Health Gateway, www.globalhealthgateway.org.au

The Global Health Workforce Alliance—WHO, www.who.int/workforcealliance/en/

The Health Systems and Policy Monitor, //hpm.org/

The International Association of Health Policy (IAHP), www.healthp.org

The International Health Economics Association, https:www.healtheconomics.org/

The Rockefeller Foundation, www.rockefellerfoundation.org/

The U.S. President's Emergency Plan for AIDS Relief (PEPFAR), www.pepfar.gov/

U.S. Global Health Policy—Kaiser Family Foundation, //globalhealth.kff.org/

United Nations Population Fund, www.unfpa.org

World Bank, www.worldbank.org/

Global Health Forums

Equity, Health and Human Development Listserver, www.paho.org/English/HDP/equidad-list-about.htm

Forum 2012 COHRED, Global Forum for Health Research, www.forum2012.org/

Geneva Health Forum, www.genevahealthforum.org/

Global Forum for Health Research, www.globalforumhealth.org/

Global Health Leadership Forum, The King's Fund, Univ. of California Berkeley, //ghlf.berkeley.edu/

Global Risk Forum, www.grforum.org

Harvard Undergraduate Global Health Forum, www.hughf.org/

Healthcare Information for All by 2015—HIFA2015, www.hifa2015.org/

Irish Forum for Global Health, //globalhealth.ie/

Norwegian Forum For Global Health Research, //globalhealth.no/

The Global Health Policy Summit, www.globalhealthpolicyforum.org/

The Lancet Global Health Portal, www.thelancet.com/global-health

World Economic Forum, www.weforum.org

Medical And Other Sciences School Based Programming

Baylor College of Medicine International Health Track, www.bcm.edu/medschool/internationaltrack/

Boston Univ. School of Medicine International Health Program, www.bumc.bu.edu/ihbusm/

Case Western Reserve Univ. Center for Global Health and Diseases, www.case.edu/orgs/cghd/

Claremont Graduate Univ.—School of Community and Global Health, www.cgu.edu/

Copenhagen School of Global Health, //globalhealth.ku.dk/

Dalhousie Univ.—Global Health Office, Faculty of Medicine, //gho.medicine.dal.ca

Duke Global Health Institute, //globalhealth.duke.edu/

Emory Univ.—Hubert Department of Global Health, Rollins School of Public Health, www.sph.emory.edu/cms/departments_centers/gh

George Washington Univ.—Department of Global Health, School of Public Health and Health Services, //sphhs.gwumc.edu/departments/globalhealth/

Georgetown School of Medicine Office of International Programs, //som.georgetown.edu/prospectivestudents/specialprograms/international/

Global Health College—Preparing Nurses for the Changing Healthcare Environment, www.global.edu/

Global Health Competency Model, Association of Schools of Public Health, www.asph.org/document.cfm?page=1084

Graduate Institute, Geneva—Global Health Programme, //graduateinstitute.ch/globalhealth

Harvard Medical International, www.phmi.partners.org/

Harvard Univ.—Department of Global Health and Social Medicine, //ghsm.hms.harvard.edu/

Johns Hopkins Center for Global Health, www.hopkinsglobalhealth.org

John's Hopkins School of Public Health—Department of International

Health, www.jhsph.edu/departments/international-health/

Karolinska Institutet—Global Health, //ki.se/ki/jsp/polopoly.jsp?d=31695&a=90146&l=en

Loma Linda Univ.—Department of Global Health, School of Public Health, www.llu.edu/public-health/glbh/index.page

London School of Hygiene & Tropical Medicine—Masters Postgraduate Certificate, Postgraduate Diploma and MSc in Global Health Policy, www.lshtm.ac.uk/study/masters/pg_ghp.html

McGill Global Health Programs—McGill Univ., www.mcgill.ca/globalhealth/

Mount Sinai Global Health—Mount Sinai School of Medicine, www.mssm.edu/research/programs/mount-sinai-global-health

Northwestern Univ. Feinberg School of Medicine—Center for Global Health, //globalhealth.northwestern.edu/MedEd/current-affiliations/Charite_Berlin.html

Stanford Univ.—Center for Innovation in Global Health, //globalhealth.stanford.edu/

Trinity College Dublin—Global Health, //global-health.tcd.ie/postgraduate/msc/

Tulane Department of International Health and Development, www.sph.tulane.edu/ghsd/

Tulane Univ.—Office of Global Health, School of Public Health and Tropical Medicine, www.sph.tulane.edu/

Umeå Universitet—Karolinska Institutet—The Swedish Research School for Global Health, www.sweglobe.net/

Univ. of Alberta—MPH Global Health, School of Public Health, www.publichealth.ualberta.ca/en/programs/mph_programs/mph_glob_hlth.aspx

Univ. of Arizona—Global Health, www.globalhealth.arizona.edu

Univ. of California—San Francisco Office of International Programs, //medschool.ucsf.edu/intlprograms/

Univ. of California—San Francisco Global Health Sciences, //globalhealthsciences.ucsf.edu/

Univ. of Edinburg—Global Health Academy, www.ed.ac.uk/schools-departments/global-health

Univ. of Iowa—Global Programs, www.medicine.uiowa.edu/md/global/

Univ. of London—International Programmes, www.londoninternational.ac.uk/

Univ. of Massachusetts—Office of Global Health, www.umassmed.edu/globalhealth/index.aspx

Univ. of Michigan—Medical School Global REACH, //globalreach.med.umich.edu/ Access the detailed "Student Handbook for Global Engagement", prepared at UM with support of the Center for Global Health, //open.umich.edu/education/sph/resources/student-handbook-global-engagement/2011

Univ. of North Carolina—UNC Gillings School of Global Public Health, www.sph.unc.edu/globalhealth/

Univ. of Oxford—MSc in Global Health Science, www.publichealth.ox.ac.uk/courses/gradstu/globalhealth

Univ. of Pennsylvania—Medical School Global Health Programs Office, www.med.upenn.edu/globalhealth/

Univ. of Virginia—The Center for Global Health, School of Medicine, www.medicine.virginia.edu/community-service/centers/global-health/home-page

Univ. of Washington—Department of Global Medicine, //globalhealth.washington.edu/

Univ. of Washington—Center for Law in Science and Global Health, www.law.washington.edu/healthlaw/ghj/

Social Networks And Global Health

Facebook Resources

CanAmerica Global Health Services, https:www.facebook.com/CanAmericaGlobal

Child Family Health International (CFHI), https:www.facebook.com/pages/Child-Family-Health-International-CFHI/36664465189

Duke Global Health Institute, https:www.facebook.com/DukeGlobalHealth

Global Health in Action, https:www.facebook.com/GlobalHealthinAction

Global Health Corps, https:www.facebook.com/GlobalHealthCorps

Global Health Delivery Project, https:www.facebook.com/globalhealthdelivery

Global Health Fellows Program II, https:www.facebook.com/GHFPII

Journal of Global Health (JGH), https:www.facebook.com/pages/Journal-of-Global-Health-JGH/233019786768057

Smart Global Health, https:www.facebook.com/smartglobalhealth

USAID for Global Health, https:www.facebook.com/USAIDGH

Washington Global Health Alliance, https:www.facebook.com/pages/Washington-Global-Health-Alliance/96771976215

Youtube Resources

Action for Global Health, www.youtube.com/user/afghnetwork

Child Family Health International (CFHI), www.youtube.com/user/cfhiglobalhealth

CSIS Smart Global Health, www.youtube.com/user/smartglobalhealth

GHTCoalition's channel, www.youtube.com/user/ghtcoalition

Global Health Bridge, www.youtube.com/user/globalhealthbridge

Global Health TV Channel, www.youtube.com/user/globalhealthchannel

Health Workforce Alliance, www.youtube.com/user/ghwavideos

Twitter Resources

CDC Global Health, https://twitter.com/CDCGlobal

Duke Global Health, https://twitter.com/DukeGHI

Gates Foundation Global Health, https://twitter.com/gateshealth

Global Health, https://twitter.com/GLOBALHEALTHorg

Global Health at Yale, https://twitter.com/YaleGH

Global Health Corps, https://twitter.com/ghcorps

Global Health Progress, https://twitter.com/GlobalHealth

Global Health TV, https://twitter.com/GlobalHealth_TV

Johns Hopkins CGH, https://twitter.com/JHUGlobalHealth

ONE, https://twitter.com/ONECampaign

Public Health Institute (PHI) Global Health, https://twitter.com/PHIGlobalHealth

USAID Global Health, https://twitter.com/USAIDGH

Email Lists

Globalhealth—Department of Global Health listserv of activities, events, opportunities at UW, //mailman2.u.washington.edu/mailman/listinfo/globalhealth

Global Health Forum listserv—Univ. of Arizona, www.globalhealth.arizona.edu/index.php?q=GHF&$2

USAID's ListServ Index, //transition.usaid.gov/cgi-bin/listserv.cgi

Canadian Federation of Medical Students (CFMS), www.cfms.org/index.php/global-health/join-the-mailing-list.html

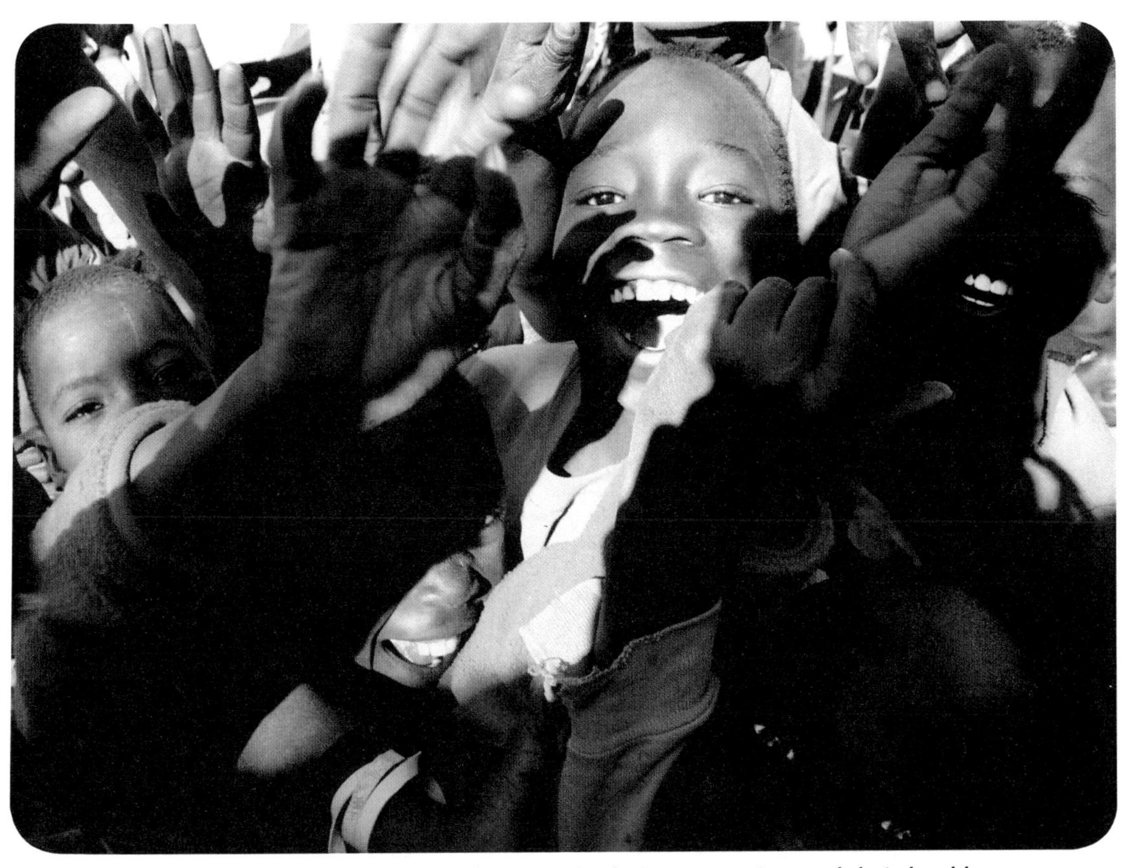

African children celebrate their youth, their community, and their health
Photographer: *Will Bynum*